JUSTICE CRUCIFIED

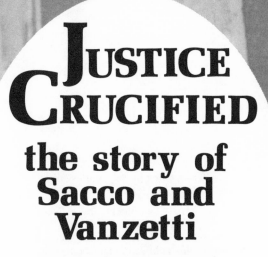

JUSTICE CRUCIFIED

the story of Sacco and Vanzetti

Roberta Strauss Feuerlicht

MCGRAW-HILL BOOK COMPANY
New York   St. Louis   San Francisco
Düsseldorf   London   Mexico
Sydney   Toronto

Book design by Joan Stoliar.

Part-opening photos courtesy of
New York Public Library Picture Collection.

1234567890BPBP783210987

Library of Congress Cataloging in Publication Data

Feuerlicht, Roberta Strauss.
Justice Crucified.
Bibliography: p.
Includes index.
1. Sacco, Nicola, 1891–1927.   2. Vanzetti,
Bartolomeo, 1888–1927.   I. Title.
KF224.S2F45   345'.73'02523   77-4913
ISBN 0-07-020638-4

for my mother and father
Lena Wesler and Isaac Strauss
in whose memory I offer this book

Foreword

I first heard of the Sacco-Vanzetti case from my mother. She did not speak to me of its historical or legal significance, nor did she know what they were. She told me that at midnight, on August 22, 1927, she and my father waited by a newsstand in a crowd of immigrants from New York City's tenements. When newspaper EXTRAS arrived with word that Sacco and Vanzetti had been executed, everyone wept.

Only later did this begin to puzzle me. Why had that polyglot assembly wept for two Italian anarchists? Why had my parents? My mother and father were neither Italian nor anarchist nor demonstrators nor demonstrative; they were apolitical Orthodox Jews from eastern Europe. My mother came to America as a child, when her family emigrated so her brothers would not be drafted into the tsar's army. My father came as a teenager with his brothers and sisters to escape an Old Testament father who beat one of their brothers to death for not going to Hebrew school. Not all immigrants sailed to America because the streets were paved with gold.

I was born and lived on the Lower East Side of Manhattan until I married. We were close enough to Little Italy so that most of our neighbors were Italian, but there were also Jews, Greeks, Spaniards, Poles, Russians: a representative sampling from southern and eastern Europe. All of the adults were immigrants, and it was apparent in the confusion of their lives and in their relationships with each other and with society how displaced these people were as they made their difficult passage between two worlds.

My father died when I was a child, but when my mother died in 1969, and I arranged for her tombstone, I realized that neither my brothers nor I knew her true surname. We knew the American version but not what it had been in the village where she was born. Surrendering one's identity was only the first sacrifice asked of immigrants; I began to wonder about the others. My mother was so anonymous her children did not know her name; Sacco and Vanzetti had to be martyred before anyone knew theirs. I decided there was a connecting thread and began to trace it through the tapestry of American history.

I don't remember what prompted the discussion with my mother about Sacco and Vanzetti; it may have been a newspaper article, for I certainly did not learn about the case in school. I attended public schools and a college populated primarily with the children of immigrants, yet we were never taught about the case, the Palmer raids, or any other negative aspect of American history. The Sacco-Vanzetti case was sometimes mentioned in passing but never explained, while the Palmer raids were not mentioned at all. The settlement of America seemed to begin and end with the Pilgrims; there was rarely more than a paragraph about those who followed, and it concerned statistics, not suffering. My son has now reached high school equally innocent of the nature of the immigrant experience. He has studied the 1920s in both private and public schools without learning, except from me, about Sacco and Vanzetti or Palmer, as though the execution of two innocent men or the arrest of more than four thousand persons in one night are matters of no consequence in a democracy.

As my interest in the Sacco-Vanzetti case grew, I discussed it with people I knew in America as well as those I met while traveling abroad, and I discovered that the names of the two men were known not only in Paris and Belgrade but in some very remote and improbable areas; they are clearly an international symbol for American injustice. I also discovered that whether in Manhattan or central Anatolia, virtually everyone had heard about the case, but virtually no one really knew anything about it.

Many of the books written about the Sacco-Vanzetti case are now out of print. Whether in print or not, most of these volumes are impenetrable, legalistic, self-serving, myopic, dated, or assume too much of the reader. There are a few excellent studies, but no credible or creditable account for the general reader and no account of any kind that places the case in immigrant or historical perspective. I know of no author who has discussed Sacco and Vanzetti in the context of the immigrant experience in America, and all seem to feel they are discharging their obligation to history by mentioning the Palmer raids of 1920.

I don't believe the story of Sacco and Vanzetti begins in 1920, the year of the major raids and the year they were arrested. If that were so, they would simply be tragic victims of an aberrant moment and could be forgotten. I believe that their story begins in 1620, with the coming of the Pilgrims or, to be more precise, in 1630, when the great Puritan migration to Massachusetts really began; that the story of Sacco and Vanzetti is the story of every unwanted immigrant and dissenter in American history; that far too many immigrants and dissenters have been unwanted; that this is not an aberration but the bequest of the seminal settlers, the Puritans; that the invidious ideas, emotions, and attitudes that killed Sacco and Vanzetti were neither born with the case nor died with it but are with us still; and that for these reasons Sacco and Vanzetti should never be forgotten.

To make the narrative whole, I have chosen not to concentrate solely on the case or its immediate background, but to take a detour through a three-hundred-year history of hate in white America. I have dwelled upon the white experience, not because most nonwhites have not suffered more than most whites, but because too little attention has been paid to what whites in America have endured at the hands of other whites. I have also dwelled upon what I deemed most relevant, detailing such dissimilar topics as Puritan theology, the labor movement, and the malevolence of Woodrow Wilson; but each excursion leads back to the main road, the road that led Sacco and Vanzetti from their remote Italian villages to between 1400 and 2000 volts shortly after midnight.

I have not only attempted to place Sacco and Vanzetti within the framework of American history and the immigrant experience but within the context of their own personalities. I wanted to scrape away the superficial images created by both idolaters and detractors and rediscover the two men as human beings. This led me in 1972 to northern Italy, where I met Vanzetti's surviving sister, Vincenzina. Miss Vanzetti not only submitted to two taped interviews, but gave me permission to use what I wished of the 115 or so letters in her possession which Vanzetti wrote to his family and friends in Italy. Miss Vanzetti has what survives of her brother's Italian correspondence; some letters seem to have been lost and others were seized by the Fascists, who regularly searched the Vanzetti home during his years in prison.

The letters Vanzetti wrote to his family in Italy are quite different from those he wrote to his friends in America; they are more blunt, more brutal, more honest. They reveal Vanzetti as an imperfect and complex man, far more interesting and believable than the plaster saint cast by his admirers. The Italian letters not only disclose much that was unknown about Vanzetti's personality and thinking, but solve a few of the lingering mysteries of the case, and help to demolish the split-guilt theory, which holds that an innocent Vanzetti died rather than betray a guilty Sacco.

I was unable to go to southern Italy, where Sacco's siblings and their descendants live, but planned to do so on another trip. When a bare purse made that impossible, I applied to almost two hundred foundations without success. The director of an Italian-American group literally said, "Are you kidding? They were anarchists!" The director of an egregiously liberal fund essentially said, "Are you kidding? We give money to minorities!" Though these reactions did not get me back to Italy, they did convince me of the need for the kind of book I was writing.

Fortunately, previously unpublished, unused, or unrevealed information, and several interviews in the Boston area with one of Sacco's grandsons, gave me considerable insight into Sacco's character, as well as the feelings of the Sacco family. I also interviewed the most relevant of the few persons still alive who knew either Sacco or Vanzetti or both, including Roger Baldwin, Sara R. Ehrmann, and Alfonsina, Lefevre, and Beltrando Brini. The taped memoirs of two of the most important figures in the case, Aldino Felicani and Gardner Jackson, both in the Oral History Collection at Columbia University and both apparently ignored by earlier writers, were illuminating. Other useful tapes were found at Columbia University and the Boston Public Library. Specifics on these and all sources are listed in the Acknowledgments, Bibliography, and Notes.

Having said what the book is or attempts to be, I should say what it is not. It is not a definitive account of the Sacco-Vanzetti case. If such a book is ever written, it will have to await the release of substantial amounts of important data and documents held in private hands. Though the case is more than half a century old, a number of vital sources are, at this time, still sealed, the most significant being the material that was in the possession of the late Aldino Felicani, head of the Sacco-Vanzetti Defense Committee. Included in the Felicani collection are legal documents, evidence used at the trial, 19 manuscripts by Sacco, 137 manuscripts by Vanzetti, the papers of the Defense Committee and the New Trial League, the papers of Fred Moore and Elizabeth Glendower Evans, and countless other invaluable items.*

This book also makes no attempt to place Sacco and Vanzetti within the framework of the Italian anarchist movement. Robert D'Attilio, surely the most assiduous researcher on the case and an authority on Italian-American anarchy, plans to write about this aspect and I willingly relinquish the field to him. I do so not only because he will do a better job than I could, but because I cannot agree with him that the specifics of Italian-American anarchy have much to do with the case. Those who persecuted Sacco and Vanzetti did not care whether they worshipped Galleani or some other prophet; that they were Italian anarchists sufficed. Nor do I think their being anarchists tells us much about Sacco and Vanzetti, though this may represent a blind spot, since I do not

*Disposition of the Felicani collection is expected in 1977, but it will remain closed for an indefinite period until it is fully catalogued.

take anarchy seriously. Carlo Tresca's daughter told me I could never believe what the anarchists of the period were like. "They were *unreal*," she said, which is very much the way I feel about them.

I believe that the behavior of Sacco and Vanzetti at all times, including their reactions to imprisonment and death, was determined primarily by factors other than their anarchist beliefs, and despite their rhetoric, I am skeptical about how deep those beliefs ran. Their being anarchists explains why they went to Mexico rather than to Canada, what they were doing the night they were arrested, and why they walked into a trap, but little else. Some of my own relatives, not Italian and not remotely radical, did many of the things Sacco and Vanzetti did; they carried weapons, fled the draft, and instinctively lied to authorities. This behavior was characteristic of a certain class of immigrants, not just anarchists, because not just anarchists but all immigrants of that class were considered to be, and considered themselves to be, outcasts.

It is not what Sacco and Vanzetti tell us about Italian anarchy that is important, but what their fate tells us about America. Thus the focus of the book is not on Sacco and Vanzetti as anarchists but on Sacco and Vanzetti as immigrants; not on who killed Parmenter and Berardelli but on who killed Sacco and Vanzetti.

Acknowledgments

Never have I written a book which has left such bittersweet memories. I cannot forget Vincenzina Vanzetti weeping on my shoulder, or the emotional interviews in which she spoke of her life, her family, and her brother; nor can I forget her grandmotherly attempts to slip caramels to my son when I wasn't looking. Just as there are no words to adequately console Miss Vanzetti for a lifetime of suffering, there are none to adequately express my appreciation to her for agreeing to be interviewed; for showing me her brother's possessions, which she reverently preserves; and for permitting me to use his letters.

Miss Vanzetti has letters which have never been published anywhere. However, the letters Bartolomeo Vanzetti wrote to Italy that are quoted or excerpted in this book have appeared in Italian in the collection, *Non Piangete la Mia Morte*, reissued as *Il Caso Sacco e Vanzetti*, by Editori Riuniti, Rome, Italy. The translation into English is by Victor Kostka.

Also in Italy, I wish to thank Mario Favro, of the Italian Committee for the Rehabilitation of Sacco and Vanzetti, who took me to Villafalletto to see Vanzetti's house and grave; Caterina Caldera, Miss Vanzetti's cousin; and Peggy Vido and her daughter Rosalba Vido, one of Italy's leading tennis stars. Mother and daughter volunteered to translate during the interviews with Miss Vanzetti and served admirably.

In the Boston area, my most poignant recollection is sitting with Nicola Sacco's grandson, Spencer Sacco, on a bench overlooking the Charles River, listening to him speak for hours about his family and the case. The following day, after I had taped an interview with him, he gave me a beautiful delft tile, though I was in his debt, not he in mine.

I recall with pleasure the afternoon spent taping the Brini family—Beltrando, Lefevre, and their mother, Alfonsina, unlined and lucid at the age of ninety-one. There were additional visits to Beltrando Brini and his forbearing wife Muriel, both of whom were consistently cooperative and hospitable.

Sara R. Ehrmann, infinitely gracious and wise, not only contributed her recollections of the case and the men, but offered many helpful suggestions and insights. Roger Baldwin, penetrating and profound at ninety-two, was kind enough to share with me his memories and opinions.

I am indebted to all of the above for agreeing to be interviewed for this book. For briefer but enlightening conversations I wish to thank Beatrice Tresca, Hymie Kaplan, and others who chose not to be identified.

Robert D'Attilio was an indispensable and unselfish source of material, advice, and leads, even though he is planning his own book and differs with many of my views. Francis Moloney, assistant director of the Boston Public Library, helped me in ways exceeding the obligations of the gentleman and scholar that he is. S. H. M. Clinton not only offered me the resources of his awesome collection of Sacco-Vanzetti material but assisted me with information and generously permitted me to reproduce several of his rare photographs in this book. My cousin, Shirley Deletetsky, served as my Boston correspondent, confidante, and hostess, making my numerous visits not only possible but exceedingly pleasant.

A letter and report from Dr. Abraham Myerson to Herbert Ehrmann, dated April 7, 1927, hereafter referred to as the Myerson report, is from the Herbert B. Ehrmann Papers, Manuscript Division, Harvard Law School Library. They are used with the consent not only of the library but of Dr. Paul Myerson and Sara R. Ehrmann. I also wish to thank Robert D'Attilio, who found the report in the Ehrmann papers; Spencer Sacco, who gave me a copy; and Mrs. James H. Chadbourn, Curator of Manuscripts and Archives at the Harvard Law School Library, for her sympathetic understanding and assistance.

Taped interviews with Albert Carpenter, Judge Elijah Adlow, Joseph Cordella, and Michael Flaherty are from the Oral History Collection of the Boston Public Library.

The Reminiscences of Aldino Felicani, Gardner Jackson, Roger Baldwin, Robert Lincoln O'Brien, and Edward S. Greenbaum are from the Oral History Collection at Columbia University. I am grateful to Elizabeth B. Mason, associate director of the collection, for suggesting tape transcripts I might otherwise have overlooked.

Source notes will be found at the end of the book. I have not used footnotes for any of the following, except where confusion might result:

—the Italian letters of Bartolomeo Vanzetti. They are footnoted only when necessary to indicate the date or the recipient.

—all quotes attributed to Vincenzina Vanzetti. They are from interviews taped June 25 and August 31, 1972, in San Remo, Italy, and from a letter to me dated July 14, 1976.

—all quotes attributed to Spencer Sacco. They are from an interview taped June 15, 1973, in Boston. Spencer Sacco's comments at the conference on Italian-American radicalism are reported separately in the Afterword.

—all quotes attributed to Beltrando, Lefevre, and Alfonsina Brini. They are from interviews taped October 12, 1971, in Quincy and Plymouth, Massachusetts. The trial testimony of the Brinis is footnoted.

—all quotes attributed to Sara R. Ehrmann. They are from an interview taped November 12, 1972, in Brookline, Massachusetts.

—all but one quote attributed to Roger Baldwin. They are

from an interview taped November 5, 1975, in New York City; the exception, from his Reminiscences in the Oral History Collection at Columbia University, is noted.

For permission to use published or copyrighted material, I would like to thank the following:

Editori Riuniti, for excerpts from *Non Piangete La Mia Morte*, copyright © 1962; reissued as *Il Caso Sacco E Vanzetti*, copyright © 1971 by Editori Riuniti, Rome, Italy. Reprinted with permission.

Alfred A. Knopf, Inc., for excerpts from Michael A. Musmanno, *After Twelve Years*, copyright © 1939 by Alfred A. Knopf, Inc., New York, New York. Reprinted with permission.

The Viking Press, Inc., for excerpts from *The Letters of Sacco and Vanzetti*, copyright © 1928 by the Viking Press, Inc., New York, New York. Reprinted with permission.

The *Atlantic Monthly*, for excerpts from William G. Thompson, "Vanzetti's Last Statement," February, 1928, copyright © by The Atlantic Monthly Company, Boston, Massachusetts. Reprinted with permission.

The *Nation*, for excerpts from Dr. Ralph Colp, Jr., "Sacco's Struggle for Sanity," August 16, 1958, and Dr. Ralph Colp, Jr., "Bitter Christmas: A Biographical Inquiry into the Life of Bartolomeo Vanzetti," December 27, 1958, copyright © The *Nation*, New York, New York. Reprinted with permission.

Columbia University, for excerpts from The Reminiscences of Gardner Jackson, copyright © 1972 by the Trustees of Columbia University in the City of New York; The Reminiscences of Robert Lincoln O'Brien, copyright © 1972 by the Trustees of Columbia University in the City of New York; The Reminiscences of Roger Baldwin, copyright © 1972 by the Trustees of Columbia University in the City of New York; and The Reminiscences of Edward S. Greenbaum, copyright © 1975 by the Trustees of Columbia University in the City of New York. Reprinted with permission.

Though I am indebted to a number of individuals and sources, all opinions and errors are my own. My most immeasurable gratitude goes to my husband, Herbert, who photographed as I interviewed, and to our son, Ira. Both assisted me in ways too numerous to recount and too meaningful to properly acknowledge.

Contents

JUSTICE CRUCIFIED

The Bridgewater and South Braintree crimes were the work of two entirely different gangs. One is as different from the other as water is from wine, and they are as easy to tell apart.

—Jack Callahan, *Outlook and Independent*, October 31, 1928

It was . . . the general opinion of such of the agents in Boston as had any actual knowledge of the Sacco-Vanzetti case, that Sacco and Vanzetti, although anarchists and agitators, were not highway robbers, and had nothing to do with the South Braintree crime. My opinion, and the opinion of most of the older men in the Government service, has always been that the South Braintree crime was the work of professionals.

—Lawrence Letherman, agent, Boston office, Department of Justice

I was crazy to come to this country because I was liked a free country, call a free country.

—Nicola Sacco

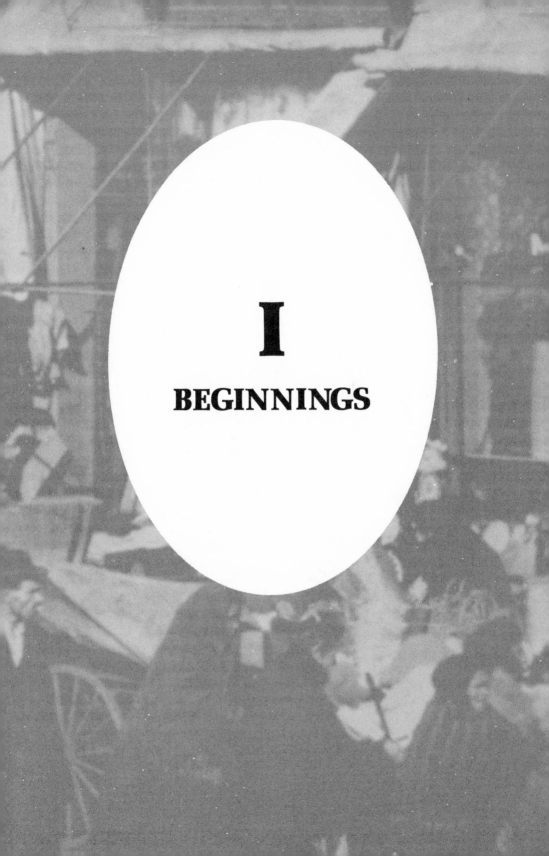

I

BEGINNINGS

1

The Crimes

At about 7:30 A.M. on the cold, damp morning of December 24, 1919, the paymaster for the L. Q. White Shoe Company of Bridgewater, Massachusetts, a driver, and a guard picked up the company's thirty-thousand-dollar payroll at the Bridgewater Trust Company. The money was placed in a galvanized iron box locked to the floor of a truck. The armed guard sat next to the driver, while the paymaster sat on the box with his back toward them.

As the truck was returning to the factory with the payroll, the driver noticed a car pull up at the intersection ahead. Three men emerged from the car and walked toward the payroll truck. One carried a shotgun; the other two had handguns.

The man with the shotgun and one of the other bandits fired at the payroll truck. The guard fired twice in return, as the driver of the truck swerved around a trolley car and raced away from the robbers. The truck skidded on the wet, slippery streets and smashed into a telegraph pole, but no one was hit, no one was hurt, and the payroll was safe.

Though nothing was stolen, the shoe company asked the

Pinkerton detective agency to investigate. A Pinkerton agent interviewed the three men on the truck, as well as witnesses who had seen the robbery attempt. But eyewitnesses to a crime are often unreliable; the action is too rapid, each person sees only one part of the picture, and many often see what they want to see or what is suggested to them rather than what actually occurs.

The men on the payroll truck and the bystanders differed in some of their observations, but agreed there were four bandits, one who remained at the wheel of the car and three who attacked the truck. Three witnesses said the man with the shotgun wore an overcoat; one said he did not. Three witnesses—not the same three—said he was bareheaded; one said he wore a black derby. Since it was inevitable at that time to identify individuals by their ethnic origin, the shotgun bandit was variously described as Greek, Russian, Polish, Austrian, Italian, or Portuguese. Despite these contradictions, a composite portrait revealed he was about forty years old, 5 feet 8 inches tall, weighed 150 pounds, and had black hair, a dark complexion, and a closely cropped black moustache, possibly beginning to gray.

The Pinkerton agent also spoke to the Bridgewater police chief, Michael E. Stewart, who was not only chief but the entire one-man force, except for a part-time assistant. Stewart confided to the Pinkerton man there were a lot of "Reds and Bolshevists" drifting into Bridgewater and that the holdup attempt was the work of an "out-of-town band of Russians."

Pinkerton operatives, less prone to fantasy, concentrated on more solid clues. They tried to track down the bandit car, retrieved an exploded shotgun shell found near the scene of the crime, and tempted underworld informers with a thousand-dollar reward offered by the shoe company. From the informers came word that a man called C. A. Barr knew something about the holdup attempt. Barr had said the criminals were Italian anarchists who lived in a shack near Bridgewater and kept the holdup car there.

On January 3, 1920, Barr was interviewed by a Pinkerton agent, Police Chief Michael Stewart, and a state police officer. The Pinkerton man reported that Barr "related a rambling statement about a machine that he had invented with which he could detect who had committed a crime no matter where it was committed." The report said nothing about Barr's claim that the crime had been committed by Italian anarchists living in a shack near Bridgewater, but it did describe him as "45 years, 5'8", 150 lbs., black hair, dark complexion, close clipped black moustache, streaked with gray."[1] Apparently the three sleuths were so bemused by Barr's bizarre tale it did not occur to them they might be talking to the shotgun bandit. For the moment, the Bridgewater crime was filed and forgotten.

Less than four months later there was a more successful and more deadly robbery at South Braintree, Massachusetts.

On Thursday, April 15, 1920, the payroll for the Slater & Morrill Shoe Company arrived, as it always did, on a morning train; the tracks of the New Haven Railroad and the South Braintree railroad station lay between the company's two factories, which were on Pearl Street, about two hundred yards apart.

In the building known as the upper factory, the money was divided into pay envelopes. The envelopes for the lower factory were stacked in wooden cases, which were placed inside two steel containers. The payroll for the lower factory, which that week amounted to $15,773.59, was always taken there by the paymaster, Frederick A. Parmenter, and a guard, Alessandro Berardelli. Both were armed, accompanied by one to three other men, and usually made the short trip by automobile. But at 3 P.M. on April 15, Parmenter and Berardelli each took a container of money and walked toward the lower factory, alone and apparently unarmed.

Berardelli led the way. About 150 feet from the lower factory, they passed two men leaning against a fence. One of the men stepped up to Berardelli, spoke to him, and shot him.

Even though Berardelli dropped his money box immediately, he was shot twice more. Parmenter, who began to run, was shot twice. Berardelli died at once; Parmenter lived for fourteen hours. One eyewitness said the bandits had to shoot Parmenter because he held on to the money, but they did not have to shoot Berardelli. Other witnesses said it seemed as though the bandits wanted Berardelli dead because he knew them.

The man who had done most of the shooting now fired once

into the air. At this signal, a large, shiny blue Buick parked nearby drove up as still another bandit emerged from a hiding place behind a stack of bricks. The robbers threw the two money boxes into the back of the Buick and piled inside. Before the car pulled away, someone fired a farewell shot at Berardelli's body; the robbers wanted to be certain he was dead.

The Buick reached the railroad crossing that bisected Pearl Street just as the tender, Michael Levangie, was lowering the gates because of an oncoming freight train. Levangie found himself looking at the barrel of a gun. "Put them up!" ordered one of the bandits. "Put them up or we will put a hole through you!"

Levangie quickly raised the gates and ran for the safety of his shack. One shot was fired at the shack as the car leaped across the tracks just ahead of the freight.

As the car sped from the scene, a gun was thrust through the missing rear window to hold off possible pursuers, though there were none. Gunshots peppered both sides of Pearl Street to discourage onlookers. Tacks were tossed onto the street—rubber-headed so they would land upright—to pierce the tires of cars that might try to follow. About two miles outside of South Braintree, the bandits abandoned the Buick in the woods and switched to a Hudson.

The crime and several of the criminals had been observed by a number of persons at different times, places, and angles. Typically, the witnesses did not agree on what or whom they saw, but there was a consensus on certain points. The daring daylight robbery was a thoroughly professional job, down to the last tack. The bandits' determination to kill Berardelli suggested he was either an acquaintance or an accomplice. There were probably five men in the Buick as it departed, two in front and three in back. Virtually everyone agreed that the driver was a pale, fair-haired young man who looked either ill or drugged. The three bandits who took part in the action on Pearl Street were described as Italians of medium height.

Investigation of the South Braintree robbery and murders was conducted by Captain William H. Proctor, head of the Massachusetts State Police, and Pinkerton detectives. Fingerprints were taken from the abandoned Buick and a careful search was made for witnesses and other evidence.

News of the crime was headlined across the state. In New Bedford, Police Inspector Ellsworth C. Jacobs remembered that he had recently seen a local thug driving a new Buick. The thug was Mike Morelli who, with his brothers, formed the nucleus of a group of criminals called the Morelli gang. Jacobs had not seen the Buick since April 15, but he had seen another car with the same license number. When asked about it, another Morelli brother, Frank, explained to Jacobs that he was an automobile dealer and had simply switched plates.

Suspicions linking the Morellis to the robbery were buried in New Bedford, however, for the case was set on a different course by Police Chief Michael E. Stewart of Bridgewater, a course the Commonwealth of Massachusetts would follow into history. On April 16, the day after the South Braintree robbery, an immigration inspector asked Stewart to help him check on an Italian anarchist, Ferruccio Coacci, who was to be deported for distributing anarchist literature. Coacci, who had agreed to turn himself in on April 15, had failed to appear, though he called the next day to say his wife was ill.

Coacci lived in a run-down house in West Bridgewater with his family and another anarchist, Mike Boda. Near the house was a shed where Boda kept a 1912 Overland automobile. Stewart could not go to Coacci's house on the evening of April 16 because he was rehearsing his part in a play, but he sent his assistant who found Coacci packed and ready to leave.

Later that night, the assistant reported to Stewart there was nothing wrong with Coacci's wife; he had just been stalling. Stewart sat in his office and brooded. It was his theory that the Bridgewater holdup was the work of a band of Bolsheviks; now he remembered Barr had said that a group of anarchists living in a shack near Bridgewater had attempted the crime.* For reasons known but to God and Stewart, the chief concluded that both the Bridgewater and South Braintree crimes were the work of the same men. Coacci was the link. He had not turned himself in on April 15 because he and his comrades were committing robbery and murder.

*Terms such as anarchist, Bolshevik, Red, IWW, and socialist were used interchangeably then by those who did not know what they meant, which frequently included the radicals themselves.

Stewart became obsessed with this idea. When he and other police officers viewed the abandoned Buick on April 17, he pontificated that "the men who did this job knew no God." Though Coacci was in the hands of immigration authorities, Stewart decided to search his house for clues. Coacci's family had moved out but Boda was still there. After looking through the house, Stewart asked Boda if he could examine the shed. Boda said it was empty; his Overland had been taken to be repaired at a garage owned by Simon Johnson.

Stewart checked the shed anyway and thought he saw tire prints which would have been too big for an Overland but just right for a Buick. When the police chief returned to the house the following morning, Boda, who was a bootlegger as well as an anarchist, decided it would be discreet to disappear for a while. But Stewart knew how to find him. He went to Simon Johnson's garage and told Johnson to call him as soon as anyone came to pick up the Overland.

Shortly after 9 P.M. on May 5, 1920, Boda appeared at the Johnson house with three other men. While Johnson stalled Boda by pointing out that the Overland had no license plates, his wife slipped into a neighbor's house and telephoned a message to Stewart: "Boda has come for his car."

At first Boda wanted to take the car even without the plates, but either he changed his mind or one of the men realized that Mrs. Johnson had left the house to make a phone call. They sensed a net closing about them, though they did not know why. Boda told Johnson he would send someone with license plates to pick up the car the following day, then he and Ricardo Orciani left on a motorcycle with a sidecar and headed toward Brockton.

The other two men left on foot, heading in the same direction. Too uneasy to wait for a trolley there, they walked about a mile, then asked a woman where the stop was. At about 9:40 P.M. the two men boarded the trolley to Brockton.

By the time Stewart reached Johnson's house the four men were gone. But either because of the direction they had taken or because the woman to whom the two men had spoken had notified the police, Stewart guessed where they were. He called the police in Brockton and told them that two foreigners, who had just tried to steal a car, were on the trolley coming from Bridgewater.

Shortly after 10 P.M., Officer Michael J. Connolly boarded the trolley on Main Street, in front of Keith's Theater. He looked down the car and saw two foreign-looking men in the last seat. Connolly walked to the rear and asked the men where they were coming from.

"Bridgewater."

"What was you doing in Bridgewater?"

They said they were visiting a friend.

"Who is your friend?"

They gave a name.

"Well," said Connolly, "I want you. You are under arrest."

The men asked why.

"Suspicious characters," said Connolly.[2]

By that time another officer had boarded the trolley. At the main trolley station in Brockton, a police car was waiting to drive the two prisoners to police headquarters. Their names were Nicola Sacco and Bartolomeo Vanzetti.

2

The Men

Nicola Sacco was born on April 22, 1891, at Torremaggiore, in southern Italy, one of seventeen children. His father sold olive oil and wine produced from his own orchards and vineyards. Sacco was christened Ferdinando, but changed his name to Nicola after a brother who died, though many of his friends continued to call him Ferdinando. Even from prison he sometimes sent letters signed with his original name or "Nando," his original nickname.[1]

At his trial, Sacco said he went to school from the ages of seven to fourteen, but his older brother Sabino has said that when young Nicola went into his father's fields to hoe, he could neither read nor write.[2] When Sacco was sixteen, he decided to become a mechanic, which he preferred to farm work. At about this time, Sabino Sacco accepted an invitation from a friend of their father's to visit him in Milford, Massachusetts. Nicola was eager to go with Sabino. "I was crazy to come to this country," he later testified, "because I was liked a free country, call a free country."[3]

Sabino and Nicola Sacco landed in Boston on April 12, 1908, ten days before Nicola's seventeenth birthday. They left for Milford the same night, finding a warm welcome but cold comfort;

they slept in an attic and were fed no more than a bowl of soup at night. Sabino immediately found a job in a foundry.

Sabino
Sacco:
My first thought was to put my brother through school; he was too young to work. He was like a puppy; he always waited for me at the factory gates. We were always together.[4]

But neither then nor ever would Nicola Sacco let anyone support him. He later told a psychiatrist, "No one can say that, in my life, I have eaten any bread which I have not worked for."[5] He got a job as a water boy with a construction company and when it became too cold to work outdoors went to work in a foundry.

Within a year or so after their arrival, Sabino, who was a socialist, had had his fill of the American dream. Returning to Torremaggiore, he used the money he had saved in America to expand his father's business.

Sabino
Sacco:
I insisted that [Nicola] return. I did not want him to work for a master in the United States. Here [in Italy] he could do business and travel.[6]

But Nicola Sacco was not yet ready to go back to Italy. Aware that he could earn more money as a skilled worker, he went to the Milford Shoe Company and paid a fifty-dollar fee to learn how to become an edge trimmer. From 1910 until he left for Mexico in May, 1917, Sacco remained at the Milford Shoe Company working at his trade. In 1912 he married Rosa Zambelli, whom he usually called Rosina. She was seventeen, he was twenty-one; they were very much in love. He wrote Mrs. Cerise Jack, who helped teach him English while he was in prison:

> I remember Mrs. Jack a years ago on our love day when I bought the first lovely blue suit for my dear Rosina and that dear remembrance still remains in my heart. . . . In morning May first nineteen twelve I dress up with my new blue suit and I went over to see my dear Rosina and I asked her father if he won't let Rosina come with me in the city town to buy something and he said yes. So in afternoon about one o'clock we both us went in city town, and we went in

a big store and we bought a brown hat, a white underdress, a blue suit, one pair brown stock, one pair brown shoes, and after she was all dress up, Mrs. Jack I wish you could see Rosina, how nice she looked, while now the sufferings of today had make her look like an old woman. But Mrs. Jack I never was ambitious to buy her diamonds and so-so, but I always bought everything that could be natural and usefull.[7]

Their first child was born in May, 1913, and Sacco named him Dante "because you know Dante was a great man in my country."[8] When Dante was old enough he would go to the factory where Sacco worked and stand beside his father's bench piling up soles. "That boy was my comrade, my friend," said Sacco. "He would say, 'Let me help, papa, I like to help.'"[9] When Sacco was through with his day's work, he and Dante raced each other home. Dante's son Spencer would later say of his grandfather, "He was very much of a father. He would take daddy fishing and things like that."

At the time Sacco was arrested, Rosina was five months pregnant; their daughter Ines never knew her father as a free man. During his trial, Rosina would bring the baby to court so Sacco could play with her during recess. "And with the lack of self-consciousness so foreign to northern races," wrote Elizabeth Glendower Evans, "he would toss the little one and fondle her as if he were in the privacy of his own home."[10]

When Sacco returned from Mexico in late August or early September of 1917, he worked in a candy factory, as a manual laborer, and in several shoe factories. One day he went to the 3-K Shoe Company in Stoughton, Massachusetts, which was owned by Michael F. Kelley who had been his mentor and superintendent at the Milford Shoe Company. Sacco asked Kelley, "Don't you remember me?" Kelley said he didn't.

"Well, I am Nick."

"You are the fellow that learned up at Milford?"

"Yes."

"Are you working now?"

"No, I am out of a job."

Michael Kelley called his son George, who helped run the factory, and said, "If you need an edge trimmer, give this fellow some consideration because I think he is a good man. If I remember him right in Milford he was a good edge trimmer."[11]

Sacco was hired by the 3-K Shoe Company in November, 1918. Kelley described him as "A good workman. Very steady. He never lost a day. He was in early and stayed late. He was a great fellow to clean up everything. He was wonderful about that."[12]

Sacco, who did piecework, sometimes earned as much as seventy-five or eighty dollars a week, a remarkable sum for an alien, or any laborer, at that time. "He was a hard worker," said Michael Kelley. "The ordinary fellow would not make as much as that because he would not have the ambition to."[13] Sacco's earnings enabled him to accumulate a substantial savings account. On May 1, 1920, four days before he was arrested, the balance was $1,508.92. After that there were only withdrawals.

During the winter of 1918/19, Sacco earned extra money by taking on the task of going to the factory every night to bank the boiler and returning at five in the morning to get the building heated before the workday began. Because of this he is sometimes described as having been night watchman and needing a gun for his duties. Neither is true; he owned a Colt .32 but it had nothing to do with his work. However the Kelleys trusted him completely; they gave him the keys to the factory "and the whole thing was in his hands there in the evening after everybody had gone home," Michael Kelley said.[14]

Sacco rented a small house in Stoughton from Michael Kelley that was directly behind Kelley's own home. Sacco's house had a garden which he tended at dawn and dusk. Kelley commented, "A man who is in his garden at 4 o'clock in the morning, and at the factory at 7 o'clock, and in his garden again after supper and until nine and ten at night, carrying water and raising vegetables beyond his own needs which he would bring to me to give to the poor, that man is not a holdup man."[15]

As a boy in Italy, Sacco had been introduced to socialism by Sabino and had joined a boys republican club. In America, Sacco moved farther left and joined a group of Italian anarchists in the Boston area. He and Rosina, a handsome pair, sometimes performed in little plays to raise funds for the anarchist cause. In 1916, he and other speakers at an anarchist meeting were arrested and fined for not having a permit.

Never a man to stifle his views, Sacco was once warned by George Kelley, "Stop talking, Nick, till this time of anti-radical excitement is past. You will surely get in trouble." He replied, "Oh, George, it is my heart that talks."[16] George Kelley said, "There never was a better fellow than Nick Sacco, nor one with a kinder heart. He couldn't kill a chicken."[17]

Though Sacco was not as philosophical as Vanzetti, he could be helpful in practical ways, such as collecting bread for the hungry strikers at Lawrence, Massachusetts.*[18] Though not as literate as Vanzetti, he read widely; a psychiatrist said his cell library was "not to be duplicated in any cell in any jail I have ever been in."[19] It was in an Italian anarchist newspaper that Sacco first heard of Bartolomeo Vanzetti before the two men ever met.

Bartolomeo Vanzetti was born on June 11, 1888, in the village of Villafalletto, near Cuneo, in northern Italy. The house he was born in still stands, though it is no longer owned by the Vanzetti family. It is a row house with faded plaster and a red tile roof, one of a series of connecting buildings enclosing an interior courtyard. Stretching out beyond the enclosure are the farmlands.

In 1880, Vanzetti's father, Giovanni, thirty-one years old and still unmarried, decided to go to America. His daughter Vincenzina has letters he sent from California; she does not know where else he may have traveled or exactly what he did.

Vincenzina Vanzetti: *His father ran a farm and was fairly well-off. My father was just his father's son; he had no profession. He just wanted to go to the United States. He must have worked; he did not have the money to stay there and do nothing. If things had gone well, he might have stayed. But since his father was old and there were four sisters to be married off, his father wrote him to come back home, and he did.*

Giovanni Vanzetti returned to Villafalletto in 1882 and married a widow, Giovanna Nivello Brunetti. After her first

*See footnote page 86.

Begin

husband died, Giovanna Brunetti and her infant son, Nalin, went to France where she worked as a wet nurse, but she returned to Italy in a few years. When she married Giovanni Vanzetti, Nalin was sent to his uncle's house to live.

Bartolomeo was the oldest of four Vanzetti children. In his autobiography, he says he went to school for seven years; Vincenzina says it was only three.*

Vincenzina   *Children went to first grade when they were seven or*
Vanzetti: *eight, and until 1914 there were only three grades, so seven plus three is ten. He got his education all by himself. My father said, "I did not have my first son, Bartolomeo, study, and I will not have any of the others study either." What a mentality!*

Even as a boy, Vanzetti approached life as a student and observer. He loved birds, so when he was twelve, he recorded in a tiny notebook descriptions of the birds he saw.† He also loved music and owned a guitar which his sister says he "fooled around with a bit." Like the other members of his family, he was a devout Catholic.

Vincenzina   *When he was a little boy, the children made an altar*
Vanzetti: *and he pretended to be the priest and made all the little boys sing the Mass.*

Another father might have recognized he had an unusually precocious son, but not Giovanni Vanzetti. The old man could easily have afforded a higher education for Bartolomeo because the farm was prosperous, but he read in a newspaper that in Turin forty-two lawyers had applied for a position that paid only thirty-five lire a month. On the basis of that article, and without considering Bartolomeo's abilities or interests, Giovanni Vanzetti decided that the boy should learn a trade, not a profession. Bartolomeo did not even get to choose his trade; since his father had opened a café in Villafalletto he wanted his son to become a pastry maker.

---

*Perhaps both Sacco and Vanzetti were embarrassed by their lack of formal education and so exaggerated it.
†Vincenzina Vanzetti still has the notebook, which is about three by five inches, with pages made of graph paper. Inside the front cover, in a clear, bold hand, is the signature, *Vanzetti, Bartolomeo*, and the date, *1900*.

At the age of thirteen, Bartolomeo Vanzetti was sent to Cuneo to become a baker's apprentice. He worked from seven in the morning until ten at night seven days a week, with three hours off twice a month. His first letters home reveal a dutiful but suffering son.

Vanzetti to his parents, Cuneo, August 23, 1901:

> Your letter made me very happy; I thank you for the gift I have received. I have studied your good advice, I agree with you and I promise I will follow it. . . .
>
> As you know I have only one pair of shoes, and if I ever have to take them to be repaired I will have to go barefoot, since I can no longer wear my old shoes. I ask you in your goodness to provide me with a new pair. . . .
>
> Please send me some goiter medicine (the air of Cuneo has already given me a goiter infection) and send directions for its use. I am happy and I like staying here. . . . I am in excellent health.

Vanzetti was neither happy nor in excellent health, though his self-diagnosis of a goiter may have been in error; it is never mentioned again. After twenty months of misery in Cuneo, he moved on to a bakery in Cavour, where he had ten hours off a month instead of six. In his autobiography he wrote, "I did not like the trade, but I stuck to it to please my father and because I did not know what else to choose."[20] He bore his wretchedness with religious resignation, expressing his misery and resentment obliquely and writing not so much what he felt as what his parents wanted to hear.

Vanzetti to his parents, Cavour, December 23, 1902:

> I am writing you this letter to give you news of me and to express to you my thoughts and emotions, which this festive season encourages me to reveal. We are at Christmas Day, that day which reminds us of the entrance of true light into the world, of the arrival of the Heavenly Child to illuminate the world, to save it from the night, to save it by

Begin»

sacrifice. This is at once a solemn and a happy day, one that should be spent around the domestic hearth, and I would give a great deal to spend it among the people I hold in most affection, and most sacred. That is what you are for me. It is not possible. Let us be patient. Let us thank God that I am living with a good family, this is a piece of luck that does not happen to everyone. I pray to Jesus with all my heart that we may all pass one thousand of these happy days of peace and love, united in our hearts if not in actuality. I also write this letter to wish you a good end to the old year and a good beginning to the new. I wish terribly to see you, and am saddened by the thought that so much time still separates us. I embrace all of you.

As time passed, Vanzetti sought sympathy more openly. "The only complaint I have concerns my feet, which are very painful," he wrote from Cavour on June 10, 1903. "In the evening, when I quit work after eighteen hours, my feet burn as if they rested on glowing coals. To tell you the truth I am tired of this miserable life."

From Cavour Vanzetti went to Turin. On November 23, 1904, writing from a hospital or clinic, he mentioned he was operated on two days earlier and "it was more painful than the first time." He did not say why he needed two operations. On January 3, 1905, he wrote he had been offered a job as a bartender and "I hope that, once I am working, I will no longer be a financial burden on you." When this job did not materialize, Vanzetti left Turin to work for a confectioner, but by May, 1906, he was back in Turin making caramels.

In February, 1907, Vanzetti became so ill with pleurisy that his father came to Turin to take him home. He was not yet nineteen years old. "And so I returned," he wrote in his autobiography, "after six years spent in the fetid atmosphere of bakeries and restaurant kitchens, with rarely a breath of God's air or a glimpse of His glorious world."[21]

After his mother nursed him back to health—"I had almost forgotten that hands could caress so tenderly"—he remained at

Villafalletto, working in the family garden. He called this one of the happiest periods of his life, but it came to a rapid and tragic end when his mother fell ill and died of cancer of the liver at the age of forty-five. Bartolomeo was nineteen, his sister Luigia was sixteen, Vincenzina was four, and the baby, Ettore, was two.

His mother's death was a catastrophic loss for Vanzetti, possibly because it left him exposed to his formidable father, and if he did not exaggerate its importance to him, he certainly exaggerated his own role. "In the last few weeks of her life," he wrote years later,

> her sufferings became so agonizing that neither my father nor her relatives, nor her dearest friends had the courage to approach her bedside. I remained alone to comfort her as best I could. Day and night I remained with her, tortured by the sight of her suffering. For two months I did not undress.
>
> Science did not avail, nor love. After three months of brutal illness she breathed her last in my arms. She died without hearing me weep. It was I who laid her in her coffin; I who accompanied her to the final resting place; I who threw the first handful of earth over her bier. And it was right that I should do so for I was burying part of myself. . . . The void left has never been filled.[22]

Peasants are realistic, sensible, and earthy; tragedy and pain are not strangers to them. It is not believable that no one would approach the dying woman; the immodest chores of the sickbed would have been taken care of by Luigia or other female relatives, not by a grown son. What Vanzetti did in this hyperbolic passage was shoulder aside his father as chief mourner and his mother as chief victim.

After his mother's death, Vanzetti said he became so despondent he considered suicide. "This desperate state of mind decided me to abandon Italy for America," he wrote.[23] His father, who had himself gone to America as a young man, did not want him to leave. Having just lost his wife, Giovanni Vanzetti did not want to lose his oldest child as well.

Begin

| Vincenzina Vanzetti: | *He wanted Bartolomeo to stay in Italy, make a place for himself, and raise a family. But there was nothing to do in Villafalletto. Bartolomeo had been to Turin and Cavour and must have found them too constricting. He went off to chase an ideal.* |

Vanzetti's ideals came later. When he left Italy he wasn't chasing anything; he was running away. He did not want to bake pastries or tend bar in his father's café; most of all he did not want any part of his father. In answer to a letter from Luigia begging him to return home he wrote, on December 22, 1914, "What would I do in Villafalletto? How would I get along with Dad?"

Vanzetti left Villafalletto on June 9, 1908, two days before his twentieth birthday. He traveled by train across France and sailed from Le Havre on June 13. His autobiography describes his first years in America as a descent into hell, but there is little indication of this in his letters home. Perhaps by the time he wrote his autobiography in 1923, his anarchist views and his conviction for two crimes he never committed had so embittered him that he deliberately recast his early years in America in a dimmer light, or perhaps he just did not want to grant his father the satisfaction of knowing he was starving and suffering in America when he could have lived in comfort at Villafalletto.

In his early correspondence to Italy, twenty-year-old Vanzetti, still playing the priest, sent pastoral letters to seventeen-year-old Luigia. This one is not dated.

> I take this occasion to remind you to be good, both to our little brother and sister and our father. Think of the tragic death of our mother, bear the children's innocent foibles and disturbances with sweetness and patience, take good care of them, keep them clean, take good care of their health, try to give them a good education and build their characters, be a good example to them.
>
> Be loving and patient with our father. Think how much he must suffer through the loss of our mother and through my departure. He has always worked and sacrificed himself for our sakes. Bear

with him when he makes nasty remarks, obey him when he is in the right. Try to make his life as easy as possible by fulfilling your duties as a daughter and a homemaker.

Be proud but not overweening, ambitious but not overambitious. Respect everyone, whoever they are, and try to get into the good graces of honest people. Be polite to gentlefolk and to your superiors, but much more polite and kinder to poor people and workers.

Be proud with the first and humble with the second. Pardon me if I lecture you, I do it because it is my duty as an older brother, besides, I am impelled by the great love I have for you, for my father and for our little brother and sister. Though we are separated by the ocean my thoughts and my heart are with you.

Heed my advice and you will be happy. Remind yourself that in doing this you will always see before you the happy faces of myself and our father. In the tranquility of your conscience you will feel our mother's benediction descending on you from above.

Vanzetti's first detailed impressions of America in his family's possession are in a letter to Luigia sent January 12, 1911, from Meriden, Connecticut. He mentions he had planned to move west but decided to stay in Meriden for awhile and instructs Luigia what lie to tell "so that father will not know that we are corresponding." The letter then goes on to limn America through the eyes of a twenty-three-year-old northern Italian immigrant, who reveals as much about himself as he does about the country.

Now I will tell you a little about America. It would take too long to tell you all of my adventures, there are enough of them to fill a book, so I will just give you a short synopsis.

As you will have understood from my first letters a tremendous financial crisis was afflicting this area at the time of my arrival. I had the good

Begi)

fortune to find work immediately in the hotels, and for ten months I lived fairly well. I worked for two months for Caldera [Giacomo Caldera, a cousin from Villafalletto who had emigrated earlier] and then for ten months at a French restaurant. However, I was unable to remain there by reason of my temperament, because my health was declining and my character does not permit me to allow injustice to occur in my presence.

I left New York for the country. I worked on farms, cut trees, made bricks, dug ditches and quarried rocks. I worked in a fruit, candy and ice cream store and for a telephone company.

At the end of the first season I had a bit of money left over, but I spent it all during the winter. This year I had a better job than the last, so I made more money. At present I am not working because of the cold. During the winter almost all outdoor work is suspended. I have the firm hope of finding a good job, since a friend of mine, an old Piedmontese, is doing his best to find me one. In the country I have become stronger and healthier. I say the country, actually the town in which I work has 30,000 inhabitants. It has a public library, a lower school and a high school and is surrounded by parks and lakes. There is no nationality on Earth that I have not found represented here.

I have suffered a great deal on finding myself surrounded by strange, indifferent and sometimes hostile people. I have had to suffer insults from people that I would have left face down in the dust, if I were a tenth as fluent in English as I am in Italian.

Here public justice is based on force and brutality, and woe betide the stranger and particularly the Italian who uses energetic methods to defend his rights, for him there are the clubs of the police, the prisons and the penal codes. Do not believe that American people are civilized, though they do have many good qualities. If you strip them of their money and their elegant clothes, they are barbarians, fanatics and criminals.

No country in the world has as many religions and religious extravagances as these blessed United States. Here he is good who is rich, even if he robs and poisons. Many have become rich by selling their human dignity, they spy on their co-workers and countrymen.

Many reduce morality to a level lower than that of the animals. Although every religion is permitted here, jesuitism is triumphant. The holy doctrines of Europe, wise and kind as they are, do not illuminate this place or its people.

In this Babylon I have remained unchanged, and cowardice has never attracted me.

I have always been generally respected, both by Americans and by Italians and even by Negroes.

No one has ever convinced me that white is black, and if there is somebody who cannot meet my eye it is because he knows that I despise him.

Know that there are many young Italians, especially from southern Italy, who do not work; they are always enjoying themselves and are generally elegantly dressed. They belong to the Black Hand and live on the fruits of their crimes. I am almost always alone, because the Italians in America are in general ignorant. I only associate with honest and intelligent people. I have been going to English school for two years and in general am doing fairly well. I understand almost everything, but have some trouble answering. I have faith only in myself, in my will, my honesty and my health. I hope to win.

Love the children, treat father as affectionately as possible, he has suffered so much for us. He has worked and is still working for our good. Practice virtue, flee vice.

Remember that if you act in this way you will fulfill your duties as a sister and a daughter. Benedictions will rain on you, and a tranquil conscience, which is indispensable to peace of mind, will afford you that consolation and that sweetness that only the good can attain. Remember also that in acting this way you will fulfill the wishes of a brother who loves you with all his heart.

After working in New York and various towns in New England as a dishwasher, farmhand, and assistant pastry chef, in factories, stone quarries, and on railroads, moving wherever there was work and starving when there wasn't any, Vanzetti settled in Plymouth, Massachusetts. There he worked on a private estate, at the Plymouth Cordage Company, until he was active in a strike and blacklisted, and as a manual laborer. In the fall of 1919, an Italian in Plymouth who had decided to return home sold Vanzetti his cart, knives, and scales, and Vanzetti became a fish peddler. When no fish were available, he chopped ice, shoveled coal or snow, dug ditches, helped lay a water main.

Originally a fervent Catholic who came to blows with a fellow worker in Turin who was a socialist, Vanzetti's earliest religious doubts arose while he was still in Italy, though he found his new religion here. "Arrived in America," he wrote, "I underwent all the sufferings, the disillusions and the privations that come inevitably to one who lands at the age of twenty, ignorant of life, and something of a dreamer. Here I saw all the brutalities of life, all the injustice, the corruption in which humanity struggles tragically."[24]

In the few hours between work, school, and sleep, Vanzetti began to read history, philosophy, political tracts, science, and literature. He mentions Marx, Mazzini, Malatesta, Kropotkin, Darwin, Tolstoy, Zola, and many others. But it was from life itself, he wrote, that he "grasped the concept of fraternity, of universal love. . . . I sought my liberty in the liberty of all; my happiness in the happiness of all."[25] By the time Vanzetti reached Plymouth in 1913 he was an anarchist.

Shortly after he arrived in Plymouth, Vanzetti took a room as a boarder at the house of another Italian anarchist, Vincenzo Brini. Brini had a wife, Alfonsina, and three children—Lefevre, then seven and a half; Beltrando, six; and Zora, who was two. Vanzetti lived with the Brinis until he left for Mexico in 1917. When he returned to Plymouth, they no longer had room for him so he boarded with the Fortini family, though the Brinis remained his friends in life and his mourners in death.

Alfonsina Brini: *Vanzetti was in the club with my husband. And he ask if they know some family they keep boarders. So my husband he said, "I'll ask my wife." That's the way he came.*

Lefevre Brini: *I remember when he came up to the house with a big valise—two valises, one big black one, one brown one. And you know, we kids, we always thought there were goodies in valises. We followed him around, but he never put them down; he was talking. I remember that so plain. Finally he put them down but we didn't dare to touch them. So mama showed him the room and he took the valises and he went in. When he first came he looked very strange to us because he had a Vandyke.* And a moustache. And sort of these high collars. He looked so different from other people because there weren't too many people around with Vandykes in our neighborhood. So he struck us as kind of odd. We thought, we'll see if we can get along with him, because he seemed to be nice. He patted us on the head and he helped my mother and father with the breakfast on Sundays.*

The Brini children more than got along with Vanzetti; they came to worship him. He was more of a father to them than their own father. He took them on walks in the woods and down to the shore, picking flowers and hunting for shells. He checked their report cards, helped them with their homework, went with them to the library, and taught them Italian, since they spoke only the Bolognese dialect, while they taught him English. In the evenings, before he went to school or read his books or argued the fine points of anarchist doctrine with Vincenzo Brini, Vanzetti would play *schira*, an Italian variation of Chinese checkers, with them. Yet in spite of his evident love for children, Vanzetti showed no interest in marriage.

Beltrando Brini: *To my knowledge, he never had a girl friend. Never interested. He never showed, that I know of, any interest in any woman, any romance.*

*Vanzetti shaved off his beard but not his moustache, which became his most memorable feature.

Begin

Vanzetti confirmed this in a letter to one of his aunts to whom he wrote, "The thought of getting married has never crossed my mind. I have never had a girl, and if I have ever been in love, it has been the kind of love that I had to stifle in my breast."[26] Since there is no indication that he stifled any love in his breast, the allusion is probably a touch of Vanzetti romanticism, designed either to ward off a probing relative or to delude himself, which he often did. "Anarchy is my beloved,"[27] he once wrote; he also said anarchism was as beautiful as a woman for him. Another time he wrote he had "renounced . . . the joys of love"[28] for his ideals, without mentioning that other anarchists, including some of his friends and heroes, found time for both.

Since Vanzetti did not have a child, Beltrando Brini became what he called his "spiritual son."[29]

Beltrando Brini: *In a sense I would say so. I'm proud of that. The one thing that prevails is the overall influence of this man upon my attitude toward making something of myself, being reliable, being honest, creating in me an image so I could lift up my head and not feel the burden of this prejudice against the Italians. He encouraged me to reach a point which I would never have done otherwise.**

He was very much interested in my education. He had a great deal of patience, infinite patience. He would sit by me while I was practicing the violin. He had a good ear for music, for pitch. I recall playing "Old Black Joe," which was in two sharps; my teacher told me the F was sharp but he didn't tell me the C was sharp. I played it without knowing I should sharp the C and Vanzetti said to me—he was very fond of "Old Black Joe," he had a good voice, he liked to sing—he said, "That note is out of tune." He knew something was wrong, he sat by and listened to me, he was an audience, and he was sort of a critic. He inspired me because he paid this much attention.

Another time, at Halloween, I had a jack-o'-lantern without a candle in it. All my friends had candles, but mine was dark. And Vanzetti happened to be going by or was visiting and he said, "Where's

*Beltrando Brini escaped the Italian ghetto in Plymouth and became an educator and a musician.

your candle?" "I don't have one." "Get one." "I haven't any money." He said, "Here's two cents. Go buy yourself some candles." Well, for two cents you could buy twenty candles. I went immediately to the hardware store and I said, "I want two cents' worth of candles." And the man gave me back nine cents. One coin wasn't a penny, it was a dime. Now, I never had much money in my pocket, as much as a dime or a nickel, but I couldn't keep the nine cents. And I felt very proud in returning it. When any person can do that to a child—bring out the best in him—I think he has had a tremendous influence.

To those who knew Vanzetti well, his humanity was so pervasive that, more than half a century later, Alfonsina Brini could weep for him and say he lived as Christ preached.

Alfonsina Brini: *I remember one time he come home with a little kitty, sick. We didn't want it in the house, it was so sick. He found a box, put it out on the piazza, and he cured it.*

Lefevre Brini: *He didn't want us children near it because it might have had something contagious. He got some boric acid and warm water and a cloth and he washed the kitten's eyes. Then he'd get some milk, warm it up, and bring it out in a saucer.*

Beltrando Brini: *He would go out there and spoon-feed it. And it recovered.*

Alfonsina Brini: *One time he lost his wallet. It was thirteen dollars that he lost, and he makes notes about it and stick them in the trees, stick them here and there, tell me if you found it. A policeman came with a wallet with sixteen dollars, somebody found it. He didn't take it because he had in his head it was thirteen not sixteen dollars.*

Lefevre Brini: *It was his wallet. You could tell. But because he thought it couldn't be his, he wouldn't take it.*

Alfonsina Brini: *He bought a pair of boots and he used it outside in the cold weather, in the mud. But there was another* man didn't have no money to buy boots. Vanzetti said, "Well, if I work this week, I'll buy another pair. You take mine."

Lefevre
Brini:

The other fellow was married and he had children and he couldn't afford to have a pair of boots like Vanzetti's. They were working together; I think this was down the shore, fishing or clamming.

Beltrando
Brini:

When I was about twelve years old, I enjoyed playing baseball. One day I was playing ball on Suosso Lane, where I lived, where Vanzetti had lived with us, and the ball went over a fence into a garden. None of the boys wanted to go into the garden to retrieve the ball. I went in there and I trampled over some of the vegetables. An old man appeared and he was very angry. I laughed in his face, didn't excuse myself, might even have said something rude.

Vanzetti saw all this. He was leaving my house and he just stood there and watched everything happen. Of all people to catch me in an act like that, he was the one for whom I'd be most ashamed. He waited until I got out of the yard and into the street. He didn't want to speak out loud with all my friends around, so he got on one knee to talk to me quietly, and gave me a lecture which put me to shame. He told me that this wasn't the thing to do, I should have asked to go into the garden, I should have been careful. At least I should have excused myself; I shouldn't have laughed in the man's face. He told me he was very much ashamed of what I had done and he hoped I'd never do it again. A couple of days after that he was arrested. That was the last time I saw him as a free man.

Alfonsina
Brini:

He wouldn't kill a fly, not that man. He kill for money? Ha! He can't be dead, that kind of man. He should live and teach humanity. Oh, God, so good, I tell you. He got this idea—anarchist—you know, I don't know much about it. But if all the men was like him, I'd like to see all anarchists!

The Bostonians, tho' their Forefathers fled thither to enjoy Liberty of Conscience, are very unwilling any should enjoy it but themselves.

—John Dunton, English bookseller, after visit to New England in 1686

Nothing is more universally human than the desire to feel that one is a member of a community of distinguished people, of an elite.

—Yves Simon

My people do not live in America, they live underneath America.

—Father Paul Tymkevich, Slavic leader

II

BACKGROUNDS

3

The Visible Saints

It is no small irony that fate or rather something as mundane as the search for work led Vanzetti to set down his two valises in Plymouth, Massachusetts, where in 1620 the Pilgrims disembarked from that most revered of all immigrant vessels, the *Mayflower*, and set down the first Puritan roots in New England. The Pilgrims were only a vanguard, however; the great Puritan migration from old England to New England came during the decade from 1630 to 1640. It was an exodus less to escape persecution than to establish it.

The name *Puritan* originated in sixteenth-century England to derisively describe those who carped at the church when it was still traumatized by the Reformation and Henry VIII's break with Rome. Henry was neither Protestant nor Puritan; purity was of no interest to him personally or theologically. The break came solely because the pope would not approve Henry's marriage to Anne Boleyn on the trifling grounds that Henry already had a wife, and since Anne was pregnant, Henry wanted a legitimate heir. Henry's concept of reform was to make the Roman Catholic Church a national church with himself rather than the pope as head, giving him the right to seize and squander its wealth and the authority to solve his complex matrimonial problems. He tolerated neither true Roman Catholics, whom he had drawn-and-quartered, nor true Protestants, whom he sent to the stake. There was no god but God, and Henry was his prophet.

When Henry died in 1547 he left three heirs born of three different mothers. His sickly nine-year-old son, Edward VI, influenced by Protestant advisers, established a Protestant reign. When Edward died in 1553, Mary Tudor ruled as a Catholic. When Mary died in 1558, Elizabeth I, the shrewd compromiser, established a Church of England that wed Protestant creed to Catholic ceremony.

Decades of weather-vane theology, dependent upon the whim of the Crown, had left England primarily Protestant, with pockets of opinionated dissenters. Most of the English accepted the Anglican church, as they accepted whatever their monarchs imposed upon them, but the Puritans were dissatisfied; the Puritans were always dissatisfied. The moderates among them wanted to reform the Church of England; the extremists wanted to establish a new church. These Separatists could not of course agree on either the form or substance of the new church to which they wanted to separate, some preferring a Presbyterian or national church but most favoring the Congregationalist idea of autonomous units, with each congregation independently covenanted to God.

The Congregationalists were the dominant Puritan strain that settled New England. They accepted Saint Augustine's concept of two churches: an invisible church which is flawless because it includes only those chosen by God for salvation, and a visible church which is flawed because though it includes only Christians—and only Christians can be saved—not every Christian *will* be saved. Regrettably, the visible church includes some of the damned.

From John Calvin came the theory of predestination which held that men were born predestined for heaven or hell. Calvin estimated that in a normal Christian community only one person in five was predestined for salvation. To beat these odds, the Puritans took from the Old Testament the concept of a covenant with God. God's covenant with Abraham had been annulled with the coming of Christ, said the Puritans; to be saved, one had to believe in Jesus with saving faith or saving grace. Just as a covenant of grace existed between God and those who had saving faith, a covenant could exist between God and groups of those who had saving faith. Thus a true church was a visible church that came as close as possible to Saint Augustine's invisible church. It was a voluntary association of visible saints, all of whom, through God's mercy and their own wisdom, were Puritans.

Queen Elizabeth and her successors, James I and Charles I, considered the Puritans nuisances at best and heretics and traitors at worst, particularly as their numbers multiplied and their theology became increasingly inflexible. After the Pilgrims had settled safely at Plymouth, and other Englishmen had set up a fishing company on the Massachusetts coast, Puritan leaders in England, who feared heightened persecution under the new bishop of London, William Laud, began seriously to consider Massachusetts as the Canaan God had promised Abraham. In Massachusetts the Puritans would not have to compromise with either church or state because they would be both. There would be no obstacles between them and God because they would be god.

There is an old Jewish folk tale which says God placed the souls of all foolish persons in a sack to distribute equally around the world, but the sack broke and all fools fell into the village of Chelm. The Puritans wished to be just as certain that all saints landed together in Massachusetts. "God sifted a whole nation that He might send choice grain over into this wilderness," said a Puritan preacher.[1]

In 1629 the Puritans obtained a commercial charter as the Massachusetts Bay Company from King Charles I, which gave them trading rights and limited powers of government in New England. Though such overseas trading companies usually had offices and shareholders in England, the Puritans who planned to go to America purchased all the stock in the company from those who chose to remain behind, which gave them unimpeded control of the colony. Taking their charter with them so the king could not easily recall it, the Puritans sailed for New England in 1630. Through manipulation and evasion, they would do what the king would never have allowed, use a corporate charter to found a theocracy. Church and commerce issued from the Puritan womb as twins, only one of them legitimate; the Puritans, who so ironly upheld authority, began by defying it.

On board the *Arabella*, one of the four ships that made the first voyage, Governor John Winthrop said in a sermon, "Thus stands the cause between God and us; we are entered into Covenant with him for this work. . . . Now if the Lord shall please to hear us, and bring us in peace to the place we desire, then hath he ratified this Covenant and sealed our Commission." A safe arrival would show that God had kept his part of the bargain; it would then be up to the Puritans to keep theirs. "We shall be as a city upon a hill," said Winthrop, "the eyes of all people are upon us." This was to be the great Puritan endeavor, to establish upon the shores of New England a society of saints whose example the rest of the world could emulate.

The Puritans founded Massachusetts Bay Colony at Salem, as well as other settlements, including Boston. They also organized themselves into small, separate congregations consisting of at least seven men who made a covenant with God and each other. The founders of each of these Congregationalist churches then selected a minister, ruling elders and, as other saints appeared, admitted new members. By 1640 there were eighteen churches in Massachusetts Bay, six in Plymouth, two in New Haven Colony, and three in Connecticut Colony.

Since the Puritans in England had been frustrated by their inability to affect government policy, they made certain that in New England only they would govern. They called their settlement a *commonwealth*, but a commonwealth is defined as "a state in which the supreme power is held by the people." In Massachusetts Bay the supreme power was held by the Puritans. The corporate charter required that the Massachusetts Bay Company be managed by a governor, a deputy governor, and a board of eighteen assistants elected annually by the stockholders. This board was to meet once a month, while the stockholders, or freemen, were to meet four times a year in general court. The general court could pass laws and regulations as necessary, as long as they were not contrary to the laws of England.

One of the first regulations passed by the general court was contrary to the laws of England; it decreed that only Puritans could be freemen and take part in government. Since non-Puritans were also emigrating to New England, it has been estimated that by 1640 some twenty thousand settlers were ruled by a Puritan minority that amounted to no more than one-fifth of the population. When the Puritan pastor Roger Williams called for separation of church and state, he was banished and went off to found Rhode Island, which became a haven for many of those the Puritans oppressed.

The Puritans in England had also been frustrated by their conflict with the Anglican church; this too was an indignity they would not countenance in New England. Scorning religious freedom as the "first born of all abominations" and "Satan's policy," the Puritans banned all other churches. Either you were a Puritan and therefore a saint or you were not a Puritan and therefore a sinner; there were no alternatives. If you were a saint you enjoyed the privileges of this world, including voting and worshipping. If you were a sinner you had no privileges, only obligations. While you lived you were obliged to contribute to the salary of the Puritan minister and attend Puritan services, though you could not be baptized or receive communion; when you died you were obliged to go to hell.

Originally, both in England and New England, one became a member of a Puritan congregation by leading a blameless life and expressing understanding and faith; whether or not it was saving faith was left to God to judge. But during the 1630s, the Puritans in Massachusetts made their church more select; the object was not to draw people in but to keep them out. To become a member of a Massachusetts congregation it was necessary to convince the church elders, who had undergone no such test, that one had actually experienced saving faith. A righteous life and good works were expected of visible saints but were not in themselves proof of saving faith. Men and women had to undergo a period of doubt and despair. If they were among the predestined, God himself rekindled their faith.

Though the covenant of faith was between man and God, the Puritan elders decided when it was genuine. Each time they admitted or rejected a member, they were anticipating God's judgment and usurping his function. If they erred, it was on the side of caution; they sanctified the few while sacrificing the many. Good Christians who were barred from the Puritan church could not worship elsewhere since there were no other churches. While the saints preached to each other, the majority of New Englanders were deprived of religious comfort, guidance, and discipline.

Under Puritan rule, society was divided into three classes, as somehow it always is. At the peak were the saints who ruled all, for clearly the men who led the community were destined for eternal life. Midway were undistinguished Puritans whose future was cloudy; they might or might not be among the saved. This uncertainty literally drove some mad. One woman in Boston drowned her child in a well; after that her doubts were relieved for she knew she was damned. At the bottom of the social structure were all those who were not Puritans, including servants, slaves, and criminals.

The Puritan certainty that they were an elect who knew God's will granted them total freedom from conscience; they were so filled with God there was no room for humanity. It was not uncommon for Puritans to have their children raised by others lest they be spoiled by parental affection. A disobedient child could be turned over to the magistrates by his parents to be whipped; a disobedient youth could be turned over to the magistrates by his parents to be executed. Since everyone else was damned they could be treated as such; nothing suffered on earth compared to the agonies of everlasting perdition. Puritans did not scruple to make fortunes from the slave trade because blacks, not knowing Christ, were already doomed. "They who never heard the Gospel, shall never answer for not believing in it," said a Puritan preacher, "because it was not so made known to them, but yet they shall answer for that habitual infidelity whereby they would have resisted it." The Puritans knew who would have resisted the gospels and who would have accepted them with the same assurance that they knew who was a saint and who was not.

This sanctified bigotry also guided the Puritans in their treatment of the Indians. The fur trade was important, but so was their security. When an English trader was killed by the Pequot

Backgrc

Indians, the Puritans retaliated with the righteousness of the Lord. A Puritan army and some Indian allies surrounded the Pequot village before dawn and set it afire. Pequots who tried to escape the flames were shot down; those who survived were sold into slavery. The entire tribe of over four hundred men, women, and children was wiped out, an act of genocide that was hailed by the great Puritan divine, Cotton Mather, who in his joy inflated the body count as he gloated that "we have sent six hundred heathen souls to hell."[2] After all, they were going there anyway.

4

The Accursed Group

All may be perfect in God's invisible church, though there have been no confirming reports, but the visible church and state established by the Puritans in seventeenth-century New England had serious problems. There were three particularly convulsive episodes which richly illuminate the Puritan mentality and its doleful legacy to freedom and justice in Massachusetts.

Each episode was linked to a serious crisis in Puritan-American history. There is a myth that crisis brings out the best in people, which may be true of such clearly defined disasters as war or earthquakes, though wars have their profiteers and earthquakes their looters. But when the crisis is only vaguely understood, when society is in disorder and authority is challenged or threatened, there is a need for explanations. If the explanations are too complex or too painful, there is a need to seek a scapegoat.

In *Community of the Free*, French philosopher Yves Simon analyzed and enunciated the characteristics and role of the scapegoat or, in his phrase, the accursed group. The accursed group is always a readily identifiable and usually unpopular minority: religious, ideological, economic, or ethnic. To make their villainy more plausible, the members of the accursed group are believed to have power and influence far beyond their capabilities. Having them to blame offers a simple, simplistic reason for whatever is wrong, relieves the community of guilt, relieves the leaders of the community of responsibility, relieves everyone of the need to confront and resolve the real problem, and relieves everyone's fear, anger, and confusion by offering them someone to persecute. "An accursed group is a very useful thing," wrote Simon, "and it is proper, prudent and comforting to have one ready at hand at all times."[1]

The first Puritan crisis involved a dissident group who were perceived as accursed because they questioned Puritan power precisely when the Puritans were struggling to maintain and expand it. In England the Puritans themselves had been dissident reformers; in Massachusetts they had redefined their mission and become as entrenched as any hierarchy they had opposed. By the mid-1630s, more immigrants were landing and pushing farther into the wilderness. Just as it became imperative to control an expanding, increasingly non-Puritan population, Puritan leaders faced insurrection not on the frontier but in Boston itself. The holier-than-thou oligarchs who ruled Massachusetts were challenged by a woman holier than they.

The dissident Antinomian movement was led by Anne Hutchinson, whom Governor Winthrop described as "a woman of haughty and fierce carriage, of a nimble wit and active spirit, and a very voluble tongue, more bold than a man." The battle with Mrs. Hutchinson and her followers was technically over the covenant of grace, but the reverberations were political rather than religious. Mrs. Hutchinson argued that since grace was a matter between man and God, no preacher was needed to certify its presence. Not only was she saying that the Puritan church was superfluous, but that the ministers were unfit to judge who had saving faith because only two of them, whom she named, had saving faith themselves.

The original Antinomians, who arose in Luther's day, believed that those with grace had no need to observe any moral law; their conscience was sufficent. This was theological anarchy; in a theocracy such as Massachusetts, theological anarchy threatened both church and state.

Anne Hutchinson was talking about pure religion; the Puritans were dealing with practical politics. In order to govern their Bible state, they had assumed worldly responsibilities they would neither acknowledge nor surrender. Religious controls served as a cover for political controls. In determining who had faith, they also determined who could vote. In giving law to saints, they also gave law to the entire community. Outward conformity had nothing to do with inner sanctity, but it was essential to preserve the Puritan dictatorship.

Whether or not it was her intent, Mrs. Hutchinson's theological questions undermined the political foundations of the Puritan state and became particularly threatening when she gathered a large following. Because they did not want to call her crime sedition and did not know what else to call it, the Puritans summoned a religious synod during the summer of 1637 to find theological grounds on which Mrs. Hutchinson could be charged. After laboring twenty-four days, the synod pronounced eighty-two opinions "unsafe," meaning heretical, and nine expressions "unwholesome." Thus armed, the Puritan leaders brought Anne Hutchinson to trial in November. Governor Winthrop was both judge and prosecutor; Mrs. Hutchinson was her own lawyer. Professional lawyers were not permitted to practice in Massachusetts since the fundamental law of the colony was the Bible. When the Puritans founded Harvard College in 1636 it was to train ministers, not lawyers.

Even with his long list of new heresies, Winthrop found it difficult to explain to Anne Hutchinson what she was accused of, since her crime lay in being a religious rather than a political Puritan. He spoke vaguely of her troubling the peace of the commonwealth but Mrs. Hutchinson demanded he be specific, and some of their exchanges were almost comic.

Hutchinson: I am called here to answer before you but I hear no things laid to my charge.
Winthrop: I have told you some already and more I can tell you.
Hutchinson: Name one, sir.

Backgr

Winthrop: Have I not named some already?

When Mrs. Hutchinson pressed him further, Winthrop snapped, "We do not mean to discourse with those of your sex"; not only was she a nuisance but a woman. It was just too humiliating.

Anne Hutchinson repeatedly demanded that she be told what she had done wrong, and Winthrop kept demanding that she prove she had done nothing wrong. Finally Mrs. Hutchinson saved the court from its own confusion by claiming that God had revealed to her "which was the clear ministry and which the wrong."

Q: How did you know that this was the spirit?
Hutchinson: How did Abraham know that it was God did bid him to offer his son? . . .
Q: By an immediate voice.
Hutchinson: So to me by an immediate voice.

Now the prosecution finally had its case. While the Puritans believed God had spoken to Abraham, they did not believe he had confided to Anne Hutchinson which of the ministers had saving faith. Her spontaneous boast of divine revelation was heresy; the court was polled and she was found guilty.

Winthrop: Mrs. Hutchinson, the sentence of the court you hear is that you are banished from out our jurisdiction as being a woman not fit for our society, and are to be imprisoned till the court shall send you away.
Hutchinson: I desire to know wherefore I am banished.
Winthrop: Say no more, the court knows wherefore and is satisfied. (Emphasis added.)

Mrs. Hutchinson was confined for four months and then put through a church trial, as though her civil trial had not already been a church trial. The purpose of the church trial was to give her the opportunity to recant her heretical views, but when she did so, the recantation was rejected. The Puritans said she was not sincere; "repentance is not in her face." The curtain fell on this divine comedy when the Puritan church formally excommunicated Anne Hutchinson not for heresy but for lying about her repentance.

Anne Hutchinson's followers were banished, disenfranchised, disarmed in the traditional meaning of being forced to surrender their weapons, or simply intimidated, and Puritan rule was preserved. Thus did Massachusetts deal with its first dissidents.

After Massachusetts Bay Colony was founded, Puritans continued to emigrate to New England, bolstering its population and providing fresh supplies of saints. But in November, 1640, the Long Parliament convened in London and for the next twenty years England was the scene of the series of events collectively called the English Revolution. For most Puritans the action was no longer in Massachusetts but in England, where they executed King Charles I and established a Puritan dictatorship. The king, facing the block, spoke a truth the Puritans were too arrogant to accept when he said, "I go from a corruptible to an incorruptible crown." Only the dead are incorruptible; men cannot be saints.

The Puritans in New England rejoiced at the success of their brethren in England and fully expected the English Puritans to use Massachusetts as a model for rebuilding the mother country. But while the English Puritans imposed a worse tyranny upon the English people than had been endured under most of their kings, England's Puritans dismissed New England's Puritans as a band of fanatics and accepted a level of religious tolerance intolerable in Massachusetts.

The English Revolution was doubly disastrous; not only did it reveal to the New Englanders that they were irrelevant but it closed off Puritan migration just as the original settlers were beginning to die out. Since new saints were no longer marching in, the Puritans had to replenish their congregations from among their own offspring; unless they could produce pious children the church was doomed. Puritan children were baptized but could not become full members of the church and receive communion unless they had saving faith. Since saving faith was not hereditary, many second-generation Puritans showed no sign of it by the time they were mature and some showed no sign of it at all.

During the 1650s, the ministry wrestled with the perplexity of what to do with these provisional Puritans. Should they be

Backgro

permitted to have their own children baptized? Should they be expelled? What if they experienced saving faith later in life?

In 1657 a synod was summoned to Boston to try to resolve these questions. It was decided that those who had been baptized and led lives free of scandal yet had no saving faith could not receive communion but could remain in the church and have their children baptized. This concession to reality caused an uproar among the orthodox, who scornfully called it the halfway covenant. Dissension over the halfway covenant capped the doubts brought on by the English Revolution. English rejection and religious compromise weakened the Puritans' sense of mission, forced them to question their identity, and brought on the second major siege of suppression, for just when the Puritans needed an accursed group on which to vent their anxieties, the Quakers appeared.

In some ways the Quakers resembled the Antinomians; several were followers of Anne Hutchinson. They believed that no church hierarchy should stand between man and God and that the Puritans had lost their "inner light." Unlike the Antinomians, however, the Quakers were not reformers trying to restore their religion to its original purity; they were a separate sect seeking the right to worship and to proselytize.

The Puritans, who believed "it was toleration that made the world anti-Christian,"[2] had in 1651 whipped several Baptists for preaching that only adults had the understanding to be baptized. When in 1656 two Quaker missionaries sailed into Boston from Barbados, the Puritan reaction was predictable. Forewarned, Puritan officials boarded the ship and confiscated all Quaker books and pamphlets, which were publicly burned by the hangman. Though there was no law prohibiting Quaker activities, the two women were imprisoned and their window boarded up so no one could be contaminated by the sight or sound of them. The women were examined for witchmarks; if any had been found they would have been hanged. As soon as possible, they were shipped back to Barbados.

A few days later eight Quakers sailed in from London and were imprisoned until they could be sent back. In October, 1656, the general court corrected the absence of anti-Quaker statutes by damning them as a "cursed sect of heretics" and passing laws to punish them and their sympathizers with fines and floggings. When a devout old Puritan suggested the laws were too harsh, he was banished in midwinter with strict orders that no one shelter him; in effect, a death sentence. He found refuge with an Indian chief, who said, "What a God have the English, who deal so with one another about the worship of their God."

Since Quakers who shipped in were shipped right out again, they began to come overland by way of Rhode Island where the Puritan exile, Roger Williams, granted freedom of worship to all. When twenty or thirty lashes of a knotted whip failed to halt the Quaker invasion, the general court passed a harsher law in 1657. For a first offense a male Quaker would have one of his ears clipped off; for a second offense, the other ear. Women would continue to be whipped for their first two offenses. For a third offense both men and women would "have their tongues bored through with a hot iron."

Three men lost an ear and one was flogged 117 times until "his flesh was beaten black and as into jelly," but the Quakers could easily match the Puritans for zealousness, and the joy with which they suffered won converts in the colony. Enraged, the general court in 1658 passed still another law, this time condemning Quakers to death, which brought a veritable stampede of eager martyrs. Among those who came were two men who had lost an ear and a woman named Mary Dyer, one of Anne Hutchinson's followers, who had already been banished twice.

The Boston Puritans chose three imprisoned Quakers at random, two men and Mary Dyer, and sentenced them to be hanged. On October 27, 1659, the three walked hand in hand to the gallows, surrounded by one hundred armed militia in the event the crowd should try to intervene. Mary Dyer watched the two men die, then she climbed the ladder and a noose was placed about her neck. At that moment she was told she had been granted a reprieve.

The hangings only served to increase Quaker activities and conversions in Massachusetts. Mary Dyer, who had been sent back to Rhode Island, returned once more, knowing what her fate would be. She was hanged June 1, 1660.

The war between the Puritans and the Quakers might have escalated into theological genocide had not events in England intervened. The Puritan reign had ended; three days before Mary Dyer's execution, Charles II rode into London in triumph. The restoration was not welcomed in Massachusetts. Puritans had executed Charles's father and there was considerable concern that the new king might seek retribution in New England, particularly since Puritan rule far exceeded the limitations set by the original charter.

The Puritans quickly released the imprisoned Quakers and banished them, but English Quakers had already reported to the king what was happening in his colony of Massachusetts. He sent a letter forbidding further executions or punishment, but though no more Quakers were hanged, the Puritans continued to whip them out of town whenever they were found.

United now against Charles, whose efforts to restore royal power in Massachusetts would lead to the third great crisis, the Puritans no longer needed an accursed group; they had an accursed king to deal with. When royal commissioners demanded greater religious toleration in Massachusetts, the Puritans faced a painful decision. If they defied Charles he might revoke their charter and Puritan rule would be ended. If they obeyed Charles and tolerated such heretics as Quakers and Baptists, the Puritans' religious monopoly would be ended. The visible saints might be assured of a place in heaven but their role on earth was definitely in doubt.

In 1674, the Quakers opened a meeting house in Boston and the Puritans, fearing the loss of their charter more than the threat to their souls, did nothing. The Baptists followed with a church of their own. Most galling was the king's order that members of his own church, the Church of England, from whose abominations the Puritans had hastened to America, be permitted freedom of worship in Massachusetts. By 1686, Anglican services were being held in Boston.

From the time of the restoration in 1660, the Puritans fought a prolonged but losing battle to retain their political and religious control of Massachusetts. The king not only forced religious tolerance upon them but in 1662 ordered them to permit all propertied freeholders to vote, whether they were Puritans or not. The Puritans, who did not surrender easily, nullified this by passing a law requiring that would-be voters who were not Puritans be approved by the ministers and the general court; for the time being, the oligarchy was safe.

In 1664 the king sent commissioners to New England to review the Massachusetts charter and force the colonists to obey the Navigation Acts. The Puritans feared for their charter because they knew it did not grant them the powers they had assumed and had taken it with them just to postpone such an inspection; they had been governing illegally from the day they landed. The Navigation Acts, which regulated, limited, and taxed colonial commerce, had been consistently evaded and violated by New England shippers who had a sharp scent for money; when Boston became a prosperous shipping center it was seen as another sign of God's favor. Some of the ministers did worry about the accumulation of private fortunes and urged the people to remember that "New England is originally a plantation of religion, not a plantation of trade," but what concerned them was that wealth is more visible than faith and that a commercial elite would arise to challenge the leadership of the religious elite.

Charles II had too many problems with Parliament, war, plague, and fire—all undoubtedly wished upon him by the Puritans—to deal with New England immediately, but in 1684 the Massachusetts charter was revoked. The king appointed a royal governor to rule the colony and the right to vote was extended to all men of property. Puritan dominance of both religious and secular life in New England would continue, but the dictatorship of the saints was over.

As the Puritan edifice crumbled, the hierarchy sought a scapegoat rather than acknowledge they had established a state contrary to reason, nature, faith, and freedom. An accursed group is always appropriate to its time and place; when the Puritans needed reassurance that God had not abandoned them entirely, they found it in witchcraft. The Puritans made their covenant with God; witches made their covenant with the devil. If the devil existed, so did God; if the devil plagued the few, God proved his affection for the Puritans by protecting the many.

It was also appropriate that when the powerful felt power-less, the powerless tried to seize power. The witch-hunts that began in Salem village in February, 1692, were a kind of peasants' revolt; they sprouted among the lowest and the least in Puritan society—a black slave, white servants, young girls—who, for as long as the hysteria lasted, held the power of life and death over some of the proudest men and women in the colony.

Before the witch-hunts had run their course, nineteen per-sons were hanged, one was pressed to death with stones, at least two died in prison, hundreds were held in custody, and hundreds more had been accused. The trials were conducted by men who had no legal training and no concept of innocence. The girls could prove the accused guilty by feigning fits. If the defendants confessed they were spared; they were hanged only if they denied their guilt. This was Puritan logic: sin, confession and repentance, forgiveness. An accused witch who did not confess was not innocent; the devil held her tongue.

Puritan injustice produced martyrs of very high quality, such as Anne Hutchinson and Mary Dyer. During the witch-hunts the victims included several women of valor, humanity, piety, and virtue. Best remembered is seventy-one-year-old Rebecca Nurse who, when the judge warned her, "You would do well if you were guilty to confess," boldly replied, "*Would you have me belie myself?*" (Emphasis added.)

The Salem witch-hunts, like the Antinomian and Quaker persecutions, exposed the Puritans as zealots not blinded by God but simply blind, morally and spiritually leprous, men devoted not to a higher cause but to self-preservation. Yet, as the original settlers, no other group left so penetrating an imprint on American history.

Calling it God's will, the Puritans planted in the stony soil of New England the seeds of intolerance, injustice, and inequality. The concept of visible saints would be stretched to embrace wealth and intellect, but the myth that an elect should determine man's fate would endure, as would the belief that this elect was entitled to choose who might inhabit their earth.

When they still held power, the Puritans inspected each newcomer before deciding whether he or she was fit to live among them. Some who came to Massachusetts were rejected as "unmeete to inhabit here" or unsuitable "to sit down among us." The concept of America as an open society was anathema to the Puritans. Immigrant historian Marcus Lee Hansen wrote, "From the very beginning their policy was to select from among those who appeared, and this exclusive attitude of New England remained a tradition throughout almost three centuries of immigration."[3]

Because the Puritan legacy was a visible elite and implacable intolerance of dissenters and aliens, three hundred years later they could properly claim among their victims the edge trimmer and the fish peddler.

5

The Oldest Prejudice

When the first United States census was taken in 1790, the total white population was 3,172,444. By analyzing family names it has been calculated that 60.9 percent were of English origin, 14.3 percent were Scotch and Scotch-Irish (ethnic Scots who had lived in Ireland), and 3.7 percent were Irish. The largest non-British group was German—8.7 percent. Dutch, French, and Swedes totaled 5.4 percent. Others who had emigrated to America in even smaller numbers included Danes, Norwegians, Finns, Spaniards, Portuguese, Poles, Italians, and Jews.[1]

While Massachusetts was candling each arrival, the other colonies were less rigid; eighteen different languages were spoken in New Amsterdam. Nonetheless, the 1790 census reveals that more than 90 percent of the first Americans came from northern or western Europe and almost 80 percent were of British origin.

At birth, America was white, Anglo-Saxon, and Protestant. The WASP would therefore be the norm; everyone else was deviant. The WASP was native stock; everyone else was an immigrant, an alien, a hyphenated-American, or an ethnic. The

WASPs established the language, the life style, and the cultural patterns to which all subsequent immigrant groups had to adjust. An immigrant's acceptability would be based on how close he came to being white, Anglo-Saxon, and Protestant or how well he could conceal it if he wasn't. As Michael Novak writes, "The entire experience of becoming American is summarized in the experience of being made to feel guilty."[2]

Since the WASP was the native—never the Indians—entomologists devoted to the preservation of the American WASP are known as nativists. They have been both militant and cosmopolitan in their determination to maintain their unique status; among those who have suffered the WASPs' sting are Catholics, Jews, nonwhites, aliens, and radicals.

The first white victims were the Catholics; historian Arthur Schlesinger, Sr., called anti-Catholicism "the oldest and most ingrained of American prejudices."[3] This too can be laid at the ulcerated legs of Henry VIII. Because his lusts and his ego overrode his kingship, the break with Rome was badly managed, leaving a bitter harvest of hate and persecution. The uncertain succession to Henry's throne, alternatingly Protestant, Catholic, Protestant, Puritan, Protestant, Catholic, and finally, Protestant, unnerved the Protestants and kept Catholic hopes alive long after both sides should have considered the matter settled.

The international character of Catholicism also troubled the English. Having confronted the Spanish armada in 1588, as well as other Catholic assaults and intrigues, English Protestants knew that some English Catholics were willing to ally themselves with a foreign power to restore a Catholic crown. To counter this threat, England was flooded with anti-Catholic propaganda which described the church in such colorful language as "bloodthirsty, unclean, blasphemic whore of the devil." As a result, many English came to view Catholics not as fellow Christians who belonged to a different and, indeed, older church, but as debased, debauched, and dangerous. Laws were passed excluding Catholics from the major professions, banishing priests and poor Catholics, and forcing wealthy ones to worship in the Anglican church.[4]

Catholics fled this persecution but few came to America; at

the time of the American Revolution there were perhaps thirty thousand Catholics in a population of 3 million. Since America was settled by English Protestants whose baggage included their biases, most of the colonies were as intolerant as the mother country. Only one Catholic, Charles Carroll, signed the Declaration of Independence because there was only one Catholic in the Second Continental Congress; Carroll's enormous wealth compensated for his religious deficiencies.[5] All of the colonies but Rhode Island had laws denying Catholics something: the right to worship or to vote or to hold office or to enter certain professions; in some colonies Catholics had to pay extra taxes.

According to Ray Allen Billington, historian of America's Protestant crusade before the Civil War, "There were two centers for the development of No-Popery sentiment in the seventeenth century: Maryland and Massachusetts."[6] America's Catholic population was concentrated in Maryland, which had been founded in 1632 by a Catholic, Lord Baltimore, but even there Catholics were outnumbered by Protestants, who ultimately banished Lord Baltimore and passed anti-Catholic laws.

Massachusetts had few Catholics within its borders as a result of the vigilance of the Puritans. In 1647 they had banned all Jesuits and priests from the colony upon threat of execution. Between hangings, the Puritans amused themselves with a game called "Break the Pope's Neck," while Harvard added intellectual substance to anti-Catholic intolerance by presenting a lecture series, later issued in pamphlet form, on the Catholic church, "their tyranny, usurpations, damnable heresies, fatal errors, abominable superstitions, and other crying wickedness in her high places."[7]

The American Revolution, won with the aid of Catholic France, brought some degree of tolerance, and the First Amendment guaranteed freedom of worship. But the Federalists, ideological heirs of the Puritans, feared and distrusted foreigners, particularly Catholics. John Adams of Quincy, Massachusetts, wrote Thomas Jefferson, "Can a free government possibly exist with the Roman Catholic religion?"[8]

The 1790s were a period of new migration to America, which included French fleeing the revolutions in France and Haiti and

Irish fleeing a failed rebellion.[9] Federalists scorned these immigrants and then were piqued when they flocked to Jefferson's Democratic-Republican party. But even Jefferson worried that pristine America would be corrupted by decadent foreigners who would "warp and bias" the American spirit and transform the country into a "heterogeneous, incoherent, distracted mass."[10] From infancy, this nation of immigrants has been hostile to immigrants; those already ashore have rejected the next shipload as foreigners.

The first arrivals in America became citizens as they landed; by 1790 immigrants were required to wait two years. A distinction was already being made between the "old" and the "new" immigration; the new immigrants were described as "the common class of vagrants, paupers, and other outcasts of Europe."[11] In 1795 the naturalization period was extended to five years; in 1798 to fourteen years, a compromise with those who contended that "nothing but birth shall entitle a man to citizenship in this country."[12]

The bill making the naturalization period fourteen years was one of the Alien and Sedition Acts passed by a Federalist-controlled Congress in 1798 in an attempt to insure the party's political survival by suppressing aliens and dissenters, for the new immigrants recognized the Federalists as elitists and the Jeffersonians as democrats and voted accordingly. Another of the anti-alien acts of 1798 gave the president, Federalist John Adams, the right to summarily expel, without trial, hearing, or explanation, any alien he considered to be dangerous. A third act gave the government the right to arrest and deport enemy aliens if America went to war, while the Sedition Act made criticism of the government, Congress, or the president a crime.

The act that gave the president the power to expel dangerous aliens expired in 1800 without being used, but the act enabling the government to arrest and deport enemy aliens remained on the books and was used by Woodrow Wilson to intern German aliens during World War I.[13] The first victim of the Sedition Act, which expired in 1801, was Mathew Lyon, an Irish-Catholic congressman who was fined one thousand dollars and sentenced to four months in prison for criticizing President Adams in a letter to a Federalist newspaper.

Backgr

When Thomas Jefferson was elected president in 1800 with the aid of the Irish and French vote, the naturalization period was restored to five years. Nativism remained strongest where the Federalists were strongest—New England. New Englanders drove away unwanted immigrants, then seethed because they settled elsewhere building up the population and political power of other states. When the first Scotch-Irish, who were Calvinists, were confronted with hostility in Massachusetts, later arrivals headed for Pennsylvania.[14] At one point a Boston mob prevented Irish immigrants from landing. A few years later, another mob tore down a Scotch-Irish Presbyterian church in Worcester, Massachusetts.[15]

These were relatively minor incidents, which served mainly to establish the continuity of intolerance in Puritan Massachusetts. During the nineteenth century this meanness of spirit broke in such force against another wave of immigrants that in the 1970s blood was still being shed in the streets of Boston because of it.*

The immigrants who were to drive the descendants of the Puritans to the wall had their own ancestors driven to the wall by that great Puritan champion, Oliver Cromwell. Previous English kings had preyed on Ireland but it was Cromwell who turned his Irish invasion into a Protestant crusade intent upon annihilating the Irish Catholics and repopulating the country with English Protestants. After slaughtering three or four thousand Catholics at Drogheda and burning a Catholic church with the congregants inside, Cromwell wrote, "I am persuaded that this is a righteous judgment of God upon these barbarous wretches."[16]

When Cromwell returned to England he rewarded his followers by granting them large estates in Ireland. Absentee landlords drained such wealth as Ireland produced, leaving the land and people impoverished. By the 1820s, the Irish were sailing to America by the thousands.

The first influx of Irish immigrants was a boon, since cheap labor was needed to push back the frontier, build transportation, and work in new industries. By 1830 there were fourteen thousand Catholics and sixteen Roman Catholic churches in New

*The Boston busing crisis was not unrelated to the treatment of the Irish immigrants by the Yankees. The Irish learned the wrong lessons, but they were taught by masters.

England, where once Quakers and Baptists had prayed at their peril. As Catholics increased in numbers, so did their desire to enjoy equality with their fellow Christians; they wanted to build their own schools and use their own translation of the Bible. Protestants responded with a massive propaganda campaign on the dangers of Catholicism.

The first anti-Catholic newspaper was founded in Boston.[17] It was followed by floods of anti-Catholic books, pamphlets, and tracts. Boston was suffering from severe economic problems, and while Irish labor might be useful in the interior, it was not wanted in the city. To deflect both anxieties and solutions, an accursed group was needed.

In 1829, a crowd of Yankees, fired up by a revivalist preacher, spent three days attacking and stoning the homes of Boston's Irish Catholics.[18] In 1833, after some Irishmen beat a Yankee to death, a mob of five hundred avengers marched on the Irish ghetto, destroying and burning.[19]

In Charlestown, across the Charles River from Boston, where health regulations permitted Protestants but not Catholics to be buried, stood a convent school built in 1818 by Ursuline nuns. Wealthy families, both Catholic and Protestant, sent their daughters to the Ursuline convent to be educated because the public schools were controlled by Congregationalists, and Boston's upper class had rejected the old-time religion for a more liberal Unitarianism.

The Ursuline convent was a hated symbol for two groups in Boston. To the laborer, it meant an unholy alliance between his economic enemy, the wealthy, and his theological enemy, the Catholics. To the orthodox ministers, the religious descendants of the visible saints, the Ursuline convent was a haven for "atheists and infidels" for the presence of Unitarians in Boston was as much a threat to the job of a Congregationalist preacher as the presence of an Irish worker was to a Protestant brickmaker.

Motivated by self-preservation as well as religious bias, streams of anti-Catholic sermons began to issue from pulpits in and about the Boston area. While the preachers were attacking the church, the anti-Catholic press focused on the convent school, falsely reporting that all Protestant pupils were being converted.

Rumors began to spread about deliciously evil doings behind the convent doors. A convent servant who had been dismissed drew wide attention by pretending to be an escaped nun. A nun who did leave the convent voluntarily returned, but by then her story had passed from mouth to mouth in Boston, gathering more sordid details as it went.

At this point the Reverend Lyman Beecher, a fiery fundamentalist, delivered three vehemently anti-Catholic sermons in three different churches in Boston demanding action, not words. The following night, August 11, 1834, a mob gathered at the school shouting, "Down with the Cross," a strange chant for Protestants. The town selectmen were notified but they insisted their one policeman could handle the situation.

At 11 P.M., reinforcements joined the crowd. The mother superior, urging the mob to disperse, made the gross error of saying, "The Bishop has 20,000 Irishmen at his command in Boston." Enraged by this threat, the crowd burst open the doors of the convent. While the nuns and their pupils fled through a rear door, the mob set fire to the school as well as a nearby farmhouse also owned by the Ursulines.[20] Later, when a futile attempt was made to get the commonwealth to pay for a new convent, a nativist editor condemned those who would "rob the treasury of the descendants of the Puritans to build Ursuline nunneries."[21]

Thirteen men were arrested for the burning of the convent, eight were tried, and one was found guilty, though he was soon pardoned at the tactful request of Boston's Catholic community. At the trial of the first accused arsonist, who was acquitted, the defense attorney told the jury, "*The prisoner at the bar cannot be convicted without Catholic testimony. We will endeavor to show what that testimony is worth.*"[22] (Emphasis added.)

The flames of Charlestown convent signaled a more virulent phase of the anti-Catholic crusade in America. In New England, assaults on Roman Catholic churches became a crowd sport. While joiners organized anti-Catholic societies, literate haters founded more newspapers and magazines, or wrote books. The classic volume on the anti-Catholic shelf was *Awful Disclosures of the Hotel Dieu Nunnery of Montreal* by Maria Monk. *Awful Disclosures*, which was published in 1836, was a best seller because, in an era parched for pornography, it was as close as most readers could get to a dirty book. It also confirmed what Protestants wanted to believe, that Catholic continence was a myth, that priests and nuns spent all their time rutting, and that the cellar of every convent overflowed with the bones of illegitimate children.*

Maria Monk's mother said her daughter had never been in a convent though she had been sent to a home for delinquents. The author herself came to a tragic end; she died in prison after being arrested for picking the pockets of her clients in a brothel. Not only had she never lived in a convent, she had not written *Awful Disclosures*; it was a collaboration by several Protestant clergymen. But though Maria Monk was discredited, the book was not; three hundred thousand copies were sold by the eve of the Civil War, and it was recirculated in 1960, when a Catholic, John F. Kennedy, ran for president.†[23]

During the decades of agitation that preceded the Civil War, both pro- and antislavery forces managed to make Catholics the accursed group. Southerners were warned that Catholics would assist blacks in a slave uprising against white Protestant plantation owners. Northern abolitionists found that some Catholic immigrants were hostile to their cause because they feared freed slaves would take away their jobs. To exacerbate matters, immigrants continued to be drawn or driven to America in increasing numbers. More than one hundred thousand came in 1845, more than two hundred thousand in 1847, more than four hundred thousand in 1854.[25] There were several reasons, chief among them the potato blight which struck not only Ireland but Germany.

Most of the German immigrants moved to the Midwest where there seemed to be room for them; there was always room if enough Indians were slaughtered or displaced. The Germans were not yet considered a problem though they included radicals

*This is not only Protestant mythology. I first heard these tales from an Orthodox Jewish relative who believed every word.
†Tens of millions of pieces of anti-Catholic hate literature were circulated during the 1960 campaign, much of it financed through tax-exempt Protestant organizations and churches.[24]

Backgr◦

escaping the unsuccessful revolutions of 1848. The Irish, however, tended to remain in the port of arrival, usually because they were too poor or ill to travel any farther.[26] By 1855, Boston had to face the shocking fact that the city contained more foreigners than natives.[27]

There is no doubt that the Irish created problems for Boston. As a result of the famine, most of them had sold their last possessions to pay for passage to America aboard ships that were little more than slavers. They arrived destitute, diseased, and often near death. The Boston Society for the Prevention of Pauperism sniffed that the city had to cope with "difficulties and embarrassments unknown to the men of an earlier day."[28] Boston gave the Irish some handouts but not equal opportunity or self-respect.* The Irish were accused both of being too lazy to work and of taking jobs away from good Americans. But peasants cannot become skilled laborers overnight; like earlier and later immigrant groups, the Irish began as unskilled workers. The women became servants and the men were a source of cheap labor which made possible the early industrialization of Boston, reviving the economy and filling the purses of the Yankee mill owners so hostile to them.[29]

Like other immigrant groups, the Irish were inclined to vote Democratic. In 1852, after Democrat Franklin Pierce was elected president with the help of Catholic and immigrant votes, the Whigs, ideological heirs of the Federalists who were ideological heirs of the Puritans, refusing to recognize that the Democrats won the immigrant vote because they were more responsive to it, decided something had to be done to limit the rights of immigrants. The Whigs allied themselves with the nativists, who hated immigrants and Catholics on principle, and workers, who feared immigrant competition for their jobs, and formed the Know-Nothing party. Members were supposed to be American-born Protestants who would swear to support only American-born Protestants for public office. Though the movement was anti-immi-

---

*Oscar Handlin writes that blacks in Boston "fared better" than the Irish. The percentage of intermarriage was higher for blacks than for the Irish, and a black "was as reluctant to have an Irishman move into his street as any Yankee."[30]

grant as well as anti-Catholic, the emphasis was anti-Catholic; foreign-born Protestants could and did join.* [31]

Using anti-Catholicism to divert the nation from the slavery issue, the Know-Nothings scored astonishing political victories in 1854. The party's greatest sweep was in Massachusetts, where the governor, all other state officers, the entire state senate, and all but two of the 378 members of the state's house of representatives were Know-Nothings.

Know-Nothings elected to Congress were unable to pass anti-Catholic or anti-immigration legislation because not enough Democrats or members of the newly formed Republican party would support them. In Massachusetts, though the Know-Nothings held all the power, they knew nothing about making it work. A committee was appointed to investigate Catholic convents, but there were no Catholic convents in Massachusetts so the members investigated Catholic schools instead. While they failed to find infant skeletons in the closets, they did run up a considerable bill for food, liquor, and whores.

The Know-Nothings failed not only in Washington and Massachusetts but everywhere they held office. Bigotry is not a positive program and will not hold a political party together for long. In 1856, the Know-Nothings nominated for president ex-President Millard Fillmore, who happened to be in Rome paying his respects to the pope at the time. Fillmore finished last in a three-way race and the people turned their attention to the real problem that was dividing the nation—slavery.

When the Civil War finally came, the immigrant groups in the North fought together for the Union, an experience that hastened their assimilation. In fact, when Irish migration had slowed but the Germans were still coming in force, bringing their radicals with them, an Irish-Catholic newspaper asked whether something shouldn't be done about restricting immigration because too many German infidels were entering the country. The Irish were clearly on their way to becoming Americans.

*Marcus Lee Hansen considered the Know-Nothing movement a revival of Puritanism, particularly in its attempt to impose virtue, which included prohibition, on immigrants. He noted, "That was the essence of practical Puritanism—the restriction of others." [32]

6

The Master Racists

In the middle of the nineteenth century, Dr. Oliver Wendell Holmes of Boston, a physician who was also a writer of monumental mediocrity, wrote that "a man of family" required among his antecedents "four or five generations of gentlemen and gentlewomen" and named this elite "the Brahmin caste of New England." Divining a gentleman or gentlewoman lay in the same mystical area as divining saving faith, but among the requirements would be money, education, and a family tree of good timber. It is significant that Holmes's definition, which became standard, required only four or five generations. Holmes himself was a sixth-generation American, but his ancestor, David Holmes, was an involuntary immigrant, a Scottish prisoner shipped to Boston in 1651 as an indentured servant. David Holmes prospered and his son John became one of the original settlers of Woodstock, Connecticut, but Dr. Holmes preferred to count back to John the settler rather than to David the servant.[1]

Well beneath the Brahmins on the social scale were the Yankees; a Brahmin had to be a Yankee but few Yankees were Brahmins. Both Brahmins and Yankees were white, Anglo-Saxon, and Protestant and had farsighted ancestors who reached America before the Revolution, but there the resemblance ended. Yankees were at best bluecollar Brahmins, men who worked as farmers, fishermen, skilled laborers, craftsmen, or small businessmen. Neither their bloodlines nor their hands were clean enough for the true Brahmin.

On balance, the Brahmins were well satisfied with themselves and their world. Boston was "that blessed centre of New England life," the "Athens of America," and the "hub of the Universe."[2] Because Brahmins were usually worldly, cultured, traveled, intellectual, and, occasionally, gifted—but most of all because they were Brahmins—their influence radiated far beyond Boston or even New England. "Maintaining a unique reputation in the nineteenth century," writes Barbara Miller Solomon in *Ancestors and Immigrants*, "the New England heart pumped its peculiar ideas through the intellectual veins of the nation."[3]

The best and the brightest of the Brahmins were liberal and humane. They scorned the Know-Nothings, accepted immigration as an opportunity to prove that everyone might benefit from a better environment, and expressed hope that the melting pot would produce a new race, uniquely American. The worst of the Brahmins had flatulent egos and constricted minds; like their Puritan ancestors they considered themselves a beacon unto the nations, and if they were ignored, it was the world's loss not theirs.

In time, the problems caused by Irish immigration and the tendency to blame the wretched for their wretchedness dimmed the Brahmin belief in assimilation, which was always more theoretical than real, and caused them to put distance between themselves and the famished, diseased, illiterate newcomers by the expedient that would later become so familiar—they moved to the suburbs. The Irish did not even get the back of the bus or horsecar; there was a separate line for them. Yankee children were forbidden to play with Irish children and were sent to private schools, while Irish children in the public schools suffered the contempt of their Yankee teachers.

Shut out of society by the Yankees and Brahmins, the Irish formed their own society in Boston; a subculture within the dominant culture.[4] The two were separate but unequal, and neither the Brahmins nor the Yankees were concerned about their eminence in the world until the Irish, politically shrewd and united by persecution, began to compete for power. By 1884, Boston had an Irish-Catholic mayor, Hugh O'Brien. The dust of the visible saints must have fluttered in their graves when he gloated that "the old Puritan city of Boston" had become "the most Catholic city in the country."[5]

Once the Yankees and Brahmins felt threatened, their air of tolerance, indifference, and gentlemanly contempt was transformed into bare-boned bigotry. Henry Adams would write, "Poor Boston has fairly run up against it in the form of its particular Irish maggot, rather lower than the Jew, but more or less the same in appetite for cheese." Adams considered the Dreyfus case a "Jew war" and believed that the honor of France was more important than justice for Dreyfus.[6] Years later Dreyfus would appeal to Adams's spiritual heirs for justice for Sacco and Vanzetti.

The addition of anti-Semitism to the list of nativist antipathies was provoked by a new wave of immigration which began in the 1880s and ended with World War I. During that period some 15 million immigrants arrived, most of them from southern and eastern Europe. The majority were Italians, Slavs, and Jews, but there were also Greeks, Syrians, Armenians, Portuguese, and other national or cultural groups. They came, like their predecessors, for political, economic, religious, and personal reasons, and certainly would have fled sooner if not for laws forbidding emigration and other political complexities.[7] Though they got a late start, they made up for it in numbers because by the time they migrated they had an advantage over earlier arrivals in the availability of steamships to provide faster, safer, and cheaper transportation.

With the Irish running the city and Jews and Italians pounding at the gates, the Brahmins saw they would soon be superfluous if not actually extinct. "Every aristocracy is tempted to build up a materialistic and racist concept of its destiny," wrote Yves Simon[8]; since the Brahmins wanted to be saved they made it a moral imperative because they were Anglo-Saxons and therefore a superior race.

The Anglo-Saxon claim to superiority originated in Europe during the middle of the nineteenth century.[9] Even before that, English anti-royalists had argued that democracy was born in the Black Forest of Germany and passed through the Teutonic branch of the Goths to the Angles and the Saxons.[10] Initially, American nativists viewed this as another sign of their strength and further proof that they could assimilate and acculturate all comers. It was always a question of absorbing the immigrants, never the other way around, and never considering that the immigrants might prefer to retain their own identities.

But the Anglo-Saxons became less optimistic about their powers of assimilation as they realized that the few cannot absorb the many, no matter how superior their genes. Escalating immigration aggravated by economic crises led to escalating racism. By the close of the nineteenth century, racist nativists were arguing that since democracy was part of the Anglo-Saxon or Anglo-Teutonic heritage, only Anglo-Saxons were fit to enjoy its rights and privileges. Immigrants who questioned the supremacy of the Anglo-Saxons were subverting the foundations of American democracy.

One of the most influential of the racist nativists was Francis Amasa Walker, a Brahmin and an economist who eventually became president of MIT. Adapting Darwinism to his own purposes, Walker said that the fittest remained in Europe while the least fit, his own ancestors excluded presumably, came to America. He called the immigrants "beaten men from beaten races; representing the worst failures in the struggle for existence." [11] Once here, this wretched refuse endangered the native stock by outbreeding them; since native Americans would not compete with foreigners for ill-paid work, they had smaller families to preserve their standard of living. In this way those not fit to survive were not only surviving but multiplying and would ultimately inherit the earth, or at least the United States.[12]

If Walker's thesis were remotely valid or honestly conceived, he might have suggested to the natives that they preserve their living standards with strong labor unions rather than twin beds, but he believed that unions were "alien." [13] Walker's solution was to turn Darwin inside out. Darwin had said that the fittest survive.

Backgro

Rather than concede that if the Anglo-Saxons were not surviving perhaps they were not the fittest, Walker and other racists argued that since the Anglo-Saxons were clearly superior and should survive, their survival had to be assured against those who seemed biologically at the point of overwhelming them. The solution was obvious: restrict immigration to America.

The first organized immigration restriction movement was born in Boston and sired by Harvard, which was founded by the Puritans to be "a nursery of knowledge in these deserts."[14] In 1894, three Brahmin graduates of the class of '89 and their friends, fearful of a world they could no longer rule by divine right and resolved to halt the pernicious invasion by foreigners, founded the Immigration Restriction League of Boston.[15]

Drawing a fine distinction, the league tried to separate itself from another nativist organization, the American Protective Association, which had a branch in Massachusetts but flourished mainly in the Midwest. The APA was primarily anti-Catholic, the league was primarily anti-immigrant; a token Catholic was even placed on the league's executive committee.

The Immigration Restriction League quickly won the support of a number of prominent Bostonians, and similar organizations were formed in other cities, often by Harvard graduates or expatriate New Englanders. When there were enough local clubs, a national Association of Immigration Restriction Leagues was organized.

Both the American Protective Association and the league exploited the severe economic depression of 1893. The APA said the depression was caused by Catholics who wanted to weaken America so Rome could conquer it more easily; members of the APA armed themselves for invasion by the pope's legions. The league said the depression was the fault of immigrants who were taking all the jobs away.

The Immigration Restriction League did not want to exclude all immigrants but only "the murder-breed of southern Europe."[16] In 1891, Brahmin Congressman Henry Cabot Lodge had introduced a bill that would presumably separate the wheat from the chaff by requiring all immigrants to pass a literacy test in their own language. It was an idea whose time had not yet come except for the league. Members of the league, permitted to test about one thousand arrivals at Ellis Island, reported a "close connection between illiteracy and general undesirability."[17] Literacy can be tested; presumably the league members determined desirability the same way their forefathers determined saving faith. Desirability was most likely linked to country of origin and outward appearance since the league concluded that a literacy test would indeed reduce the number of immigrants from southern and eastern Europe.

It was an invidious conclusion, falsely preconceived and totally invalid. Many of the immigrants from eastern and southern Europe were highly literate; some of the poorest of the Jews were so learned that the Brahmins later complained they were too intellectual, too serious, and lacking in "warm-heartedness,"[18] an odd complaint coming from the sons of the pioneers. If certain groups of immigrants tended to be illiterate it was because their various conquerors or despots would not open schools for them or because every hand was needed to nurse the soil, not because they were uneducable. Only a morally vacuous intellectual could believe a literacy test accurately measured character or desirability, yet in 1895 the league drafted a new literacy bill and Lodge, by then a senator from Massachusetts, sponsored it.

The Immigration Restriction League and its supporters in Boston and elsewhere lobbied hard for the bill, which was passed by both houses of Congress. Democratic President Grover Cleveland vetoed it with the apt observation that it discriminated against recent arrivals by calling them undesirable and that the same had been said about the ancestors of some of America's best citizens.

The bill was reintroduced and passed by the Senate in 1898, but died in the House when everyone was distracted by the Spanish-American War. Many Brahmins opposed the war and American imperialism, some because they retained a fragment of idealism, others because they feared that no matter how many Filipinos America slaughtered, by annexing the Philippines, Hawaii, Puerto Rico, and other nonwhite territories, the country was opening arteries through which even lower races would filter into the national bloodstream.

As the twentieth century began, the Immigration Restriction League became stronger, bolder, more militant, more political, and more openly bigoted. It supported Republican politicians who supported immigration restriction (the Puritans begat the Federalists who begat the Whigs who begat the Republicans). It also allied itself in common cause with anti-Catholic organizations and opposed a proposal to ease crowding in eastern cities by relocating immigrants in less populated areas of the country, warning southerners who were interested in the plan because they needed cheap labor that southwestern Europeans were "brownish." [19] The league did not want a solution unless it was the final one—barring all unwanted immigrants.

Despite its flagrant racism, or possibly because of it, the league gained in membership and attracted increasingly reputable sponsors. Among the vice presidents of either the Boston or national organizations were Henry Holt, the publisher, Owen Wister, the author, and a number of university presidents led by Abbott Lawrence Lowell of Harvard.[20]

If the league were sincerely concerned about the quality of immigrants rather than their race, it could have disbanded in 1903 when Congress passed an immigration bill excluding "all idiots, insane persons, epileptics . . . paupers; persons likely to become a public charge; professional beggars; persons afflicted with a loathsome or with a dangerous contagious disease; persons who have been convicted of a felony or other crime or misdemeanor involving moral turpitude; polygamists . . . prostitutes" and pimps.

But barring the poor, the sick, and the degenerate did not suffice for the Immigration Restriction League of Boston. Just when their resolve should have been shaken by scientific evidence that character is determined by environment rather than heredity, the racists of the league seized upon the pseudoscience of eugenics to prove the reverse; if superior plants and animals could be bred by selective mating, why not superior people?

In the last decades of the nineteenth century, an English

scientist, Sir Francis Galton, studied genetic patterns and suggested the human race would profit if only the better people bred. When Galton's ideas crossed the ocean, racists seized upon the fact that physical characteristics are transmitted genetically to include personal characteristics as well. Good Americans were the result of good breeding; industriousness and intelligence were as much a genetic mandate as blond hair and blue eyes. Continued nonselective immigration would mongrelize the Anglo-Saxon race.[21]

The ideas of the eugenicists were so appealing to the Immigration Restriction League that the group considered changing its name to the Eugenic Immigration League. Two anthropological studies, neither written by an anthropologist, were also important in providing and disseminating propaganda for the league. The first was *The Races of Europe* by William Z. Ripley, a league adviser who taught economics at Harvard. Ripley divided the Caucasian race into three groupings—Teutonic (tall, blond); Alpine (stocky); and Mediterranean (slender, dark)—and worried about the problem of reversion: if a superior race bred with an inferior race, the superior race might revert to the latent, inferior characteristics of some distant ancestor (excepting the Puritans).[22]

The second book was *The Passing of the Great Race* by Madison Grant, a New York aristocrat, lawyer, and amateur scientist. Grant wrote there was no way of successfully mixing races because the lower type would always triumph: "The cross between any of the three European races and a Jew is a Jew."[23] For Grant, the blond Nordic (Teutonic) race was "white man par excellence"[24] while the immigrants from southern and eastern Europe were "the weak, the broken, and the mentally crippled of all races drawn from the lowest stratum of the Mediterranean basin and the Balkans, together with hordes of the wretched, submerged populations of the Polish ghettoes. Our jails, insane asylums, and almshouses are filled with this human flotsam and the whole tone of American life, social, moral, and political, has been lowered and vulgarized by them."[25] To preserve the Nordic race from this plague, Grant opposed both democracy, which did violence to the natural aristocracy of the Nordics, and immigration, which threatened their purity.

Backgro⟩

Thus, by the eve of America's entry into World War I, when Adolf Hitler was just a dispatch runner in the German army, the Immigration Restriction League of Boston and its scientific and intellectual allies, such as Abbott Lawrence Lowell of Harvard, were propagating the idea of a master race.

7

Pests and Pogroms

To accommodate both racists and reality, immigrants were
assigned new places in the ethnic hierarchy. The "new"
immigration that was unwelcome in 1790 became the
"old" immigration by 1880, to distinguish them from even more
unwelcome arrivals. Germans and Scandinavians could at least
claim Teutonic or Nordic blood, and most of them were Protestant. Most of the Irish were not, but like the other old groups they
were too well settled to uproot. The new immigrants who came
after 1880 were rarely Protestant, and since they were still pouring
in, it might be possible to stop the flow.

Slavs, Jews, and Italians had been represented in small
numbers in America since colonial times. When they began to
come in bulk, the Slavs were accepted with the least difficulty,
possibly because they tended to be blond and blue-eyed. There
had been one earlier substantive migration of Jews, who came
from the German states between the 1830s and the 1850s, but most
of them were skilled and well educated and they were generally
accepted along with other German immigrants. In 1862, General
Ulysses S. Grant expelled "Jews as a class" from Tennessee

because he thought some of them were selling Confederate cotton, but the order was revoked by Lincoln.

Italians sometimes joke that the first Italian immigrant to reach America was Columbus. In 1621, four Italian craftsmen were sent to Jamestown by the Virginia Company of London to encourage glass manufacture in the colony. The colonial secretary reported that "a more damned crew hell never vomited." Other Italians followed in small groups, and by 1855 they were living in the slums of New York.[1]

The Brahmins were particularly perplexed by the Jews and Italians who came after 1880 because of a conflict in stereotypes. Some Brahmins were Hebrew scholars; for them Jews were the patriarchs of the Old Testament. But the Jews from eastern Europe were peddlers, not patriarchs; they did not look as though the Lord would engage them in direct conversation, and if he wouldn't, neither would the Brahmins. Other Brahmins were Renaissance scholars; for them Italians were Michelangelo and Leonardo. A man of culture enjoyed Italian music and art, and a trip to Italy was often part of a Brahmin education. When real Jews and real Italians arrived in their strange clothes, clutching their possessions in bundles, the Brahmins could not believe such splendid fellows as the Old Testament Hebrews or the Renaissance Italians could have fallen so low; here were living examples of what poor breeding could do to great races.

Of the groups that affronted the sensitivities of the Immigration Restriction League and other racists, the Italians probably suffered the greatest discrimination. Centuries of foreign occupation and exploitation had left Italy one of the poorest countries in Europe. With too many people trying to live off the land and too few cities or industries to absorb the overflow, Italians, particularly peasants from southern Italy, turned with hope toward America. It was their misfortune that during the decades when the league was whipping up hatred of immigrants, immigration to the United States reached its peak, and the largest number to come from any single country were Italian.[2]

The racists distinguished between northern and southern Italians. The northern Italians, often blond and blue-eyed, had that faintly Teutonic touch. The darker southern Italian, said one of the founders of the Immigration Restriction League, was partly Negroid.[3] Woodrow Wilson, in his *History of the American People*, published ten years before he became president, wrote that Italians from the "lowest class from the south of Italy" lacked skill, energy, initiative, and intelligence, and that "the Chinese were more to be desired."

Literate racists led the way and the mobs responded; no other whites in America suffered the brutality inflicted upon the Italian.[*] The largest mass lynching in American history took place in New Orleans, where there was a sizable Sicilian community. Sicilians, even more than other southern Italians, bore the stereotype of being violent, criminal, and linked to the Mafia or Black Hand.

On October 15, 1890, David C. Hennessy, the New Orleans superintendent of police, was ambushed by five men. A friend claimed that when he asked Hennessy who shot him, the chief replied, "Dagoes." Though Hennessy was conscious and coherent for nine hours before he died, he said nothing more about his attackers, but based on the rumored word "Dagoes," the mayor ordered the police to "arrest every Italian you come across."

Of the several hundred Italians arrested, nineteen were indicted for the crime, even though only five men took part in the assault. The mayor announced to an already aroused community the police had evidence Hennessy "was the victim of Sicilian vengeance."

The evidence did not convince the jury, which found six of the first nine men tried not guilty and could not agree on the other three. The judge ordered all nineteen Italians returned to prison, including the six who were acquitted. The following morning, March 14, 1891, an integrated lynch mob estimated at between twelve and twenty thousand whites and blacks marched on the jail. The leaders broke in and shot eleven of the Italians. In order

[*]In 1969, Dr. Ralph Bunche told me, in a private interview, that when he was a boy in Detroit, his white playmates, the children of immigrants from central Europe, let him join them in throwing snowballs packed with rocks at Italian immigrant children. The story embarrassed Dr. Bunche and he asked that it not be published during his lifetime.

to satisfy the bloodlust of the crowd which was, according to a *New York Times* report, "crazy to know what was going on within," two of the victims who were not quite dead were dragged outside and publicly hanged.[4]

Even more extraordinary than the lynching of eleven innocent men was the reaction. Future president Theodore Roosevelt thought it "rather a good thing" and boasted that he had said so at a party where "various dago diplomats" were present.[5] The *New York Times* headlined its story "Chief Hennessey [*sic*] Avenged," called the lynchers "a very respectable mob" and editorialized that the lynching was a "terribly effective method of inspiring a wholesome dread in those who had boldly made a trade of murder." The *Times* also lamented that "these sneaking and cowardly Sicilians, the descendants of bandits and assassins, who have transported to this country the lawless passions, the cutthroat practices, the oathbound societies of their native country, are to us a pest without mitigations. . . . Our own murderers are men of feeling and nobility compared to them."[6] Bishop Phillips Brooks, the Episcopal leader of Boston, said that southern Italians and Sicilians should either mend their ways or stop coming to America "to murder and be murdered."[7]

Italians were lynched not only in Louisiana but in Pennsylvania, West Virginia, Colorado, Mississippi, Florida, North Carolina, and Illinois.*[8] On March 21, 1894, several hundred Italians were driven out of Altoona, Pennsylvania, by an armed mob. There was worse terror in the mining town of West Frankfort, Illinois, in August, 1920. It began with a number of robberies which the people blamed on the Black Hand. When two teenagers, believed to be members of the gang, were found murdered, not only the Black Hand but every Italian in Altoona was held accountable. Mobs stormed the Italian district killing, beating, burning, and ordering the people out. Italians streamed away from Altoona carrying the few possessions they could salvage. Though

---

*From 1882–1962, almost three times as many blacks (3,442) as whites (1,294) were lynched, even though blacks were only about 10 percent of the population. But black lynchings were concentrated in the South; in twenty-two states more whites were lynched than blacks.[9]

seven hundred state troopers were summoned, the rioting lasted for three days.*[10]

Italians were victimized not only personally but economically. In a report issued in 1910 showing the relative status of different groups of workers, southern Italians ranked last. At the top of the economic ladder were English-born Englishmen, who earned $673 annually. The comparable income for native Americans was $666, for northern Italians $480, for blacks $445, and for southern Italians $396.[12]

The report was issued by the Dillingham Commission, named after one of its members, Senator William P. Dillingham. When Theodore Roosevelt, a collateral or New York Brahmin, became president in 1901 after McKinley's assassination, the Immigration Restriction League, still peddling its literacy test, had an ally in the White House. The new president proposed such a test, but Congress did not include it in the Immigration Act of 1903. By that time Roosevelt was more conscious of the power of the ethnic vote so he waited until 1907 to rid himself of the issue by appointing a commission of senators, congressmen, and experts to study the immigration problem.

Rabid restrictionists such as Abbott Lawrence Lowell of Harvard expressed concern about getting the commission to report in their favor; those who had influence used it.[13] When the Dillingham report was finally issued, it was a racist's dream. Commission investigators abroad, who had helped gather data, found illiteracy was related to poverty; the report said it resulted from "inherent racial tendencies." Old immigrants were pronounced more literate in English than new immigrants, without noting they had been in America generations longer. The report concluded that the new immigrants were inferior to the old ones, southern Italians were inclined to be criminal as well as poor, and an "illiteracy" test was essential.[14]

*John Higham, author of *Strangers in the Land*, the standard work on American nativism from 1860–1925, writes, "No pogrom has ever stained American soil, nor did any single anti-Jewish incident in the 1920s match the violence of the anti-Italian riot in southern Illinois."[11] The word *pogrom* is not restricted to persecution of Jews in eastern Europe; it can happen here and it did, both in Altoona and in West Frankfort.

Backgr

Because of the ethnic vote, a new literacy-test bill was not passed until after the elections of 1912. Republican President William Howard Taft vetoed it during his last days in office, an act of singular integrity because he had just lost the election to Woodrow Wilson and owed nothing to anyone.

But the racists would not retreat. Another literacy bill was passed by Congress and sent to President Wilson in January, 1915. During his campaign, Wilson had had an awkward time explaining his bigoted writings to ethnic voters and he was not about to make the same mistake again; he vetoed the bill. *

Early in 1917—again, after the elections—an immigration act incorporating the literacy test was passed by Congress and vetoed by Wilson. But this time Congress had the votes to override the veto and the bill became law. After a quarter of a century of mountainous labor, the aging Harvard boys of the Immigration Restriction League had finally brought forth their mouse.

The literacy clause excluded "all aliens over sixteen years of age, physically capable of reading, who cannot read the English language, or some other language or dialect, including Hebrew or Yiddish." Once an alien passed the test, which meant reading aloud thirty to forty printed words in the language of his choice, he could bring in his wife, minor children, adult daughters, parents, and grandparents whether they were literate or not and whether they accompanied him or were sent for later. Exemptions from the test were granted to persons escaping religious persecution, laborers whose skills were unavailable in America, and diplomats.

By the time the literacy test was finally enacted, it was as irrelevant as the men who conceived it. World War I had been more effective than any test in cutting off immigration. Besides, the new immigrants were not as illiterate as the Brahmins wanted to believe; there was almost always one member of the family who could read.

---

*By this time England and Germany were at war with each other, which put considerable strain on the Anglo-Teutonic theory. The nativists responded by excising the Teutonic strain from the Anglo-Saxon heritage; somehow, the Germans had lost it in the Black Forest.

The importance of the Immigration Act of 1917 lay less in what it did to the rights of immigrants trying to enter America than what it did to the rights of those already here. Under pressures caused by World War I and its aftermath, America would no longer simply try to bar unwanted immigrants at the gate; Americans would turn their hate inward and try to expel the aliens in their midst.

8

Economic Wars

Anti-immigrant feeling in America was erected on twin pillars, political and economic. Brahmin racism was primarily a reaction to the erosion of their political power. In the same way, those who held economic power had no intention of losing or sharing it. Yves Simon wrote, "To be assured of cheap labor, it is not enough that the privileged portion of society have control over money, government, the police, culture, and techniques. It is also necessary that the public conscience—and above all the collective conscience of the privileged class itself—willingly accept a concept of society which represents the extreme poverty of the working class as a thing both good and natural. . . . Peacefully to enjoy the advantages of cheap labor, they have need of an ideology which represents the workers as second-class men."[1]

The history of the labor movement in America parallels the history of the immigrant because immigrants provided the labor, yet whenever there was an economic crisis of any sort, the immigrant was blamed. One business journalist wrote, "If the master race of this continent is subordinated to or overrun with the communistic and revolutionary races, it will be in grave danger of social disaster."[2] The disasters businessmen feared were higher wages or a shorter workday, but to fend them off, they used immigrants as the accursed group; whenever there was labor strife it was blamed on alien radicals or radical aliens. The fact that most immigrants were conservative did not save them from being painted Red together with the few extremists among them. "There is no such thing as an American anarchist," stormed an angry writer.[3]

Periods of major anti-immigrant agitation coincided with periods of major economic unrest, or union activity, or both. The *New York Times* called strikes and boycotts "entirely un-American" and said that "those who employ them have no real conception of what American citizenship is or implies."[4] Presumably a good American was the manufacturer who said, "I regard my employees as I do a machine, to be used to my advantage, and when they are old and of no further use I cast them in the street."[5]

It was true that the relationship between capital and labor or owner and worker had changed during the course of American history, but this was because of population and industrial growth, not foreign agitators. On the frontier, individualism was essential for survival. What could not be made at home was produced by craftsmen, who were well paid because they were scarce. A skilled laborer could earn twice as much in the colonies as he could in England; in 1630, the Massachusetts General Court, its Puritan heart unfailingly in the wrong place, tried to limit wages by law.[6]

Even before the American Revolution industries such as armaments, textiles, and shoemaking were functioning, but labor was in such short supply that wages were high. To increase the labor supply, indentured servants and slaves were imported; England also sent over convicts. Some indentured servants sailed willingly, binding themselves to work for a certain number of years in return for their passage; others were kidnapped.

The first seeds of the American labor movement were planted in colonial times when skilled workers organized according to craft. The first strike may have been in 1677 when cartmen in New York refused to remove refuse until the city paid them a higher fee.

Backgro

After the American Revolution, work became less of a craft and more of a job. To speed production for an expanding market—expanding because of increased immigration—the factory or mill system was introduced. Many products no longer represented the skill of one man but the work of a number of men, each dully repeating one part of a process. What was gained in speed was lost in quality, as well as in the concern the laborer had for his task and the employer had for the laborer.

By 1800, unions were being formed by skilled workers to protect themselves against the unskilled and semi-skilled who earned much less for doing part of a job rather than the whole. Unskilled workers did not organize until much later because most of them were grateful to be employed; many were women and children. Though it was limited and local, much that is characteristic of unionism—organizing, strikes, wage demands, boycotts, closed shops—had appeared on the American scene by the beginning of the nineteenth century, introduced by native Americans. Those who attacked unionism as un-American were blind to history as well as justice.

From the beginning, the reaction of the owners was to break strikes and jail strikers. Yet by the 1830s, America had its first industrial union, and skilled workers had won a ten-hour day everywhere but New England where mill owners denied the shorter day to artisans because they feared unskilled factory workers would also demand it. In Lowell, Massachusetts, the workday averaged more than twelve hours, or over seventy-three hours per week.[7] In Holyoke, Massachusetts, a manufacturer decided his workers were sluggish in the mornings because they ate breakfast; to increase production, breakfast was banned.

Those who protested were fired and blacklisted. Since no one would accept such working conditions if there were alternatives, mill owners began to hire immigrants too impoverished to ask questions. The foreign element in the factory system, which manufacturers would later condemn so bitterly, was introduced by the manufacturers themselves, the better to exploit, for if one group of immigrants grumbled there was always a hungrier horde waiting to take their place. The manufacturers soon learned how to divide the immigrants from the native workers and from each other by using them as strikebreakers. Said Jay Gould, "I can hire one half of the working class to kill the other half,"[8] and he was right.

After the Civil War came industrialization, as after water-power came steam. The American economy boomed; railroads, mining, and manufacturing changed the face and feeling of the nation. The giant industrialists never opposed immigration; they needed men like they needed coal, and used them with as much indifference. With the full development of the factory system, work became even more unskilled and impersonal. Where there had once been communication between the owner of a small shop or mill and his employees, there was now a chasm between the industrialist and his serfs. A New England manufacturer observed that when people "get starved down to it, then they will go to work at just what you can afford to pay."[9]

In this situation, one worker trying to bargain with his employer was like one grain of sand trying to build an embankment. Labor could match the power of capital only by organizing, bargaining collectively, and striking. The factory by its very nature made large unions possible; if so many men could work together they could also strike together.

Blaming foreign agitators, industrialists used their considerable influence with the press, politicians, and the courts to crush union activity. Strikes were condemned as unpatriotic, un-Godly, and criminal. The *Albany Law Journal* editorialized, "A mob of strikers is entitled to no more leniency than a mob of lynchers or common ruffians."[10] Strikes were halted by court injunctions and strikers were prosecuted for conspiracy. Officials were always willing to send in police, the militia, and even the army to break strikes and murder strikers. During one coal strike in Pennsylvania a posse fired on a group of some one hundred and fifty unarmed strikers—all of them immigrants—killing twenty-one and wounding forty; this was a single incident among many. In Reading, Pennsylvania, federal troops sent in to break a railroad strike killed eleven persons. During the same strike, troops killed twenty in Pittsburgh.

Despite the setbacks and the corpses, the union movement advanced; by the 1880s, the major demand was for an eight-hour workday. The movement began with the unions but picked up support from radicals, some of the press, and even a few politicians. Though it was a national crusade, agitation for the shorter day was hottest in Chicago, which was not only a center for active unionism but active radicalism. The bitter accusations against foreign agitators had, in some instances, a kernel of truth; there were radicals in America, some of them foreign born. Their various utopias ranged from total freedom for the individual to total subjugation by the state, but their assorted methods of faith healing would have found no audience if industry had not been so intransigent. Workers wanted a raise or a shorter day, not a revolution. In blocking modest reform, industry was, in a very real sense, its own accursed group.

On May 1, 1886, nearly one hundred thousand persons in Chicago struck and demonstrated for the eight-hour day, but there was no rioting or violence. May 2 was uneventful because it was a Sunday. On Monday, May 3, there were more demonstrations. Striking union members, locked out of the McCormick Harvester factory, attacked strikebreakers and smashed factory windows. Almost two hundred policemen raced to the scene, firing and clubbing. One striker was killed, several were shot, and many were beaten.

On Tuesday, May 4, there were more clashes between groups of workers and the police. A protest meeting was called for 7 P.M. in Haymarket Square by Chicago revolutionaries who were economic communists and political anarchists. Though the organizers expected thousands, perhaps twelve hundred appeared. Embarrassed by the small turnout, the radicals moved the meeting from Haymarket Square to a nearby alley. Three speakers harangued the crowd, which gradually drifted away, driven by boredom and a sudden, cold drizzle. By 10 P.M. only a few hundred remained.

At about 10:20, just as the last speaker had said, "In conclusion . . . " about 180 policemen suddenly appeared. A police captain ordered the crowd, which was small, soaked, and, until that moment, entirely peaceful, to disperse. In reply, a dynamite bomb sailed through the air and exploded near the first group of police. Immediately the police opened fire. The bomb killed seven policemen and wounded more than sixty. The police killed several persons and wounded about two hundred.

While the *New York Times* declared the Chicago radicals

guilty before any were brought to trial and hoped they "shall suffer the death they deserve," a small newspaper in Topeka, Kansas, asked editorially, "We do not say [the bombers] are in the right, but are they wholly to blame? Is there not some reason for these outbreaks? To cure an evil it is necessary to eradicate the cause. . . . The proper way would seem to be to lay all prejudice aside and inquire into the cause of this growth of Anarchism."

For the police, the prosecutors, and public opinion, the proper way was to hang a few anarchists. The bomb thrower was never positively identified, but thirty-one persons were indicted and eight anarchists were tried. Of the eight, six either had not been at the rally or had left before the bomb was thrown. None were accused of throwing the bomb; they were charged with being accessories to the bombing and with conspiracy to murder.

The eight men were found guilty; seven were sentenced to hang and one was sentenced to fifteen years. One of the men facing death, who did make bombs even though he was not at the rally, committed suicide in his cell by exploding a bomb in his mouth.

The Haymarket affair became a national and international issue and a forerunner of the Sacco-Vanzetti case in that the men were tried primarily for their ideas rather than their acts. The governor of Illinois, inundated with pleas and petitions for clemency balanced by outraged demands that the men be executed, took a middle course; he commuted two of the sentences to life imprisonment. The other four men were hanged on November 11, 1887.[11]

The Haymarket bomb blew up the negative perception of immigrants into monstrous caricature. Because five of the men who were tried were German-born radicals, the incident indelibly inked in the public mind the image of the immigrant as bomb thrower and confirmed for many the fraudulent claim that labor agitation was the work of foreign ideologues.* The fight for the eight-hour day was temporarily halted; trapped between extremists of the Left and Right, it was the worker who lost.

*Of the other three, one was of German descent but American born, one was an Englishman, and one was a 100 percent American whose ancestors came on the second voyage of the *Mayflower*. The Anglo-Teutonic tree bore some very strange fruit.

Backgr

Before the Immigration Restriction League of Boston was founded to exclude immigrants on the basis of race or national origin, attempts were being made to exclude or deport alien radicals. These attempts would succeed before the literacy test because fear of radicals exceeded fear of illiterates. In 1892, during the Homestead strike, a Russian-born anarchist, Alexander Berkman, shot and stabbed Henry Clay Frick, the manager of the Carnegie Steel Company. Though Frick survived, the image of America's throat bared to alien assassins was reinforced, particularly since foreign revolutionaries were killing off kings, queens, presidents, tsars, prime ministers, generals, and diplomats at a terrifying rate. In September, 1901, all fears seemed to be confirmed with the assassination of President William McKinley. The assassin, Leon Czolgosz, was American-born, but his parents were Polish; he was a madman, but he claimed to be an anarchist. [12]

At the same time that Theodore Roosevelt pleased his friends in the Immigration Restriction League by proposing a literacy test, he also pleased his friends in industry by proposing the exclusion of anarchists. In addition, he recommended an "economic fitness" test to bar the poor. [13]

When the Immigration Act of 1903 was passed, there was still no literacy test and the restriction based on economic fitness was limited to paupers and beggars. But McKinley's assassination had its effect. For the first time in American history, immigrants were excluded because of their ideas; the law barred "anarchists, or persons who believe in or advocate the overthrow by force or violence of the Government of the United States or of all government or of all forms of law, or the assassination of public officials." Immigrants could be barred not only for their beliefs but for their associations; the bill excluded anyone "who is a member of or affiliated with any organization entertaining and teaching such disbelief" in organized government. If an excludable anarchist or anarchist-by-association slipped by, he could be deported within three years after his entry.

The anarchist exclusion clause did not end the wars between capital and labor because the belief that union activity would cease if not for alien radicals was just a fallacy. Labor grievances were not the mischief of outside agitators, they were real and had to be dealt with. The clause was not even effective in barring foreign anarchists. When Aldino Felicani, who was to become the guiding spirit of the Sacco-Vanzetti Defense Committee, fled Italy in 1914, he was a well-known anarchist who had been tried twenty-four times, jailed repeatedly, and ultimately came to America to avoid a long prison term. [14] Yet he managed to slip in regardless of the anarchist exclusion clause and regardless of the fact that he did not have a passport. [15]

The law not only failed to keep out anarchists, but it also failed to recognize that anarchists are made, not born. Neither Sacco nor Vanzetti were anarchists when they left Italy; conditions in America turned them into radicals.

As America moved into the twentieth century, it was still the land of opportunity; Andrew Carnegie had the opportunity to earn more than $23 million in one year, untaxed, while the average annual wage was between $400 and $500. [16] Two-thirds of America's wealth was held by 2 percent of the population, while two-thirds of the population shared 5 percent of the wealth. Between one-third and one-half of the people lived at subsistence level. [17]

Even those who were not radical could see that some sort of leveling was needed, though its acceptability depended largely on its source. The respectable drive for reform was led by the Progressive movement which, in 1912, ran a presidential candidate who finished second in the three-man race. The candidate was ex-President Theodore Roosevelt, a man of infinite variety, who was a Progressive that year because he wanted to regain the White House and had already lost the Republican nomination to Taft. Roosevelt's campaign rhetoric was occasionally so inflammatory that he was accused of trying to overthrow the government; had he landed at Ellis Island and delivered some of his speeches he would have been barred from the country by his own immigration legislation. [18]

The Progressives were the right wing of the reform movement; they accepted the system but wanted it to work for more people. Farther left was the Socialist party led by Eugene Debs. Debs, originally a union leader and a Democrat, switched to socialism when Democratic President Grover Cleveland sent in

Backgrd

federal troops to break the Pullman strike in 1894. Every four years, from 1900 to 1912, Debs dutifully ran as Socialist candidate for president. In 1912, when reform was in the air, he polled over nine hundred thousand votes, but he never stood a chance of being elected and he never stood for anything more radical than an orderly, constitutional, socialist-oriented government.[19]

At the extreme left was the IWW, formally the Industrial Workers of the World, informally the Wobblies. Founded in Chicago in 1905, the IWW was a union which tried to organize those at the very bottom of society—migratory workers, unskilled workers, immigrants, blacks. The IWW did not want to work within the system; it wanted to replace it. In 1908 control of the organization was seized by anarcho-syndicalists who believed in one big union—industrial, international—organized not only to win specific benefits but ultimately to overthrow world capitalism and rule in its place. The anarcho-syndicalists were not interested in conventional politics and, as frequent victims of employer or state violence, they sometimes advocated it in turn. The IWW alternated between being an effective union and a sassy revolutionary movement; in either capacity the Wobblies were magnets for the wrath of the authorities.[20]

In 1909, a U.S. Steel subsidiary in McKees Rocks, Pennsylvania, decided to change the wage system to piecework. The workers, most of them immigrants, sent a committee of forty men to management to ask for an explanation. The forty were promptly fired. The IWW called a strike, and the company called in hundreds of state police and special deputies. During the battles between strikers and police, a dozen persons were killed and almost a hundred were injured. In a nostalgic, Old World touch, arrested immigrant strikers were dragged down the streets behind the horses of the state troopers. But in the end the IWW won the strike and the company was forced to return to a fixed-wage system.

For the next few years, the IWW concentrated on a free-speech campaign in the West, mainly to publicize the plight of migratory workers. At street rallies the Wobblies recruited new members, attacked working conditions, and usually had a few things to say about religion and capitalism. Regardless of what the

First Amendment says about free speech, Wobblies were banned, arrested, hosed by firemen, beaten, branded, and tarred-and-feathered. Female Wobblies were sent to jail to be raped.

In November, 1916, some three hundred Wobblies sailing from Seattle to Everett, Washington, for a free-speech demonstration were met by a band of police and armed vigilantes. In the exchange of gunfire, two vigilantes and five Wobblies were killed. The five Wobblies were a Frenchman, a German, a Swede, an Irishman, and a Jew.[21]

Seventy-four Wobblies were arrested and charged with murdering the two vigilantes; none of the vigilantes were arrested for murdering the Wobblies. One Wobbly was put on trial first; an IWW lawyer named Fred Moore was a member of the defense team. When the first Wobbly was acquitted, the other seventy-three were released. *

Though most IWW activities, particularly the free-speech campaign, took place in the West, the devil came to Massachusetts during a strike of textile workers in Lawrence. Though Brahmin money helped build Lawrence, the principal mills were now owned by the American Woolen Company whose president, William Wood, was the son of a poor Portuguese fisherman; the young often assimilate very quickly.

Lawrence, Massachusetts, was a one industry town; some forty-thousand men, women, and children worked in the woolen and cotton mills. They earned an average of $8.76 per week—though wages sometimes sank as low as $2.30—and paid $1 to $6 weekly just for rent. Because one income was insufficient, entire families labored; half of the employees in the four mills owned by the American Woolen Company were girls between the ages of

*Less fortunate was the IWW's most famous martyr, Swedish-born Joe Hill. In January, 1914, Hill was accused of murdering a grocer and his son in Salt Lake City, Utah. Hill was found guilty and executed on November 19, 1915, after sending a telegram to IWW leader Bill Haywood with the unforgettable message, "Don't waste time in mourning. Organize." The trial of Joe Hill, like the Haymarket affair, aroused a storm of national and international interest and protest. It has been argued that Joe Hill could no more get a fair trial in Mormon Utah than Sacco and Vanzetti could get a fair trial in Puritan Massachusetts. Hill's guilt was not proved beyond a reasonable doubt and he should not have been convicted or executed, but his alibi was not persuasive and it is possible that he did commit the crime.

Backgrou

fourteen and eighteen. A doctor reported that a "considerable number" of these teenagers died within two or three years of employment. Thirty-six out of every one hundred adults in the mills died of malnutrition, overwork, tuberculosis, or occupational diseases before the age of twenty-five. [22]

In an attempt to bring some relief to the textile workers, the Massachusetts state legislature passed a law cutting the workweek for women and children all the way back from fifty-six hours to fifty-four hours, effective January 1, 1912. When pay envelopes were distributed on January 11, women weavers in one of the mills were the first to discover that because of the shorter workweek they had been docked thirty-two cents. The women left their looms shouting, "Short pay! Short pay!" Other workers joined them and by the following day, thousands of textile workers in Lawrence were on strike.

When the strike began, the IWW had only about three hundred paid members in Lawrence. Joseph Ettor, an experienced IWW organizer, immediately went to the mill town, where he was soon joined by Arturo Giovannitti, a radical poet and editor, who took charge of strike relief. Later, the IWW sent in its heavy artillery, including Bill Haywood, Elizabeth Gurley Flynn, and an Italian radical leader named Carlo Tresca.

The IWW demanded that the workers not only receive full pay but a 15 percent increase. On behalf of the mill owners, the mayor of Lawrence called out the local militia, while the governor sent in the state militia. One of the officers later told a magazine writer, "Our company of militia went down to Lawrence during the first days of the strike. Most of them had to leave Harvard to do it; but they rather enjoyed going down there to have a fling at those people." [23]

The brave Harvard lads would certainly enjoy a fling at those people who were mongrelizing the master race, for if ever a strike was an ethnic experience, it was at Lawrence. Some twenty-five nationalities took part; the largest numerically were Italian, but there were also some rare specimens for Massachusetts, such as Turks and Syrians. The only way to bring unity out of such diversity was to organize on the basis of nationality. Each national group had its own headquarters and sent representatives to the strike committee's central headquarters, where all activities were coordinated. *

Because the strikers were poor, cold, hungry, and afraid, they almost gave in within a few days. But history has remarkable ways of repeating itself. In 1963, Dr. Martin Luther King, Jr., tried to desegregate Birmingham, Alabama, with a series of nonviolent public demonstrations. His campaign was faltering when Public Safety Commissioner Bull Connor turned high-pressure hoses on the demonstrators, strengthening their resolve and winning them national sympathy. In January, 1912, when the strike at Lawrence was crumbling, the militia turned fire hoses on the strikers and the icy bath did more to revive their spirits than a hundred union organizers.

The strikers were not only hosed down but beaten and assaulted by the militia; a Syrian teenager died after being bayoneted in the back. Despite this brutality, the IWW, which had been violent elsewhere, decided to remain nonviolent in Lawrence. Yet the union was immediately blamed when, within a week after the strike began, the police found twenty-eight sticks of dynamite in three different places in Lawrence. The *New York Times* editorialized that "the strikers display a fiendish lack of humanity" and recommended they be placed "beyond the comfort of religion until they have repented," a curious penalty for so many anarcho-atheists. The IWW insisted it was a frame-up; a Boston newspaper reported the details of the story before the dynamite was found.

On January 29, John Breen, an undertaker, member of the school board, and son of a former mayor, was arrested for planting the dynamite to discredit the IWW. Breen remained free on bail and when tried and convicted was fined five hundred dollars. In contrast, some thirty strikers who threw chunks of ice at the militia who were hosing them were sentenced to a year in jail.

---

*Personal interview, Hymie Kaplan, October 11, 1971. Kaplan, a distant relative of mine, was active in the Lawrence strikes of 1912 and 1919. He recalled that during one of the two strikes, probably 1919 though he wasn't certain, Nicola Sacco and another man came to Lawrence with a truckload of bread Sacco had collected from his fellow shoeworkers for the starving strikers. "It was highly appreciated, believe me," Kaplan said.

Backgro█

Breen implicated William Wood, president of the American Woolen Company, in the plot against the Wobblies, but Wood was acquitted.

The night Breen was arrested, a striker, Anna LoPizzo, was shot to death when police stormed a picket line. The strikers said she was killed by a police officer. The authorities, in an attempt to break the strike by picking off its leaders, accused Joseph Ettor and Arturo Giovannitti, who were at a meeting three miles away at the time of the shooting, of being accessories to the murder because they incited and provoked violence. Three months later, a worker named Joseph Caruso was charged with the murder itself.

Breen had remained free on bail while awaiting trial, but Ettor, Giovannitti, and later Caruso, went directly to prison. Ettor and Giovannitti were imprisoned for eight months without trial, Caruso for five. By the time the three men were finally tried in September, the strike was over; it was over even before Caruso was arrested.

The strikers had soup kitchens and other forms of aid which came to thirty-three cents per striker per day. By February, some of them had reached the point where they could no longer feed their families. A decision was made to evacuate a group of the strikers' children to sympathetic families in New York City. Margaret Sanger, future pioneer of the birth control movement, was put in charge because she was a nurse, a socialist, and "an American."[24] She later told a congressional committee that of the 119 children, only four wore underwear; the rest were too poor. "Their outerwear was almost in rags," she said, "their coats were simply torn to shreds."[25] When the children were examined in New York, all were found to be suffering from malnutrition.

Several weeks later another ninety-two children were evacuated. Fortunately, all starving, ragged children look alike whether they are immigrant or native; newspaper photographs of these young refugees shocked an indifferent nation. The press became more sympathetic to the strikers and criticism began to rain upon the mill owners of Lawrence. The owners and city officials decided to lock the doors of the deathcamp; they decreed that no more children could leave the city. On February 24, when another convoy was scheduled to depart for Philadelphia, fifty policemen and two companies of militia surrounded the railroad terminal in Lawrence. They tore youngsters apart from their parents, clubbed mothers and children, threw some of them into a patrol wagon, and carted them off to jail.

Now the country was thoroughly sickened, and several congressmen demanded an investigation. It was blocked in the Senate by Henry Cabot Lodge, but the House held a hearing early in March. One witness, a fourteen-year-old girl, described how two weeks after she went to work a machine pulled her scalp off and she was hospitalized for seven months .[26]

At this point the textile owners knew they had lost. The American Woolen Company announced pay increases ranging from 5 to 20 percent, as well as other concessions, and the other companies followed.

The strike was over, but Ettor and Giovannitti remained in jail, where Caruso joined them in April. In some ways the Ettor-Giovannitti case was a preamble to the Sacco-Vanzetti case. Throughout the country and in Europe there were protest meetings, demonstrations, and rallies, mostly to raise funds for the defense. An Ettor-Giovannitti Defense Committee was organized; all of its members were indicted by Massachusetts authorities, but released on bail. One of the attorneys at the trial was Fred Moore.

Ettor and Giovannitti had witnesses to prove they were speaking elsewhere the night Anna LoPizzo was shot. Joseph Caruso had witnesses to testify he was home eating supper. Caruso said he was not a member of the IWW but planned to join as soon as he was free. On November 26, 1912, the three men were acquitted. It was still possible for Italian radicals to get a fair trial in Massachusetts.

9

Silencing Dissent

When World War I began in Europe in 1914, the anti-immigrant crusade had gone stale. The Immigration Restriction League was still pushing its literacy test and industry was still concerned about alien anarchists, but the public was largely indifferent. New immigrants were assimilating just as the old ones had, and since economic concessions were being made to reformers out of fear of radicals, the radicals kept losing their constituency.

The initial reaction in America to the war itself was confusion; no one seemed to know what it was about. Both the Allies and the Central Powers had sympathizers, but it was agreed almost unanimously that the war was none of America's business. President Wilson called for neutrality[1] and even Theodore Roosevelt, who loved nothing better than a good war, wrote, "It would be folly to jump into the gulf ourselves to no good purpose."[2]

But as the war grew bigger, bloodier, and longer, it became apparent that the world had grown too small for America to ignore what was happening over there. A debate over war policy began which lasted several years, leaving the country bitterly divided;

even after Wilson had resolved his own doubts, he had not resolved the doubts of others.

Opposition to America's involvement came primarily from isolationists, immigrants, pacifists, progressives, and radicals. Many of these people were articulating an ideal expressed by the Puritans and the founding fathers, that Europe was so steeped in corruption the future lay in America. If all of Europe was overrun with oppression, it did not matter who won a war the savagery of which seemed matched only by its pointlessness.

Immigrants who had risked their lives to flee European tyranny could not understand why they should be expected to risk their lives to preserve it. Many German-Americans favored their country of origin and were outraged when America sold arms to England but not to Germany, a policy Wilson defined as neutrality. Wilson responded by saying the German-Americans spoke with "alien sympathies."[3] Theodore Roosevelt, who quickly concluded there was some good to the war after all, blasted "professional German-Americans" who "spiritually remain foreigners in whole or in part." All Americans, he said, should have "the simple and loyal motto, America for Americans."[4]

Many Irish-Americans hated England far more than Germany, particularly after the Easter Rising of 1916, an Irish revolt against English rule. One of the rebels was so badly wounded he had to be carried before the firing squad in a chair; this was the sort of delicate touch that made Americans other than the Irish wonder why the English should be considered morally superior to the Germans.[5]

Pacifists opposed all wars, and progressives wanted to see the world rebuilt, not destroyed. Social worker Jane Addams wrote, "Was not war in the interest of democracy for the salvation of civilization a contradiction in terms, whoever said it or however often it was repeated?"[6] Radicals believed in class war, not in countries quarreling over colonies and markets and national honor. Eugene Debs wrote, "The workers have no country to fight for. It belongs to the capitalists and plutocrats. Let them worry over its defense, and when they declare wars as they and they alone do, let them also go out and slaughter one another on the battlefields."[7] A Wobbly said:

Backgrou

You ask me why the IWW is not patriotic to the United States. If you were a bum without a blanket; if you had left your wife and kids when you went west for a job, and had never located them since; if your job never kept you long enough in a place to qualify you to vote; if you slept in a lousy, sour bunk-house, and ate food just as rotten as they could give you and get by with it . . . if every person who represented law and order and the nation beat you up, railroaded you to jail, and the good Christian people cheered and told them to go to it, how the hell do you expect a man to be patriotic? This war is a businessman's war and we don't see why we should go out and get shot in order to save the lovely state of affairs which we now enjoy.[8]

In opposition to the doves were a large flock of pro-British hawks led by Theodore Roosevelt who, aging and ailing, longed to lead one last charge up some Bavarian version of Kettle Hill.* Like Roosevelt, other prominent hawks such as Massachusetts Senator Henry Cabot Lodge believed in the inherent superiority of the Anglo-Saxon; once the war began, Germans were no longer Teutons, as in tales told by the racists, but Huns, as in Attila, who raped nuns and mutilated children for sport, or so the English said.†

---

*In *Ragtime* (New York: Random House, 1975) p. 259, E. L. Doctorow writes, "Roosevelt accused Wilson of finding war abhorrent. He thought Wilson had the prim renunciatory mouth of someone who had eaten fish with bones in it. But the new President was giving the Marines practice by having them land at Vera Cruz. He was giving the army practice by sending it across the border to chase Pancho Villa. He wore rimless glasses and held moral views. When the Great War came he would wage it with the fury of the affronted. Neither Theodore Roosevelt's son Quentin, who was to die in a dogfight over France, nor the old Bull Moose himself, who was to die in grief not long thereafter, would survive Wilson's abhorrence of war." The old Bull Moose died of a coronary embolism, not grief, and he once said of his four sons, "I would rather one of them should die than have them grow up weaklings." Roosevelt got what he wanted.

†For details on the English propaganda effort to bring America into the war, see Phillip Knightley, *The First Casualty* (New York: Harcourt Brace Jovanovich, 1975), pp. 120 ff. Knightley says (p. 82) the English propaganda organization in World War I served as a model for Goebbels in World War II.

On April 2, 1917, President Woodrow Wilson asked Congress to declare war on the Central Powers: Germany, Austria-Hungary, Bulgaria, and Turkey. He gave as his reason, "The world must be made safe for democracy," a noble sentiment irrelevant to the only war in progress at the moment. "It is a fearful thing to lead this great peaceful people into war," he said, "but the right is more precious than peace, and we shall fight for the things which we have always carried nearest our hearts,—for democracy, for the right of those who submit to authority to have a voice in their own Governments, for the rights and liberties of small nations, for a universal dominion of right by such a concert of free peoples as shall bring peace and safety to all nations and make the world itself at last free. To such a task we can dedicate our lives and our fortunes. . . ."[9]

It is said that after the speech Wilson returned to the White House and wept.[10] Perhaps when the fog of rhetoric had lifted he remembered that neither the life nor fortune he had dedicated was his own; the lives would be those of unknown soldiers while the fortunes amounted to the $2 billion loaned to the Allies by American bankers which would be lost if the Allies lost. "We are going into war upon the command of gold," said Senator George Norris.[11] Novelist John Dos Passos wrote about "making the world safe for cost plus democracy." British historian A.J.P. Taylor tartly concluded, "In the last resort, the United States went to war so that America could remain prosperous and rich Americans could grow richer."[12]

It is difficult to believe Wilson went to war solely for economic reasons, but it is difficult to understand why he went to war at all. Since he was an Anglo-Saxon racist who had said, "England is fighting our fight. . . . She is fighting for her life and the life of the world,"[13] and since the Allies were faltering badly, Wilson may have believed that by saving England he was saving civilization. Historian William Leuchtenburg concludes that America entered World War I with a "sense of mission," with the conviction that "American Christian democratic ideals could and should be universally applied" making it the "duty of 'peace-loving' Americans to resort to killing to impose virtue abroad."[14] In that sense America went to war not only because Wilson was a racist but because he was a Puritan.

Wilson was a Puritan not only in his sense of mission but in

Backgr

his refusal to suffer opposition. "Woe be to the man that seeks to stand in our way in this day of high resolution," he said, and he meant it. * 15 He knew he had drummed the country into a war that many still opposed or doubted; enlistments were so poor a draft law had to be passed, causing many Americans to flee the country. People simply did not believe that this war would either make the world safe for democracy or be "the war that will end war"—a phrase coined by H.G. Wells which justifies his reputation as a master of science fiction.

In order to convert Americans to his crusade, Wilson created a brainwashing organization called the Committee on Public Information. It was headed by a journalist, George Creel, who said its purpose was to win the "hearts and minds"—those were his words—of the American people for the war. 16 Under the heavy hands of Creel and his associates, the country was deluged with war propaganda; it choked every channel of communication and cloaked every aspect of American life. No totalitarian state could have done better; in movies and in men's clubs, in classrooms and in churches, Americans were assured that this was the best of all possible wars. Most people succumbed because most people believe their government no matter what it tells them. America became so "propaganda-demented" that one writer described a church-sponsored meeting in New England at which a speaker demanded that the Kaiser be boiled in oil and the "entire audience stood on chairs to scream its hysterical approval." 17

Once America was at war with Germany, German-Americans supported the war or at least did not openly oppose it. But this did not spare them retribution. Reaching back to the antialien acts of 1798, Wilson put sixty-three hundred Germans into concentration camps. 18 German aliens not imprisoned were required to register with the government and forbidden to move without permission. Naturalized Germans were threatened with loss of citizenship.

The effect of presidential persecution and government propaganda was to turn America into a nation of paranoiacs. Since

*The apotheosis of Wilson by liberals is inexplicable. Brought up "between the Bible and the dictionary," as Dos Passos wrote, no American president was so imperious, hypocritical, self-deluded, intolerant, vindictive, inflexible, or paranoid. No president came closer to destroying civil liberties, and no other president made a mockery of his office by refusing to resign when incapacitated by a stroke, leaving his wife to govern at her whim. Nixon knew when it was time to quit; Wilson did not.

the enemy was thousands of miles away, an accursed group had to be found closer to home. At first it was the German-American. Rumors swept the country that they were poisoning wells, spreading epidemics, and planning insurrections. Actually, they were busy changing their names and keeping out of sight, but an aroused nation boycotted German opera and christened sauerkraut "liberty cabbage." Individual Germans were flogged, tarred-and-feathered, and lynched.[19]

German-Americans were not the only victims, as suspect thy neighbor became government policy. Attorney General Thomas Gregory urged every American to be a "volunteer detective" and to "feel free to bring . . . suspicions and information" about spies and subversives to the Justice Department. Within a month, Gregory was receiving a thousand accusations a day; the daily total later rose to fifteen hundred. Gregory acknowledged that most of these accusations were "utterly worthless"—many people were either hysterical or trying to settle personal grudges—but he continued to encourage Americans to report "disloyal acts" and "seditious utterances."[20]

In addition to freelance witch-hunters, covens were formed. A month before America declared war, Albert M. Briggs, an advertising executive, asked Gregory for permission to organize a group of volunteers to assist the Justice Department. Both Gregory and President Wilson consented to the formation of the American Protective League. At its peak, the APL had 1,400 units and 350,000 members. This private organization, whose members were mainly small businessmen and other armchair patriots, was not only authorized to check on the loyalty of free men but specifically assigned by the Justice Department and the War Department to investigate government employees and prospective military officers.

APL sleuths were not only oblivious to the meaning of the arcane term civil liberties, but incompetent to the point of low comedy and high tragedy. They conducted over 3 million loyalty investigations without finding any spies, but they did use their semi-official position to make arrests (though they had no authority to do so), ruin careers, accuse each other of subversion, procure prostitutes and bootleg liquor for army camps, round up draft

Backgrou

evaders, act as strikebreakers, break up political meetings, and intimidate aliens, union members, radicals, and Democrats. Gregory knew of these outrages but he did not disband the organization; it served to enforce conformity.[21]

In his zeal to save democracy abroad, Woodrow Wilson seemed determined to destroy it at home. There were already several statutes on the books which would have protected the nation from any real threat of conspiracy or treason, but Wilson considered them inadequate because the conspiracy statute made prosecution of an individual difficult, if not impossible, and the treason law applied to acts, not words. An espionage bill was introduced which some members of Congress and the press feared was an attempt to silence dissent. Wilson assured them, "I shall not expect or permit any part of this law to apply to me or any of my official actions, or in any way to be used as a shield against criticism." He also said the bill was "absolutely necessary to the public safety."[22] It was passed by both houses of Congress and signed by Wilson on June 15.

Though the Espionage Act of 1917 dealt with espionage, the protection of military secrets, subversion of the military, and obstruction of the draft, it also established an extraordinary new offense: "Whoever, when the United States is at war, shall willfully make or convey false reports or false statements with intent to interfere with the operations or success of the military or naval forces of the United States or to promote the success of its enemies . . . shall be punished by a fine of not more than $10,000 or imprisonment for not more than twenty years, or both."

When Wilson said the law would not be used as a shield against criticism, he did not add, as he later did, that he would only tolerate criticism that was "patriotic and intelligent."[23] Criticism of the war or of the president was both unpatriotic and unintelligent and therefore a false statement subject to the heavy penalties of the Espionage Act. Freedom of the press was similarly gagged. Censorship of the press was supposed to be voluntary, but publications were also subject to the rule about false reports and false statements.

As soon as the ink on the Espionage Act was dry, Postmaster General Albert S. Burleson ordered local postmasters to send him publications that might "embarrass or hamper the Government in conducting the war." Within a month, issues of fifteen major publications had been banned from the mails; some publications were destroyed by being denied their special mailing rates. Burleson refused to issue guidelines on what was acceptable and what was not, saying that to do so would be "incompatible with the public interest."[24] Magazines were banned for criticizing AFL leader Samuel Gompers, for suggesting the war be paid for by taxes instead of loans for printing Jefferson's opinion that Ireland should be a republic. Inevitably the absence of sane or comprehensible rules had a chilling effect by initiating a self-censorship that was worse than censorship itself.

After a few months, Attorney General Gregory decided that while the Espionage Act was effective against organized propaganda, it did not cover spontaneous or casual antiwar statements, so he asked Congress to amend it. The Sedition Act of 1918 created a whole new grabbag of punishable offenses to sweep in those who "willfully utter, print, write, or publish any disloyal, profane, scurrilous, or abusive language about the form of government of the United States, or the Constitution of the United States, or the military or naval forces of the United States, or the flag of the United States, or the uniform of the Army or Navy of the United States, or any language intended to bring the form of government of the United States [or the Constitution, military forces, flag, or uniform] into contempt, scorn, contumely, or disrepute." An American who said the uniform was baggy now faced twenty years in prison.

The Sedition Act also made it an offense to "advocate any curtailment of production in this country of any thing or things, product or products, necessary or essential to the prosecution of the war." This was the strikebreaking provision, for while some Americans might think the purpose of the war was to beat back the Germans, others would find it a good cover for beating back the union movement.

The Alien and Sedition Acts of 1917 and 1918 were directed at dissent from any source, native or immigrant, conservative or radical. The alien radical was specifically dealt with in the Immigration Act of 1917. The act of 1903 had barred anarchists or

Backgro

those who believed in or advocated the overthrow of the government and declared they could be deported within three years after their arrival. The act of 1917 broadened the definition of unwanted radicals to include those who "advocate or teach the unlawful destruction of property"—an anti-union, particularly anti-IWW, clause. The period during which alien radicals who entered illegally could be deported was extended to five years. Aliens like Sacco and Vanzetti who entered legally, believing in government and law and believing that America was a free country, only to become radicalized by the immigrant experience, could now be deported at any time.

For those determined to expel all alien radicals, the 1917 act left two loopholes: the five-year cutoff period for deporting aliens who had entered as radicals, and the wording for those who became radicals after entering which made them deportable for "advocating or teaching" their beliefs, thus requiring proof of individual guilt or illegal behavior. The Deportation Act of 1918 eliminated the time limit; a politically undesirable alien could be deported at any time whether he was undesirable when he entered or became so later. The need for overt acts was also eliminated; belief in the wrong ideas or membership in the wrong organization was sufficient to make an alien deportable. Woodrow Wilson's arsenal against freedom of conscience and expression was now complete.

There were 1,956 prosecutions under the Espionage and Sedition Acts. [25] Though the accused were entitled to a jury trial, there is very little value in trial by jury for political offenses a jury finds repugnant. In *Free Speech in the United States*, Zechariah Chafee, Jr., writes, "It is only in times of popular panic and indignation that freedom of speech becomes important as an institution, and it is precisely in those times that the protection of the jury proves illusory." *[26] Chafee quotes Judge Charles F. Amidon of North Dakota, who said:

*Chafee's book is dedicated to President Abbott Lawrence Lowell of Harvard: " . . . So long as he was President no one could breathe the air of Harvard and not be free." The irony of this will become apparent. Those who did not breathe the air of Harvard were not so fortunate.

Only those who have administered the Espionage Act can understand the danger of such legislation. When crimes are defined by such generic terms, instead of by specific acts, the jury becomes the sole judge, whether men shall or shall not be punished. Most of the jurymen have sons in the war. They are all under the power of the passions which war engenders.

For the first six months after June 15, 1917, I tried war cases before jurymen who were candid, sober, intelligent businessmen, whom I had known for thirty years, and who under ordinary circumstances would have had the highest respect for my declarations of law, but during that period they looked back into my eyes with the savagery of wild animals, saying by their manner, "Away with this twiddling, let us get at him." Men believed during that period that the only verdict in a war case, which could show loyalty, was a verdict of guilty.[27]

A verdict of guilty was brought in against 877 persons.[28] Chafee writes, "Almost all the convictions were for expressions of opinion about the merits and conduct of the war. . . . The courts treated opinions as statements of fact and then condemned them as false because they differed from the President's speech or the resolution of Congress declaring war."[29]

Rose Pastor Stokes, a socialist who had left the party to support the war, wrote a letter to a newspaper in which she said, "I am for the people, and the government is for the profiteers." A jury found this was a deliberately false statement calculated to interfere with and cause insubordination in the armed forces and to obstruct the draft. Mrs. Stokes was sentenced to ten years.

Reverend Clarence Waldron handed five persons a pamphlet in which he said war was not Christian. Reverend Waldron received a very un-Christian term of fifteen years.

D.H. Wallace, a former British soldier, said that "when a soldier went away he was a hero and that when he came back . . . he was a bum, and . . . that the soldiers were giving their lives for the capitalists, that 40% of the ammunition of the allies or their guns was defective because of graft." Wallace, sentenced to twenty years, went mad and died in prison.

Most of the Espionage and Sedition Act prosecutions were hit-and-run cases, people snared at random for saying the wrong thing at the wrong time, but some were aimed at specific targets. War often offers a nation the opportunity to do some vigorous domestic housecleaning. While America did not enter World War I just to wipe out the Wobblies, it seemed as good a time as any.

Like immigrants who were judged by how close they came to the Anglo-Saxon center, unions were judged by how well they conformed, and the Wobblies clearly were not conformists. The IWW was the most threatening of the unions because it was radical, independent, unpredictable, skillful at organizing and leading immigrant workers, and willing to take on tough battles.

When America entered the war, those Wobblies who liked a brawl under any auspices went off to fight in the armed forces. The union leadership opposed the war in principle but did nothing to oppose it in practice; they even advised their members to register for the draft. For all of their inflamed and sometimes ill-advised rhetoric, the Wobblies now were interested in only one thing—organizing workers. Nothing mattered more to them than the union, and they knew that the moment they gave the government any justification, the war would be used as an excuse to crush it.

Since 1915, the IWW had been busy in the West, organizing farm workers as well as the lumber, oil, mining, and construction industries. In 1917, though the war sent copper prices soaring, wages were cut. The IWW called a strike against the copper companies, which was immediately labeled subversive and pro-German. One July day, vigilantes in the mining town of Bisbee, Arizona, seized close to twelve hundred strikers and sympathizers, penned them on a cattle train, and shipped them to New Mexico under armed guard.

The prisoners were kept in the desert for thirty-six hours without food or water, beaten, and then jailed for three months without charges. In February, 1918, the President's Labor Mediation Commission, headed by Secretary of Labor William B. Wilson, investigated the copper strike and the Bisbee incident. They found that the strike really was a strike and not a German plot and that about one-third of the Bisbee victims were Wobblies, one-third were members of the AFL, and one-third didn't belong to any union at all. They also found that many of the men supported the war, were registered for the draft or had already served, bought Liberty Bonds, and gave to the Red Cross.[30] In time, twenty-one of the vigilantes were indicted but none were convicted; wartime juries rarely got hysterical enough to protect the innocent.

The Bisbee kidnappings had been rather ham-handed; President Wilson had his own plans for dealing with the Wobblies whom he called "a menace to organized society" and "worthy of being suppressed."[31] During the first six months of the war, AFL-affiliated unions took part in 518 labor disputes while the IWW took part in just three.[32] AFL strikes were negotiated, mediated, and settled, but when an IWW strike in the Pacific Northwest in the summer of 1917 halted lumber production, the government decided to strike back. Troops were sent in to raid IWW halls, break up meetings, and arrest Wobblies without warrants or charges.

President Wilson appointed a judge to investigate the union. Bill Haywood offered to turn over the IWW files, but the offer was not accepted. On September 5, 1917, the Justice Department raided IWW halls as well as members' homes all across the country, seizing tons of letters, records, literature, and other union materials. On September 28, one hundred and sixty-five IWW leaders were indicted for obstructing the war, encouraging resistance to the draft, and conspiring to cause insubordination in the armed forces.[33]

A total of 184 Wobblies were tried in three separate groups—in Chicago, Sacramento, and Wichita. The show trial in Chicago began on April 1, 1918, and dragged on into August. Though there were ninety-nine defendants, including Bill Haywood,* the prosecuting attorney said, "It is the IWW which is on trial here." One of the defense attorneys was again Fred Moore.

When the trial ended the jury had to evaluate five months of

*While testifying, Haywood said, "I have a dream that there will be a new society sometime in which there will be no battle between capitalist and wage earner."

Backgrou

testimony against ninety-nine individuals; it took them less than an hour to find everyone guilty. Haywood and other top Wobblies received the full term of twenty years; the other defendants received ten years or less. Fines came to almost $2,500,000, wiping out the union treasury.

In Sacramento, prison conditions were so foul that five Wobblies died before their trial began. The forty-six survivors were found guilty. The group of thirty-four in Wichita, Kansas, suffered most. Jailed in various hellholes for over two years before they were tried, some died and others lost their minds. In December, 1919, long after the war was over, the remaining Wobblies were found guilty of wartime conspiracy charges. Besides the three federal trials, a number of Wobblies were tried and convicted under various state sedition or syndicalist laws. Though some isolated units remained, President Wilson had his way; the IWW had effectively been suppressed.

The single most prominent victim of Wilson's vendetta against his critics and the First Amendment was Eugene Debs. The war divided the Socialists as it divided the rest of the country; some supported it while others were opposed. But there was no doubt where Debs stood. "I abhor war," he said. "When I think of a cold, glittering steel bayonet being plunged into the white, quivering flesh of a human being, I recoil with horror." * Debs also recoiled with horror at the mounting suppression of dissent. "It is extremely dangerous to exercise the constitutional right of free speech in a country fighting to make democracy safe in the world," he said. He wrote one of his friends convicted under the Espionage Act that if she was sent to prison, "I shall feel guilty to be at large." [34]

He would not feel guilty long. On June 16, 1918, during a Socialist convention in Canton, Ohio, Debs spoke in public to a crowd of about twelve hundred, including Justice Department agents and members of the American Protective League who were checking the audience for men with draft cards so that Debs could be accused of obstructing the draft. "The master class has always

---

*Even for Debs, one of the few idealists of his day, human flesh was white.

declared the wars," said Debs, "the subject class has always fought the battles. The master class has had all to gain and nothing to lose, while the subject class has had nothing to gain and all to lose—especially their lives."[35]

Debs was arrested on June 30. A reporter asked him if he wanted to repudiate his views. "I do not," Debs replied. "If necessary, I shall die for those principles."[36] His trial began on September 9, in a federal courtroom in Cleveland. The prosecutor called Debs "the palpitating pulse of the sedition crusade." Debs made no attempt to deny anything he had said; he simply asked for permission to speak to the jury, which was granted.

For almost two hours Debs talked about socialism, capitalism, exploitation, revolution, dissent, war, and peace. He said he believed as the founding fathers did "that a change was due in the interests of the people, that the time has come for a better form of government, an improved system, a higher social order, a nobler humanity and a grander civilization." He said he opposed an unjust war, just as Lincoln had opposed the war with Mexico, and concluded by telling the jury that their verdict did not much matter "so far as I am concerned. . . . What you may choose to do to me will be of small consequence. . . . I am not on trial here. . . . American institutions are on trial here before a court of American citizens."[37]

Debs was so eloquent that several members of the jury wept. The following day, dry-eyed, they found him guilty. Before being sentenced, Debs said, "Your honor, years ago I recognized my kinship with all living things, and I made up my mind that I was not one bit better than the meanest of the earth. I said then, I say now, that while there is a lower class, I am in it; while there is a criminal element, I am of it; while there is a soul in prison, I am not free."[38]

The judge told Debs he was deluding himself, that he might believe he was serving humanity but actually he "would strike the sword from the hand of this nation while she is engaged in defending herself against a foreign and brutal power." Then he sentenced the sixty-three-year-old Debs to ten years in prison.

While Debs appealed to the Supreme Court, he remained free and the war ended; the war was over before any Espionage Act appeals reached the Supreme Court. Zechariah Chafee, Jr., comments, "We cannot rely on the Supreme Court as a safeguard against the excesses of war legislation. A statute enacted early in a war is likely to receive its first authoritative interpretation many months later when the war is over."[39]

There is a more cogent reason for not relying on the Supreme Court; the justices are not necessarily more immune to patriotism, prejudice, or hysteria than the rest of the population. The Supreme Court repeatedly upheld the Espionage Act. The first decision, *Schenck* v. *United States*, involved a case where there was a direct attempt to persuade young men to resist conscription. The court unanimously ruled against the defendants, and Justice Oliver Wendell Holmes set down his famous guidelines on the limitations of free speech:

> We admit that in many places and in ordinary times the defendants in saying all that was said . . . would have been within their constitutional rights. But the character of every act depends upon the circumstances in which it is done. . . . The question in every case is whether the words used are used in such circumstances and are of such a nature as to create a clear and present danger that they will bring about the substantive evils that Congress has a right to prevent.[40]

A week later, the Supreme Court upheld Debs's conviction. Holmes wrote the Debs decision without once mentioning his own doctrine of "clear and present danger," possibly because there was no way to claim that Debs presented a clear and present danger to the conduct of the war or the functioning of the draft. Debs went to prison on April 13, 1919, five months after the war ended. Woodrow Wilson, who couldn't abide anyone who practiced morality instead of preaching it, refused to pardon the sick old man. "I know there will be a great deal of denunciation of me for refusing this pardon," Wilson told his secretary. "They will say I am cold-blooded and indifferent, but it will make no impression on me. This man was a traitor to his country and he will never be pardoned during my administration."[41] When Debs heard this, he said of Wilson, "It is he, not I, who needs a pardon."*[42]

To Justice Holmes's intense indignation, he received mail criticizing his decision in the Debs case. He wrote his friend, Sir Frederick Pollock:

> I am beginning to get stupid letters of protest against a decision that Debs, a noted agitator, was rightly convicted of obstructing the recruiting service so far as the law was concerned. I wondered that the Government should prese the case to a hearing before us, as the inevitable result was that fools, knaves, and ignorant persons were bound to say he was convicted because he was a dangerous agitator and that obstructing the draft was a pretence. How it was with the Jury of course I don't know, but of course the talk is silly as to us. There was a lot of jaw about free speech, which I dealt with somewhat summarily in an earlier case.[43]

Holmes could not seriously believe Debs was obstructing the recruiting service, but as a Civil War hero wounded in action three times, he may have been as offended by Debs's apparent lack of patriotism as any member of the jury. Holmes was also a charter member of the Brahmin caste of New England; his father minted the phrase. As Anne Hutchinson and Mary Dyer could affirm, the visible saints never did have much patience with noted agitators, nor did the great dissenter have much patience with fools, knaves, and ignorant persons rude enough to point out his inconsistencies.

Holmes's letter on the Debs decision has been quoted often enough but not fully enough. Holmes went on to speak of Felix Frankfurter, then a professor of law at Harvard, and note the prejudice against Frankfurter because he was a Jew. "It never

---

*In 1920, Debs, still in prison, received over 900,000 votes as Socialist candidate for president. He was finally pardoned on Christmas Day, 1921, by President Warren G. Harding. Those two butts of liberal scorn, Harding and Coolidge, pardoned the political prisoners jailed by the liberal hero, Woodrow Wilson.

occurs to me until after the event that a man I like is a Jew," wrote Holmes, "nor do I care, when I realize it. If I had to choose I think I would rather see power in the hands of the Jews than in the Catholics',—not that I wish to be run by either."[44]

10

The Red Scare

World War I ended on November 11, 1918, but not in America, which went to war with itself as peace brought a doubtful dividend in the form of a national nervous breakdown.

By the time the war was over, the enemy had changed; the Allies were far more concerned about Communists than Germans. The Bolshevik Revolution in Russia and the temporary success of Communist revolts in Hungary and Bavaria caused the Allies, including England, France, and America, to send troops to Russia to assist the counterrevolution and make the world safe for capitalism. The assistance was futile and counter-productive; it served to unite the Russian people against foreign intruders and to freeze the West into a cold war mentality as early as 1918. Joe McCarthy was an eleven-year-old boy feeding chickens on his father's farm in Wisconsin when President Woodrow Wilson was stumping the country hinting that Republicans who opposed the League of Nations were Bolshevik dupes.

There were not only Communists abroad but in America as

well. By September, 1919, the left wing of the Socialist party had broken away and founded the Communist Labor party. At the same time, the extreme left wing of the Socialist party broke away and founded the Communist party. America now had two Communist parties, a Socialist party, and odd-lots of anarchists, syndicalists, Wobblies, and assorted other radicals ranging from the most benign to the most explosive. Their numbers were small but their existence was real, and when America sank into a psychological, economic, and leadership slump, the Left was there to be sacrificed, though those who felt the full force of the terror were not simply radicals but alien radicals, and often just aliens.*

The psychological slump was due to disillusionment with the war. Those who believed Wilson's evangelical exhortations learned from returning veterans, from secret treaties published by the Bolsheviks revealing the Allies had agreed on how to divide the spoils, and from the Paris peace talks that this war was no different from any other in its cupidity and cynicism. In one memorable moment at the peace conference, Wilson asked the Australian representative if his country was prepared to defy the appeal of the whole civilized world. "That's about the size of it," the Australian replied.†[1]

The economic slump began when war industries halted production; suddenly 9 million workers and 4 million returning veterans were crowding the job market. As unemployment rose, so did prices; Americans were trapped in that most vicious of all economic nightmares, depression and inflation. Some veterans, finding that while the war had not trained them for civilian employment it had at least taught them how to use a gun, turned to crime, and the country was embarrassed and terrified by a wave of robberies committed by ex-soldiers.

*Possibly the flu pandemic of 1918–19, which killed more than a half-million Americans, contributed to the paranoia. There was fear in the air, and giving it a name made it more bearable, even if it was the wrong name.

†A.J.P. Taylor wrote, "It was particularly embarrassing for [Wilson] when the Japanese maliciously tried to write the principle of race equality into the League Covenant. Wilson had to buy them off by presenting them with Shantung, the former German sphere in China."[2]

Red Scare

What America needed badly was strong and reassuring guidance from the White House, but no one was home. Wilson had gone to Paris for the peace conference that began in January, 1919, coming like the Messiah to create a perfect world. When he returned to America, it was to tour the country to win support for the League of Nations, which Congress might have approved if Wilson had been willing to compromise or his ego had allowed him to invite Henry Cabot Lodge, his most influential enemy in the Senate, to go to Paris with him. In October, Wilson suffered a paralytic stroke, and the American people had no president for the next seventeen months until Harding was elected and inaugurated.*

Even if Wilson had remained healthy and at home, the Red Scare of 1919 and 1920 might not have been averted. When the war ended, there were, according to the American Civil Liberties Union,† 1,472 political prisoners either in jail or awaiting trial. Asked to pardon them, Wilson replied, "I do not think the men you refer to are in any proper sense political prisoners. They have in fact violated criminal statutes of the United States."[4]

Wilson would neither free political prisoners nor cease his search and destroy missions. Because Congress did not officially end the war until July, 1921, the administration tried to maintain the fiction that hostilities continued so as to be able to use the Espionage and Sedition Acts, though with characteristic prescience, Wilson urged Congress to pass a peacetime sedition law. Publications continued to be closed down or barred from the mails and, early in 1920, three men were tried in Syracuse, New York, for distributing circulars calling for amnesty for political prisoners. They were convicted and sentenced to prison for, among other crimes, disloyal language and obstruction of recruit-

*Since Wilson was followed by Harding, Coolidge, and Hoover, it may be argued that America had no president until 1932.
†The ACLU, founded by Roger Baldwin in October, 1917, as the National Civil Liberties Bureau, was an outgrowth of an earlier pacifist group. When the NCLB protested wartime violations of civil liberties, its publications were banned from the mails and the government stopped just shy of persecuting it out of existence. Baldwin, a Harvard man whose ancestors arrived on the *Mayflower*, was jailed as a conscientious objector just before the war ended. The ACLU adopted its present name in January, 1920.[3]

ing, even though the war had been over for fourteen months.

The Red Scare in America followed a consistent action-reaction pattern. When something traumatic happened—strikes, riots, bombings—the public blamed the Bolsheviks; ever since the Russian Revolution most radicals were called Bolshevik no matter what their creed, just as earlier radicals had been called anarchist, a term still used but not as often.

Because prices were outracing wages and workers could no longer be silenced by false appeals to their patriotism, there were some thirty-six hundred strikes in 1919, involving over 4 million persons.[5] The National Association of Manufacturers and other employer organizations responded by calling unionism "nothing less than bolshevism" and "the greatest crime left in the world," but labor was no longer listening.[6]

Four of the strikes were spectacular enough to cause national headlines and hysteria. The first was in Seattle where, in February, sixty thousand workers took part in a general strike in support of shipyard employees demanding higher pay. Though there was no violence and the strikers made certain the city had food and fuel, Seattle was paralyzed. The workers had proved their power in a stunning display of strength that amounted to overkill. Many Americans had not yet accepted the idea of even one striking union; a united front of striking unions was terrifying.

The Russian Revolution had begun with a general strike in Petrograd, so the nation's press covered the Seattle story with screaming scare headlines such as "Reds Directing Seattle Strike—To Test Chance for Revolution" and reported it as the first move of the Bolsheviks to take over America. Politicians suggested the strike leaders be sent back to Russia. The mayor had federal troops sent in. Seattle's labor leaders were so startled and intimidated by the reaction they called off the strike on the fifth day.

The other three major strikes took place in the fall. On September 9, the Boston police struck because the police commissioner refused to let them affiliate with the AFL and fired nineteen union leaders from the force. No one could be less radical than the Irish-Catholic cops of Boston, but the press described the strike as a war between Boston and bolshevism. "Lenin and Trotsky are on their way," said the *Wall Street Journal*. President Abbott Lawrence Lowell of Harvard, always public-spirited when it came to anti-immigrant or antiunion activity, urged his students to join a volunteer police force. President Wilson called the strike "a crime against civilization.

The police agreed to return to work while the issues were settled by mediation but on September 14, Governor Calvin Coolidge of Massachusetts uttered the line that was to make him president: "There is no right to strike against the public safety by anybody, anywhere, anytime." All the striking police were fired.

The Boston police strike was barely cold when some 365,000 steel workers walked out in late September in support of a wage increase, an eight-hour day, and other demands. The chairman of the board of directors of U.S. Steel refused even to meet with union leaders, while the *Wall Street Journal* praised him for "fighting the battle of the American Constitution." Press assistance came from all sides. The *New York Times* said the workers wanted "control of the industry," while the radical press helped no one by calling the strike "open class war." The ranting of the radical press did as much to hurt the cause of unionism and fuel the fears of uneasy Americans as the antilabor pieties of the major newspapers; it is likely that at least some radicals were as anxious as the industrialists for the unions to fail so they could have an all-out confrontation.

When the strikers refused to go back to work, spies infiltrated union locals, and police, sheriffs, and vigilantes were used to break up meetings and smash heads. Attempts were made to subvert the strike by pitting white against white and black against white. The steel companies instructed spies to "stir up as much bad feeling as you possibly can between the Serbians and Italians. . . . Call up every question you can in reference to racial hatred between these two nationalities. . . . Urge [the Serbians] to go back to work or the Italians will get their jobs."[7] Black strikebreakers were brought in, which caused such riots that troops had to be summoned. In January, 1920, the steel strike ended with nothing gained and twenty lives lost.

The fourth major strike involved the United Mine Workers who, led by John L. Lewis, voted to walk out on November 1 because the coal operators would not meet their demands. The Seattle strike had frightened the country because it revealed the potential power of a united labor movement, the police strike because it left a city unprotected, the steel strike because steel was so vital to the economy, and the coal strike because winter was coming. Before the strike began the coal operators were howling that something had to be done about the "insurrection," and the *New York Tribune* said the miners were "red-soaked in the doctrines of Bolshevism."

The attorney general obtained an injunction to prevent union leaders from taking part in the strike, but the men walked out as scheduled. Three days later, on November 4, the Commonwealth of Massachusetts voted for governor. Coolidge, who was running for reelection, was as undistinguished as governor as he would be as president, but many people believed he had saved Boston from the Bolsheviks during the police strike. Against the backdrop of the steel and coal disputes, the nation watched the election results in Massachusetts to see if the commonwealth would rather be dead than Red. Coolidge's easy victory was proclaimed "A Defeat of the Soviets" and a telegram was sent to Coolidge in Wilson's name saying, "I congratulate you upon your election as a victory for law and order." *

On November 8, at the request of the attorney general, the courts ordered the union leaders to end the coal strike. John L. Lewis sensed the public mood and conceded. "We are Americans," said Lewis, "we cannot fight our government." Lewis did not explain, nor did anyone, why men seeking higher wages should have to fight not only their employers but their government, or why starvation should be equated with patriotism.

In addition to the strikes in 1919 there were riots, many of them antilabor or antiradical. On May Day, mobs in Boston, New York, and Cleveland assaulted marchers, raided meetings, and trashed Socialist party headquarters. The attackers were not arrested but hundreds of radicals were charged with rioting and disturbing the peace.

*Before law and order became a code phrase referring to nonwhites, it referred to poor whites, immigrants, strikers, and radicals.

The most serious of the riots, however, were racial. Blacks had also fought (in segregated units) to make the world safe for democracy. A black editor warned that the white American "will find that in teaching our boys to fight for him he was starting something that he will not be able to stop."[8]

The worst of the race riots were in Omaha and Chicago. In Omaha, a maniacal mob of whites, determined to lynch a black prisoner, shot at police, set fire to the prison, cut the hoses of firemen who tried to extinguish the blaze, and almost hanged the mayor when he tried to intervene. Even after the mob had lynched their victim, troops had to be called in to restore order.[9]

The Chicago riot began when a black teenager, playing with his friends on a homemade log raft floating in Lake Michigan, was hit on the forehead, either accidentally or deliberately, by a stone thrown by a white man. Before anyone could help him, the boy sank into the water and drowned. By nightfall, blacks and whites were stoning each other on the beach and a black policeman had killed a black rioter. The Chicago riot lasted for seven days; when it was over, the militia had been called in, twenty-three blacks and fifteen whites were dead, and over five hundred persons were injured.[10]

Instead of blaming racism, the whites blamed radicalism. In a year when seventy-two blacks were lynched, the *New York Times* mournfully observed that "Bolshevist agitation has been extended among the Negroes." The *Boston Herald* found "the sinister influence of the IWW and of bolshevism . . . clearly evident." Rather than investigate racism, segregation, and lynch law, the Justice Department decided to investigate black radicalism. The investigation was assigned to the General Intelligence Division of the Bureau of Investigation.

The Bureau of Investigation, known since 1935 as the Federal Bureau of Investigation, was proposed to Congress in 1907 and 1908 by Attorney General Charles Joseph Bonaparte.[11] The reaction was negative; both the House and Senate recoiled at the consequences of setting up a "central police or spy system in the Federal government." A newspaper called the idea "absolutely contrary to the democratic principles of government."

Backgr

Congress adjourned May 30, 1908; on July 1, the attorney general established the Bureau of Investigation. When members of Congress demanded an explanation, they discovered that the industrious new organization, by tailing them and checking their mail, had already compiled dossiers of personal information and turned them over to President Theodore Roosevelt. Roosevelt indignantly denied that the investigators had opened congressional mail; he said that "through . . . accidental breaking . . . the contents are exposed." [12] Then he published the private correspondence of one of his senate critics; undoubtedly the letters had been exposed when the envelopes accidentally broke open. Thus, with the aid and encouragement of the president, the Bureau of Investigation initiated its long career of congressional blackmail while J. Edgar Hoover was in knickers.

During World War I the bureau distinguished itself by the zeal with which it pursued draft evaders. [13] Its favorite tactic was the mass raid or dragnet. No one knew what was going to happen until agents of the bureau drove up to the target area and pounced. Men were arrested on the street, in hotels, flophouses, and barber shops, in parks, theaters, and office buildings, in cars, trains, and trolleys. Though the draft age was from twenty-one to thirty, every male was presumed to be a draft evader whether he was fifteen or seventy-five or a multiple amputee, unless he could prove otherwise by showing his draft registration card.

In a series of raids in the greater New York area, seventy-five thousand men were seized; one newspaper called the raids "the greatest carnival of arrests that the city ever knew." At first the bureau claimed 25 to 30 percent of those arrested were draft evaders, which still meant that 70 to 75 percent were innocent. It was later discovered that only one out of two hundred, or one-half percent were draft evaders; the other $99^{1}/_{2}$ percent had been seized, searched, and imprisoned without warrants or justification. Among those swept in by mistake were members of draft boards, policemen in civilian clothing, and foreign diplomats. There were also large numbers of men who were carrying their draft cards, but the agents were too eager to arrest everyone in sight to stop long enough to check.

The raids were halted because of their absurdities and

excesses, but their subliminal effects were more invidious than their apparent ones. They implanted three concepts in the public mind: civil liberties do not concern the government and therefore need not concern the people; draft evaders and other dissenters are outcasts who warrant neither constitutional protection nor public sympathy; it is acceptable to imprison thousands to trap one offender. These truths being self-evident, the public would be not only quiescent but acquiescent when the Bureau of Investigation used the techniques perfected in the draft raids to hunt alien radicals.

The Bureau of Investigation, whose only genuine skill seemed to be survival, turned to the radical problem when the war ended. Actually, radicals were not entirely new to the bureau; in September, 1917, its agents had conducted the mass raids on IWW homes and halls. In September, 1918, when a bomb exploded in a government building in Chicago killing four and wounding many others, the bureau, before investigating, blamed the IWW even though leaders of the union were in the building requesting bail at the time, making it unlikely their comrades would try to blow them up. The bureau arrested a number of Wobblies anyway, but no one was convicted and the bombing of September, 1918, was never solved.[14]

The following April the bureau had its investigative abilities taxed again, for 1919 was not only a year of strikes and riots but of bombings as well. On April 28, a package was delivered by mail to the office of Seattle's mayor. When it began to leak acid, it was found to contain a homemade bomb. On April 29, another package was delivered to the home of a former senator from Georgia. When his maid opened it, her hands were blown off.

A New York City postal clerk, who read newspaper accounts of the two bombs, remembered that he had put aside sixteen similar packages because of insufficient postage. The sixteen packages were checked; all contained bombs. A nationwide search was ordered and eighteen more bombs were located. No one else was hurt, but someone or some group had planned to blow up thirty-six prominent Americans on May Day, including Justice Holmes, John D. Rockefeller, J.P. Morgan, and several

Backgr<

government officials, among them the new attorney general, A. Mitchell Palmer.

The press and public went wild with outrage, demanding that someone be lynched, and quickly. The *New York Times* said that "Bolsheviki, anarchists, and IWWs" were to blame.[15] Radicals insisted the bombs were planted in order to discredit them, though it was unlikely that the Bureau of Investigation would blow up the attorney general just to score points. The absurdity of mailing bombs with insufficient postage suggests a foreigner or foreigners unfamiliar with the postal system.

The Bureau of Investigation and police in New York and other cities worked feverishly to find the bombers. Arrests were always forthcoming, but never came. Instead, on the night of June 2, bombs exploded in eight different cities, killing two persons. In Washington, D.C., as Attorney General Palmer was preparing for bed, he heard a loud explosion; an elk's head fell from the wall and crashed at his feet. Downstairs, the front door and all of the windows of his home had been blown in.[16] The bomber had apparently tripped and blown himself up before he could throw the bomb into the house. Possibly there had been two bombers since the police retrieved what appeared to be parts of two left legs, though they insisted only one man was involved, which led a Washington newspaper to comment it was no wonder he tripped since he had two left feet.[17] Flyers were scattered about the street which said, in part, "There will have to be murder; we will kill. . . . We are ready to do anything and everything to suppress the capitalist class." The flyers were signed, "The Anarchist Fighters."

The public again reacted with outrage and demands for hasty punishment. A new director, William J. Flynn, was appointed to the Bureau of Investigation, which kept announcing that arrests would be made before nighttime, that Lenin was responsible, that they were working hard and making progress. "This is the biggest job in the business of crime detection in America today," said Attorney General Palmer. On August 1, 1919, to intensify the search for the bombers and to deal with radicals generally, the Bureau of Investigation established an anti-radical or General Intelligence Division and put in charge a young man with a future,

J. Edgar Hoover. But neither Hoover nor Flynn nor anyone else could break the case; no one ever found out who was responsible for any of the bombings of 1919.[18]

When the GID investigated black radicalism after the race riots of 1919, J. Edgar Hoover personally prepared the report, which said that while black radicals had not instigated the riots, they had exploited them.

According to Hoover, there could "no longer be any question of a well-concerted movement among a certain class of Negro leaders of thought and action to constitute themselves a determined and persistent source of a radical opposition to the Government, and to the established rule of law and order." He was also critical of the "ill-governed reaction" of black leaders toward race rioting, their "threat of retaliatory measures in connection with lynching" (just hang there and be quiet), their demands for social equality, their anti-southern feelings, and their views of the peace treaty and the League of Nations. Behind all this Hoover found shocking insubordination—"race consciousness . . . openly, defiantly assertive of its own equality and even superiority." He concluded that certain blacks constituted a "radical opposition to the Government and to the established rule of law."[19]

The Hoover report was typical of the official attitude of the time. Rather than concede that the strikes and riots and even the bombings, unjustified as they were, reflected legitimate grievances, men of responsibility continued to deflect reform by crying Bolshevik. A Senate investigation of domestic radicalism, headed by Senator Lee Overman, was held early in 1919, immediately after the Seattle strike. What seemed to titillate the members of the Overman committee most was not domestic radicalism but sex in Russia. One witness, Archibald E. Stevenson, a New York attorney associated with the Bureau of Investigation, was questioned about this.

Overman:　　Do they have as many wives as they want?
Stevenson:　In rotation.

*　　*　　*

Overman:　　Do you know whether they teach free love?
Stevenson:　They do.[20]

Stevenson also testified that the presence of so many aliens in America increased the dangers of radicalism and urged that "foreign agitators" be deported.

Overman: What do you think about our immigration laws?
Stevenson: I think they ought to be very much more stringent.

Another senator interrupted to say, "But you cannot base exclusion altogether on mere educational lines. Some of these fellows . . . can read and write and yet they are anarchists and socialists." Stevenson agreed that "These people who are coming over here are, in many instances, very extraordinarily well-read people." The fervor of the Immigration Restriction League had been futile; the literacy test had accomplished nothing. But Overman suggested another solution the league would have approved.

Overman: Would it do to pass a law that no person should enter this country unless he is a white man—an Anglo-Saxon—for the next ten years?
Stevenson: If it could be done I think it would be a good thing.[21]

The Overman committee also heard some contrary views. A clergyman testified that "all the agitators in the world cannot stir up discontent in this country unless the soil is ready for the sowing of the seed of discontent." A YMCA official who had recently returned from Soviet Russia suggested that the future of radicalism in America depended on whether or not the unemployed could find jobs. The head of the American Red Cross mission to Russia said that "If we answer the economic wrongs which fester and make centers of resentment . . . we can meet and answer the agitation and unrest."[22]

But these sensible opinions of sensible conservatives were ignored. The final report of the Overman committee suggested that the Bolshevik revolution in America would begin in about fifteen minutes. It recommended a peacetime sedition act and the exclusion or deportation of more aliens. One newspaper headlined the story, "Red Peril Here."

A second investigation that had a baleful influence on public opinion was conducted by a committee of the New York State legislature headed by state Senator Clayton R. Lusk. The ubiquitous Archibald Stevenson, who had provoked the demand for an investigation by writing a report on the dangers of radicalism in New York City, served as assistant counsel to the committee.

On June 12, the day the Lusk hearings began, twenty agents of the Bureau of Investigation and ten state police raided the Russian Soviet Bureau in New York. The Russian Soviet Bureau claimed its function was to handle commercial relations between Russia and the United States, but it was primarily a propaganda organization. The purpose of the raid was to gather publicity and evidence for the Lusk committee; the idea came from Stevenson and the raid was carried out in the best bureau tradition. Agents and police rushed in without warning, cutting telephone lines and destroying material on sight, though enough remained to carry off two tons of documents which, according to the committee, proved that the Russian Soviet Bureau was the clearinghouse for all radical activity in the country, that radical publications preached the word to at least a half million followers, and that the revolution would begin with the union movement.

On June 21, the Lusk committee raided the socialist Rand School in New York City and the headquarters of the local IWW. Now Lusk announced that radicals controlled over one hundred unions and the Rand School was in league with the Russian Soviet Bureau to bolshevize American labor. Stevenson announced the Rand School was bolshevizing the blacks. Lusk and Stevenson in chorus pronounced the Rand School the headquarters for the Bolshevik revolution in America, and the committee filed suit to have the school's charter revoked. When it came time to support its charges in state supreme court, the Lusk committee wasn't ready. After repeated delays because the committee couldn't seem to find any evidence, a judge threw the case out. But the dramatic raids and the lurid charges, not the action of the court, harvested the headlines.

The press contributed to the hysteria by continuously front-paging stories on radicals and radicalism, whether they were credible or not. The publishers were satisfying their proclivities, since most of them were conservative businessmen who either

Backgro

believed the stories or wanted others to believe them; they were also filling their purses. When the war ended newspaper sales had dropped, and it became an economic imperative to find a new sensation; scare stories about radicals seemed to suffice. There was little attempt to look behind the smoke to see if there was fire, or how large the fire really was. What passed for investigative reporting just confirmed everyone's fears. The *New York World* published an exposé which estimated that there were five million Bolsheviks or parlor pinks in America.

In order to preserve its interests, big business also had a front seat on the anti-Bolshevik bandwagon. Ever since the first worker had asked for more porridge, business had branded union activity un-American. When labor agitation increased after the war, so did employer agitation. DuPont, Morgan, and Rockefeller money was poured into patriotic societies which inundated the nation with propaganda warning that every threat to corporate earnings, including unions and the income tax, was Bolshevik.[23]

In addition to the societies which fronted for big business, two other groups were hyperactive during the Red Scare. One was the Ku Klux Klan, for whom all Catholics, Jews, blacks, aliens, and unions were un-American. Since the Klan enjoyed a spectacular surge in membership in 1920, its logic must have seemed very persuasive to people corroded by decades of racist propaganda emanating from more reputable sources—men with four or five generations of gentlemen among their ancestors, and presidents of Harvard.[24]

The other group was the American Legion, founded in May, 1919, by veterans whose goal was "to foster and perpetuate a one hundred percent Americanism."[25] This is a phrase that occurs often in the course of American history, particularly in times of crisis when the country is trying to define itself. Just as the Puritans sought signs of saving faith, the American Legion in 1919 sought signs of 100 percent Americanism. Since the signs were elusive, the positive was deduced from the negative. The Puritans were certain that Indians and blacks lacked saving faith; the legionnaires were equally certain that no Wobbly could be a 100 percent American even if he did fight beside them in France.

On the first anniversary of Armistice Day, November 11, 1919, the American Legion in Centralia, Washington, decided to show how to deal with those who were not 100 percent Americans. The legionnaires were aided and abetted by the local lumber trust, which was fearful of IWW attempts to organize lumberjacks.

Some of the legionnaires marched in the Armistice Day parade carrying rubber hoses, gas pipes, and coils of rope, strange implements to celebrate the end of the war. Knowing the parade route took the marchers past the IWW hall, the Wobblies rightly suspected they would be attacked. Some members remained in the hall while others were stationed at various points outside. All were armed.

The marchers went by the hall once and nothing happened. Then they turned to march past again. This time some of the legionnaires rushed the hall. One of the Wobblies inside was Wesley Everest, a veteran wearing his uniform. "I fought for democracy in France and I'm going to fight for it here," Everest said. "The first man that comes in this hall, why, he's going to get it."

As the legionnaires smashed through the door, shots rang out from Wobblies inside and outside the hall. Three legionnaires fell dead. A number of Wobblies were arrested, but Everest ran from the building. A posse caught up with him as he tried to cross a nearby river. He fired, killing another legionnaire, the nephew of the lumber trust leader who had planned the attack.

When his gun was empty, Everest was seized by the mob which beat him and knocked his teeth out with a rifle butt before dragging him to prison by a strap around his neck. That night the lights went out in Centralia while a lynch mob broke into the jail. "Tell the boys I died for my class," said Everest.

Everest was beaten, thrown into a car, and castrated. Then the lynchers drove him to a railroad bridge where they hanged him three times before they let him die. As his body swung from the girders, the lynchers fired at it. The coroner wrote, "Everest broke out of jail, went to the . . . bridge, and committed suicide. He jumped off with a rope around his neck and then shot himself full of holes." [26]

The Centralia incident triggered a new series of assaults

Backgrou

against the Wobblies in Washington; they were raided, beaten, and jailed. In Congress, the dead legionnaires were hailed as martyrs. "The shots that killed these boys were really aimed at the heart of this nation by those who oppose law and seek the overthrow of government," said one senator. A Presbyterian publication called for every radical to "swing at the end of a rope."

No 100 percent Americans questioned what the four martyrs were doing when they were shot, nor did anyone investigate Everest's lynching, though eleven Wobblies were tried for murdering the legionnaires. It was quite a trial; the judge had delivered a funeral eulogy for the legionnaires attacking the IWW, and the American Legion received corporate contributions to pay fifty men four dollars a day to sit at the front of the courtroom dressed in uniform. Three witnesses who testified that the Wobblies did not fire until the hall was attacked were arrested for perjury.

One defendant was released in the course of the trial; the jury found another insane, acquitted two, and found two guilty of manslaughter and five guilty of second degree murder. The judge refused to accept the manslaughter verdicts and sent the jury back to reconsider. They returned with two acquitted, one insane, and seven guilty of second degree murder. When the convicted men received prison terms ranging from twenty-five to forty years, the public protested; they wanted them hanged.[27]

At a victory loan pageant in Washington, D.C., a man who refused to rise for the national anthem was shot three times in the back by a sailor while the onlooking crowd cheered and applauded. A man who murdered an alien for saying "To hell with the United States" was acquitted by a jury within two minutes.[28] With the president, Congress, government officials, state legislators, the press, businessmen, and patriotic organizations all seeing Red, and radicals providing just enough bombs and bombast to make it believable, the American people inevitably began to see Red too.*

*It is interesting to speculate whether prohibition, the last crusade of the Puritans, ratified in January, 1919, and effective one year later, added to the tension.

11

America's Reign of Terror

With Wilson paralyzed in the White House, too ill to rule, too obstinate to resign, the country was ripe for a demagogue who would stretch out his hand to part the Red sea so the people could cross unharmed while the waters poured over the evil Bolsheviks who pursued them. Such a savior would surely be swept into the White House in November, 1920.

The man who saw the potential and was in a position to exploit it was Attorney General A. Mitchell Palmer. Palmer was a Pennsylvania Quaker, a three-term congressman who had refused the position of secretary of war because he didn't think "a man of peace" was suitable for such a post. Instead Wilson appointed him judge, alien property custodian, and in March, 1919, attorney general.[1]

At first there was hope Palmer would be more liberal than his predecessor, Thomas Gregory, but Palmer's ambitions and the two attempts on his life may have warped his judgment. Besides, as a Quaker, he hated radicals who were often atheists and sometimes violent. It probably never occurred to Palmer that

Quakers were once considered radicals, just as it never occurred to the 100 percent Americans who feared revolution that some of them had ancestors who had led one.

It was after Palmer's home was bombed in June, 1919, that he requested and received from Congress $500,000 to set up the General Intelligence Division of the Bureau of Investigation, under J. Edgar Hoover. Hoover announced that "civilization faces its most terrible menace of danger since the barbarian hordes overran West Europe and opened the dark ages."[2] To save civilization from the menace of danger, no sacrifice was too great, no act too unconstitutional.

The money appropriated by Congress was to be used for the "detection and prosecution of crimes," but Hoover ordered his men to search for seditious activity and evidence "which may be of use in prosecutions . . . under legislation . . . which may hereafter be enacted."[3] In the hope that a peacetime sedition law would be passed, Hoover had the GID investigate activities that were not yet criminal.

Agents put together dossiers on suspected radicals, using information obtained from undercover informers, neighbors, friends, and enemies, which guaranteed a grab bag of gossip, misrepresentation, and hearsay. They also gathered books, pamphlets, and other writings on or by radicals and monitored radical meetings. If a meeting was open, a stenographer was sent to take notes; if it was closed, an undercover agent attended.

After the GID accumulated its vast collection of chyme, the problem was how to digest it. Before going to the Justice Department in 1917, Hoover had worked for the Library of Congress and was familiar with its card-indexing system. He set up a similar system for the GID, covering radical individuals, organizations, and publications. These cards were cross-indexed with listings of radicals and organizations in key cities. Working like dervishes, GID agents soon had, or claimed to have, files on a half-million radicals. Common radicals rated just a card with basic information on why they were dangerous and where they could be arrested. Important radicals were honored with more substantial biographies; three months after the GID was founded, Hoover claimed "a more or less complete history of over 60,000 radically-inclined individuals,"[4] a research and writing achievement any author would envy.

In addition to this prodigious literary output, the GID prepared weekly reports for government officials on the latest developments within the radical movements. It also found time to conduct an extensive propaganda campaign. Antiradical articles and cartoons were sent to newspapers and magazines to be used without charge. Always hungry for handouts to fill the spaces between the ads, many publications printed this Justice Department material without identifying it as propaganda, so readers accepted it as reporting.

Letters signed by Attorney General Palmer were sent to the press for dissemination to the public to impress both with the mounting dangers of bolshevism. One of Palmer's letters restated the old charge that Soviet Russia was trying to incite a revolution in the United States and added the new one that "the entire movement is a dishonest and criminal one." Elsewhere the letter said, "Its sympathizers in this country are composed chiefly of criminals."[5] Palmer not only nourished the hysteria but planted the concept that radicals were not just radical but common criminals as well.

The propaganda had its desired effect. The public began to demand that the Justice Department do something about the accursed Bolsheviks, which was exactly what Palmer had in mind; he wanted the people to look to him for salvation. But he had to save them dramatically and quickly to be in a position to compete for the Democratic nomination.

Though the United States technically was still at war, Palmer was uncertain whether the courts would continue to uphold the Espionage and Sedition Acts, and peacetime sedition laws were stalled in Congress. The solution to Palmer's dilemma lay in the pernicious hostility to immigrants that has persistently tainted the American dream. According to Hoover, 90 percent of all radicals in America were foreign born.[6] That meant 54,000 alien radicals based on the biographical file, or 450,000 based on the entire index. If they were deported, everyone from the lynchers of the Ku Klux Klan to the Brahmins of the Immigration Restriction League

Backgrou

would be content, and Palmer could begin to write his Inaugural address. The best part of the plan was that it did not depend on any sedition act, passed or unpassed; the Deportation Act of 1918 provided for the expulsion of alien radicals at any time.

On August 12, 1919, William J. Flynn, director of the Bureau of Investigation, sent confidential instructions to his agents which read, in part, "The bureau requires a vigorous and comprehensive investigation of anarchistic and similar classes, Bolshevism, and kindred agitations advocating change in the present form of government by force or violence, the promotion of sedition and revolution, bomb throwing, and similar activities. *In the present state of the Federal law this investigation should be particularly directed to persons not citizens of the United States, with a view of obtaining deportation cases.*" [7] (Emphasis added.)

After the general strike in Seattle, fifty-four alien radicals were shipped east on a train labeled the "Red Special" to be deported from Ellis Island. But this was early in 1919 and public opinion had not yet solidified against the alien radical; only three were actually expelled. By the fall, the events of the chaotic year had not only tipped public opinion in the opposite direction, but had unbalanced it.

On Friday evening, November 7, 1919, the Bureau of Investigation, led by Flynn himself, opened its war against alien radicals in true bureau style. GID agents, supplemented by local police and detectives, burst into the Russian People's House in New York City without warning and with a minimum of warrants. The Federated Unions of Russian Workers, which was on Hoover's list, had a one-room office in the building; the other rooms were used for classes for Russian immigrants. Some of the two hundred men and women who were in these classrooms when the invasion began later reported, in sworn statements, what had happened.

Mitchel Lavrowsky, fifty years old, formerly a high school principal and teacher in Russia said:

> At about 8:00 o'clock in the evening, while I was teaching algebra and Russian, an agent of the Department of Justice opened the door of the school [room], walked in with a revolver in his hands and ordered

everybody in the [room] to step aside; then ordered me to step toward him. I wear eyeglasses and the agent of the Department of Justice ordered me to take them off. Then, without any provocation, [he] struck me on the head and simultaneously two others struck and beat me brutally. After I was beaten and without strength to stand on my feet, I was thrown downstairs and while I rolled down, other men, I presume also agents of the Department of Justice, beat me with pieces of wood, which I later found out were obtained by breaking the banisters. I sustained a fracture of my head, left shoulder, left foot, and right side. Then I was ordered to wash myself and was taken, as I now understand, to . . . Park Row [the New York office of the Justice Department] where I was examined by various people and released about 12:00 midnight.[8]

Nicolai Melikoff, one of the students, described how the agents searched everyone, taking twenty dollars from his pocket which they never returned. He said that one detective "knocked me down . . . sat on my back, pressing me down to the floor with his knee and bending my back until blood flowed out of my mouth and nose. I was then taken to a sink where I was ordered to drink some water and was also ordered to wash my face. After this, I was thrown downstairs." He too was taken to Park Row and released after questioning.[9]

Semeon Kravchuck was walking toward the school when he was stopped and ordered into the building "where I was immediately attacked and brutally beaten."[10] Peter Karas, who lived in the neighborhood, was only out for a stroll, but two agents stopped him, beat him, and sent him to Park Row for questioning.[11]

The victims were ordered to wash off the blood because the press was waiting outside to report on how the brave Bureau of Investigation was beating back the Red menace, omitting such details as their ripping out banisters to do so. The next day's *New*

Backgrou

York Times reported the raid in a six-column headline: "Raids on Radicals Here and In Other Cities."* The article said that on the second anniversary of the Bolshevik Revolution in Russia, "The Federal government, aided by municipal police in New York and several other large cities, last night dealt the most serious and sweeping blow it has yet aimed at criminal anarchists."

The *Times* described how the agents "had gone systematically through the building in search of incriminating literature of any kind. Doors were taken off, desks were ripped open, and even the few carpets were torn up to find possible hiding places for documents." Though the immigrants had been told to wash up, there was a limit to what could be concealed. The *Times* reporter noted that "A number of those in the building were badly beaten by the police during the raid, their heads wrapped in bandages testifying to the rough manner in which they had been handled." [12]

The following day the *Times* reported that thirty-three men captured in the raid, "most of them with bandaged heads, black eyes, or other marks of rough handling," and two women had been taken to Ellis Island "where an effort will be made to deport them as anarchists and revolutionists." About 150 others were freed, including anyone who could prove he was a citizen. The *Times* said that those who were released "also had blackened eyes and lacerated scalps as souvenirs of the new attitude of aggressiveness which has been assumed by the Federal agents against Reds and suspected Reds. Twelve of the men who were roughly handled and later released said they were soldiers [presumably the *Times* meant veterans]. The others said they were teaching or attending classes at the People's House, where automobile repairing and the English language and other subjects were being taught." [13]

The same night as the New York raid, and during the following day, raids were conducted against radicals or suspected radicals in some fifteen other cities, most of them in the Northeast,

*Since this was during the period of the coal strike, the front page also contained a story quoting the chairman of the Coal Operators' Committee as saying "Lenin and Trotsky are financing the present radical movements among labor in the United States."

but including Baltimore, Detroit, Chicago, St. Louis, Akron, and San Francisco.

Possibly the worst abuses were in Connecticut. In Bridgeport, sixty-three men who had gathered to discuss buying an old car to teach themselves to become auto mechanics were arrested by federal agents. Sixteen were released, but the other forty-seven were jailed in Hartford. Friends who came to visit them were also arrested, until ninety-seven aliens were being held. Some were beaten, tortured, and threatened with death. They were kept in what amounted to solitary confinement for five months until a lawyer finally intervened. Even then most of the men were not freed, but transferred to Deer Island in Boston Harbor.[14]

In Detroit, Alexander Bukowetsky was arrested at a concert given by the Union of Russian Workers. Beaten, abused, jailed for six months while the government tried to decide whether or not to deport him, Bukowetsky movingly expressed the feelings of the bewildered aliens caught in Palmer's trap when he said, "When I came to America I came with the thought that I was coming to a free country,—a place of freedom and happiness, and I was anxious to come,—to get away from the Czaristic form of government. As much as I was anxious to come here to America I am a hundred times more anxious to run away from Americanism to return to Soviet Russia, where I will at least be able to live."[15]

The Justice Department had managed to make Soviet Russia look good by comparison, yet Palmer's office announced, "This is the first big step to rid the country of these foreign trouble makers."[16] Local officials, following Palmer's lead, stalked alien radicals all across the country. In New York, the Lusk committee had over five hundred persons arrested.[17]

If the American people had been rational, they would have evaluated the labors of the federal and local police with skepticism. Palmer claimed the Union of Russian Workers had four thousand members. J. Edgar Hoover should have had them indexed according to city as well as name and affiliation, but of all the hundreds arrested, only 199 were deportable members of the URW, a batting average of 5 percent. Yet Palmer was lauded by Congress, the press, and the public. Seeing the White House looming larger, Palmer exaggerated the radical threat in a report to the Senate and urged passage of a peacetime sedition act so citizens as well as aliens could have their heads broken by the Bureau of Investigation.

For the public, catharsis would not be complete until the aliens were actually deported. This had been done previously in small numbers—sixty had been sent off since 1917—but not in wholesale lots, because though the attorney general could arrest aliens, only the secretary of labor could deport them. To Palmer's intense frustration, both the secretary of labor, William Wilson, and the assistant secretary, Louis F. Post, had little liking for mass arrests and deportations.

On November 25, the Russian People's House was raided again. This time the agents announced they had found a "secret room" containing material "for 100 bombs." Since this was the sixth raid on the Russian People's House and no such room had been discovered sooner even though the raiders had all but chewed up the plaster, and since no one was arrested in connection with this alarming discovery, it is not unreasonable to suspect that the explosive materials had been planted by the GID to obtain explosive headlines.

When news of the "Reds' Bomb Shop" swept the country, public and congressional opinion forced the secretary of labor to concede that alien members of the Union of Russian Workers should be deported. J. Edgar Hoover personally took on the task like an experienced travel agent. He arranged for the use of an army transport, the *Buford*, which was immediately nicknamed the "Soviet Ark," and invited members of the House Immigration Committee to come to New York to see the Reds sail in the sunset.

The *Buford* carried 249 aliens and 250 soldiers to guard them. It sailed on December 21, 1919, for Finland; the aliens went the rest of the way to Russia by train. Of the 249 deported, 199 were arrested during the November raids, 7 were assorted criminals or misfits, and 43 were radicals arrested earlier, including Emma Goldman and Alexander Berkman, who had tried to assassinate Henry Clay Frick. Three of the aliens were women. At least a dozen of the men aboard were forced to leave behind their wives and children; in some cases wives did not know what had happened to their husbands until the boat sailed. The GID explained that news of the sailing of the *Buford* had to be "kept quiet and secret," which meant that everyone knew about it except the families of the victims.

Though a few individuals were troubled by the symbolism of America not just rejecting the oppressed but sending them back, the sailing of the *Buford* was greeted with glee. After all the tension and the talk, this was finally action. Though most of the passengers were innocent of any crime except being foreign born, the *Boston Evening Transcript* said the *Buford's* voyage was as important as Columbus's while another newspaper hoped that "other vessels, larger, more commodious, carrying similar cargoes, will follow in her wake."

Palmer's act had played in Peoria; the encore had to be bigger and better. J. Edgar Hoover announced there would be as many more Soviet Arks as necessary to clean out his index file. He also made the statement, surprising even for that period, that actual deportation would not necessarily wait until each case was concluded. The government was prepared to ship first and ask questions later.

Having promised more arks, Palmer and Hoover had to fill the holds. They decided that membership in either one of the two American Communist parties that had recently been organized made an alien deportable, even though only the secretary of labor could make such a ruling. While GID agents were infiltrating the Communist parties, a reshuffling of responsibilities in the Labor Department made it possible for Palmer to get the department's cooperation. The secretary of labor was ill and Louis Post was busy taking his place. The acting secretary, John W. Abercrombie, happened also to be a member of the Justice Department, so he readily agreed to sign more than three thousand warrants for the arrest of aliens who were Communists. Abercrombie also changed the rules for deportation hearings so aliens effectively lost the right of counsel. Deportation was not a criminal but an administrative procedure, which meant aliens suffered the onus of being criminals without having any of their rights. They were granted only a closed hearing before an immigration official who was judge, jury, and prosecutor.

Hearing rules specified that "at the beginning of the hearing . . . the alien . . . shall be apprised that he may be represented by

Backgro

counsel." This was a hollow privilege since most aliens could not afford a lawyer or did not know how to find one. At Palmer's request, even that right was eliminated; Abercrombie changed the rules to read, "Preferably at the beginning of the hearing . . . or at any rate *as soon as such hearing has proceeded sufficiently in the development of the facts to protect the Government's interests*, the alien . . . shall be apprised that thereafter he may be represented by counsel."[18] (Emphasis added.)

An already confused, terrified alien, often speaking only poor English, could easily be trapped by the hearing officer into incriminating himself; only after the government had its case was the victim to be informed he could have a lawyer. Palmer admitted that examining aliens with attorneys present "got us nowhere."[19]

On December 27, 1919, a confidential letter was sent by Frank Burke, assistant director of the Bureau of Investigation, to district chiefs. "The tentative date fixed for the arrests of the COMMUNISTS is Friday evening, January 2, 1920," it said. The letter included the following information and instructions:

> The grounds for deportation in these cases will be based solely upon membership in the COMMUNIST PARTY of America or the COMMUNIST LABOR PARTY.
>
> If possible you should arrange with your undercover informants to have meetings of the COMMUNIST PARTY and the COMMUNIST LABOR PARTY held on the night set. . . . This, of course, would facilitate the making of the arrests.
>
> It is not the intention nor the desire of this office that American citizens, members of the two organizations, be arrested at this time. If, however, there are taken into custody any American citizens, through error, and who are members of the COMMUNIST PARTY of America or the COMMUNIST LABOR PARTY, you should immediately refer their cases to the local authorities.*

*This was so they could be prosecuted under state sedition or syndicalist laws.

Particular efforts should be made to apprehend all of the officers of either of these two parties if they are aliens; the residences of such officers should be searched in every instance for literature, membership cards, records and correspondence. The meeting rooms should be thoroughly searched. . . . All literature, books, papers and anything hanging on the walls should be gathered up; the ceilings and partitions should be sounded for hiding places.

I have made mention above that the meeting places and residences of the members should be thoroughly searched. I leave it entirely to your discretion as to the method by which you should gain access to such places.

On the evening of the arrests, this office will be open the entire night and I desire that you communicate by long distance to Mr. [J. Edgar] Hoover any matters of vital importance or interest which may arise during the course of the arrests.

I desire that the morning following the arrests you should forward to this office by special delivery marked for the "Attention of Mr. Hoover" a complete list of the names of the persons arrested, with an indication of residence, or organization to which they belong, and whether or not they were included in the original list of warrants. In cases where arrests are made of persons not covered by warrants, you should at once request the local immigration authorities for warrants in all such cases and you should also communicate with this office at the same time.[20]

January 2, 1920, was a night to remember; over four thousand persons were arrested in thirty-three cities. Agents of the Bureau of Investigation did not restrict their activities to meeting halls or to the warrants they had in hand; they marched into homes, restaurants, dance halls, bowling alleys, schools, and shops and arrested everyone they found. They also seized passers-by, loiterers, and those who made the error of asking what the devil was going on.

Following instructions, the agents searched for membership lists. When they were found, the agents sped to the homes of those on the lists, hauled them out of bed in the middle of the night, and arrested them without warrants; that could be taken care of in the morning.

Because the press had noted the excessive brutality of the November raids, agents had been warned that "violence towards any aliens should be scrupulously avoided." However meeting-rooms and homes were smashed and trashed in the search for incriminating material. Told to take everything, including what was on the walls, agents in Massachusetts seized a suspicious looking sign which said "No smoking" in Cyrillic.[21] Though some three thousand warrants were available, Hoover's filing system had failed again; there were no warrants for most of those arrested.

Some of the worst abuses took place in the Boston area. In Lawrence, Mr. and Mrs. Hymie Kaplan were awakened during the night. Agents looking for evidence ripped open their mattress and the mattress on which their young children slept. They found nothing, but arrested Kaplan anyway, though he was not a member of either of the Communist parties. At the time he was working as a union organizer for the conservative AFL.*

In Lynn, agents arrested all thirty-nine men at a meeting because they were speaking "a foreign tongue." The men were not plotting to overthrow the government but setting up a Jewish cooperative bakery. Only one of them happened to be a Communist, and he was a citizen.[22]

In Boston, agents with neither an arrest nor a search warrant awoke a woman in her apartment at dawn. Because they would not permit her to go into the next room, she dressed in a closet while the men ransacked the apartment. Though she was an American citizen she was imprisoned for several hours and property taken from her was not returned.[23]

Only a few of those arrested were fortunate enough to be released at all. Hundreds of prisoners in the Boston area were thrown into unheated cells on Deer Island. On their way to the

*Personal interview, Hymie Kaplan. Kaplan was certain that in the Boston area the purpose of the Palmer raids was mainly to harass union activists on behalf of the textile owners.

harbor, they were marched through the streets in chains so news photographers could show the public how dangerous they looked.[24]

The immediate reaction of press and public to the raids was uncritical approval; not just hundreds but thousands of the accursed group had been netted. A few newspapers and individuals murmured about civil liberties, but the *Washington Post* admonished them that "There is no time to waste on hair-splitting over infringement of liberty."

Palmer assured the public he had "halted the advance of 'red radicalism' in the United States" and that the material seized (including the No Smoking sign, presumably) proved that the aliens who ran the radical movement in America received their marching orders from Lenin and Trotsky. He also reinforced the insidiously racist image of the alien as not just radical but genetically criminal and defective. "Out of the sly and crafty eyes of many of them," he said, "leap cupidity, cruelty, insanity, and crime; from their lopsided faces, sloping brows, and misshapen features may be recognized the unmistakable criminal type." Palmer offered these gratuitous and irrational observations because America was enduring a crime wave, now due primarily to prohibition, as well as the availability of unemployed veterans as hired guns. Rather than attempt to explain why the Bureau of Investigation failed to catch criminals or bombers, Palmer would say of the radicals, "Each and every adherent of this movement is a potential murderer or a potential thief, and deserves no consideration." If enough of them were deported, the country would be simultaneously cleansed of radicalism, unionism, crime, and all other evils.

The Palmer raids marked the pinnacle of mass action directed against aliens in America because ultimately they frightened citizens as well. A few days after the January raids, the New York State legislature refused to seat five members because they were Socialists. The Socialist party was legal in New York and the men had been freely elected by their constituents. Two months earlier, the House of Representatives had refused to seat a Socialist congressman from Wisconsin; when the voters chose him again in a special election, the House still refused to seat him. Both liberals and conservatives felt that the refusal to seat legally elected representatives subverted the democratic process more than any Bolshevik could; the day might come when Democrats refused to seat Republicans or vice versa.

A peacetime sedition bill was passed by the Senate on January 10, a week after the Palmer raids, but it died in the House when citizens realized it would give the government the right to do to them what had just been done to aliens. The ACLU and another reform group, the National Popular Government League, conducted a joint investigation of the Palmer raids and other abuses committed by the attorney general's office. Their report, issued by the National Popular Government League in May, 1920, was signed by twelve illustrious attorneys, all of whom had supported the war and none of whom could be accused of disloyalty. It carefully documented Palmer's violations of the Fourth Amendment, in his casual disregard of warrants as well as the unreasonable searches and seizures; the Fifth Amendment, in forcing aliens to incriminate themselves; and the Eighth Amendment, in demanding excessive bail and using cruel and unusual punishments. Palmer was also excoriated for employing undercover agents to entrap aliens and spending government funds for propaganda.

The report also included a summary of the trial known as *Colyer* v. *Skeffington.* Held before Judge George W. Anderson, the case arose when eighteen of the aliens arrested in the Boston area went to federal court, which forced the disreputable deeds of the Justice Department to become a matter of public record.

Anderson: And you took seven citizens and put them in cells and kept them overnight, as you say now?
Agent: I found out later that they were citizens.
Anderson: Is that your notion of liberty under the law?
Agent: I had no other way of finding out they were citizens. They didn't tell me as such until the next morning.[25]

The government's counsel said that the federal agent was only obeying orders. Judge Anderson replied, "Well, that may be true, but it is the business of any American citizen, who knows anything about Americanism, to resign if given such instructions."[26] When the judge discovered that an alien arrested January 2 had a warrant dated January 17, he commented, "This case seems to have been conducted under that modern theory of statesmanship that you hang first and try afterwards."[27] The government's counsel objected to this remark and tried to justify the actions of the Justice Department, which led Judge Anderson to retort, "A more lawless proceeding it is hard for anybody to conceive. Talk about Americanization! What we need is to Americanize people that are carrying on such proceedings as this."[28]

Palmer failed not only because his excesses were alarming but because he did not meet the rising expectations he had encouraged. He had arrested more than four thousand persons, or enough to fill a fleet of arks, but the Justice Department itself had to release more than one-third of the prisoners because they were not deportable.

Palmer promised that the remaining twenty-seven hundred would be expelled, but Assistant Secretary of Labor Louis Post, better late than never, was now making the decisions. After reviewing the evidence, Post concluded:

> As a rule, the hearings show the aliens arrested to be working men of good character who have never been arrested before, who are not anarchists or revolutionists, nor politically nor otherwise dangerous in any sense. Many of them . . . have American-born children. It is pitiful to consider the hardships to which they and their families have been subjected during the past three or four months by arbitrary arrest, long detention in default of bail beyond the means of hard working wage earners to give, for nothing more dangerous than affiliating with friends of their own race, country and language, and without the slightest indication of sinister motive, or any unlawful act within their knowledge or intention.[29]

Post ruled that evidence unlawfully obtained could not be used; he revoked the change in the rules that denied aliens an attorney until after the government had its case; he refused to accept guilt-by-association, saying that inclusion on a membership list did not make a man a Communist since many of the aliens were listed only because they had belonged to organizations which had merged with one of the Communist parties; and he ruled that party membership alone was not grounds for deportation "unless supported by proof of individual activities or declarations tending to show knowledge of the character of the organization." [30]

By the time Post was through, some twenty-two hundred deportation warrants had been cancelled. Only 556 persons were ordered deported, plus a few left from earlier raids, or a total of less than six hundred. When over four thousand persons are arrested, 556 deportations are not impressive, not when the public has been promised a cast of thousands. People did not cease to fear the Red menace, but they did cease to believe Palmer. In March, 1920, he had announced his candidacy; in order to boost it he decided to ride the Red Scare once more by declaring the Bolsheviks would rise on May Day. The GID warned there would be assassinations, bombings, a general strike.

America went on a national alert. Militia were mobilized, police were assigned to twenty-four-hour duty, important persons and places were heavily guarded. In Boston, trucks with mounted machine guns were parked at strategic points. In Chicago, which seemed to have an inexhaustible supply of radicals, 360 persons were held in preventive detention.

May 1 came and went without incident; no assassinations, no bombs, no general strike. The public, no longer titillated by Palmer, just tittered. When a wagonload of bombs exploded on Wall Street on September 16, killing thirty-three and wounding over two hundred, Palmer raced to New York and said it was a revolutionary plot, but no one paid any attention. When the Bureau of Investigation maintained its flawless record by not finding the bombers, no one was surprised.

The Democrats nominated James Cox for president in 1920, the people elected Republican Warren Harding, with Calvin Coolidge, who had saved Boston from the Bolsheviks, as vice-president, and America sank into the stupor that is usually referred to as normalcy.

There were no further wholesale assaults on aliens and no

more nights of terror, except for individuals. But it is difficult to redirect the mood of a nation or alter perceptions evolved over a period of three hundred years. The Puritan concepts that truth is vested in a select group of visible saints and that both aliens and alien thoughts are abominations remained the worm that ate at the core of democracy in America.

Generations that followed redefined and altered these delusions to their advantage. The instant the supremacy of the white Anglo-Saxon settlers was challenged, the accursed groups became Catholics, aliens, radicals, or all three. Times changed, places changed, people changed, but periods of crisis recurred, and the latest aliens or dissidents were always to blame. When Brahmins feared for their survival the scapegoats were first the Irish, then the newer immigrants. When industrialists feared for their profits, unions became the diabolic spawn of alien radicals. During World War I, the Puritan in the White House viewed every critic, pacifist, and draft evader as an enemy. In the traumatic aftermath of the war a new dimension was added to the caricature; aliens were not only radical but criminal.

By 1920, the Puritan legacy, the cant of the nativist racists, the economic wars, the World War, the crime wave, and the Red Scare had conditioned the American people to fear and despise certain groups: aliens from southern and eastern Europe, particularly Italians; Catholics; radicals; draft evaders; and, of course, criminals. The fatal circumstance would be for Italians who were baptized Catholic but had become atheists, anarchists, and draft evaders to be accused of robbery and murder. America and the Puritan Commonwealth of Massachusetts were ready for the Sacco–Vanzetti case.

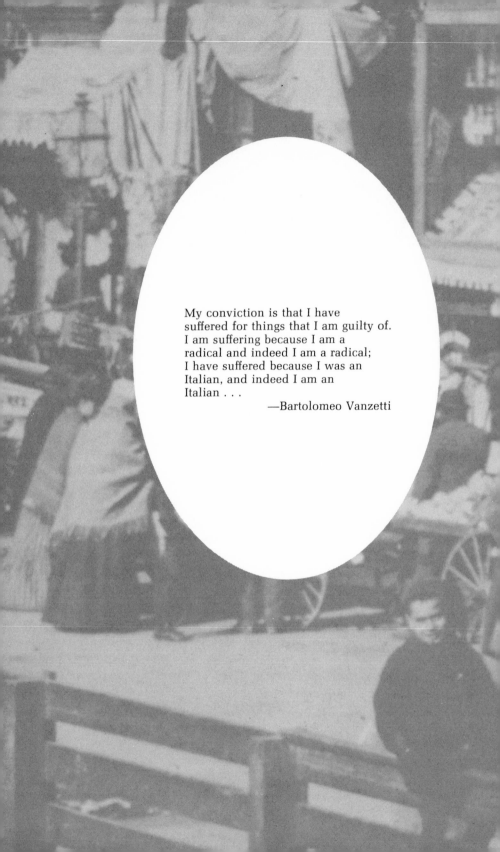

My conviction is that I have
suffered for things that I am guilty of.
I am suffering because I am a
radical and indeed I am a radical;
I have suffered because I was an
Italian, and indeed I am an
Italian . . .

—Bartolomeo Vanzetti

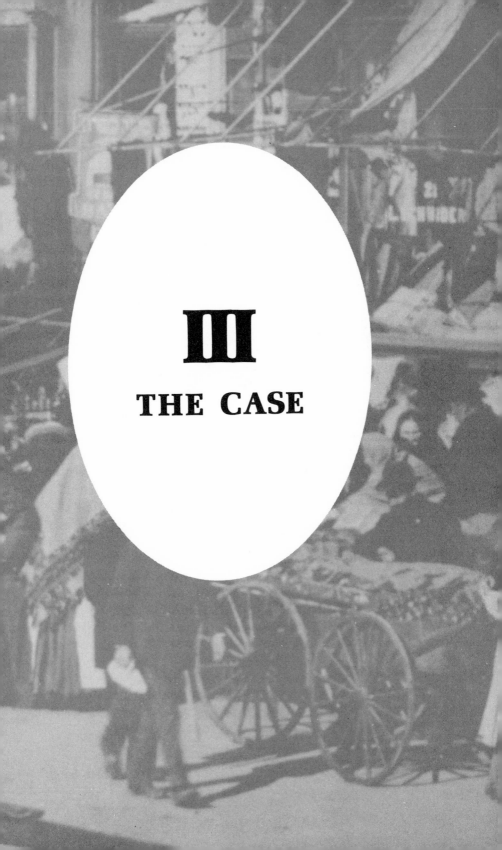

III

THE CASE

12

Into the Trap

The lives of Nicola Sacco and Bartolomeo Vanzetti and the history of the United States began to converge at about the same time. Though both men sailed to America in 1908, they did not know each other in Italy and did not meet here until May, 1917;[1] what brought them together was the anarchist movement.

At a conference on Italian-American radicalism held in Boston in November, 1972, one of the speakers, Professor John D. Baker, discussed the views of John Dos Passos on "Italian Anarchism and the American Dream."[2] In *Facing the Chair*, a small book Dos Passos wrote on the case as a propagandist for the two men, he sarcastically attacked the American view that anarchy was "garlic-smelling" and an "outlaw creed," saying:

> For half a century Anarchy has been the bogy of American schoolmasters, policemen, old maids, and small town mayors. About the time of the assassination of McKinley a picture was formed in the public mind of the anarchist; redhanded, unwashed for-

eigner whom nobody could understand, sticks of dynamite in his pocket and bomb in the paper parcel under his arm, redeyed housewrecker waiting only for the opportunity to bite the hand that fed him. Since the Russian Revolution the picture has merged a little with that of the sneaking, slinking, communist Jew, enviously undermining Prosperity and Decency through secret organizations ruled from Moscow.[3]

Baker said Dos Passos believed that Italian-American anarchism "was born of the Christian dream of a perfect world . . . predicated on a second coming of Christ . . . transformed over the centuries into a secular dream of a city of God instituted by men." Baker also said Dos Passos felt that anarchy was not a "foreign import . . . with no connection to the American culture," but the same ideal "that gave birth to the Puritan experiment in Massachusetts" and later motivated Jefferson and others who hoped that "in the virgin land of a new world mankind had a final chance to begin anew."[*][4]

But the dream failed the Italians as it failed so many others. Dos Passos wrote, "Many Italians planted the perfect city of their imagination in America. When they came to this country they either killed the perfect city in their hearts and submitted to the system of dawg eat dawg or else they found themselves anarchists."[5]

Sacco and Vanzetti would not submit to the system and so found themselves anarchists. Though they would be linked for eternity, there is no indication they were close friends; they were comrades fighting for the same cause.[†] Before his arrest, Vanzetti

---

*Professor Baker was savaged by anarchists present who were furious at the impertinent notion that anarchy could flow from Christian ideals. No one pointed out that the perfect city of the anarchists was far more idealistic than the perfect . city of the Puritans, since the former was inclusive and the latter was exclusive. Vanzetti himself did not object to being compared to Christ; he did so in his autobiography and his letters.

†Because they spent most of the seven years following their arrest in separate prisons, Sacco and Vanzetti exchanged letters which were courteous rather than warm. Sacco signed his "Your faithful comrade, Nick Sacco" or "Your faithful comrade now and forever, Ferdinando Sacco."

The

never mentioned Sacco in his letters to his family, and he seldom mentioned him afterward though he referred to the Brinis and other friends. The Brinis kept open house for local and visiting Italian radicals, but they never heard of Sacco until his arrest.*

As anarchists, both Sacco and Vanzetti opposed World War I. On December 15, 1914, in a letter to his Aunt Edvige, Vanzetti wrote:

> You say the war is just, and since justice gives strength, you hope for victory. . . . I do not believe it, nor does anyone believe it that has eyes in his head, ears to hear with or a mind that thinks. Justice, or the belief that one's cause is just, can give an individual or a people the strength to accomplish great things, or to die heroically. Nothing more. . . .
>
> The poor are those who must conduct the war and pay for it with their blood, their tears, their misery and their lives. Nor will victory be of any benefit at all to the poor. . . .
>
> All the nations that are now at war are sure that they have right and justice on their side. This is not possible, thus we have the proof that no people can even know relative justice, much less the absolute right. If the opposite were the case there would no longer be wars. . . .
>
> I rest my case for the present. If I were to write down all of my thoughts on this subject, I would write a book. So console yourself if I do not for the moment return to Italy, and to the thousand dangers that would surround me in that country.

Once America entered the war, Vanzetti and Sacco seemed to feel a thousand dangers surrounding them here. On May 18, 1917, a law was passed requiring every male between the ages of twenty-one and thirty—meaning those who had not reached their thirty-first birthday—to register for the draft on June 5. Though aliens were required to register, they would not be drafted unless

*Personal interview, Beltrando Brini.

they had begun the process of becoming citizens. Yet Sacco and Vanzetti, who had met only a week or so earlier, joined other Italian anarchists in fleeing to Mexico at the end of May, just before registration day.

The escape to Mexico, which would weigh so heavily against them, is one of the enduring mysteries of the case. Why did Sacco and Vanzetti run from the draft when, as aliens, they could not be drafted?

As Vanzetti explained in a letter sent to his family from Monterrey on July 26, 1917, there were two reasons. "I intend to return to the United States as soon as I have understood how conscription in the United States works," he wrote. "Here at least I am safe from it. . . . What is more it seems that the threat in the United States of conscription and deportation is just a bluff . . . if this is so then so much the better for me."

Aliens who have emigrated from a land where the government cannot be trusted will not trust the government of the land to which they have come. Anarchists don't trust government on principle. For alien anarchists like Sacco and Vanzetti, the wording of the draft law, insofar as they understood it, must have seemed deceptive. If the government was not going to draft them, why did they have to register?*

Vanzetti also mentions deportation, which both men dreaded.

---

*The draft law was as confusing as Congress could make it. Section 2 said that the draft "shall be based upon liability to military service of all male citizens, or male persons not alien enemies who have declared their intention to become citizens. . . . " Section 5 read: "All male persons between the ages of 21 and 30, both inclusive, shall be subject to registration. . . . All persons so registered shall be and remain subject to draft. . . . " The law baffled not only Sacco and Vanzetti but countless others; almost every day the government issued a new clarification. In essence, every male of draft age had to register; only then could he apply to his draft board for an exemption. Newspaper accounts of the period reveal that many young men fled to Mexico, Canada, or Cuba, even though the penalty for failing to register was one year in prison. Sacco and Vanzetti were not only exempt as aliens but Sacco had a dependent wife and child. But the two men apparently did not understand the law at first and, as anarchists, did not want to register with the government. My own relatives who were aliens but not radicals also failed to understand that the law exempted them and took whatever evasive action they could; one of my uncles fled to Canada.

The

<table>
<tr><td>Spencer
Sacco:</td><td>What Sacco went to Mexico for, rather than this business about dodging the draft, was he feared deportation proceedings against him.</td></tr>
</table>

Sacco, Vanzetti, and their comrades knew that under the Immigration Act of 1917 they could be deported for their anarchist activities. Why aliens were so troubled by this puzzled Americans in 1920, and still does. What was deportation but a free ride home?

This view is distinctly American; it does not consider what an anarchist might face when he was expelled for his activities. If he was undesirable here, he might be even more undesirable in his native land. A deported Italian anarchist faced the possibility of spending the rest of his life in forced exile, if not actually in prison.

Sacco and Vanzetti chose to go to Mexico to avoid both the draft and deportation because Italian anarchists had an escape route from Mexico to Italy which enabled them to return home rather than to exile.[6] This was never mentioned during the trial or the appeals because it would have closed the route to other anarchists.

The fears of Sacco and Vanzetti were not without foundation. While they were in Mexico, the police came to the Brini house in Plymouth one day looking for clues to Vanzetti's whereabouts. Since they could not have been seeking him as a draft evader, their visit must have had something to do with his anarchist activities.

<table>
<tr><td>Lefevre
Brini:</td><td>Was I ever frightened! They just came to the house, it was around supper time. And I knew what they were looking for, because I was warned by my parents. So in they come and I knew where there was something, so I went and got it and I hid it under my blouse. It was a letter from Mexico with [Vanzetti's] address.* I remember one thing they asked about—friends. If Vanzetti had friends. I remember the policeman</td></tr>
</table>

*Anyone who thinks Vanzetti was capable of pulling off a brilliant payroll robbery in broad daylight should consider that, as an anarchist in hiding, he sent letters to America with his return address.

saying, "Well, who comes here at night?" "Nobody comes here at night," I remember saying. At the time, there was nobody coming to the house. My father used to go out a lot to play cards in the club.

Sacco and Vanzetti returned to America after three or four months, partly because they finally realized they could not be drafted and weren't about to be deported, and partly because they found life in Mexico intolerable. Since they faced a one-year sentence for not registering for the draft, both took the precaution of using different names for a while. Sacco, the devoted family man, went directly back to Massachusetts; as he explained at the trial, "I leave my wife here and my boy. I could not stay no more far away from them." Vanzetti wandered about the country, stopping in St. Louis, Youngstown, Ohio, and Farrell, Pennsylvania. From Youngstown he wrote his family on September 26, 1918, "I am working and am in excellent health. I am calm, and have so far stayed out of danger. Please, do not worry on my account. I would have a lot of things to tell you about America but . . . it seems that it is no longer permitted to tell the truth, so I will be silent."

It was not until September 1, 1919, that Vanzetti wrote his father, "I have returned to Plymouth, have taken up my real name once again and I am writing from the house of the Brinis, though, unfortunately, I no longer live with them. They can no longer put me up, firstly because the children are growing up and need more room, secondly because Alfonsina must go to work to help out her family. So much for the progress made by the workers!"

Though Sacco and Vanzetti had been concerned enough about their fate to go to Mexico, the government had concentrated its repression during the war on native radicals and the IWW. It was only when Palmer needed headlines to propel him to the White House and was uncertain how long the courts would uphold the Espionage and Sedition Acts that attention returned to the alien radical. In May, 1919, Luigi Galleani, a leading Italian anarchist whose followers included Sacco and Vanzetti, was taken into custody and deported. In June came the bombing of Palmer's home with copies of an anarchist flyer scattered at the site.

J. Edgar Hoover's GID agents traced the flyer to a printing shop in Brooklyn. In February, 1920, they seized Roberto Elia, a printer at the shop, and Andrea Salsedo, a typesetter who also published his own anarchist newspaper,[7] and took them to the Bureau of Information office at Park Row for questioning. Since there were no warrants for their arrest and the GID had no intention of releasing them until they could get information leading to the bomber or bombers, the two men were imprisoned at the bureau's headquarters; according to the GID, Salsedo and Elia "voluntarily" agreed to accept their hospitality. The GID also claimed that Salsedo "was never mistreated at any time and never was struck, intimidated, or threatened" though the agents did mention that unless he cooperated he might be jailed or deported.[8]

Elia reported the story somewhat differently. He said that Salsedo, tortured and beaten by GID agents, said to him, "I do not want to die. We have done nothing, but we are in a trap. What are we to do? I will admit that I printed [the flyer] because I cannot stand any more."

Salsedo told William J. Flynn, director of the Bureau of Investigation, who was in on the kill himself, that he had printed the flyer and that Elia had nothing to do with it; he also gave Flynn the name of the man he said had ordered it. Even after Salsedo's confession, the GID continued to hold the two men in their Park Row prison while the investigation continued.

The prolonged detention of Salsedo and Elia concerned their fellow anarchists. On Sunday, April 25, a group including Sacco, Vanzetti, Ricardo Orciani, and Aldino Felicani met at the Italian Naturalization Club in East Boston to discuss what they could do to help the two men. They decided to send someone to New York to find out what was happening. Vanzetti, the fish peddler and laborer who had no steady job and would therefore lose no pay, was chosen.

In New York, Vanzetti met with Luigi Quintiliano, secretary of the Italian Workers' Defense Committee. Quintiliano had little information about Salsedo and Elia, but he warned Vanzetti that more Justice Department raids were expected and that the Boston anarchists should rid themselves of their literature so there would be no incriminating evidence when their homes were searched.

The following Sunday, May 2, when the East Boston anarchists met again, Vanzetti reported what Quintiliano had told him. Orciani said Mike Boda had a car that could be used to pick up the literature cached in various homes in the Boston area. The anarchists also agreed to hold a public meeting May 9 to raise funds for the defense of Salsedo and Elia; Vanzetti would be the speaker.

Early the following morning, May 3, as a GID report noted somewhat petulantly, "Salsedo put an end to his part of the arrangement by jumping from the fourteenth floor of the Park Row Building." Assistant Secretary of Labor Louis Post, after investigating, found that Salsedo had been "lawlessly a prisoner . . . held incommunicado in a secret prison controlled by detectives of the Department of Justice, that this prison was fourteen stories above the street, and that his body struck the pavement with an impact that turned it to pulp."[9]

Post did not attempt to determine whether Salsedo's death was murder or suicide. The Bureau of Investigation insisted it was suicide and called it "inexplicable." Since Salsedo had been illegally imprisoned in the building for eight weeks without any clue to his fate, it may have been suicide but it was hardly inexplicable. Meanwhile, the bureau, faced with a sudden glare of publicity because of the pulp on the pavement, quickly turned Elia over to immigration authorities who deported him.

Even before Salsedo's death, alien anarchists knew how vulnerable they were. In an undated letter written during that period of postwar turbulence, Vanzetti told his father, "I have saved up enough to be able to return to Italy in case the necessity to do so should arise."

Sacco acted more decisively. Toward the end of March, 1920, he had received a letter from his brother Sabino telling him that their mother had died. George Kelley, the superintendent at the 3-K shoe factory, later testified that Sacco told him "he was very sorry to think that he wasn't at home when she died, that [his family] had wanted him to come home previous to her death and that he thought now that as long as he had an opportunity, that he would go home while his father was still alive."[10]

Sabino's letter came at a time when Sacco was receptive to

The C

the idea of going home. He decided to return to Italy not just to visit but permanently. He had had enough of America. There was money to be made and he had made it, but the freedom he had sought was an illusion; his views made him an outlaw. He had saved fifteen hundred dollars, which would go a long way in Italy, either as an investment in the family business or in any other way he chose; and if he did not leave voluntarily with his family, he might be forced to leave involuntarily without them and be sent into exile, or worse.

> Spencer   *The family was going back to Italy to live. There is*
> Sacco: *no doubt about that at all. That is a matter of family*
>   *fact.*

Shortly after receiving the news of his mother's death, Sacco went to the office of the Italian consul in Boston and inquired about getting a passport.* He was told he would need two copies of a photograph of his family. On the afternoon of April 15, 1920, Sacco brought the photographs to the Italian consulate. That same afternoon a gang of bandits robbed the payroll at the Slater & Morrill Shoe Company in South Braintree killing the paymaster and guard.

Because Sacco's photographs were too large, he had others taken toward the end of April which he brought to the consulate. The last day he worked was Saturday, May 1, though he stopped by the 3-K factory on Monday, May 3, to pick up his tools and work clothes and to say goodby.[11]

The news of Salsedo's death that morning stunned the anarchists. Arrest and deportation were bad enough but, as far as they were concerned, this was murder. Disposing of the literature became more urgent; none of them wanted to be guests of the Justice Department and share Salsedo's fate.

Vanzetti, who had no work because the fish were not running locally and prices were too high in Boston, spent Monday afternoon, Tuesday, and Wednesday at Sacco's home in Stoughton.[12] On Tuesday, May 4, Sacco went to Boston to pick

---

*Italians returning home could use a form called a *foglio di via*, which was cheaper than a passport; that is what Sacco applied for.

up his *foglio di via*. He planned to leave for New York on Saturday, May 8, with his pregnant wife, Rosina, and their seven-year-old son, Dante, to board a ship for Italy.[13]

On Wednesday, May 5, Boda and Orciani came to Sacco's house on Orciani's motorcycle. At about 7 P.M., Sacco and Vanzetti left for Bridgewater; Boda and Orciani followed later on the motorcycle.[14] All were headed for Simon Johnson's garage to pick up Boda's Overland so it could be used to gather the incriminating literature. As Sacco explained at the trial, "The best way to take by automobile, could run more fast, could get more fast, could hide more fast."[15]

Sacco and Vanzetti took a trolley to Brockton where they had to wait for another trolley to Bridgewater. While waiting, they had coffee in a lunchroom where Vanzetti drafted an announcement for the meeting to be held May 9, though the primary purpose would no longer be to raise funds for Salsedo. He read the text to Sacco who felt that, like so much of what Vanzetti wrote, it was too long. The very practical Sacco suggested Vanzetti cut it so it would cost less to print. Vanzetti rewrote the announcement on the trolley to Bridgewater and gave it to Sacco, who put it in his pocket to take to a printer.[16]

When they got off the trolley at Elm Square in West Bridgewater, they walked until they saw the lights of Orciani's motorcycle outside the Johnson house.[17] Boda had already asked for his car. Mrs. Johnson had already gone next door to telephone the police. The trap set by Police Chief Michael E. Stewart was about to spring shut.

The (

13

Bricks Without Straw

When Sacco and Vanzetti were arrested the night of May 5, 1920, there was no evidence to link them to the robberies at South Braintree or Bridgewater. There was only Stewart's hunch, based in part on C. A. Barr's assertion that Italian anarchists had attempted the Bridgewater holdup, that both crimes had been committed by radicals.* All Sacco and Vanzetti had done was go with a comrade to pick up his car. For this they were executed seven years later.

Stewart rushed to the Brockton police station to question Sacco and Vanzetti. They were Italian anarchists, which confirmed his suspicion they were guilty; evidence could come later. Two other factors doomed them. They were armed when they were arrested, and they lied when they were questioned that night and the following day.

Many persons, willingly or unwillingly, contributed to the fate of Sacco and Vanzetti; their own contribution was to carry

---

*Stewart had been active in rounding up radicals during the Palmer raids. Because he was a victim of Palmer's propaganda, Sacco and Vanzetti became victims as well.

weapons. If they had not been armed, there would have been no question of a gun taken from a dying guard, of whose bullet killed him, of contradicting the claim they had gone to Mexico because they were pacifists. For the seven years Sacco and Vanzetti fought for their lives, and the half century or more since their deaths, the guns have troubled their sympathizers and armed their opponents. The weapons did not kill Parmenter and Berardelli; in the end they helped to kill Sacco and Vanzetti.

Sacco carried a loaded Colt .32 automatic pistol in his waistband and extra cartridges in his pocket. Vanzetti carried a loaded Harrington & Richardson .38 revolver. Though he had no extra cartridges, he had several shotgun shells in his pocket.

Why were they armed? Herbert B. Ehrmann, who became one of their attorneys when it was too late to save them, wrote that the carrying of weapons by Italians in southeastern Massachusetts "was not unusual" and called it "a cultural pattern without significance."[1] It was a cultural pattern of great significance; it signified not that Italians were dangerous, but that they were afraid. Carrying guns may not have been unusual, but neither was it universal; Aldino Felicani said he carried a gun,[2] Beltrando Brini said his father did not. An Italian neighbor of Vanzetti's who, when summoned before Governor Fuller expressed his view that Vanzetti was innocent, nonetheless said to me in exasperation, "Now what the hell was he doing in Brockton with a gun in his pocket?"*

Vanzetti later testified, "I got the revolver because it was a very bad time, and I like to have a revolver for self-defense."

Q: How much money did you . . . carry around with you?
Vanzetti: When I went to Boston for fish, I can carry eighty, one hundred dollars, one hundred and twenty dollars.
Q: What do you mean by "It was a bad time"?

---

*In the immigrant, predominantly Italian section of New York in which I grew up in the 1930s, I never saw a gun used, but my mother did, to settle a personal quarrel fatally. My father never carried a weapon because he would never use one, but I had an uncle who carried a knife and used it frequently.

The C

Vanzetti: Bad time, I mean it was many crimes, many holdups, many robberies.[3]

In a long letter dated December 5, 1926, in which Vanzetti tried to summarize the entire case for his sister Luigia, he wrote that when they were arrested:

> Sacco had his pistol with him—and I had an old revolver that had been given me a short time before, when I went to New York for the defense of Elia and Salsedo (you will have heard of them). I also had three or four shotgun shells that I had taken from Sacco's house to give to an old friend of mine who hunted, and lived in Plymouth. All of this may seem rather strange and in need of an explanation.
>
> Sacco was about to go to Italy and his wife was getting the trunks ready. I saw the shells on the mantlepiece and asked him if he was going to use them. He told me that he would shoot them off into the forest if he had time, and if not he would throw them out. At that point I put them in my pocket and said that I would sell them to a sympathizer and give the money to the cause. . . .
>
> I was almost always unarmed, the only exception being when I was going somewhere particularly dangerous, or when I was carrying a large sum of money with me. I had the revolver with me then because I had been traveling around constantly, for political reasons, since my return from New York.

Vanzetti was not given the revolver when he went to New York; he had bought it several months earlier. When he returned from New York he went back to Plymouth and could have left his revolver there before going on to Boston and then to Sacco's house. Because being armed conflicted with his image of himself, Vanzetti did not want to tell the truth to Luigia any more than he wanted to tell it to the authorities. But what was the truth?

There are two possible truths; the one usually cited is that they were armed in self-defense. Being an Italian, an alien, and an anarchist was so dangerous at the time that even the meekest man might carry arms, but if he did, the value was more psychological than real. Contrary to their reputation for violence, anarchists surrendered without a fight; no one seems to know of any shootouts between anarchists and the authorities. The question of whether Sacco and Vanzetti reached for their guns became a controversial issue at the trial; the arresting officer said they did but both of them denied it.

There may be another reason Sacco and Vanzetti were armed, one that has never previously been considered. They lived in a unique, conspiratorial world of Italian anarchists, with its own factions, its own codes, and its own justice, which sometimes meant judging or even executing an adversary.

Sacco and Vanzetti may have carried weapons not so much to protect themselves from robbers or federal agents as to protect themselves from other anarchists. Since they would never admit this, they bore through their lives and into death the onus of being armed.*

The fact that Sacco and Vanzetti lied when they were first questioned gave persuasive ammunition to the prosecution and became the cornerstone of the "consciousness of guilt" theory. By this reasoning, Sacco and Vanzetti lied because they were conscious of their guilt. But what guilt were they conscious of? Given the period in which they lived, the death of Salsedo, the arrests and deportations of their comrades, the warnings about new raids, they assumed they had been arrested because they were alien anarchists. They were guilty of that, so they lied to protect themselves and their associates. As far as Sacco and Vanzetti were concerned, they were at war with the government and the

*I have an unimpeachable source for this information who does not wish to be identified. One anarchist historian said it had absolutely no validity; another considered it improbable but not impossible. The son of an Italian anarchist of the period said it would not surprise him because of the vehemence of the arguments he heard and the readiness with which these men labeled each other "traitor." Errico Malatesta, the Italian anarchist philosopher, was shot in the leg by an Italian anarchist during an anarchist meeting in West Hoboken, New Jersey.

The (

government was at war with them; in wartime you do not aid the enemy.*

This attitude was shared by the authorities, who lied to Sacco and Vanzetti. No one told them they were arrested on suspicion of robbery and murder. Vanzetti later testified he had asked repeatedly why he had been arrested and had been told only, "Oh, you know, you know why."[4] The fact that Sacco and Vanzetti assumed they were arrested for their beliefs is not consciousness of guilt but consciousness of innocence. Men who had been involved in a daring crime only three weeks earlier would have found it more prudent to admit to anarchy and be deported rather than face a capital charge and possible execution.

The night of their arrest, Chief Stewart did not question them about the robbery but about their beliefs.

Stewart:	Are you a Communist?
Sacco:	No.
Stewart:	Anarchist?
Sacco:	No.
Stewart:	Do you believe in this government of ours?
Sacco:	Yes. Some things I like different.[5]

* * *

Stewart:	Are you an anarchist?
Vanzetti:	Well, I don't know what you call him. I am a little different.
Stewart:	Do you like this government?
Vanzetti:	Well, I like things a little different.
Stewart:	Do you believe in changing the government by force, if necessary?
Vanzetti:	No.

---

*This is not just anarchist reasoning but immigrant reasoning, particularly if the immigrants come from nations ruled by tyrants. The immigrants I knew lied instinctively to any figure representing authority or the state, whether it was helpful, harmful, or irrelevant.

| *Stewart:* | Do you subscribe for literature or papers of the Anarchistic party? |
| *Vanzetti:* | Sometimes I read them.[6] |

Both men told Stewart they had gone to West Bridgewater to visit a friend; they were not about to tell the authorities they were getting a car in order to gather up anarchist literature before the next raid. They also denied knowing Boda or Coacci; whatever trouble they were in, they were not going to get their friends involved. Neither Sacco nor Vanzetti was asked about the robbery and murders at South Braintree, yet Pinkerton detectives were informed the following morning that the "Brockton police had under arrest two Italians . . . who were implicated . . . in the holdup."[7]

On May 6, Sacco and Vanzetti were questioned by the district attorney of Norfolk County, Frederick G. Katzmann. Katzmann was interested in the holdups, not deportation cases, but Sacco and Vanzetti had no way of knowing this. Katzmann did not tell them what they were suspected of, nor did he ask them directly about the two crimes. He entrapped them by asking indirect questions that would not arouse their suspicions so if they lied or were evasive he could say it was consciousness of guilt. Katzmann asked Sacco if he knew Berardelli. Sacco said no. Katzmann asked Sacco if he had heard about the South Braintree murders. Sacco said he had read about them.[8] Katzmann did not ask Vanzetti where he was on April 15, he asked him where he was on the Thursday before Patriots Day, April 19. Vanzetti said he did not remember.[9]

If Sacco and Vanzetti were guilty, even these oblique queries would have put them on guard, and they would have had ready answers and alibis. But they still believed they had been arrested as anarchists, so on most questions they lied to Katzmann, just as they lied to Stewart, to protect themselves and their friends.

Katzmann did not begin his case with evidence incriminating the two men; there was none. He began by accepting Stewart's wild hunch that the same Italian anarchists were responsible for both Bridgewater and South Braintree, then sought evidence to fit

The (

the criminals rather than the crimes.* His initial assumption was that the gang that committed the two robberies consisted of five anarchists—Sacco, Vanzetti, Orciani, Boda, and Coacci—four of whom were such poor conspirators they could not pick up a used car without being caught. This theory quickly evaporated. Orciani could prove he was at work when both robberies were committed. Coacci had already been deported but nothing could be found to link him to the crimes in any way. Boda was such a singularly small man he would have stood out in any crowd, yet no witness saw anyone remotely resembling him.

That left only Sacco and Vanzetti. Actually, it left no one, once their fingerprints were checked with those on the Buick used in the South Braintree holdup. Their fingerprints were obviously not on the car since the prosecution never offered them as evidence.[10] The prosecution also failed to trace the stolen money to Sacco and Vanzetti. Neither man had changed his life style since the robbery, nor did they have the money in their possession. Well, perhaps they had robbed for the cause; anarchists sometimes did that sort of thing.†

The best rebuttal to this theory can be found in a document that has never before been published, a report from Dr. Abraham Myerson to Herbert Ehrmann on a psychiatric examination of Sacco conducted April 7, 1927. Dr. Myerson reported that Sacco said he "believed in expropriation, but not in expropriation for any individual or for himself, because that was robbery, banditry; that he never could in his philosophy or in his character have taken a pistol and robbed a lot of workmen of their payroll."[11] Sacco would not steal for himself and if he stole for the cause he would not have victimized his fellow workers.

Katzmann would not have understood Sacco's logic even if he had heard it, but the district attorney very sensibly asked the Boston office of the Justice Department to check whether the

---

*Sara Ehrmann, Herbert Ehrmann's widow, asked whether she thought Katzmann was convinced of the guilt of Sacco and Vanzetti, replied with a question: "What do people really believe after they have taken a certain position? What do they believe?"

†On the assumption that Coacci might have taken the money back to Italy when he was deported, his trunk was intercepted and searched. The money was not found.

anarchist movement had received a substantial infusion of funds after the payroll robbery. When the answer was negative, the prosecution suppressed this information, just as they suppressed the fingerprint evidence and anything else that confirmed the innocence of Sacco and Vanzetti. Not until August 22, 1927, did the Justice Department admit that its agents had investigated and reported that the anarchist movement had not received money after the crime for which Sacco and Vanzetti were executed that night.

Katzmann's case disintegrated further when he discovered Sacco had worked on December 24, 1919, the day of the Bridgewater holdup. Payroll records were not that clear, since Sacco was paid by the piece not by the day, but the amount of money he earned that week plus the testimony of his employers and coworkers indicated he was at the 3-K factory that day. At this point even the most zealous prosecutor might have dropped the case against Sacco and Vanzetti and resumed his search for the criminals, but not Katzmann. He had two thin threads to work with which he would weave into a hangman's noose. First, Sacco had not been at work on April 15, the day of the South Braintree crime. He claimed he had been at the Italian consulate to see about his *foglio di via*, but he would have to prove it to a Yankee jury. Second, it would be less difficult to convince a jury that Vanzetti took part in the South Braintree holdup if he were convicted of a previous crime.

On May 26, there was a preliminary hearing on the South Braintree murder charge, but it involved only Sacco. On June 11, Vanzetti was indicted for the attempted robbery and murder at Bridgewater. Normally a prosecutor would try the murder case first, since it was more important than attempted robbery, but Katzmann reversed the order; he would try Vanzetti first. Once he secured Vanzetti's conviction he would try both men for the murders at South Braintree; when dealing with a five-man gang, it is twice as convincing to have two defendants as one. Katzmann knew Vanzetti had an excellent alibi for his whereabouts on the day of the Bridgewater crime, but he also knew the alibi had a fatal flaw: Vanzetti's witnesses were Italian.

The

With the arrest of Sacco and Vanzetti, another key figure enters the story, Aldino Felicani. Unlike Vanzetti, whose anarchy may have been born of rebellion against his father, Felicani became a socialist because his father and uncles were.[12] By the time he reached his late teens, Felicani had moved farther left and was working for an anarchist printer and agitator.[13] During a six-month term in an Italian jail, Felicani shared his cell for several weeks with Benito Mussolini.[14]

In 1911, when a young anarchist soldier he knew was put in a mental institution for shooting an officer, Felicani led a national campaign to have the soldier tried or freed.[15] Though Felicani was forced to flee to America to avoid a long prison term in Italy, the ultimate success of the campaign would affect his judgment in the Sacco-Vanzetti case. Like many other radicals he believed the people, not the courts, were the true judges and therefore public agitation was more important than a good lawyer.

In America, Felicani worked for *La Notizia*, an Italian-language socialist daily published in Boston.[16] He was a typesetter but often wrote copy as well. In 1919 he met Vanzetti, and they soon became close friends.

Aldino Felicani:	*I liked Vanzetti very much. We thought alike. . . . I didn't have to ask Vanzetti if he did this crime. . . . I knew he didn't do it. . . . I knew Nicola Sacco . . . but besides . . . conversations when there were five or six of us together, we had no intimate relationship. Vanzetti was my real friend.*[17]

Felicani asked four or five other Italian anarchists who knew Sacco and Vanzetti because they had fled to Mexico together to form a committee to help the two men but they were reluctant. Undaunted, Felicani asked the owner of *La Notizia* if he could receive contributions for Sacco and Vanzetti at the newspaper office. The owner agreed and Felicani finally found a few Italian radicals who would let their names be used.[18] This was the beginning of the Sacco-Vanzetti Defense Committee, which would last as long as the case and would itself create controversy over whether it assisted or destroyed the two men.

Felicani sent out appeals for contributions for the defense. To each appeal he added names of people not present at committee meetings to make the organization seem larger than it was.[19] The first contributions came from Italians who were either anarchists, sympathizers, or friends of Sacco and Vanzetti. Donors sent ten cents, fifteen cents, twenty-five cents, fifty cents, or one dollar; it took as many as two hundred contributions to put together forty or fifty dollars.[20]

With money raised and borrowed, Felicani sought an attorney for Vanzetti. A friend suggested a criminal lawyer named James M. Graham. At their first meeting Graham asked Felicani for five hundred dollars and said he would do his best.[21] Meanwhile, Vanzetti's friends in Plymouth hired another lawyer, John P. Vahey. Felicani said Vahey claimed he had great influence and was in a position to help Vanzetti because "he knew the whole business there."[22]

He certainly did. In 1924, John Vahey, Vanzetti's lawyer, and Frederick Katzmann, Vanzetti's prosecutor, became law partners.

The

14

Plymouth:
I Could Tell He Was
a Foreigner

The trial of Bartolomeo Vanzetti for attempted robbery and murder at Bridgewater began on June 22, 1920, in Plymouth, Massachusetts. Vanzetti's lawyers were John P. Vahey and James M. Graham, the prosecutor was District Attorney Frederick G. Katzmann, and the judge was Webster Thayer. One of the jurors was a foreman at the Plymouth Cordage Company, which had blacklisted Vanzetti for his role in a strike. The juror was not challenged by the defense attorneys.

The attempted robbery in Bridgewater had occurred at about seven-thirty in the morning of December 24, 1919, when four bandits tried to hold up a payroll truck. One bandit had a shotgun; two others had handguns. Katzmann contended that Vanzetti was the shotgun bandit.

The district attorney relied primarily on the eyewitness testimony of three men. He knew, though the defense did not, that the three men had changed their testimony considerably from the time they first spoke to a Pinkerton agent the day of the holdup to the time of Vanzetti's trial six months later.*

*Ehrmann says the defense did not find out about the Pinkerton reports on the Bridgewater crime until June, 1927.

163

Alfred Cox, the paymaster who sat on the money box bolted to the floor of the truck, originally described the shotgun bandit as "a Russian, Pole or Austrian, 5'8", 150 pounds, dark complexion, 40 years of age, was without a hat and wore a long dark overcoat with the collar up. He had a closely cropped moustache which might have been slightly gray." [1]

Benjamin Bowles, the town constable who was also a guard for the shoe company, sat next to the driver of the truck and had exchanged fire with the shotgun bandit. Bowles described him as "5'7", 35 or 36 years, 150 pounds, had a black closely cropped moustache, red cheeks, slim face, black hair, and was an Italian or a Portuguese. He had no hat on and had a black overcoat on with collar up." [2]

Frank Harding, a bystander who saw the robbery attempt, described the shotgun bandit as "slim, 5'10", wore a long black overcoat and black derby hat. I did not get much of a look at his face but think he was a Pole." [*][3]

Two of the three key witnesses had told the Pinkerton man that the bandit had a closely cropped moustache; the third said he hadn't seen the bandit's face clearly and mentioned no moustache at all. Vanzetti's outstanding feature was his big, bushy moustache which under no circumstances could be considered closely cropped.

On May 18, Cox, Bowles, and Harding testified at a preliminary hearing. With Vanzetti sitting before them as the suspect, the three men began to change their descriptions. Cox, who had seen a "dark" complexion changed it to "medium," which was closer to Vanzetti's coloring. Asked to identify the shotgun bandit, Cox said, "I think it is this man behind the rail, the man with the moustache," though he added, "I think there is a doubt." [4] Bowles still described the moustache as "short croppy," but included facial descriptions suited to Vanzetti whom he positively identified as the bandit. [5] Harding, who had not seen the bandit's face clearly, now decided he had a dark moustache and Vanzetti was the man. [6]

*The futility as well as the indignity of ethnic identification is proven by having the same man identified as Russian, Austrian, Italian, Portuguese, and Polish (two votes). How can a Mediterranean type (Italian, Portuguese) be mistaken for a Slavic type (Russian, Polish)? And what does an Austrian look like?

The

At the trial in Plymouth, the testimony changed again. Cox decided the moustache wasn't cropped after all, but "trimmed." Under cross-examination, however, he indicated he still wasn't "positive" Vanzetti was the bandit, though "he looks like the man."[7] Bowles was positive, and he now described the moustache as "bushy."[8] Harding, who "did not get much of a look at his face," offered a complete description, including "heavy dark moustache."[9]

Why had the three witnesses made the moustache fit the man rather than their memories? In the six months since the crime their memories had faded; in the meantime, officers of the commonwealth had arrested a man and said he was the bandit. All three witnesses had been taken to the Brockton police station and seen Vanzetti in the psychological framework of an accused prisoner; Bowles admitted he had discussed the case with Chief Stewart. It was easier to let the moustache grow than to contradict the commonwealth. Besides, all three men worked for the shoe factory that was the object of the robbery attempt and may have felt obliged to help convict at least one criminal.

Another prosecution witness, a woman, identified Vanzetti as the man at the wheel of the car, which was not very helpful to Katzmann's case because Vanzetti couldn't drive. Even if he did, he could not also have been the shotgun bandit because other witnesses said the driver remained in the car during the robbery attempt.

A fourteen-year-old high school student, Maynard Freeman Shaw, who was delivering newspapers when he saw the holdup attempt, contributed a new dimension to ethnic caricature when he was asked to describe the shotgun bandit.

Shaw: No hat on and I was just getting a fleeting glance at his face, but the way he ran I could tell he was a foreigner, I could tell by the way he ran.[10]

                  *   *   *

Vahey: You could tell he was a foreigner by the way he ran?
Shaw: Yes.
Vahey: What sort of a foreigner was he?
Shaw: Nation?
Vahey: Yes.

Shaw:	Why, European.
Vahey:	What?
Shaw:	Either Italy or Russia.
Vahey:	Which was it, Russia or Italy?
Shaw:	There I can't say exactly.
Vahey:	Does an Italian or a Russian run differently from a Swede or Norwegian?
Shaw:	Yes.
Vahey:	What is the difference?
Shaw:	Unsteady.
Vahey:	Both the Italians and the Russians run unsteadily?
Shaw:	As far as that goes I don't know.
Vahey:	You don't know how a Swede runs, do you?
Shaw:	No.
Vahey:	Does a Swede run cross-legged?
Shaw:	No.
Vahey:	You don't want to have this jury think, do you, that you can tell what the nationality of this man was by the way he ran? Do you want them to believe that?
Shaw:	Yes, I do.
Vahey:	Now what nationality did he belong to?
Shaw:	Let me say that I believe—well, the first thing that came into my mind was that he was an Italian or a Russian. I would not say,—he might be a Mexican for what I know. I would not say he was an Alaskan or an African.
Vahey:	You mean by that he was not a colored man?
Shaw:	No.
Vahey:	You eliminate the African, do you, from your consideration?
Shaw:	Yes.
Vahey:	He was either a Russian or an Italian or a Greek or a Brazilian or a Mexican—either one of those?
Shaw:	Yes.
Vahey:	Or a Jap?
Shaw:	Might be.
Vahey:	Would you say that he might be a Jap?
Shaw:	No.

The

Vahey:	You would not say that he was a Jap or a Chinaman or an African,—those three are eliminated absolutely, are they?
Shaw:	Yes, *nor an American.*[11] (Emphasis added.)

Shaw testified he had seen the three bandits close together, about 150 feet from where he was hiding behind a tree, yet he could not describe anyone but the shotgun bandit. Though he said he had only "a fleeting glance at his face," Shaw was able, with Vanzetti in the courtroom, to describe the length of the bandit's hair ("about an inch and a quarter or an inch and a half"), his moustache ("it was dark but it was not black"), and his complexion ("there was a foreign look in it, sort of sallow").[12] From that fleeting but obviously intense glance, Shaw had identified the shotgun bandit as Vanzetti, after discussing the matter at the Brockton police court with Chief Stewart.

Besides the eyewitness testimony, the prosecution produced as evidence five shotgun shells. Four were supposedly found in Vanzetti's pocket when he was arrested; one was a spent shell found at the scene of the Bridgewater crime. The man who found the exploded shell and some shot—the pellets within the shell— said they were small pellets normally used for hunting birds and small game. This would indicate the robbers did not intend to murder anyone.

In his book, *The Case That Will Not Die*, attorney Herbert Ehrmann pointed out several peculiarities about the shells.[13] First, the prosecution said there were four shells in Vanzetti's pocket while Vanzetti said there were only three, though when pressed in cross-examination he said he really didn't know and wouldn't insist. In his letter to Luigia, he said three or four, but that was six years later and by then he was no longer certain of the number and probably didn't think it mattered. Since Vanzetti did not testify at his first trial, it was not until the trial at Dedham that he explained why the shells were in his pocket. As he wrote Luigia, he saw the shells lying on a shelf in Sacco's house and since Sacco didn't want them, Vanzetti decided he would sell them to a friend to raise a little money for the cause. Sacco testified that the shells were there because a friend and his wife had once visited and brought a gun and a box of shells for "playing and shooting in the wood."[14] The shells that were not used were put in a closet where Rosina Sacco found them when she was cleaning the house and packing for the trip to Italy.[15]

The reason the number of shells was important was that there was a second peculiarity. If they came out of a single box, they should have been the same brand, but three of the unfired shells introduced at Plymouth were Peters and one was a Winchester. A spent Winchester shell had been found at Bridgewater; a spent Peters shell was found near the abandoned Buick after the South Braintree crime. The prosecution, looking ahead, was covered for both cases.*

Third, there was no proof that the shells offered as evidence at Plymouth were the shells removed from Vanzetti's pocket since they had not been marked in any way. Michael J. Connolly, the policeman who arrested Sacco and Vanzetti, testified that he had searched Vanzetti.

Q: Did you find some shells?
Connolly: I did.
Q: How many?
Connolly: Four.
Q: I will ask you to look at these shells and see whether or not those are the shells?
Connolly: They look like the same ones.

Vahey protested that "they look like the same ones" was insufficient identification, but Judge Thayer admitted the shells as evidence.[16]

Finally, the fact that Vanzetti was carrying shotgun shells of any type in his pocket the night of May 5 did not prove he was the shotgun bandit of the previous December 24, a point Vahey made in trying to block the introduction of the shells entirely, but Thayer ruled this was a question for the jury to decide.

In presenting Vanzetti's case, the defense dwelt at length on the size of his moustache. Hoping to dent the credibility of the

*In the end, the spent Peters shell was not used as evidence at Dedham. The prosecution had found other ways to snare Vanzetti.

The (

prosecution's three major witnesses, defense counsel showed, during cross-examination, that their descriptions had changed since the preliminary hearing. The defense also offered a number of Vanzetti's friends and acquaintances in Plymouth to say he always wore his moustache the same droopy way and that it had not been trimmed or cropped in December, 1919. John Vernazano, Vanzetti's barber, testified he had shaved Vanzetti and cut his hair for the past five or six years.

Graham:　　Have you ever trimmed or cut his moustache?
Vernazano:　No sir; sometimes I did trim a little round on the bottom.

*　　*　　*

Graham:　　Point to where you mean on your own moustache.
Vernazano:　Just two or three hairs cut off there, right on the top of his lip.
Graham:　　Did you ever cut the ends of it or trim the ends of it?
Vernazano:　No, no, no.
Graham:　　Did you ever see it trimmed?
Vernazano:　No.
Graham:　　Did you ever see it any different from what it is today?
Vernazano:　Never; always he had a long moustache.[17]

Two Plymouth police officers, who were not Italian, also testified for Vanzetti, but Katzmann sent them spinning. John Gault, an officer for five years, said he had known Vanzetti about four years and saw him three or four times a week and that his moustache always looked the same. Under cross-examination, Gault said he did not know if Vanzetti's moustache had been trimmed on December 24 and did not remember if he saw him that week.[18] No one made the point that a moustache trimmed or closely cropped on December 24 would have been obvious for quite some time afterward.

Joseph Schilling, a Plymouth police officer for ten years, testified he saw Vanzetti two or three times a week and his moustache "always looked the same to me."

Katzmann:　Are you telling this jury that it was always the same?
Schilling:　No, I would not.

Katzmann:	Are you telling this jury that the ends were never cut off?
Schilling:	No, sir, I would not.[19]

Vanzetti's defense at Plymouth was not limited to the length of his moustache. He had an exceptionally strong alibi for the morning of December 24, and many witnesses to confirm it. Unwilling to practice his trade of pastry maker, which he hated, Vanzetti earned his living as necessary doing odd jobs or peddling fish. Often he just spent his time clamming, picking flowers, wandering in the woods, rowing his own little boat, or chatting with friends.[20] On most days Vanzetti would have difficulty proving his whereabouts, or even knowing them himself, but not the day of the Bridgewater crime.

When Italians began to emigrate to America in large numbers, they tended, like other immigrant groups, to settle in clusters. Italians from the same area or city or village clung together in the new land and tried to keep their customs, where possible. Most of the Italians in Plymouth came from the area around Bologna, and it was traditional for them to eat eels on Christmas Eve. They bought their eels from the fish peddler, Vanzetti, on the morning of December 24.

Though Vanzetti sold local fish when they were available, he also bought fish from wholesalers in Boston. Shortly before Christmas, he ordered a barrel of eels from the Corso & Cannizzo Company to be shipped to him COD. He then went to his Italian neighbors taking orders for the eels, which were delivered by American Express on Tuesday, December 23, to 35 Cherry Street, where Vanzetti boarded with the Fortini family.

The barrel was heavy and so were the orders; Vanzetti realized he would need help to get all the eels delivered early enough the following day to allow the women to salt and cook them for supper. He went to his old friends, the Brinis, brought them their own order of eels, and asked twelve-year-old Beltrando to help him in the morning.

Beltrando Brini:	*He intended to get a horse and wagon to deliver his eels, rather than [use] his pushcart, because he had*

The ❶

> *more orders than he cared to push in a cart. And I*
> *was quite enthused about riding on the horse. I was*
> *more than anxious to help him; I had never ridden*
> *on a horse and wagon before.*

After making arrangements with Beltrando, Vanzetti returned to the Fortini house where he worked until midnight wrapping the individual orders in newspaper.[21]

On the morning of December 24, Carlo Balboni, on the way home from his job on the night shift at the Plymouth Cordage Company, stopped at the Fortini house at 6:15 A.M. to pick up two pounds of eels from Vanzetti.[22] Then Vanzetti drank some warm milk for breakfast and went to the baker from whom he intended to borrow the horse and wagon. But the baker was also busy that day; even though he had a truck, he told Vanzetti he needed both the truck and the wagon to get his own orders delivered.[23]

At about 7:30 that morning, just as the holdup was beginning in Bridgewater, Beltrando Brini, on his way to meet Vanzetti, saw him delivering an order of eels on Court Street.[24] Beltrando asked Vanzetti where the horse was, and Vanzetti told him it was not available.[25]

Beltrando   *I was very much disappointed that he couldn't get*
Brini: *the horse. I would have helped him in either case,*
       but you know, I had my spirits high—riding on a
       horse and wagon, driving a horse—and he didn't
       have any. But he apologized. He felt very bad about
       it. And I'm sure he would have been glad to have
       had it because he had quite a load of fish. The
       pushcart wasn't very light; I couldn't budge it.

Before Beltrando could set out with Vanzetti, his father came by on his way from the bakery where he had gone to put his homemade bread in the oven to bake. Mr. Brini told Beltrando to go home and get his rubbers because the streets were muddy.[26] Beltrando had to hunt for a while before he found the rubbers under the cellar steps.[27] When he went out again he walked to the Fortini house where Vanzetti was loading his wheelbarrow;[28] Vanzetti had a pushcart and a wheelbarrow and used both that morning.[29] By then it was 8 A.M.; Beltrando knew because he heard the eight-o'clock whistle at the Plymouth Cordage plant.[30]

From 8 A.M. until 1:30 or 2 P.M., Beltrando Brini helped Vanzetti deliver eels to the Italian community in Plymouth.[31]

Beltrando
Brini: *I was with him all that morning.*

Fourteen Italians confirmed or corroborated Vanzetti's alibi,[32] though many more had purchased eels from him.

Beltrando   *I heard that some didn't want to testify. Everyone*
Brini: *was scared; you know, it was in the air. We felt that*
              Italians didn't amount to anything, that anything we
              said wasn't valid because we weren't the people to
              say it. We were without power. No one cared to
              listen to us. It didn't make any difference even if we
              were innocent; we didn't amount that much to
              society. They wanted to prove the opposite. Some-
              one wanted to find a scapegoat for those crimes.

There was reason for the Italians to be afraid. Besides the ubiquitous antialien, anti-Italian atmosphere of the time, the abuse of Vanzetti's Italian witnesses at the Plymouth trial deserves a special chapter in the annals of immigrant history. Katzmann tried to prove the witnesses were lying about their recollections of December 24 by asking them about other dates chosen at random, which is a fallacious ploy. A person is likely to remember what happens on a special day, such as the day before Christmas, especially when there is a special custom involved; he is also likely to remember what happened on a day when something extraordinary occurred, such as a payroll robbery that a friend is accused of committing. Very few people remember what they were doing November 21, 1963, but almost everyone over a certain age knows what he was doing the following day when he heard the news of John F. Kennedy's assassination. In the same way, when later learning a particular day was significant, one often recalls details that would be forgotten otherwise.

A fair example of Katzmann's scorching style and its intimidating effect on the immigrant witnesses was his cross-examination of Mary Fortini, Vanzetti's landlady.

The

Katzmann:	What day was Vanzetti arrested?
Fortini:	I think on Wednesday.
Katzmann:	What Wednesday?
Fortini:	I don't know.
Katzmann:	Two months ago, was it not?
Fortini:	I don't know.
Katzmann:	Three months ago, wasn't it?
Fortini:	I don't know.
Katzmann:	A week ago, was it not?
Fortini:	I don't know.
Katzmann:	Yesterday, was it not?
Fortini:	I don't know.

*   *   *

Katzmann:	What time did Vanzetti get up on the day after Christmas?
Fortini:	I don't remember.
Katzmann:	What time did Vanzetti get up the first day of this year?
Fortini:	I don't know.
Katzmann:	What time did Vanzetti get up on Washington's birthday of this year?
Fortini:	No, I don't know.

*   *   *

Katzmann:	What time did he go to bed the Saturday night before Easter morning of this year?
Fortini:	I don't know, no, sir.[33]

Katzmann was not through amusing himself and the jury. He had questioned Mrs. Fortini through an interpreter; now he asked her if she spoke English. She said no.

Katzmann:	You talked to the officers the day they came to your house in English, did you not? *
Fortini:	I don't understand him and he don't understand me.[34]

After a few more questions through the interpreter, Katzmann asked Judge Thayer for permission to examine Mrs.

---

*Katzmann was not the man to make fun of other people's English.

Fortini in English. Thayer did not ask Katzmann why; he merely replied, as though it were a matter of great indifference to him, "Go ahead, if you care to."

Katzmann: Do you know what language I talk? Do you know my language?

Fortini: No.

Katzmann: What is a horse—do you know?

Fortini: I don't understand nothing.

Katzmann: Do you know what a horse is?

Fortini: No, sir.

Katzmann: Do you know what a Brini is?

Fortini: No, sir.

Katzmann: Do you know what a Balboni is? That is something you hang out on the line washday, isn't it?

Fortini: Me don't understand you. You come in my country and you don't understand nothing, and me just the same.[35]

Neither Thayer nor Vanzetti's attorneys tried to halt the sadistic flaying of Mrs. Fortini. If Katzmann had asked whether you hung a Thayer or a Vahey or a Graham out on washday, there would have been outrage in the courtroom, but Italian names and Italians could be mocked with impunity.

Katzmann was a brilliant prosecutor, scoring points both fair and foul. Since the defense asked every witness who knew Vanzetti about the size of his moustache, and Vincenzo Brini, Beltrando's father, had testified that half a pig was delivered to his house the night of December 23, Katzmann opened his cross-examination of Brini by asking, "I suppose Mr. Brini, that you can remember that Vanzetti's moustache was not trimmed about last Christmas time because you bought a pig the night before—is that right?"[36] With one wisecrack Katzmann had demolished Vincenzo Brini and every other witness who verified the length of Vanzetti's moustache. To underscore his contention that all the Italian witnesses were lying for Vanzetti, Katzmann's first question to the baker, Enrico Bastoni, was, "I suppose, Mr. Witness, you want to tell the truth here, don't you? I am asking you if you

The

desire to tell the truth here?" Bastoni replied well enough, "That is what I came here for."[37]

The one witness Katzmann absolutely had to destroy was Beltrando Brini, who knew better than anyone what Vanzetti was doing at the time of the Bridgewater robbery attempt. Brini, who was thirteen years old when he testified at Plymouth, remembers he was on the stand somewhere between two and three hours.

Beltrando Brini: *Katzmann tried to show that my story was mainly a story, memorized, learned by heart, repeated and prepared for my friend. "Who did you tell this to?" "My mother." "Who else?" "To my father." "Did you tell it to anybody else?" "Yes, to the attorney." "Who told you what to say?" "Nobody told me what to say." "But you kept saying this over again—did you finally memorize it?" "You can't help but memorize it when you say a thing over and over again." He was trying to show it was a lesson learned by heart. And he asked me how I happened to remember—trying to test my memory of that particular day. And there was some ridicule in that. I was exasperated a couple of times, besides the fact that I was frightened. And another thing that riled me was that the defense attorney would never object or come to my defense. He never came to the assistance of any of the witnesses.*

Neither did Judge Thayer, though the judge helped Katzmann nicely by observing at one point, "You brought out the fact that he [Beltrando Brini] has rehearsed this [his testimony] and rehearsed it on many occasions, that he learned it by heart."[38] Thus the judge confirmed the prosecutor's allegations and helped discredit Beltrando Brini as a witness.

Besides trying to show that Beltrando had memorized a story to help his friend Vanzetti, Katzmann tried to trick the boy into revealing Vanzetti was an anarchist.

Katzmann: Did Vanzetti come sometimes to your house and talk to your papa?

Beltrando: Yes.

Katzmann: Would you stay in the room when they were talking? Did you hear what they were saying when they were talking together?

Beltrando: Yes.

Katzmann: Did you hear them talk about our government?

Vahey: I pray your Honor's judgment.

Beltrando: What do you mean by our government?

Thayer: He may answer yes or no.

Beltrando: No.[39]

Young Brini slipped out of that trap, no thanks to Thayer, but Katzmann tried again.

Katzmann: What society do your papa and the baker and Vanzetti belong to, do you know?[40]

This time the lawyer's objection was upheld, but Katzmann resumed the same line of questioning with only one objection from Vahey to which Thayer did not even respond.

Katzmann: Did your papa and Vanzetti and the baker belong to any society or organization?

Beltrando: No.*

Katzmann: Did you ever hear Mr. Vanzetti making any speeches to the Italians?

Beltrando: No.

*   *   *

Katzmann: Did you ever hear him saying he was going to Bridgewater?

Beltrando: No.

*   *   *

*Beltrando Brini, at thirteen, knew very little of his father's or Vanzetti's beliefs. Brini told me Vanzetti would "come down to the house and spend evenings with my father on political philosophy, and they would argue back and forth. They wouldn't agree. There would be variations, little refinements. Of course it was a lot beyond me and I couldn't understand what would keep my father up so long and late in the night with Vanzetti, talking."

The

Katzmann:	Did you ever hear him talk about a man named Sacco?
Beltrando:	No.
Katzmann:	When he was talking with your papa or the baker? Did you ever see a man named Sacco there at Plymouth?
Beltrando:	No.
Katzmann:	Did you ever hear Vanzetti talk about a man named Mike Boda?
Beltrando:	No.[41]

Though the questions about Sacco and Boda related to another case to be tried after Katzmann won his conviction in this one, neither Vanzetti's attorneys nor the judge interceded; in fact, one of Vanzetti's lawyers, James Graham, blurted out in the courtroom that Vanzetti was under suspicion for the South Braintree crime. Katzmann wanted the jurors to know about South Braintree and Vanzetti's anarchism while the defense tried to conceal both, though between newspaper accounts and word of mouth the jury probably knew anyway.

Because of Vanzetti's anarchist beliefs, his attorneys did not want him to testify. This was June, 1920; A. Mitchell Palmer's credibility had waned but not the popular fear of alien radicals. Vanzetti had the right not to testify; every defendant has that right, and the jury is always instructed not to hold this against him, but jurors are human and the natural reaction to a man who will not take the stand in his own defense is to assume he is concealing his guilt. If Vanzetti had testified, however, it would have given Katzmann the opportunity to cross-examine him on his views. These views were irrelevant to the holdup attempt, but Thayer would undoubtedly have found reason to allow this line of questioning, as he did at Dedham, and the jury certainly would have reacted negatively.

Vanzetti later wrote that Vahey "asked me how I would explain from the stand the meaning of Socialism, or Communism, or Bolshevism, if I was requested by the district attorney to do so. At such a query, I would begin an explanation on those subjects, and Mr. Vahey would cut it off at its very beginning. 'Hush, if you will tell such things to the ignorant, conservative jurors, they will send you to state prison right away.'"[42] Vanzetti claimed Vahey could have prevented Katzmann from asking him political questions, which the Dedham trial proved was not true. He also said Vahey prevented him from testifying "because he feared that I might have convinced the jury of my innocence."[43] Even though Vahey later became Katzmann's law partner, there seems to be no justification for this bitter accusation. Weighing the reaction of the jurors to Vanzetti's silence against their reaction to his turning the courtroom into a radical platform, Vahey advised Vanzetti to stay off the stand. After all, the case against him was weak—three witnesses who saw the wrong moustache—and Vanzetti's alibi was strong—countless witnesses who bought eels from him that morning.

Vanzetti's first trial ended without a word from the defendant. The last statement Katzmann managed to get on record was that the night of Vanzetti's arrest he carried a loaded revolver.[44]

The transcript of the Plymouth trial is fragmented at this point and records only a portion of Judge Thayer's charge to the jury. It included the line, "Because the [defendant's] witnesses are Italians no inference should be drawn against them,"[45] an echo of the words spoken at the trial of one of the men accused of burning Charlestown convent: *The prisoner at the bar cannot be convicted without Catholic testimony. We will endeavor to show what that testimony is worth.* Read, "The prisoner at the bar cannot be acquitted without Italian testimony. You can decide what that testimony is worth."

The jury withdrew to deliberate at 10:50 A.M. on July 1. At 3:40 P.M. they returned to ask if they could return a verdict of assault with a dangerous weapon. Thayer informed them they could "if the weapon, such as a gun, as has been described in this case, was found to be a dangerous weapon and at the same time you find that the defendant did not intend to kill . . . you would return the verdict of guilty of an assault with a dangerous weapon. In order to maintain the allegation complete [Vanzetti was accused of assault with intent to rob and assault with intent to murder] you must find an intent to murder. . . . So you see, gentlemen, that depends upon what you find with reference with [*sic*] that one word, 'intent.'"[46]

The jury had already decided Vanzetti was guilty; the only question was, how guilty? In order to resolve the question of intent, the jurors decided to open the shells, which were in the juryroom as part of the evidence, to see what size shot they contained. Small shot cannot kill a man; buckshot can. When the shells were opened, they contained buckshot.

The jury returned in half an hour. Vanzetti was found guilty of assault with intent to rob and assault with intent to murder. Thayer thanked the jurors for their "splendid and efficient services" and concluded, "You may go to your homes with the feeling that you did respond as the soldier responded to his service when he went across the seas to the call of the Commonwealth."[47] Though it would not be an issue until the next trial, Thayer apparently knew Vanzetti was a draft evader.

The next day Thayer and Katzmann learned the shells had been opened in the juryroom, but did nothing. According to one of the jurors, Katzmann said "he did not want it known."[48] At the end of 1920, Vanzetti's new attorney heard of the incident and questioned the jurors about it. Herbert Ehrmann, who did not enter the case until 1926, pointed out that not only was secretly opening the shells a violation of Vanzetti's rights—jurors are not supposed to consider evidence not openly on record—but there was no proof the shells in the juryroom were the shells found in Vanzetti's pocket, nor was there proof they were the shells offered as evidence; they were still not marked in any way. Four loaded shells and one exploded shell had been put in evidence but as most of the jurors remembered it, only three loaded shells and the exploded shell were in the juryroom.[49]

The jury foreman, Henry S. Burgess, said he opened two shells, both Winchesters, but only one Winchester had been introduced as evidence.[50] He also recalled that the shells were marked "B" which meant small pellets, yet they were filled with buckshot.[51] Ehrmann wondered if the shells might have been refilled by hand, particularly since one of the jurors felt they opened so easily they may have been opened before.[52]

In 1927 Ehrmann personally examined two shells allegedly found in Vanzetti's pocket and found them "in perfect condition" and clearly identified as containing buckshot. If these had been the shells shown at Plymouth, Katzmann would certainly have made the point that they were lethal, and the jurors would not have had to open them.[53]

Not only is the provenance of the shells in serious doubt, but even if they were found in Vanzetti's pocket and even if they did contain buckshot, they were found on May 5, not December 24. If Vanzetti were the shotgun bandit, the shells he carried the night he was arrested were not necessarily the same as the shells he used during the robbery attempt six months earlier. The jury had determined his "intent" based on evidence that was not only extremely questionable but totally irrelevant.

Vanzetti was sentenced by Judge Webster Thayer on August 16, 1920. To make it impossible for him to demand a new trial on the grounds that the shells had been secretly opened, Thayer did not sentence Vanzetti on the charge of assault with intent to murder.[54] For assault with intent to rob, Vanzetti received twelve to fifteen years.

Now that Vanzetti was a convict, Katzmann moved quickly. He relieved Captain William H. Proctor, an experienced officer who was head of the state police, of the responsibility for investigating the South Braintree crime, because Proctor believed Sacco and Vanzetti were innocent. Proctor was replaced by the inexperienced one-man police force, Chief Michael Stewart of Bridgewater, who had intuited that "the men who did this job knew no God," had trapped Sacco and Vanzetti, and was convinced of their guilt.

On September 11, 1920, Sacco and Vanzetti were indicted for the robbery and murders at South Braintree. Motions for separate trials for the two men were denied by Judge Thayer; Katzmann wanted the Plymouth conviction to reflect not only on Vanzetti but on Sacco as well.

The trial of Bartolomeo Vanzetti at Plymouth seems no more than a prologue to the trial of both Sacco and Vanzetti at Dedham, but it was a prologue without which the play might not have taken place or might have ended differently. If Vanzetti had been acquitted at Plymouth, it is doubtful he would have been tried at Dedham; there was too little evidence against him. Failure in the first trial might have convinced Katzmann to drop the charges against Sacco; even if not, Sacco alone might have had a better chance than Sacco linked to a convict.

What happened at Plymouth assured Katzmann that Sacco and Vanzetti could not have a fair trial because Vanzetti had not had one. The Yankee witnesses against him had changed their testimony and were far outnumbered by the Italian witnesses, but the Yankee jury believed the Yankee witnesses. If the Dedham trial was to prove there was no justice for Italian radicals in Massachusetts, the Plymouth trial proved there was no justice for an Italian in Massachusetts. If there had been no conviction at Plymouth, there probably would have been no conviction at Dedham; there probably would have been no trial.

Thus it was the racism so carefully planted by the Puritans, so tenderly nurtured by their descendants, that killed Sacco and Vanzetti. If eating eels on Christmas Eve had been a Puritan custom, Vanzetti would have been acquitted.

15

The Cutting of the Throat

Vanzetti's reaction to the guilty verdict was described by his friend Aldino Felicani who said that he was "beside himself."[1] The Brinis, who were closer to Vanzetti than his family in Italy, were stunned.

Alfonsina Brini:
He [Beltrando] was so mad when they found him guilty here. Oh, so mad. He went up and down the street, swearing. "I was with him myself. That means nothing." Oh, so mad.

Lefevre Brini:
I still remember that time. Boy! Poor kid. If anybody knew, he knew. I used to visit Vanzetti down at the Plymouth county jail every day. Every day I used to take a walk down to see him and bring mayflowers or violets. We were kids; we were sure that he would be freed. You know—justice? We knew he wasn't there, he was here. My brother and I said, "How can it be? They can't do anything to him. It's impossible!"

Beltrando   *I didn't realize what was afoot. I didn't realize that*
Brini: *this was, you might say, an intentional device to*
             incriminate him before a more serious charge. I
             think perhaps other people mentioned it and it may
             have come to my attention, but I didn't, at that time,
             put much emphasis on it.

As an anarchist and an outlaw in two countries, Aldino Felicani did not harbor naive ideas about justice; he would leave that to the Brini children. Though the verdict surprised him, Felicani was one of the few persons who sensed from the beginning that issues beyond common criminality were at stake. Every morning he took the first train from Boston to Plymouth to cover the trial. Katzmann and his assistant usually rode the same train, and Felicani said they would turn and look at him and say, "What does this fool want?"[2]

Felicani wanted the public, or at least the part that he could reach—the Italian community—to know what was happening at Plymouth. He attended the morning sessions of the trial and returned to Boston about 1 P.M. to begin his story. At 5 P.M. he would get the Brockton newspapers, which were also covering the trial, and find out what had happened during the afternoon. From then until midnight he worked on *La Notizia*, always including an article about the Plymouth trial. He says his was the only account of the trial to appear in any Boston newspaper.[3]

During the trial, Felicani, an experienced propagandist, wrote letters to *La Notizia* from mythical persons in various cities to show that people everywhere were aroused. After Vanzetti was found guilty, real letters began to arrive; Felicani received messages of sympathy and interest as well as contributions from Italians who weren't radical. They had seen one sample of American justice; in preparation for the second trial they began to organize committees to raise money for the defense of Sacco and Vanzetti.[4]

Felicani knew that the issues involved extended beyond the Italian community and that support would have to also. Though leftist ideologies are often irreconcilably hostile to one other, this was less true in the 1920s when radicals seemed to shift easily from one *-ism* to another. The fact that they all opposed the

Cutting of the Throat   183

American system, and were opposed in turn, encouraged a loose but sympathetic alliance.

Having obtained some support from socialists and Wobblies, as well as anarchists, Felicani decided to approach the Communists. He took Mrs. Sacco, who was pregnant, and Mrs. Coacci, whose husband had been deported, to Communist party headquarters in Boston to ask for help for them. He was told, "The Sacco-Vanzetti case is a criminal case. We are not interested in criminal cases." Felicani comments wryly, "That was the first type of Communist cooperation in the Sacco-Vanzetti case."[5]

The people most astonished by Vanzetti's arrest and conviction were not in Massachusetts but in Villafalletto. Vanzetti, Felicani, and the Brinis knew he was innocent, but they also knew what conditions in America and particularly in Massachusetts had produced the verdict. The young Brinis may have believed in justice but their elders knew how little there was for alien anarchists in America.

For Vanzetti's father, Giovanni, his sisters, Luigia and Vincenzina, and his brother, Ettore, what had happened to Bartolomeo was a mystery too great to comprehend, a humiliation too terrible to be borne. The old man had not wanted his son to go to America; he had urged him repeatedly to come home. Now Bartolomeo was not just a rebel and a heretic but a criminal.

Vincenzina *We learned about his arrest from the newspapers,*
Vanzetti: *then friends wrote. They were all Italians living around Boston. For many years it was a cause of constant suffering. We shut ourselves up at home. My reaction was a feeling of pain.*

Vanzetti's first letter to his family after his arrest is dated October 1, 1920. It was sent from Charlestown prison where he was serving his term for attempted robbery. By then he had not only been convicted of the first crime but indicted for the second. Vincenzina Vanzetti believes he wrote home sooner, but if he did, the letters have been lost or were confiscated by the Fascists.

The

Dearest father,

I have restrained until this moment the desire to write to you, since I had hoped to be able to give you some good news.

Things have continued to go badly, so I decided to write to you. I know how painful this occurrence in my life must be for all of you, it is this thought that makes me suffer the most. I beg you to be as strong as I am, and to pardon the pain that I am involuntarily causing you. I know that several people have written to you, but I do not know if you are in possession of all the facts, since several letters and collections of newspapers that friends sent to Italy have never been received. This fact forces one to admit that either the Italian or the American authorities are censoring all mail that concerns me. I do, however, know that you have received some letters and are therefore acquainted with the nature and outcome of my trial; it was a true crime against legality. A friend sent me your greetings, your conviction that I am innocent, and the happy news that you are feeling well. These are consolations of incalculable worth. Yes: I am innocent, despite everything I am feeling well, and I do my best to remain in good health. Now they are accusing me of murder. I have never killed or wounded or robbed, but if things go as they did in the other trial they would find even Christ, whom they have already crucified, guilty. I have witnesses that I will call in my defense, and I will fight with all of my energies. The weapons are unequal, and the fighting will be desperate. I will have against me the law with all of its immense resources; the police with its ages of experience in the art of condemning the innocent, a police whose actions are both uncontrolled and uncontrollable. Also arrayed against me are political and racial hate, and the great power that gold has in a country, and in a time, when the depth of human degeneration has been plumbed. The lust for gold has forced certain wretches to tell all sorts of vile lies about me. I have nothing to oppose this formidable coalition of enemies but my popularly acknowledged innocence, and the love and care of a handful of generous souls who love and aid me. The general public proclaims my innocence, demands my liberation. If you knew how much they have done, are doing and will do for me, you would be proud.

I hope that my Italian comrades will not deny me their support. In fact I'm sure they won't.

I have asked for the transcript of my trial. It will be translated into Italian and into other languages, and sent to Italy and to the other European nations.

Take heart therefore and be optimistic. Justice is always triumphant in the end, and so it will be in my case. Do not let this adversity oppress you, let it rather be an incentive to life, to living. Who knows what surprises destiny carries in its breast for us mortals? Who would have thought, a few days before my arrest, in what conditions I would now find myself? Who, therefore, can predict, from the terrible condition in which I now find myself, what tomorrow has in store for me? Let us, therefore, have faith and continue the struggle. . . .

I wish to tell you and all my loved ones one other thing. Do not keep my arrest a secret. Do not be silent, I am innocent and you have nothing to be ashamed of. Do not be silent, broadcast the crime that has been committed against me from the rooftops. Tell the world that an honest man is being sent to jail to restore the reputation of the police, which has been lost in a hundred scandals and a hundred failures. The police have not been able to find one single criminal in all this rising sea of crime. I am being sent to jail because of an old sadist's attachment to his power and his position, and because of

The (

his desire to see me deprived of my liberty and my blood. Do not be silent, silence would be shameful.

For the moment I don't need any money. If I should need some I will let you know. The prisons here are much better than in Italy; I say this by intuition and from what I have heard, since I have never been in prison in Italy. We all have our own cells. Our furniture consists of an adequate bed, a closet, a table and a chair. The electric lights are on until nine at night. We are given three meals a day, and a hot drink once or even twice daily. We are allowed to write two letters a month, and an additional letter every third month. The warden allowed me to write several extra letters, this is one of them. There is a library which contains the world's scientific and artistic masterpieces. We work eight hours a day in a healthy atmosphere. We are allowed out into the courtyard every day. The inmates? Except for a few victims of circumstance, who are more to be pitied than censured, they are wretches. I treat everyone as well as I can, but I remain mostly in the company of those few who are able to understand me, know my case and honor and love me. If you have kept the last letters that I sent you, send them back to the address of one of my friends, and insure them at the post office. They may be of great use to me.

I finish on a happy note: it is almost certain that there will be a retrial for the things that I was first accused of.

Be strong, therefore, and encourage my sisters and little brother, as well as all my relatives and friends.

In a second, undated letter to his father written during the same period, Vanzetti sounded less strained and more genuinely optimistic since Felicani's efforts at propagandizing had begun to produce results.

I know that many people have written to you, and some have come to visit you in person, so you know all about what is happening to me. I will, therefore, tell you that if things went so badly, it is because those that were supposed to defend me did exactly the opposite.

Now I have a new lawyer, a faithful and able man. The first trial will be retried, the second one has been postponed until March. You must already know that . . . the workers of Italy . . . and other generous persons have taken an interest in the case. Mexican, Spanish and French workers are also coming to my aid, both with monetary contributions and in other ways.

In this day and age it is not possible to sacrifice a man simply because he loves liberty and justice.

Know that while I was a prisoner in Plymouth, the population of that town treated me as if I had been their own son.

I had visitors every day. I was given so many flowers and cigars, and so much fruit and candy, that I was forced to refuse some of what was so generously offered.

Every Sunday they brought me lunch. . . .

Every day, almost all of the Italian press in America takes up our defense.

Last Sunday I received a letter signed by 200,-000 workers of New York. They declared their solidarity to my cause, begged me to keep my hopes up, and declared their belief in my innocence.

My health is good, and I hope the same is the case with you; though I understand that this event in my life must be most painful to you, as you are not as accustomed to adversity as I am. It would however be unreasonable to become discouraged at this point.

The new lawyer, the "faithful and able man" Vanzetti mentions, was Fred Moore. Before Moore was finally fired, he

The (

would be called many things other than faithful or able. Spencer Sacco referred to his hiring as "the cutting of the throat."

As Felicani tells it, after the Plymouth trial he was "desperate" to find a new lawyer. He says he did not go to Carlo Tresca, one of the most important Italian radicals in the country, Tresca came to him. Tresca told Felicani he was handling the case all wrong; radicals should be defended by a radical lawyer. Tresca and Elizabeth Gurley Flynn recommended Fred Moore.[6] Radicals had confidence in Moore. He was a veteran of the IWW trial in Chicago and had helped win acquittals for a Wobbly accused in the Everett massacre and for Joseph Ettor and Arturo Giovannitti after the Lawrence strike.

Undoubtedly Tresca, Elizabeth Gurley Flynn, and Felicani remembered what they thought were Moore's triumphs, particularly the Ettor-Giovannitti case which also involved Italian radicals. They may not have known or cared that Moore could be eccentric, irresponsible, and had the curious habit of disappearing when he was needed in court or elsewhere.[7] They also may not have known how little he had to do with the Ettor-Giovannitti case. When Herbert Ehrmann checked on his predecessor, he found that the defense at Lawrence had been handled by two experienced, conservative lawyers, and that Moore had done little more than run errands and round up witnesses.[8]

Fred Moore entered the Sacco-Vanzetti case in August, 1920; the first check to him was dated August 19.[9] He told Felicani that he would prepare the case and when the time came he would hire local lawyers.[10] As far as Sacco and Vanzetti were concerned, the time did not come until it was too late. What happened in the courtroom was of secondary importance to Moore; he saw the Sacco-Vanzetti case as political persecution, which it was, and he devoted his energies to fighting it in the streets, not the courts.

Moore told Felicani that the Sacco-Vanzetti Defense Committee should be properly organized and should set up its own office. Since space was available at 32 Battery Place, where *La Notizia* was printed, Felicani opened the committee's first office there.[11] Moore opened a separate office and gave himself a salary of $150 a week, plus expenses.[12] Expenses turned out to mean as much money as he could get his hands on.

Aldino Felicani:	*There was no limit to Moore's spending money. . . . I never saw anything like it, and of course this established, from the beginning, a very difficult business between me and Moore.*[13]

Despite their quarrels over finances, Felicani gives Moore full credit for arousing and expanding interest in the case. With help from Tresca, Elizabeth Gurley Flynn, and others, Moore reached for support not only within radical circles but beyond them, to the AFL, the ACLU, and what Felicani calls "the Americans"—those who were neither Italian, nor ethnics, nor even radical. Felicani says Moore "penetrated to elements that we would never have been able to reach without him."[14] As word of the injustice spread, help came from an unexpected source, a small band of liberal women, several of them Brahmins, who became Sacco and Vanzetti's most stalwart supporters, sustaining them with money, time, and affection. Elizabeth Glendower Evans, the most dedicated of the group, served as surrogate mother for both men.

Even though the pitch of propaganda rose, Vanzetti was dissatisfied. He wanted more, said Felicani, not for his sake "but for that of other people who might be in the same situation someday."[15]

Perhaps he did. But Vanzetti's letters home reveal a desperate need to reassure his father he was innocent as well as a desperate need to be loved and respected, or to prove he was. Some of the letters were just laundry lists of supporters, as though by recording all of the people who believed in him, Vanzetti could make his father believe in him too.

In his comments about propaganda, Felicani says, "Sacco felt the same way. Of course, Vanzetti was more of a reflective type."[16] As usual, Sacco is just an afterthought; Felicani often forgets to mention him at all. Vanzetti speaks of Sacco in his letters only when he has to; it is as though he were bearing this enormous tragedy alone. Sacco, who preferred human love to universal adulation, just wanted the trial over with so he could either go to his wife or to the executioner. His wishes were

The Ca

consistently ignored both by the Defense Committee and by Moore, and he came to hate Moore.

Fred Moore has been and can be blamed for many things, but not for turning the Sacco-Vanzetti trial into a political case. It *was* a political case. The two men were being tried because they were Italians, aliens, and anarchists; that was the commonwealth's decision, not Moore's.

What Moore and Felicani did was organize, agitate, and propagandize to let the whole world know it was a political trial, so Massachusetts could not do its dirty work in secret. Whether, in the end, this was productive or counterproductive is debatable. There are those who believe the agitation kept Sacco and Vanzetti alive through seven years of appeals, alerted the world to the injustice of their execution, and possibly spared others the same fate.

Roger   *It helped in the sense that it dramatized the defects*
Baldwin: *of the system of justice in Massachusetts. . . . The*
            suspicion that these men were being tried for their
            political opinions and their activities, and for being
            foreigners in a hostile community . . . that was nec-
            essarily an international issue used against the
            United States. I think, on the whole, although it
            didn't save them from execution, that it did assist in
            correcting some of the excesses of the time; the
            witch-hunting of the time.

The other view, as stated by Herbert Ehrmann, is that the agitation rallied "what is known today as the Establishment to the defense of the Massachusetts administration of justice." [17] He felt that Sacco and Vanzetti might have been convicted, agitation or not, but later appeals might have succeeded if the propaganda campaign had not united the authorities against the two men.

Felicani and Moore had turned initially to their natural sources of support: Italians, radicals, non-Italian immigrants, and labor unions. But during the Red Scare, these were the accursed groups. Sacco and Vanzetti were arrested and tried because they were alien radicals; to have more alien radicals rush to their defense only confirmed the danger to the community. Besides, the descendants of the Puritans were not about to permit such rabble to criticize their justice or tell them how to run their courts. When support for Sacco and Vanzetti finally came from other elements of society, it was either too little or too late.

What Fred Moore can be blamed for is concentrating so heavily on the battle in the streets that he neglected the battle in the courtroom. He may have felt he had to win hearts and minds the world over, but his first obligation was to win the hearts and minds of the twelve members of the jury. He not only did not win over the jurors or the judge, he seemed to go out of his way to provoke them.

Already a subject of distrust in Massachusetts for the unpardonable sin of being from out of state, he outraged the stiff-necked Yankees by his bohemian behavior. He refused to cut his long hair, an object of suspicion even then, and often removed his jacket, vest, and shoes in the courtroom. It may seem petty of the jurors to condemn him for this, but it was even pettier for Moore to insist upon it. Moore seemed to think he had nothing to lose, but his conduct reflected on his clients; unfairly but inevitably it was they who suffered the reaction to Moore's offensive manners.

Moore's personal life became the subject of much rumor and speculation; it was said he was a womanizer. This was certainly irrelevant to the guilt of Sacco and Vanzetti, but when a trial is held only because the community is aroused, it is senseless to have a defense lawyer who arouses it further. While both Sacco and Vanzetti led flawless personal lives, Moore's behavior fitted the image of the radical who is not only dangerous but decadent; a threat to the prevailing morality as well as the prevailing politics. Again, it was not Moore who was hurt, but his clients.

There was also the problem of Moore's tendency to disappear for reasons that could only be guessed at, not confirmed.

Roger   *I heard that he was found one day in the public*
Baldwin: *library when he should have been in court, reading*
and completely dazed. Whether he took drugs I
don't know, but I heard that he did.

<table>
<tr>
<td>Aldino
Felicani:</td>
<td>I used to go to Moore's room . . . and . . . find him a human wreck. . . . The thought came to me that he was using morphine, or something like that. . . . I said, "I will strangle that son-of-a-bitch if he isn't good in court."[18]</td>
</tr>
</table>

Albert Carpenter, who was an investigator for Moore, said Moore had cancer and that "he sometimes was in such pain that he would go off by himself and you wouldn't see him, maybe, for two or three days. And then he'd feel better and be back on the old job again. . . . I knew all of the time what the trouble was but he asked me never to divulge my knowledge of his cancerous condition."[19] Another Moore apologist has said that when Moore was overtired or overworked, he went to the library to relax.

Neither story explains why Moore should go to the library when he was needed in court, or where he was when he couldn't be located in the library, or why Felicani found him a wreck in his room, or why he disappeared for long periods during the IWW trial in Chicago. If Moore took drugs for pain or any other reason, or suffered from some physical or mental ailment, it would have been fairer to his clients and his associates to confide in them rather than to leave them dangling.

Moore's private life and problems would have mattered less if he had kept his promise to stay in the background and turn over the courtroom duties to competent local lawyers. But he didn't. He waited until the last possible moment to call in three prominent and successful attorneys from Quincy, the McAnarney brothers, John, Thomas, and Jeremiah. Years later, John McAnarney told the Lowell Committee, the ultimate judges in the case:

> Mr. Moore came to our office and stated that he had been recommended by one of the judges of the Superior Court to see if he could get the McAnarney brothers to take the defense of these two men. I heard the story and told him on account of the pressure of my other work I personally could not take the case but, if he was willing, my brother J. J. [Jeremiah] McAnarney who was one of the trial lawyers of

Norfolk County, he would undoubtedly take on the case . . . and that T. F. [Thomas] . . . would help out . . . but I wanted in the first place, because of the nature of the crime, I wanted to find out something about these men myself as to their innocence or guilt. That led to my going to Dedham, me and my brothers. I had a session of a whole afternoon with Sacco and his wife; I think at that time Vanzetti was serving his fifteen years at Charlestown. It was later I had my interview with him.

I have closely examined Sacco and put him through every test I could think of. . . . I took Moore out and talked with him over an hour. I wanted to find out if he was holding back anything from me that would have any bearing on the innocence or guilt of these men. As a result of my conference with Sacco and Moore, I came to the conclusion that Mr. Sacco was innocent of that crime. I told my brothers they could go and secure his acquittal as far as they could with a free conscience. I live in Quincy and the offense took place in South Braintree. It was a horrible crime and I did not want to have anything to do with it and have my office concerned in keeping them from getting their right punishment but, if they were not the right fellows, I wanted them acquitted.[20]

For the record, Jeremiah and Thomas McAnarney were counsel for Vanzetti, and Moore was counsel for Sacco. John McAnarney said this was just a "trial maneuver" to give each lawyer the right to argue before the jury and to cross-examine witnesses, but that all the lawyers worked for both men. He also emphasized that Moore was chosen by a "committee of radicals," not by Sacco or his wife.[21]

McAnarney was asked if at a certain stage of the trial he or his brothers "took the laboring oar." He replied, "At no time was the laboring oar taken out of Mr. Moore's hands. That was the unfortunate part of it."[22]

The C

Even before the jury selection was completed, the antagonism between Moore and Judge Thayer reached such a pitch that Jeremiah and Thomas McAnarney told their brother they feared the case was already lost. "It was obvious there would be a miscarriage of justice and they begged I should go out and take charge of it," said John McAnarney. He agreed to do so if he could get an even more distinguished attorney, William G. Thompson, as co-counsel. "I pleaded with him [Thompson] for a long time to come out on the case," said John McAnarney, "and I told him in substance in my opinion it meant the lives of these two men and the best opinion I could form at the moment [was] they were innocent.

"Mr. Thompson yielded and we met at the courthouse. We first saw Mr. Moore and we labored for a long time in one of the anterooms to get him to withdraw from the case. He positively refused to do so."[23] At that point Judge Thayer was considering whether to permit Moore to serve as defense counsel since he was not a member of the Massachusetts bar. When Thayer ruled Moore could remain, Rosina Sacco wept with despair since she and her husband wanted to be rid of him.[24] Sacco somehow perceived Moore would be a burden to the case, while Vanzetti and Felicani were so pleased with Moore's work as a propagandist they were blind to the damage he did in the courtroom.

Though Thayer permitted Moore to serve as counsel, the hostility between lawyer and judge continued. Thomas McAnarney said that "whenever he [Moore] would address the court it was quite similar to waving a red flag in the face of a wolf."[25] The McAnarneys became so desperate to save Sacco and Vanzetti by getting Moore out of the case they offered to turn their fee over to Thompson and, said Thomas McAnarney, "we would go on with the case, having got into it, without any compensation at all if we could get Mr. Moore to retire. Well, Mr. Moore wouldn't retire." In Moore's mind, the Sacco-Vanzetti case was his; by making it important he had made himself important. He was not about to be forced out while he was molding his masterpiece.

Thomas McAnarney gave the Lowell Committee examples of the friction in the courtroom and how it was kept out of the record:

Mr. Moore would make an objection or make some remark, and it would be perfectly clear that it got under Judge Thayer's skin. Judge Thayer would respond by telling him that he might be practicing law outside in the West or in California, but not in Massachusetts. . . . The counsel would go up to the desk, have a conference at the bench or something— you know it isn't ordinarily done in a murder case, but we would go to the bench, and I remember beckoning at one time for the stenographer to come forward. I wanted something taken down. The Judge made the remark, "To hell with him. We don't want him. We will send for him when we want him." After that I made no further effort to get the stenographer.*[26]

Whatever damage Moore did to the Sacco-Vanzetti case during the trial and afterward may have been irrelevant since it is likely he lost it before it ever began.

According to Felicani, a Norfolk County court interpreter named Angelina DeFalco visited him at the offices of *La Notizia* early in January, 1921. Mrs. DeFalco, who claimed to be a friend of District Attorney Katzmann, told Felicani he could buy Sacco's freedom. When Felicani asked about Vanzetti, Mrs. DeFalco replied that he would be more of a problem because he was a convict but that he too would be acquitted if the committee paid enough.†

Mrs. DeFalco explained that the district attorney, his assistants, and the foreman of the jury would be bribed, and after a mock trial Sacco and Vanzetti would be acquitted.[27] The Defense Committee would have to agree to hire two other lawyers, Francis Squires and Percy Katzmann, the district attorney's brother. Frederick Katzmann would then step aside and let an assistant handle the case.[28]

*Those who have concluded from reading the trial transcript that the trial and the judge were entirely fair—a conclusion I find insupportable—might at least wonder what Thayer wanted suppressed.

†Advocates of the split-guilt theory forget that because of his previous conviction Vanzetti bore a presumption of guilt that pulled both men down.

The C

A few days later, Mrs. DeFalco invited Felicani to dinner at her home. She indicated that people he should speak to about the case would be there. When Moore heard about this, he refused to let Felicani go because he feared some kind of trap. Shortly before the dinner, Felicani called Mrs. DeFalco to say he couldn't come because he was waiting for someone to arrive from New York with a large sum of money for the committee. He suggested she come to his office the following morning to "discuss terms." When she agreed, a primitive listening mechanism was installed in the *La Notizia* building so that everything Mrs. DeFalco said could be heard in the basement where a stenographer would record it;[29] there are no new ideas, only new devices.

Later that evening, Felicani and two other men drove by Mrs. DeFalco's home and saw a car parked outside. When they checked the license number the next day, they found the car belonged to attorney Francis Squires.[30]

There were four others at the morning meeting between Mrs. DeFalco and Felicani. According to Felicani's account, she said it would cost forty thousand dollars to acquit both men. She wanted five thousand dollars immediately and said the committee would have all summer to collect the balance.[31]

On the basis of Mrs. DeFalco's conversations with Felicani and other members of the Defense Committee, Moore decided to put the courts of Massachusetts on trial. He brought charges against Mrs. DeFalco and, in a blaze of blinding ego, asked for and received permission to prosecute the case himself.

Since Mrs. DeFalco had not received any money, she was charged with attempting to solicit law business without being a member of the bar.[32] Mrs. DeFalco testified she had been approached by the Defense Committee, not the other way around.[33] Squires testified he had been told by Mrs. DeFalco the committee wanted to retain him as a lawyer. Percy Katzmann testified he never discussed the case with Mrs. DeFalco until after her arrest. Both Squires and Percy Katzmann denied authorizing Mrs. DeFalco to approach the Defense Committee on their behalf. District Attorney Frederick Katzmann testified he had never heard of Mrs. DeFalco until she was arrested.[34]

Moore was so anxious to strike a blow against the courts he did not stop to consider how weak his case was. Several of his witnesses were anarchists too principled to take the oath before testifying; when it was one witness's word against another's, radicals with emotional and ideological interest in the case were not more credible than two reputable lawyers and a district attorney. Felicani said Mrs. DeFalco approached him, but there was no proof he did not approach her; trial testimony revealed she saw or spoke to Felicani and other members of the Defense Committee several times. Mrs. DeFalco claimed she represented the two lawyers and the district attorney; there was no proof they authorized her to do so. Squires's car was parked outside Mrs. DeFalco's home the night of the dinner; there was no proof he did not believe he had been summoned by the committee to take over the case.

Squires and the two Katzmanns were cleared by Judge Michael Murray, who reprimanded Mrs. DeFalco as "imprudent and unwise" but found her not guilty. Judge Murray criticized those who "without warrant . . . lessen the public confidence in those entrusted with the administration of . . . our law" and called the attempt to discredit District Attorney Katzmann "reprehensible."[35]

Herbert Ehrmann noted that during the following decade, two Massachusetts district attorneys were removed from office, an attorney general was impeached, and a number of leading trial lawyers were disbarred, all because of corruption.[36] But Judge Murray could not have anticipated this, nor did it mean that Squires or the Katzmann brothers were guilty. Ehrmann felt that if Mrs. DeFalco approached Felicani on behalf of the three men, Moore should either have hired Squires and Percy Katzmann or declined to, but he was in no position to turn the offer into a public scandal.[37]

Moore's lunge for the jugular ended up slashing the wrong throats. An outside agitator and a cabal of anarchists had challenged Massachusetts justice; this must have appeared to the public as the act of men made desperate because Sacco and Vanzetti were guilty. Moore had also accused Katzmann of offering to throw the case for money. Whatever Katzmann's original motives were for trying Sacco and Vanzetti, he now had a more cogent one; he had to gain a conviction to prove he couldn't be bought. Finally, Moore's unproved allegations backfired by

The

uniting the judiciary of Massachusetts against him and his clients. Moore drew the lightning, but Sacco and Vanzetti were to burn.

Vanzetti to his father, January 30, 1921:

I have nothing in particular to tell you, but I am writing this letter to exchange a few words with you; tell you of the excellent state of my health and of the good spirits in which I find myself. I hope that the same is the case with you, with my sisters and with Ettore. I beg you to do your utmost to be in good spirits and in good health. I am also writing because I know that my letters are always welcome, and that you await them anxiously. Today the sky is gray and cloudy; my room is rather dark, so I am not reading as I want to preserve my eyesight. For this reason I went to the Catholic and to the Protestant masses this morning. I go because I like to hear the music and the singing—both performed by the prisoners— and so as to ascend and descend the eleven steps that lead to the church, as the exercise is both beneficial to my health and agreeable. After the last mass we were allowed into the courtyard for an hour, we were also permitted to talk. Then we had lunch, it was excellent. In a little while I will go to the theater. I do not know if there will be a film or music and song. In any case I will spend two entertaining hours there. After supper I will study a bit of English, a bit of arithmetic and I will read a passage or two from a good book. After having done a few exercises I will go to bed. This is the manner in which I pass Sunday in prison when it is cloudy. When the sun illuminates my room I spend little or no time in church and read instead. Speaking of books, four beautiful new books, all written in Italian, were just given to me. My friends make sure that I always have money, so in addition to the regulation food I buy oil, butter and fruit. How many free people would like, if only they were able, to feed their children what I am eating here!

For what concerns the trials, things are going better every day.

We are sure that I will have a retrial for the first accusation, and it is not humanly possible that I will be found guilty.

As for the trial that is still pending, I have irrefutable proofs of my innocence. My defense will no longer be handled by . . . accomplices of the prosecutor, but rather by able and honest men. By now the press, and this includes the big English-language papers, are forced, in the name of truth, to be favorable to us. Just a few days ago, Mr. Palmer, the head of the federal pigs, was publicly attacked by members of Congress. . . . They accused him of trampling the law underfoot in his treatment of the Reds. . . .

If this is not sufficient there is also another scandal that is now coming to light. My lawyer just had an Italian woman arrested. She was working as an interpreter in the court in which I was tried. She was asking the "Committee for the Defense" of Sacco and myself for $50,000 [sic]. She said this would be used to get rid of our old lawyers, and hire the prosecutor's brother . . . to defend us. . . .

What a pigsty! What a travesty of justice! What dogs!

The Italians here have done a lot for me. I have the support of the Society of the Sons of Italy, of the labor unions, and of many political and economic clubs. Not only the workers but also professional people are helping me.

My reputation before my arrest was excellent. My trial was a police frameup that disgusted everyone. My reputation is now better than it was before. All honest men demand my liberation, capitalists and priests are of course excluded. Not only the Italians but also many Americans are on my side. . . . The Spanish and Mexican workers have also rallied to my side.

The

Ah yes, I will never be able to say that the population is not grateful to me. It has done a great deal for me, and is ready to do a great deal more, to do whatever is necessary to have Sacco and myself once more in the forefront of the sacred battle for liberty and justice. . . .

In America things are going very badly. There is a great deal of unemployment, and enough misery to soften the heart of a tiger. Those responsible could not care less. It is well known that good Christians do not have a heart in their breast.

Vanzetti to his father, May 24, 1921:

Next week on the 31st of May, my second trial will start. . . .

The purpose of this letter is to restate my innocence once again, and to tell you that I have a good lawyer to back me up. I am also supported by an array of generous souls who have not and will never abandon me. I also write to tell you that both my physical health and my mental state are good. When you receive this letter the trial will probably be over; let us hope that I will be declared innocent. You are not aware of the present condition of this nation. This is no longer the America that . . . excited your admiration.

In any case the world is not what it once was. We are living in a sorry time. This is a time of corruption, a time in which power is desperately assailed and defends itself desperately. There is nothing so extraordinary as to be surprising.

I could even, despite my innocence, be found guilty a second time. But, by God, this error will not endure. Time is a gentleman and will prove us right.

The trial of Nicola Sacco and Bartolomeo Vanzetti for robbery and murder at South Braintree began on May 31, 1921, in Dedham, Massachusetts. The defense lawyers were Fred Moore, the McAnarney brothers, and William J. Callahan, a young Brockton attorney who was originally retained to represent Vanzetti at Plymouth and then replaced by Vahey. The prosecutor was Frederick G. Katzmann, assisted by Harold P. Williams. The judge was Webster Thayer, who presumably requested the assignment. Thayer should have disqualified himself, or been disqualified, because of his hatred of anarchists; in April, 1920, he had rebuked a jury for acquitting an anarchist who had done nothing but express his views.* [38]

Thayer should also have been disqualified because he had already judged Vanzetti at Plymouth. Thomas McAnarney later said Thayer believed Sacco and Vanzetti were guilty "from the mere fact that he sat on Vanzetti's trial . . . and had sentenced him to . . . 12 to 15 years . . . and that same man coming before him charged with a somewhat similar crime, I couldn't help but feel we were up against a stone wall."[40]

The stone wall was even thicker than the attorneys realized. Katzmann had to redeem his reputation and Thayer had to save the republic. Then there was the foreman of the jury, Walter H. Ripley, former chief of police in Quincy. An Italian policeman would later testify that Ripley "was a very strong man against the Italians; he had a very strong feeling against Italians. He never would address an Italian as an Italian but he would address him as 'Dago' or other names like that. . . . He always said that if he had the power of it he would keep them out of the country."[41]

When Ripley was on his way to the jury panel at Dedham, he discussed the Sacco-Vanzetti case with a friend he had known for thirty-eight years, a contractor named William H. Daly. Daly later said in a sworn affidavit that he had expressed his own opinion to Ripley that the two "ginneys" were innocent. Ripley replied, "Damn them, they ought to hang them anyway!"[42]

*Judge Elijah Adlow, formerly chief justice of the Boston Municipal Court, has said that Thayer's phobia dated back to an incident in 1919, when Judge Albert F. Hayden sentenced May Day demonstrators in Roxbury to heavy prison terms and two months later had his front porch blown to splinters by a bomb.[39]

The C

16

Dedham: The Prosecution

The transcript of the trial of Sācco and Vanzetti runs to 2,266 printed pages, from the clerk's opening statement to the jury's verdict. The record has convinced some, including the jury, that Sacco and Vanzetti were guilty. It has convinced others, including two of the outstanding legal scholars of the period, Supreme Court Justice Louis Brandeis and Professor Felix Frankfurter, that they were innocent. Many persons such as foreman Ripley determined guilt or innocence without seriously considering the record, for what happened in the courtroom at Dedham was strangely irrelevant to the Sacco-Vanzetti case; the biases that influenced the judge and jury were implanted long before the trial began and the best efforts and evidence for the defense came after it ended.

Sacco and Vanzetti were tried for the crime that took place in South Braintree on April 15, 1920, when a band of five robbers seized the payroll at the Slater & Morrill Shoe Company, killed the paymaster, Frederick A. Parmenter, and the guard, Alessandro Berardelli, and departed in a shiny new Buick. Though over fifteen thousand dollars was stolen, the prosecutor did not try to link Sacco and Vanzetti to the spoils, since he could find no links, nor did he identify the other three bandits, since he did not know who they were. These two essential elements were never part of the prosecution's case.

Instead, the commonwealth offered sixteen witnesses who were supposed to identify Sacco as one of the criminals, a remarkable investigative achievement since at the preliminary hearing at Quincy a year earlier, Sacco was not positively identified by anyone. One witness, Lewis L. Wade, had said, "I do not want to make a mistake. This is too damn serious, but he looks like the man."[1] When Wade was called upon to identify Sacco at Dedham, he equivocated. "Well, he resembles,—looks somewhat," Wade said vaguely. Pressed for a more positive statement, Wade replied, "Well, I ain't sure now. I have a little doubt." Judge Thayer intervened to ask, "What is your best recollection, if you have any; what is your best judgment?" Wade responded, "Well, my best judgment is this: If I have a doubt, I don't think he is the man."[2] Lewis Wade, who had worked for Slater & Morrill for sixteen years, was fired by the company shortly afterward.

Louis DeBeradinis had seen the bandit car go by as it made its escape; a robber on the front seat had pointed a gun at him. Asked by Assistant District Attorney Harold P. Williams to describe the man, DeBeradinis replied, "He had a long face . . . and awful white, and light hair." Williams insisted DeBeradinis had said, when he saw Sacco in the Brockton police station, "I have an idea that is the one that pointed the revolver at me. I am not sure that is the man. It looks to me, but I am not going to say for sure." DeBeradinis insisted he had said, "The one I saw was light, and Sacco was dark." The examination continued with the assistant district attorney and his witness haggling over who had said what to whom.[3]

Of the prosecution's sixteen witnesses against Sacco, only seven identified him with varying degrees of certainty and credibility. William S. Tracey had noticed two men standing outside a drugstore near the robbery site; he assumed they were waiting for a trolley. He believed that one of the men was Sacco. "While I wouldn't be positive," he said, "I would say to the best of my recollection that was the man."[4] Tracey had seen the two men at

The

about 11:35 A.M. No evidence was offered that the two men Tracey had seen took part in the crime three-and-one-half hours later, nor had Tracey seen the holdup.

William J. Heron saw two men in the South Braintree railroad station between 12:30 and 1 P.M. the day of the robbery. Heron was "pretty sure" Sacco was one of them.[5] He said the two men spoke Italian but admitted he himself did not speak or understand Italian and wasn't certain he knew the difference between Italian and French or Spanish. Like Tracey, Heron did not see the robbery.

Louis Pelser said he saw the robbery from a window in the Rice & Hutchins shoe factory, which overlooked the holdup site, and claimed he saw one of the bandits shoot Berardelli. Pelser said of Sacco, "I wouldn't say he is the man, but he is the dead image of the man I seen."[6] During cross-examination it developed that Pelser had previously told the defense he had not seen the shooting and had told the police he had not seen enough to be able to identify anyone. One of Pelser's coworkers testified that when the shooting began, Pelser, like the rest of the men, ducked under a workbench in the shop.[7]

Carlos E. Goodridge rushed out of a poolroom when he heard the shooting and saw the getaway car. One of the men pointed a gun at him; Goodridge identified him as Sacco.[8] Three other witnesses testified Goodridge had told them he couldn't identify anyone in the car; another said Goodridge had mentioned only a "young man with light hair." The defense tried to introduce the fact that Goodridge not only had a long criminal record but was on probation on a larceny charge, which may have affected his willingness to cooperate with the prosecution. After a conference at the bench which Thayer would not allow the stenographer to record, the judge ruled this evidence inadmissible.

Lola Andrews was looking for a job on the morning of April 15. At about 11:30 A.M.—the same time William Tracey saw the man he thought was Sacco standing outside a drugstore—Mrs. Andrews passed an automobile parked near the Slater & Morrill factory. A sickly-looking, fair-haired man was sitting on the back seat while a darker one bent over the hood. When Mrs. Andrews left Slater & Morrill fifteen minutes later, the lighter man was standing behind the car, while the darker one was lying with his head and shoulders beneath it, repairing something. Mrs. Andrews asked the darker man for directions to the Rice & Hutchins office; she identified him as Sacco.[9] Five witnesses testified that Mrs. Andrews had lied or changed her story. One was a woman who had been job hunting with her that day and said there had been no such encounter. A sixth witness, trying to verify Mrs. Andrews's account, testified that Mrs. Andrews had said she tapped Sacco on the shoulder to get his attention. In *The Legacy of Sacco and Vanzetti*, Professor Edmund Morgan wondered why Mrs. Andrews asked directions of the man beneath the car when another was standing nearby, and how she managed to tap him on the shoulder.[10]

Mary Splaine, from a second floor window at Slater & Morrill, saw the Buick depart. She said a man was standing between the front and rear seats, leaning out of the car window. Though he was in view for less than four seconds, and the street was sixty feet away, Miss Splaine identified the man as Sacco. Under cross-examination she admitted she had originally picked out a rogues-gallery photo of another man as the one she had seen leaning out of the car. This man's photo was also selected by other witnesses, but he had an unimpeachable alibi since he was in prison the day of the robbery. When Miss Splaine saw Sacco with a group of other prisoners, she did not identify him as the bandit; at the preliminary hearing in Quincy she had said, "I don't think my opportunity [to see him] afforded me the right to say he is the man."[11] Yet at Dedham she identified Sacco without hesitation. "From the observation I had of him in the Quincy court and the comparison of the man I saw in the machine, on reflection I was sure he was the same man," she said.[12]

Frances Devlin, who worked in the same room as Mary Splaine, also saw a man leaning out of the car. At Quincy she was asked, "Do you say positively that he [Sacco] is the man?" She replied, "I don't say positively."[13] By the time she got to Dedham, she was positive.[14]

Professor Morgan, in analyzing the testimony of witnesses such as Miss Devlin and Miss Splaine, noted that before one's imagination can be altered to fit a prejudice or suspicion, it is first

The

opposed by memory, but eventually memory is erased and imagination triumphs.[15] The Braintree police chief, Jeremiah Gallivan, who was present at the preliminary hearings in Quincy as well as the trial in Dedham, put it more piquantly when he said, "I couldn't understand it, how they [the witnesses] got stronger in Dedham than they was in Quincy."[16]

The defense produced seventeen eyewitnesses to the robbery. Two said they couldn't tell whether or not Sacco was one of the robbers; the other fifteen testified he was not one of the bandits they saw either before, during, or after the crime.

Of the thirty-three eyewitnesses called by both sides, only seven identified Sacco. Three said they saw him before the robbery: Tracey, who spotted him in front of a drugstore before noon; Heron, who was "pretty sure" Sacco was at the railroad station at 12:30 or 1 P.M., and Lola Andrews, who tapped him on the shoulder while he was under a car, head first. A fourth witness, Pelser, said Sacco was the "dead image" of the man who shot Berardelli; a coworker said Pelser was under a bench at the time. Three more witnesses said they saw Sacco after the holdup: Goodridge, the man on probation; and the two women, Splaine and Devlin, whose memory improved with time. The seven persons who claimed to have seen Sacco dressed him variously in a dark suit, in green pants with a brown shirt, or in a gray shirt with no jacket.

Katzmann began his case with sixteen persons he thought would identify Sacco, though nine disappointed him. He had only four witnesses to testify against Vanzetti, each weaker than the next, even though Vanzetti had a much more memorable face than Sacco; it was impossible to miss that moustache.

One of the witnesses was Michael Levangie, the gate-tender at the railroad crossing in South Braintree, who was ordered by the bandits to raise the gates for them. Interviewed by a reporter within half an hour after the robbery, Levangie was asked if he could identify the men. Levangie replied that he was too scared to see anyone. Three other men spoke to or overheard Levangie after the incident. He repeated the same story, that he had seen a gun pointed at him and run for the safety of his shanty. He did tell one man that the driver had a light complexion; the one point on which virtually everyone agreed was that the driver of the car was pale, fair haired, and sickly looking.

When questioned by a Pinkerton detective on April 18, Levangie had changed his description of the driver to "black hair, dark complexion, clean shaven, and long hooked nose"[17] which, while markedly different from the original description, still did not describe Vanzetti; the moustache was missing. Yet when Levangie saw Vanzetti at the Brockton police station he decided he recognized him and at Dedham, Levangie testified that Vanzetti drove the bandit car.*[18]

Levangie's testimony putting Vanzetti in the driver's seat was a doubtful boon for the prosecution.† The assistant district attorney, in his opening remarks to the jury, had already described the driver as "this light-haired man with an emaciated face" adding "as they came across [the tracks] he [Levangie] noticed on the front seat an Italian with a moustache, I believe with a slouch hat on, whom he identified as the other defendant, Bartolomeo Vanzetti."[21]

This put Vanzetti on the front seat next to the driver, until Levangie insisted Vanzetti was the driver. But as the trial developed, the man most of the witnesses described on the front seat

*An inquest was conducted April 17, 1920, two days after the robbery and murders, but the minutes were not made available to the defense until 1927. In the minutes as released in 1927, Levangie described the driver as having a "dark complexion, dark brown moustache." The moustache was emphasized by the device of asking Levangie about it again in a separate question.

Ehrmann made the following points: on April 15, immediately after the shooting, Levangie said he could not recognize any of the men, but the driver had a light complexion. On April 18, Levangie changed his description of the driver but the man was still clean shaven. On April 21, four days after the inquest, the police issued descriptions of the bandits. The driver was reported as "age 25, 5 feet 7 inches, 130 pounds, light complexion, dimple in cheek, sallow skin." All of the bandits are described as smooth shaven; there is no moustache anywhere. How could Levangie have said on April 15 and April 18 that the man was smooth shaven and on April 17 given him a moustache? If the inquest testimony, when finally released, had differed markedly from the trial testimony, it would indicate Levangie had committed perjury at Dedham. Ehrmann wondered, "Was the brown moustache in the original transcript or was it inserted at a later date?"[19]

†There was also a witness ready to testify that Sacco was the driver of the holdup car, but the prosecution, having two drivers already, did not call upon her. Neither Sacco nor Vanzetti owned a car or knew how to drive.[20]

The C

alongside the driver did not look at all like Vanzetti, so it was necessary to move him again, which Katzmann did in his summation to the jury. Katzmann acknowledged Levangie was wrong when he said Vanzetti drove the car, ignored the opening statement about Vanzetti sitting next to the driver, and glibly suggested to the jury "the possibility, no the likelihood or more than that, the probability that at that time Vanzetti was directly behind the driver in the quick glance this man Levangie had of the car."[22]

The second witness who identified Vanzetti was Austin T. Reed, the gatetender at the railroad crossing at Matfield, about twenty miles from South Braintree. Reed put Vanzetti on the seat beside the driver and testified Vanzetti had called out to him, "What to hell I was holding him up for?"[23] Moore pounced on this in cross-examination.

Moore: And his salutation to you was in a loud, bold voice, in the English phraseology that you saw fit to give, something I believe to the effect, "What in hell did you stop us for?"

Reed: Yes, sir.

            *   *   *

Moore: And the voice was loud and full and strong back forty feet. Is that right?

Reed: Yes, sir.

Moore: What?

Reed: Yes, sir.

Moore: With a running motor?

Reed: Yes, sir.

Moore: And a train passing,—approaching?

Reed: Yes, sir.

Moore: The quality of the English was unmistakable and clear?

Reed: Why—

Moore: Is that right? Answer yes or no. What?

Reed: Yes.[24]

By 1927, Vanzetti had had the enforced leisure to become fairly proficient in English, but it was still neither unmistakable nor entirely clear. In 1920, it was awkward and broken; when

Vanzetti testified the jurors themselves would hear how badly he spoke.

The prosecution had only two other witnesses against Vanzetti when the trial began. Austin Cole, the conductor of the trolley on which Sacco and Vanzetti were arrested, testified that both men had boarded his car in West Bridgewater on the evening of either April 14 or 15; he wasn't sure which.[25] This testimony, if true, brought Sacco and Vanzetti together, but it did not relate to the crime at South Braintree.

John W. Faulkner said he saw Vanzetti on a train on the morning of April 15 carrying a black bag, and that Vanzetti got off at East Braintree.[26] Faulkner's description of the coach in which he rode was contradicted by the conductor, the ticket agent at East Braintree, the assistant trainmaster, and the railroad company. The ticket agent at East Braintree said he had seen a tall man with a black bag get off the train a number of times, but it was not Vanzetti. The conductor testified he had taken no fares from Plymouth or any stop near Plymouth to any Braintree stop the morning of April 15. The ticket agents at Plymouth and nearby, stations did not sell tickets to any Braintree stops that morning, and none of them recognized Vanzetti.

A fifth witness against Vanzetti turned up among the men summoned for the jury panel. When Harry E. Dolbeare saw Vanzetti in the courtroom he thought he remembered seeing him in South Braintree on the morning of April 15 in an automobile with a "tough looking bunch."[27] There was no further indication this was the holdup gang.

Thus the five witnesses against Vanzetti were Levangie, who barely glimpsed him, changed his story several times, and finally put him in the wrong seat in the car; Reed, who at a distance of 40 feet, with a train approaching, heard him curse in unmistakable and clear English; Cole, who said he saw him on a trolley at another time and place; Faulkner, who said he saw him on a train but was contradicted by every responsible person who could have confirmed his story; and Dolbeare, who said he saw him in a car on the morning of the robbery.

Professor Morgan commented, "If there could be weaker evidence of identity of two human beings, it rarely appears as a

The C

basis for conviction in court records. . . . A reading of the record almost forces the conclusion that no reasonable jury could have been satisfied by the identification testimony alone of the guilt of either Sacco or Vanzetti."[28] Even Judge Thayer conceded this. In denying a defense motion for a new trial based on the discovery of another eyewitness, Thayer wrote, "These verdicts did not rest, in my judgment, upon the testimony of the eyewitnesses, for the defendants, as it was, called more witnesses than the Commonwealth who testified that neither of the defendants were in the bandit car." [29]

What did the verdicts rest on? The prosecution also presented physical evidence against Sacco and Vanzetti. They failed to present such pertinent physical evidence as the fingerprints on the abandoned Buick or the stolen money; instead they offered a gun, a cap, and a bullet. The cap and bullet were intended to link Sacco to the crime; the gun was Vanzetti's.

In his opening statement to the jury, Assistant District Attorney Williams mentioned that Vanzetti carried a revolver the night he was arrested, but he gave it no particular emphasis; he said Vanzetti would be implicated by eyewitness testimony. At some point during the trial—perhaps after realizing how feeble the eyewitness testimony was—the prosecution developed a new theory. The revolver in Vanzetti's pocket was no longer an ordinary .38 caliber Harrington & Richardson; it became the gun that belonged to the slain guard, Berardelli.

Berardelli usually carried a Harrington & Richardson revolver, but none was found on his body, so the prosecution decided to put the absent revolver in Vanzetti's pocket. Before it could be absent it had to be present, yet the prosecution offered no evidence that Berardelli was carrying his gun at the time of the robbery or that any of the robbers was seen taking it from him. Since Berardelli was shot immediately, without resistance, no one ever explained why a bandit would waste time rummaging in the dying man's pockets—he wore both a jacket and an overcoat—to look for his gun. The entire argument rested on one witness who said he saw a bandit push what might have been one of the money boxes into the car with his right hand while he held what "looked like a white gun"[30] in his left hand. Another witness with a better view said the bandit had used both hands to pick up the money box while a third witness said the two money boxes were put into the car by two other bandits, but since Vanzetti's gun was nickle-plated, it became Berardelli's "white gun."

The prosecution put Berardelli's widow on the stand and asked her to examine Vanzetti's gun. She said it looked like her husband's. Further questioning revealed that about three weeks before he was shot, Berardelli had taken the revolver, which was loaned to him by Parmenter when he was hired as a guard, to a repair shop because the spring was broken. On cross-examination, Mrs. Berardelli was asked if the revolver came back from the repair shop. "I don't know," she replied.[31]

Later, the defense called Aldeah Florence, a neighbor with whom Mrs. Berardelli boarded for four months after her husband's death. Mrs. Florence testified that three or four days after Berardelli's funeral, Mrs. Berardelli told her, "If he had taken my advice and taken the revolver out of the shop he would not be, maybe he would not be in the same condition he is today."[32] Katzmann did not call Mrs. Berardelli back to the stand to contradict Mrs. Florence, which confirms that Mrs. Florence was telling the truth. Another prosecution witness, James Bostock, a millwright who did a lot of repair work for Slater & Morrill, testified Berardelli had shown him the revolver the Saturday night before the shooting.[33] But Bostock also did not hold up under cross-examination. He changed his story to say Berardelli had shown him the gun once, the first time Bostock asked him if he carried one. It was no longer the Saturday night before the shooting but "one morning right at the elevator."[34] Bostock also said Berardelli let him hold the gun.

Jeremiah
McAnarney: What did you do then?
Bostock: I looked at it.
McAnarney: Did you, really?
Bostock: Yes, sir.
McAnarney: Have you a distinct recollection of anything on that revolver?
Bostock: No, sir, not one particularly. I couldn't tell it if I saw it again.

McAnarney: And that is the only time you saw it?

Bostock: Yes, sir. I have seen it a number of times in his possession.

McAnarney: But you couldn't tell it again?

Bostock: No, sir.

McAnarney: And you don't know whether this [Vanzetti's] is the revolver?

Bostock: No, sir.[35]

Berardelli's gun had been taken for repairs to the Iver Johnson Sporting Goods Company, which did not record the serial number. Lincoln Wadsworth, who worked for the company, testified he had received Berardelli's .38 for repairs and that Vanzetti's revolver was "the same caliber and make,"[36] by which Wadsworth meant only that it was a Harrington & Richardson .38, not that it was Berardelli's, though that is how everyone, including the jury and the defense attorneys, interpreted Wadsworth's statement.* Neither Wadsworth nor anyone else at Iver Johnson had any records to show the gun had been picked up, though it was no longer at the shop.

The prosecution also summoned George F. Fitzemeyer, the repairman at Iver Johnson. Fitzemeyer bulldozed all previous testimony by saying Berardelli's revolver was a .32 not a .38 and that it needed a new hammer, not a new spring. Asked to examine Vanzetti's revolver, Fitzemeyer said it had a new hammer, which suggested it might be Berardelli's after all, even though it was the wrong caliber.

The prosecution's testimony on Berardelli's gun produced

---

*In 1927, Wadsworth, who had been a special agent for the Justice Department and could not be accused of harboring secret sympathies for anarchists, voluntarily testified for the defense before the Lowell Committee. He told the committee he had tried to explain to the assistant district attorney that while it was possible that Vanzetti's revolver and Berardelli's were the same, it was just "a very slim chance." Wadsworth said that "Mr. Williams did not seem to want to have that at all, so that I just let be on it. And then in the courtroom I felt sure I would have a chance to say the same thing that I have said here, but when the time came to be cross-examined I simply was not, that was all, and I went down on the records . . . that that was the pistol." Wadsworth was asked whether he thought Vanzetti's revolver was Berardelli's. He replied, "There are thousands of times more chances that it was not than that it was."[37]

nothing but contradictions and chaos, while the defense was able to trace the history of the revolver Vanzetti carried. When Vanzetti was arrested, he had lied about the gun because he bought it from a fellow anarchist he did not want to implicate, but at the trial a Maine Yankee named Rexford Slater testified he had bought the gun from his mother-in-law and later sold it to Ricardo Orciani. Orciani did not testify but a man named Luigi Falzini said he bought the gun from Orciani and sold it to Vanzetti in January or February of 1920.

Yet carefully picking his way through the wreckage of his evidence, Katzmann, in his summation to the jury, reconstructed the crime to say that Sacco had taken the gun from the dying Berardelli (even though it was still in the repair shop) and given it to Vanzetti (in whose pocket it was transformed from a .32 to a .38). To accept this, the jury not only had to ignore the testimony but believe that Vanzetti, who could be naive but whose instincts for self-preservation were strong, who was cautious enough to leave the country when he thought he might be drafted and to change his name when he thought he might be arrested as a draft evader, who had gone to New York to find out about Salsedo and knew he might be picked up by the government at any time as an alien anarchist, was out on the night of May 5 on a potentially hazardous anarchist mission carrying a gun which belonged to a man murdered in a sensational robbery only three weeks earlier, when he had his share of the loot with which to buy himself another weapon.

The other two pieces of physical evidence were the cap and the bullet. Fred L. Loring, who worked for Slater & Morrill, testified he had found the cap about 18 inches from Berardelli's body immediately after the shooting.[38] The prosecution knew this was untrue; the defense did not.* Loring did not find the cap near Berardelli's body; he found it in the middle of the street on the evening of April 16, almost 30 hours after the robbery. The cap was turned over to Chief Gallivan of the Braintree police, who showed it to the Pinkerton man working on the case. The

---

*Ehrmann discovered the truth about the cap in 1927 by checking a 1920 newspaper which reported when it had been found.

The Ca

Pinkerton man noted it was "an old dark color heavy winter cap about 6 $7/8$ size."[39]

Though at least two witnesses said the man they thought was Sacco wore a hat, not a cap, and the cap had been found so long after the murder it could have been lost by any passing workman, the prosecution decided to make it fit Sacco. The police went to Sacco's home and, without a warrant, seized some of his clothing, including one of his caps.* The cap they confiscated was size 7 $1/8$, which made it clear the found cap was too small to belong to Sacco. But Katzmann already knew the cap wasn't Sacco's; his skill was in building his case before a jury so willing to believe they never noticed he was using all mortar and no bricks.

Assistant District Attorney Williams called George Kelley, Sacco's superintendent at the 3-K factory, to testify that Sacco sometimes wore a dark cap, which he hung on a nail while he was working. Williams then asked Kelley if the cap found on the street "is alike in appearance to the cap that you have described as being worn by Sacco." Kelley looked at the cap and replied, "The only thing I could say about that cap, Mr. Williams, from hanging up on a nail in the distance, it was similar in color. As far as details are concerned, I could not say it was."[40]

Williams then tried to introduce the found cap as evidence against Sacco. When Jeremiah McAnarney objected, Judge Thayer came to Williams's assistance.

Thayer: I would like to ask the witness one question: whether,—I wish you would ask him, rather,— according to your best judgment, is it your opinion that the cap which Mr. Williams now holds in his hand is like the one that was worn by the defendant Sacco?

Moore: I object to that question, your Honor.

Thayer (to Williams): Did you put it? I would rather it come from Mr. Williams. Will you put that question?

Williams: Mr. Kelley, according to your best judgment, is the

---

*Before the Plymouth trial, Chief Stewart searched Vanzetti's room, without a warrant and without success, looking for the dark overcoat worn by the shotgun bandit.

	cap I show you alike in appearance to the cap worn by Sacco?
Kelley:	In color only.
Thayer:	That is not responsive to the question. I wish you would answer it, if you can.
Kelley:	I can't answer it when I don't know right down in my heart that that is the cap.
Thayer:	I don't want you to. I want you should answer according to what is in your heart.
Kelley:	General appearance, that is all I can say. I never saw that cap so close in my life as I do now.
Thayer:	In its general appearance, is it the same?
Kelley:	Yes, sir.
Moore:	I object to that last question and answer.
Thayer:	You may put the question so it comes from counsel rather than from the Court.
Williams:	In its general appearance, is it the same?
Kelley:	Yes.
Williams:	I now offer the cap, if your Honor please.
Thayer:	Admitted.[41]

With Thayer's help, the prosecution had gotten a cap found thirty hours after the robbery admitted into evidence as Sacco's cap, found near the body of Berardelli. They then offered as evidence the cap taken from Sacco's home. Moore objected because it was seized without a warrant, but Thayer admitted it anyway. During Sacco's cross-examination he was given his own cap and asked if he could identify it. "It looks like my cap," he replied. He was asked to put it on, which he did. Asked to put on the cap found in the street, Sacco tried, but it was too small. "Can't go in," he said.

Katzmann:	Can't go in?
Sacco:	No.
Katzmann:	Try and pull it down in back and see if it can't go in?
Sacco:	Oh, but it is too tight.

Katzmann, who knew very well what the answer was, asked Sacco, "What is the difference in size between those two hats?" Sacco said he didn't know, but that the second cap was too tight.

The

Katzmann:	Is it any tighter than that hat [Sacco's cap]?
Sacco:	Yes, lots.
Katzmann:	Lots tighter?
Sacco:	Yes.
Katzmann:	You are sure of that?
Sacco:	I am pretty sure. I can feel it.

Katzmann tried to get Sacco to say the second cap was tighter because it was made of heavier material. Sacco replied, "I don't say if it is material." But Katzmann was not to be defeated; he had another ploy to distract both Sacco and the jury. The found cap had a tear in the lining. Seizing upon George Kelley's observation that Sacco hung his cap on a nail, Katzmann asked Sacco to examine the lining of his own cap.

Sacco:	I never saw that before.
Katzmann:	What is it?
Sacco:	I don't know.
Katzmann:	Don't know what that is?
Sacco:	It is a hole.
Katzmann:	It is a hole?
Sacco:	Yes.
Katzmann:	And you never saw that before?
Sacco:	No.
Katzmann:	Still you say that is your hat?
Sacco:	Sure. Never saw that [hole] before.[42]

Katzmann wanted to prove that since Sacco hung his cap on a nail, and both caps had holes in the lining, both caps belonged to Sacco. The size of the found cap was never mentioned, nor was the fact that when it was found it had no hole. Chief Gallivan of the Braintree police testified in 1927, "That cap was whole when it was given to me, but I am the fellow that tore it."[43] Gallivan opened the lining seeking a name or some other kind of identification, which he did not find. Since the prosecution received the found cap with the hole made by Gallivan the conveniently matching hole in Sacco's cap supported the claim that both caps belonged to Sacco and made false evidence credible.

The most important, complicated, and controversial physical evidence presented at Dedham was based upon the prosecution's assertion that the bullet that killed Berardelli came from Sacco's gun. Because this would clinch the case against Sacco, what is most significant in evaluating it is that when the trial began, the prosecution had no intention of making any such claim.

When Sacco was arrested he had a loaded Colt .32 automatic pistol in the waistband of his trousers and over twenty loose cartridges in his jacket pocket; the exact number was never verified. All of the bullets fired during the robbery came from either a .32 automatic or a foreign pistol of comparable make, which made Sacco's gun immediately suspect. The commonwealth's leading ballistics expert, Captain William Proctor, examined the six bullets taken from the two bodies, four from Berardelli, two from Parmenter. He found that five of the bullets could not have been fired by Sacco's gun because they came from a weapon with a right twist, while Colt automatics had a left twist, that is, the spiral grooves inside the barrel twisted to the left. The one bullet that could have been fired from Sacco's gun was the shot that killed Berardelli. Since the surgeon who did the autopsies marked each bullet with a Roman numeral as he removed it, this is known as bullet III.

As Proctor later explained in an affidavit:

> During the preparation for the trial, my attention was repeatedly called by the district attorney and his assistants to the question: whether I could find any evidence which would justify the opinion that the particular bullet taken from the body of Berardelli, which came from a Colt automatic pistol, came from the particular Colt automatic pistol taken from Sacco. I used every means available to me for forming an opinion on this subject. . . . At no time was I able to find any evidence whatever which tended to convince me that the particular model bullet . . . came from Sacco's pistol and I so informed the district attorney and his assistant before the trial.[44]

Understandably displeased with this opinion, the prosecution called in a second expert, Charles J. Van Amburgh. While it is not known what Van Amburgh said at that point, it is reasonable to assume he also doubted that the bullet was fired from Sacco's gun, because Katzmann, in a private conversation with Moore which the jury never knew about, told the attorney he would not attempt to offer proof that any particular bullet came from any particular gun, obviously because there was no such proof.

Several days after the trial began it finally occurred to Moore that if the prosecution was unwilling to present ballistics evidence, it meant the evidence was in Sacco's favor; if Katzmann could not use the tests to convict Sacco, Moore could use them to clear him. Before proceeding, however, Moore and Thomas McAnarney took the precaution of carefully explaining to Sacco that the tests would show whether or not the fatal bullet was fired from his gun. McAnarney said that Sacco told them to "experiment all they wished."[45] Since Sacco knew whether or not he was guilty, his immediate acquiescence is incontrovertible proof of consciousness of innocence.

On June 5, while the trial was in progress, Moore asked Thayer's permission to have ballistics tests conducted, and the judge consented. But the attorney had made a fatal misjudgment. As an experienced lawyer, Moore had been wise enough to check with Sacco to be sure of his innocence, but as an experienced radical, he had forgotten that the ballistics evidence was in the hands of the commonwealth.

The tests were conducted on June 18 by three experts. Proctor and Van Amburgh represented the prosecution; James E. Burns, a ballistics engineer at the United States Cartridge Company, represented the defense. A number of bullets were fired from Sacco's gun, then compared with the six bullets presumably extracted during the autopsies and four spent shells presumably found at the scene of the crime. Three of the spent shells could not have been fired from Sacco's gun; one could have, which theoretically mated the fatal bullet with its shell. Since careful records were not kept of the evidence found, Ehrmann wondered if the convenient shell was a coincidental act of God or deliberate manipulation, such as the extra shotgun shell of the necessary make found in Vanzetti's pocket or the hole in Sacco's cap.[46]

After the ballistics tests, the three experts offered three different opinions. Proctor said there was no proof Sacco's gun had fired the fatal bullet. Van Amburgh said it might have. Burns said it definitely did not.* Proctor told Katzmann and Williams that if he was asked at the trial whether bullet III was fired from Sacco's pistol "I should be obliged to answer in the negative," Therefore, Williams phrased his questions with deliberate deceit, and Proctor cooperated fully.

Williams: Have you an opinion as to whether bullet 3 was fired from the Colt automatic [Sacco's gun] which is in evidence?

Proctor: I have.

Williams: And what is your opinion?

Proctor: My opinion is that it is consistent with being fired by that pistol.[47]

Since Proctor was not asked to clarify that statement during cross-examination, the jury assumed he was saying Sacco's gun fired the fatal bullet. In his affidavit dated October 20, 1923, more than two years after the trial was over, Proctor explained that what he said was correct:

> Bullet number 3 in my judgment, passed through some Colt automatic pistol, but I do not intend by that answer to imply that I had found any evidence that the so-called mortal bullet had passed through this particular Colt automatic pistol and the district attorney well knew that I did not so intend and framed his question accordingly. Had I been asked the direct question: whether I had found any affirmative evidence whatever that this so-called mortal bullet had passed through this particular Sacco's pistol, I should have answered then, as I do now without hesitation, in the negative.†[48]

---

*Ballistics experts often disagree; they also err. Ehrmann gives examples of serious ballistics errors in *The Case That Will Not Die*, pp. 263 and 281–82.

†Proctor's affidavit seems disingenuous. He must have agreed to cooperate with the prosecution for some reason; perhaps he feared for his job. When he finally spoke up, the jury, influenced by his misleading testimony, had rendered its

By carefully wording its questions, the prosecution had made a negative opinion sound positive. The jurors did not hear any of the private discussions or deals; all they heard was the head of the state police say that the fatal bullet was "consistent with" being fired from Sacco's pistol. In his charge to the jury, Judge Thayer said Proctor had testified that Sacco's gun fired the fatal bullet.[49]

The prosecution's second ballistics expert, Van Amburgh, asked directly whether bullet III came from Sacco's gun, was somewhat evasive. "I am inclined to believe that it was fired, No. 3 bullet was fired, from this Colt automatic pistol," he said.[50] As for the spent shell, Proctor said it was fired from the same make of weapon as Sacco's, but he was never asked whether it was actually fired from Sacco's gun. Neither was Van Amburgh, which suggests the prosecution's experts were unwilling to commit themselves. Burns and another ballistics expert testified for the defense that neither bullet III nor the shell were fired from Sacco's pistol.

The dispute over ballistics evidence continued after the trial was over and, indeed, after Sacco and Vanzetti were dead. In 1923, during appeals for a new trial, two new experts argued for the defense that bullet III was not fired from Sacco's gun; two experts for the prosecution said that it was. Proctor had already given his affidavit to the defense, but Van Amburgh compensated for it by being no longer "inclined to believe" but "positive." During or after the presentation of this evidence, the barrel of Sacco's gun was switched, deliberately or accidentally, by either the prosecution or the defense. There is no certainty therefore that the original barrel is presently on the gun, or has been since 1923.*

In 1927, tests were conducted for the prosecution by Major Calvin Goddard, using a comparison microscope. Because Goddard had already said that bullet III and the shell had been fired by Sacco's gun, the defense refused to cosponsor the tests or send its own experts, though Herbert Ehrmann attended as an observer. Not surprisingly, Goddard confirmed his opinions about the

---

verdict, and there was no way to change it. The scenario is similar to Lincoln Wadsworth's testimony on whether Vanzetti's gun could have been Berardelli's in the duplicity of the prosecution, the density of the defense attorneys in not properly cross-examining the witness, and the seizure of conscience that came too late.
*See page 286 ff.

bullet and shell. However something more significant occurred. For the first time Ehrmann closely examined the four bullets allegedly taken from Berardelli's body. The doctor who did the autopsies had marked the bullets by scratching the bases with a needle; this was evident on bullets I, II, and IIII, which had fine, straight lines. The marks on controversial bullet III, however, were thick, ragged, and wobbly; they seemed to have been made with another instrument.[51] Even Goddard admitted there was a difference.[52]

A question arose which still hangs over the Sacco-Vanzetti case: was bullet III removed from Berardelli's body during the autopsy or was it fired by the prosecution from Sacco's gun and substituted for the fatal bullet?

Though new ballistics tests were conducted as recently as 1961, none of the tests are meaningful except perhaps those conducted before the trial, since there is no assurance the experts were testing the authentic bullet or the authentic gun barrel. Whether bullet III is authentic or not can be resolved by the undisputed fact that when the trial began, Katzmann did not intend to use ballistics evidence and Sacco did not object to the testing of his gun.

The

17

Dedham: The Defense

Vanzetti had not testified at the Plymouth trial for fear his views would be held against him; in the end his silence was held against him. At Dedham, both Sacco and Vanzetti had to testify no matter what the consequences. Only an explanation of their background and beliefs could justify their mysterious behavior the night they were arrested, their being armed, their lies. In 1927, John McAnarney told the Lowell Committee, "They [his brothers] consulted with me, and I take full responsibility of [*sic*] this branch of the defense, as to whether or not the radicalism of the defendants should be disclosed. I reminded them of the statement of Judge Sherman, 'If your client is innocent, put him on the stand and tell the truth; if he is guilty, keep him off the stand.'"[1]

Vanzetti testified first. His alibi for April 15 was so feeble it had to be true; any story invented for or by him would have been more convincing.

According to Vanzetti, he spent the morning of April 15 selling fish. About noon he met a cloth peddler, Joseph Rosen, who offered him a piece of material for a suit at a bargain price because there was a hole in it. Since Vanzetti's friend and former landlady, Alfonsina Brini, had worked in a woolen mill, he decided to get her opinion of the cloth. Vanzetti knew she was home because she had been ill, so he and Rosen went to the Brini house and showed Mrs. Brini the material. Rosen then left and waited outside while Vanzetti spoke to Mrs. Brini. When Vanzetti came out of the house he bought the cloth. Then he took his cart and went off to sell the rest of his fish.

Afterward, he went down to the shore where he saw Melvin Corl, a fisherman he knew, who was painting his boat. While they chatted, two other men came by. After an hour and a half or more, Vanzetti pushed his cart back to the Fortini house. It was a typical Vanzetti day.[2]

Rosen, Corl, Mrs. Brini, and her daughter Lefevre corroborated Vanzetti's story, as did several minor witnesses. In cross-examination, Katzmann used the device for discrediting witnesses that had worked so well at Plymouth; he asked them what they were doing on other days or times chosen at random, and when they couldn't answer, it appeared they were lying for Vanzetti. Corl, the fisherman who was with Vanzetti about the time the robbery was taking place in South Braintree, said he remembered the date because he had finished painting his boat the following day, which made it possible to use the boat again on April 17, his wife's birthday. After Katzmann mauled Corl's memory by flinging other dates at him, Jeremiah McAnarney tried to undo the damage by making the only relevant rebuttal.

McAnarney: Well, in your life there has only been one friend of yours in the last year that was in any way connected with a murder or charge, has there not?

Corl: Yes.

McAnarney: Whether or not the fact that Mr. Vanzetti was charged with murder and you learned of that along the 5th or 6th of May, helps you now to fix your mind back on what transpired on the 15th?

Corl: Yes, sir.[3]

Katzmann saved his greatest scorn for the Brinis, Alfonsina and Lefevre. He hammered at Mrs. Brini on the stand, trying to

The C

prove she couldn't possibly be sure the incident with the cloth peddler took place April 15. Mrs. Brini, who used an interpreter, insisted she remembered the date because her illness had become worse the previous day, and a doctor came to see her the morning of the 15th.

Alfonsina
Brini:

*Too bad you can't talk with your language, because they break you—they break you up when they want to. You testify one thing, they start something else. Bad people there. You know, they make their law the way they want it.**

The defense either considered Mrs. Brini a poor witness or feared Katzmann would use her to introduce the Plymouth conviction because the following day, rather than have Katzmann cross-examine her further, they agreed to put the following on record: "It is agreed by counsel for the Commonwealth and counsel for the defendant as follows: that this witness, Alphonsin [*sic*] Brini has, in another case, testified on behalf of the defendant Vanzetti as to his whereabouts different from the place set forth in that case."[4]

Mrs. Brini had not testified as to Vanzetti's whereabouts at the time of the first robbery, her son had. She had testified that she saw Vanzetti the night before the robbery and on Christmas Eve. But Vanzetti's lawyers did not bother to check this, so they agreed to Katzmann's statement that Mrs. Brini had lied for Vanzetti in another case. In his summation, Katzmann called her "a stock, convenient and ready witness as well as friend of the defendant Vanzetti."[5]

Having disposed of the mother with the help of Vanzetti's lawyers, Katzmann went to work on the daughter. Fifteen-year-old Lefevre Brini, who left school at the age of fourteen to go to work,[6] was home on April 15 taking care of her sick mother. She testified she was setting the table about noon when Vanzetti came with the cloth peddler, and she knew it was April 15 because "it was just one week after I left my work to take care of my mother, who came home from the hospital."[7]

Katzmann: Will you tell this jury, Miss Brini, if when you saw

*Interview with author.

	the cloth on a day with Mr. Vanzetti and the gentle-man named Rosen, if at that time you then said to yourself, "I am looking at this cloth one week since I left my work." Did you?
L. Brini:	I don't understand you.

*   *   *

Katzmann:	Did you think at all, Miss Brini, on the day when the cloth was there, of remembering what day it was?
L. Brini:	I did not, no, then, but I did when I thought of it.[8]
Lefevre Brini:	*I was scared to death. I ran a temperature the night before. I don't think I was on the stand very long, but it was long enough to get me real mad at Mr. Katzmann. Ma had come home from the hospital, and I was taking care of her. I remember the man that came to the door with the cloth. Katzmann didn't change my testimony any, but he tried to. He got me all rattled. He didn't change anything about what I knew and what I said, because I knew darn well you can't be in two places at the same time.**

Since Vanzetti was virtually a member of the Brini family, and Lefevre Brini admitted she and her family kept information about him from the authorities when he was in Mexico, the question must fairly be asked: Did they lie for him on the stand? It is impossible to talk to Beltrando Brini and not believe he was telling the truth when he testified he was delivering eels with Vanzetti at the time of the first crime. The details are too clear in his mind; his agony at the injustice is too real. No one, least of all a guileless man like Brini, could sustain a fraudulent role for so many years, particularly since he had little to gain and much to lose; his defense of Vanzetti could have destroyed his career. It is equally impossible to disbelieve Alfonsina and Lefevre Brini. Alfonsina Brini repeated her story when interviewed ten months before she died at the age of 92; so did Lefevre Brini, who still weeps over what was done to an innocent man.

To assume, for a moment, that mother, daughter, and Corl lied for Vanzetti out of friendship, that still leaves the cloth peddler, Joseph Rosen, who was a stranger to him. The immigrant

*Interview with author.

The (

attitude was to stay away from trouble, and the courts meant trouble, authority, the law. Rosen could have had no motive to testify for Vanzetti except the desire to tell the truth.

Sacco had a better alibi than Vanzetti for his whereabouts on April 15, but he did not have the one alibi that would have saved him; he was not at work that day. If he had been, there would have been no Sacco-Vanzetti case. For the jury, if Sacco was not at work he was robbing a payroll in South Braintree; no other explanation would do.

When Sacco received the letter from Sabino telling him that their mother had died, he had decided it was time to return to Torremaggiore. On April 15, he took the day off from work to bring the photographs for his *foglio di via* to the Italian consulate in Boston. He left Stoughton on a morning train shortly before 9 A.M. and arrived in Boston about 9:35. In Boston he went to the Italian section, the North End, bought a copy of *La Notizia*, read for a while, strolled, met a friend and chatted, and priced some suits and straw hats but didn't buy any. By then it was nearly noon. He ran into another friend, Professor Felice Guadagni, and together they went to Boni's restaurant for lunch. After lunch, Sacco went to the Italian consulate. He arrived there about 2 P.M. and spoke to a clerk, Giuseppe Andrower.[9]

Sacco: I said, "I like to get my passport for my whole family." He asked me,—he said, "You bring the picture?" I said, "Yes," so I gave it to him, see, a big picture. He says, "Well, I am sorry. This picture is too big." "Well," I says, "can you cut and make him small?" "No," he said, "the picture we cannot use, because it goes too big." I says, "Can you cut?" He says, "No, no use, because got to make a photograph just for the purpose for the passport, small, very small,"—so I did.*[10]

Sacco was at the Italian consulate only ten or fifteen minutes. He then went to a café where he again met Guadagni. Guadagni introduced him to Antonio Dentamore, a former Catholic priest

*Sacco had passport photos taken by a Stoughton photographer. Edward Maertens, who confirmed this at the trial. The second question Maertens was asked, after his name, was his nationality (Belgian).[11]

who at the time was an editor at *La Notizia*, which had changed owners and was no longer a socialist newspaper. After leaving the café, Sacco shopped for groceries. Shortly after 4 P.M., he took a train back to Stoughton where he did more shopping before returning home about 6 P.M.[12] In cross-examination, Sacco was asked why he didn't go to the consulate in the morning and come back on the noon train. He replied, "Well, I think to pass all day when I been in Boston. . . . I have been working all the time. I will stay, take all day if I have a chance."[13] The decision of the hard-driving Sacco to take a full day off was another link in the chain of circumstances that cost him his life.

A large number of witnesses corroborated Sacco's story. The superintendent at the 3-K factory, George Kelley, testified that at the beginning of that week Sacco asked for a day off so he could go to the Italian consulate to take care of his *foglio di via*.

Kelley: I told him at that time that if he was caught up he may have the day off. At that time, there was no mention of the day. It went along about Wednesday, and he came to me and said he was going in tomorrow.[14]

Jeremiah McAnarney later tried to clarify that point. He asked Kelley whether the agreement was that Sacco would not take the day off until he had broken in the man who was replacing him.

Kelley: I couldn't say as to that, no. The understanding was that the work would be caught up or he would not go.

McAnarney: I see.

Kelley: And when it was caught up, I was willing that he should go.

McAnarney: And that was the fact and that was what did take place, wasn't it?

Kelley: Yes.

McAnarney: When he got the work caught up, he took that day?

Kelley: Yes.[15]

The payroll had to be heisted on a Thursday because that

Th

was when it was delivered. To believe Sacco guilty one must believe that the carefully plotted crime hinged on whether or not he could finish his edge trimming in time to take the day off to participate.

Among the witnesses who testified to seeing Sacco in Boston on April 15 was Guadagni, a former professor of Italian and Latin, who joined him for lunch at Boni's. In the restaurant Guadagni introduced Sacco to Albert Bosco, another editor at *La Notizia*, and John D. Williams, an advertising agent. Both men testified for Sacco, as did Dentamore, who by the time of the trial was in charge of foreign exchange at a bank.

When Katzmann asked Sacco's witnesses why they remembered the date as April 15, several recalled that at noon that day, Italian newspapermen in Boston had held a luncheon in honor of James T. Williams, Jr., the editor of the *Boston Evening Transcript*, and this was a subject of general discussion. Guadagni had been invited but had not gone; when Dentamore met Sacco in the café shortly before 3 P.M., he had just come from the event.

Sacco's witnesses cannot be discounted without conjuring up an elaborate conspiracy created for him but not for Vanzetti, involving at least four men who were not motivated to lie for a friend or for the cause. One was Dentamore, who had left the priesthood for personal reasons and was not a radical, who had an important job he could jeopardize, and who, upon hearing that Sacco was going to Italy, asked him to deliver a message to an Italian politician they both knew. The second was John D. Williams, the advertising agent who, like Dentamore, had never even met Sacco until April 15. It was known that Williams was a socialist, though not an anarchist, but the prosecution challenged his memory rather than his motives. The third was Giuseppe Andrower, the clerk in the Italian consulate, who had returned to Italy but sent a deposition from Rome.

In the deposition, Andrower said he had been in charge of "answering questions and giving information to the public" as well as dealing with passports and visas. Shortly after Sacco's arrest, Guadagni, who was a member of the Sacco-Vanzetti Defense Committee, went to the consulate and asked Andrower if he remembered Sacco's visit. Andrower did not until Guadagni showed him the photograph that Sacco had with him on April 15. The deposition read, in part:

> I first saw the photograph marked "B" on April 15th, 1920, in the office of the Royal Italian Consulate at Boston, Massachusetts . . . at about two or quarter past two in the afternoon. . . . The photograph marked "B" was first exhibited to me by Mr. Sacco. Early in April Mr. Sacco came to the Royal Italian Consulate for information how to get a passport for Italy. I gave him the information and told him that he should bring two photographs, one to be attached to the passport and the other for the records of the office. He then left and on April 15th, 1920, as I have stated before, he returned with a photograph the same as exhibit "B." I told him that this photograph was too large for use on a foglio di via or an Italian passport.[16]

Andrower was asked by the American vice consul, before whom he made the deposition, how he knew the date was April 15.

> April 15th, 1920, was a very quiet day in the Royal Italian Consulate and since such a large photograph had never been before presented for use on a passport I took it in and showed it to the Secretary of the Consulate. We laughed and talked over the incident. I remember observing the date in the office of the Secretary on a large pad calendar while we were discussing the photograph. The hour was around two or a quarter after two as I remember about a half an hour later I locked the door of the office for the day.

Andrower also said he remembered the date because "there was much less business than on the previous and following days. There were only about thirty or forty people in the office applying for passports that day and we usually had about two hundred."[17]

The C

A functionary of the Italian government had no reason to lie for Sacco, whom he did not know, since the Italian government was not concerned about the fate of the two anarchists. Judge Thayer later said the Italian consul visited him at his home to assure him his government "had no interest in this case."[18]

A fourth witness for Sacco was even more convincing than the others because not only was he a stranger, but it was sheer chance that he testified at all. James Matthews Hayes was a mason and contractor who had been highway surveyor in Stoughton, where he lived. He went to Dedham because a defense investigator wanted information about a highway laborer in Stoughton who had seen the bandit car. While Hayes was there, he decided to sit in on the trial. Sacco spotted Hayes in the courtroom and told Jeremiah McAnarney that Hayes had been a fellow passenger on the train from Boston to Stoughton on the afternoon of April 15. McAnarney called Hayes into an anteroom and asked him if he knew where he had been that day. After Hayes checked, he was called to the stand.

McAnarney:	As the result of [our] conversation did you go back home and make an investigation with reference to trying to find out if you could place yourself on the 15th of April, 1920?
Hayes:	Yes, sir.

*   *   *

McAnarney:	What investigation did you make?
Hayes:	I found that on the 15th of April I had gone to Boston.
McAnarney:	Tell us now how you remember that you went to Boston on the 15th of April?
Hayes:	I remembered that by a perusal of my time books and by other incidents that happened previous to that.

*   *   *

McAnarney:	Have you got your time book with you?
Hayes:	Yes, sir.

Hayes testified that he had gone to Boston on the afternoon of April 15 to buy some items to repair his car and to check on a concern in which he had recently bought some stock.

McAnarney: About what time did you arrive in Stoughton, if you remember, definitely?

Hayes: Between five and six.

McAnarney: That is on the 15th day of April?

Hayes: Yes, sir.

McAnarney: Did you know Sacco?

Hayes: No, I never knew Sacco. Never met him.

McAnarney: And until I spoke to you and asked you to try and place yourself on April 15th, had you ever given it a thought as to where you were?

Hayes: No, sir, I never had any occasion to.

McAnarney: Whether Sacco was on that train or not you don't know?

Hayes: I don't know.

McAnarney: But you came out on that train?

Hayes: Yes, sir.[19]

When Katzmann made his usual demand that Hayes tell him what he had done on other dates, Hayes had a reply that finally silenced the district attorney; he said he could answer if it was recorded in his time book. Then Sacco was called to the stand.

McAnarney: Mr. Sacco, where did you see this man [Hayes]?

Sacco: I remember that I might have seen him in the—I remember that I have seen him the 15th day of April in Boston.

McAnarney: Well, where did you see him?

Sacco: I saw him on the train coming home to my house.

* * *

McAnarney: And from that time that you saw him on the train, when did you next see this man?

Sacco: I saw him in court last week.[20]

Hayes was asked to leave the courtroom while Katzmann cross-examined Sacco.

Katzmann:	On what side of the coach did you sit?
Sacco:	I remember that I sat on my right, as you go to Stoughton.

*   *   *

Katzmann:	How far from the front or how far from the rear? Locate the seat.
Sacco:	About the center.
Katzmann:	Where did this man sit you are now speaking of?
Sacco:	On the left, right aside of me.
Katzmann:	On the aisle side of the seat? That is, next to the aisle?
Sacco:	Near the aisle, on the side.
Katzmann:	And where were you sitting? Next to the aisle or next to the window in your seat.
Sacco:	I was sitting near the aisle.[21]

Hayes, who had not heard this exchange, was brought back into the courtroom to be cross-examined by Katzmann.

Katzmann:	In coming out from Boston to Stoughton, on which side of the coach were you seated, left or right?
Hayes:	I was seated on the left.
Katzmann:	And whereabouts in the car?
Hayes:	About midway in the car.
Katzmann:	And on which side of the seat?
Hayes:	On the inside of the seat.
Katzmann:	That is, next to the window or next to the aisle?
Hayes:	Next to the aisle.
Katzmann:	Have you talked this over with Mr. Sacco before he took the stand?
Hayes:	No, sir.
Katzmann:	Or his counsel?

Hayes:	No, sir.
Katzmann:	Has anybody asked you before I asked you in which part of the coach you were seated?
Hayes:	No.
Katzmann:	Or which part of the seat?
Hayes:	No, sir.[22]

Hayes had proved that Sacco was on a train from Boston to Stoughton in the late afternoon of April 15. An American advertising agent, a clerk from the Italian consulate, a banker, and a Yankee businessman had placed Sacco in Boston from about 1 P.M. until after 4 P.M. If Sacco was in Boston, he could not have been in South Braintree murdering Berardelli at 3 P.M.

On their alibis for April 15, Vanzetti had fared poorly and Sacco had done well, particularly when he recognized Hayes in the courtroom and the train story was confirmed in every detail. If this had been a criminal trial, the alibis of Sacco and Vanzetti would have been their most important testimony, but it was not just a criminal trial, it was a political trial as well. Not until 1926 was the defense able to produce evidence that the prosecution was cooperating with the Justice Department,* but there were sufficient signs at Dedham to indicate this was no ordinary trial.

John McAnarney later said:

> A prospective juror entering that court was first met by a[n armed] guard. . . . He was held up by a guard at the door. That is notice number one that [this] is an unusual case. I have defended many cases in Norfolk County for murder and nothing like that happened.
>
> You get in the door and at the foot of the stairs another guard held you up. That is notice number two. The human mind is so constant that those men [the jury] could not help attaching these guards to the defendants. They wasn't there on account of the government. They were there to guard those men.

*See pages 324 ff.

The

You get to the head of the stairs and again there was another [guard] and in the courtroom the guards were there.

The jurors passed from the courtroom out into what used to be our law library, that room was used by the jurors. Up and down parading in that corridor was another guard.

All that spelled in the minds of those jurors that here was a situation that was unusual. Those men were there . . . to guard the community from these defendants and from their friends.[23]

In the courtroom, Sacco and Vanzetti sat in a cage. True, all defendants in murder trials sat in the cage, but the jury wasn't judging all defendants, it was judging two Italian anarchists. Not only were they caged in a heavily guarded courtroom—itself an overwhelming presumption of guilt—but six times a day, in the morning, in the evening, and during luncheon recess, they were marched through the streets of Dedham between the jail and the courthouse encapsulated in a convoy of guards. They must have seemed a horrendous threat to the community to require such extraordinary force to contain them.

In order to prove their innocence—that the prosecution had to prove their guilt beyond a reasonable doubt was a fiction—Sacco and Vanzetti not only needed alibis for April 15 but for May 5 and 6 to explain what they were doing when they were arrested and why they had lied. In justifying his decision to have them testify, John McAnarney said:

> I saw no way that those men could avoid going on the stand and telling fully and frankly their connection with the commonistic [sic] movement or the radical movement they had been allied with. The only thing to do was to take the full responsibility of that and, if they did that much, [it would explain] their conduct which otherwise would be very suspicious . . . their being up trying to get the car at the Johnson house, their being on the electric car

with revolvers on them, lying to the officers and the district attorney before they knew they were charged with murder. . . . They were firmly convinced and they believed at that time they were taken into custody on account of radicalism. I told my brothers it was up to them to tell the whole story . . . so the facts might be put plainly before the jury. By no other theory could the actual facts be brought to the foreground other than the fact they explain the whole situation and accounted for their behavior and consistently so.[24]

Judge Thayer and other apologists for justice in the Commonwealth of Massachusetts would blame the defendants for introducing the subject of anarchy into the trial. But they were forced to introduce the subject of anarchy to explain themselves; the commonwealth was not forced to use it to impale them, but it did.

Vanzetti was led through his direct testimony by Jeremiah McAnarney who apparently did not want him to use an interpreter, perhaps because he suspected that a Yankee jury would resent the indication that after thirteen years in America, Vanzetti could still not speak adequate English. Resorting to an interpreter only once in direct examination and once in cross-examination, Vanzetti told about his early life in Italy, his years as an itinerant laborer in America, and his alibi for April 15. After April 15, there were no fish to sell, so Vanzetti spent most of his time looking for work. "I don't find no work and no fish," he said.[25]

He mentioned visiting the Italian Naturalization Club in East Boston, but did not say this was where he met with his anarchist friends. He said, "We decided to send a man to New York . . . and I was the man that they decided to go," but when McAnarney asked what the purpose of the trip was—to find out what was happening to Salsedo—Katzmann objected and was upheld by Thayer.[26]

Vanzetti said that after returning to Plymouth from New York he went to Boston on May 1 and stayed with a friend. On

The C

May 3 he went to the piers to buy fish, but it was too expensive so he took a train to Sacco's home in Stoughton. He then described how, on the night of May 5, he, Sacco, Orciani, and Boda went to the Johnson garage to get Boda's car.

McAnarney: What were you going to get the automobile for?

Vanzetti: We were going to take the automobile for to carry books and newspapers.

McAnarney said he didn't understand the answer and repeated the question.

McAnarney: What were you going to get the automobile for?

Vanzetti: For to take out literature, books and newspapers, from the house and the homes.

McAnarney: What house and homes did you want to take the books and literature from?

Vanzetti: From any house and from any house in five or six places, five or six towns. Three, five or six people have plenty of literature, and we want, we intend to take that out and put that in the proper place.

McAnarney: What do you mean by a "proper place"?

Vanzetti: By a proper place I mean in a place not subject to policemen go in and call for, see the literature, see the papers, see the books, as in that time they went through in the house of many men who were active in the radical movement and socialist and labor movement, and go there and take letters and take books and take newspapers, and put men in jail and deported many.

Katzmann asked that Vanzetti's remarks be stricken from the record, but Thayer did not reply, and Vanzetti just kept talking.

Vanzetti: And deported many, many; many have been misused in jail, and so on.

McAnarney asked Vanzetti whether rounding up the literature had anything to do with what he had learned in New York.

Vanzetti: Yes. What we read in newspapers, too.[27]

There was no further explanation of either the radical raids or the arrest and death of Salsedo. Instead McAnarney had Vanzetti recite the details of his arrest and asked him if he had told his interrogators about wanting the car to pick up the literature.

Vanzetti: No, I don't tell them that thing.
McAnarney: You withheld that from him. You never told that to them before?
Vanzetti: No.
McAnarney: Why not?
Vanzetti: Because in that time there, there was the deportation and the reaction was more vivid than now and more mad than now.
McAnarney: The action?
Vanzetti: The reaction. What you call "reaction." It mean the authority of this country and every country in the world was more against the socialist element in that time than before the war and after the war. There were exceptional times.[28]

Instead of developing this theme, or letting Vanzetti develop it, McAnarney just let it drop. Instead of trying to make the jury understand what radicals faced and what Sacco and Vanzetti feared, McAnarney, who probably didn't understand it himself, went on to the delicate matter of Vanzetti's flight to Mexico to avoid the draft.

McAnarney: Did you at one time go away from Plymouth?
Vanzetti: Yes, sir.
McAnarney: And when was that, please?
Vanzetti: I should say it was in the year 1917, before the registration.

*   *   *

The

McAnarney:	Why did you go away?
Vanzetti:	I go away for not to be a soldier.[29]

McAnarney did not ask Vanzetti to explain why he opposed the war, he asked about the various places Vanzetti traveled before returning to Plymouth. Nor did McAnarney make any attempt to get into the record the fact that many native Americans also fled the draft and that, as an alien, Vanzetti could not have been drafted, which might have eased the sting; it is foolish rather than criminal to run from the draft if you are not subject to it.

McAnarney, who could switch subjects faster than an automatic slide projector, then asked Vanzetti if he drove an automobile.

Vanzetti:	No.
McAnarney:	Did you ever drive one?
Vanzetti:	No, sir, I am not able.[30]

Next, McAnarney asked several questions to enable Vanzetti to deny John Faulkner's testimony that he was the man with the black bag who got off the train at East Braintree the morning of the robbery. Abruptly, McAnarney sprang the big question but destroyed its impact by naming the wrong month.

McAnarney:	Were you at South Braintree on the 15th day of May, 1920?
Vanzetti:	No.
Katzmann:	*April.* (Emphasis added.)
McAnarney:	April, 15th day of April, 1920. Did you take part in any shooting or anything that occurred there?
Vanzetti:	No, sir.
McAnarney:	On the 15th day of April, 1920?
Vanzetti:	No, sir.[31]

Suddenly it was back to the alibi of the cloth peddler. Vanzetti identified the piece of cloth he bought and it was admitted into evidence. Flick, and McAnarney returned to the night of the arrest.

McAnarney:	Why did you not tell Mr. Stewart the truth

| | that night when he arrested you and talked with you at the station? |
| Vanzetti: | I was scared to give the names and the addresses of my friends as I know that almost all of them have some books and some newspaper in their house by which the authority take a reason for arresting them and deport them. |

*   *   *

McAnarney:	Tell us all you recall that Stewart, the chief, asked of you?
Vanzetti:	He asked me why we were in Bridgewater, how long I know Sacco, if I am a radical, if I am an anarchist or communist, and he asked me if [I] believe in the government of the United States.
McAnarney:	Yes.
Vanzetti:	If I believe in the violence, if I believe in the use of violence against the government of the United States.[32]

Instead of following this up, McAnarney asked about Mike Boda, then changed the subject again.

McAnarney:	What was the purpose of the meeting that you were going to speak at on May 9th?
Vanzetti:	The purpose of that meeting was to help the political prisoners, but especially to help Salsedo and Elia.
McAnarney:	Who was Salsedo?[33]

When Katzmann objected, McAnarney dropped the question even before Thayer ruled and went back to asking about Boda. Another fast switch and McAnarney had Vanzetti deny that he had called out to Austin Reed, the gate tender at Matfield, without making the point that Vanzetti did not speak unmistakable and clear English. McAnarney also asked Vanzetti about Harry Dolbeare's testimony that he was in an automobile in South Braintree the morning of April 15.

240

Vanzetti:	No, that is not true. I never been in Braintree, down near Braintree, near South Braintree, or East Braintree.[34]

Then it was back to Boda again. McAnarney asked Vanzetti when he had learned about the plan to use Boda's car to pick up the literature and that the car was in a garage in Bridgewater.

On these trivial points, the direct examination of Vanzetti ended. This was the defendant's best opportunity to tell his story and his own lawyer had bungled it; the facts had not been put plainly before the jury, as John McAnarney had advised. Many of Jeremiah McAnarney's questions were disjointed, irrelevant, or illogical, and the rapidity with which he skipped from one subject to another would have confused the most attentive juror. McAnarney had gotten on record that Vanzetti was a radical and a draft evader without giving him the opportunity to justify his acts or to explain how the prevailing attitude toward radicals and draft evaders affected his behavior. The attorney spoke of "conscious guilt," but he seemed unaware that it related to Vanzetti's being an alien anarchist or that America wanted such men to feel guilty. He never mentioned that people like Sacco and Vanzetti were considered virtual outlaws, subject to deportation or, in Salsedo's case, death.

Vanzetti's own lawyer did not understand him or his background well enough to know how to present his case. Katzmann did not understand Vanzetti either, but he understood the jury very well: good, hardworking Yankees. Patriotic, too. The foreman, Walter H. Ripley, saluted the flag when he entered the courtroom each morning. Thus Katzmann's opening question to Vanzetti flew straight as an arrow.

Katzmann:	So you left Plymouth, Mr. Vanzetti, in May, 1917, to dodge the draft, did you?
Vanzetti:	Yes, sir.[35]

Neither judge nor attorneys objected. With that query, the real trial of Sacco and Vanzetti began.

18

Dedham: The Heretics

Katzmann's cross-examination of Vanzetti and later of Sacco left no doubt that the trial was simultaneously criminal and ideological. The criminal charge was murder but the ideological charge was heresy.

Katzmann:	When this country was at war, you ran away so you would not have to fight as a soldier?
Vanzetti:	Yes.
Katzmann:	Is that true?
Vanzetti:	It is true.
Katzmann:	Did you ever work in Springfield, Massachusetts?
Vanzetti:	Well, I have worked not really in the town of Springfield, Massachusetts, but in a shanty near Springfield.
Katzmann:	In a shanty near Springfield?
Vanzetti:	Yes, in a shanty, you know, the little house where the Italian work and live like a beast, the Italian workingman in this country.
Katzmann:	Where the Italian man lives and works like a beast?

Vanzetti:	Yes.

*   *   *

Katzmann:	What did you put [that] in for?
Vanzetti:	I put it for to tell you if I refused to go to war, I don't refuse because I don't like this country or I don't like the people of this country. I will refuse even if I was in Italy.[1]

Instead of following this effective thrust with his views on war and exploitation, Vanzetti began to ramble about good people and bad people and how hard he worked, until Katzmann interrupted. He had asked Vanzetti about Springfield because he thought he could get him to admit he drove a truck on that particular job, but Vanzetti denied it.

Katzmann:	Are you certain that you did not drive that automobile truck?
Vanzetti:	Oh, yes, I am certain of that.
Katzmann:	Sure of that?
Vanzetti:	Nobody can prove I ever drove one automobile in my life.[2]

Katzmann asked that this reply be stricken from the record, and it was. After some other questions, Katzmann brought up his interrogation of Vanzetti on May 6, the day after the arrest. At that time Katzmann had advised Vanzetti he did not have to answer and that what he said could be used against him, but did Vanzetti really understand what Katzmann meant? A lawyer would have advised Vanzetti to be silent; he would also have demanded to know why Vanzetti had been arrested. But there was no lawyer present, just Vanzetti, Katzmann, and a stenographer taking down every word. Obviously Vanzetti felt he had to answer; what would happen to him if he didn't? What had happened to Salsedo? In the courtroom Katzmann asked Vanzetti if he had frightened him. Vanzetti replied, "I was not frightened that you punch me. I was disturbed."[3] It was a fear Vanzetti could not articulate in English and Katzmann could not comprehend in any langauge.

Katzmann:	You were willing, were you not, to answer such questions as I asked you?
Vanzetti:	I am not willing or unwilling. I was there like

a piece of paper in my hand, and the policemen take me out and down as they liked. I do
not know the rule of the jail. I do not know
very well the language. I speak a little better
now after one year in jail than then. I never
was arrested before. I don't know anything
about trials, jails.[4]

Katzmann used what he claimed was the stenographic
record of his interrogation of May 6 to show Vanzetti had lied.
Vanzetti admitted this, though he said he didn't remember all of
the questions or answers that Katzmann read. Katzmann tried to
show that some of the lies—the price of Vanzetti's revolver or the
date he left Turin—bore no relation to Vanzetti's claim that he was
concealing information because he feared he had been arrested as
a radical, but they also bore no relation to the charge of murder
and robbery. Vanzetti was obviously upset, distraught, bewildered. He explained in court, "I wasn't in a good mental condition."[5]

Vanzetti tried to distinguish between deliberate lies, which
he acknowledged, and errors or memory lapses. He said he lied
"because I have some purpose";[6] he was trying not to incriminate
himself or any of his comrades. He had denied knowing Mike
Boda because "if I . . . tell you the truth [about Boda] I must give
you the name of plenty of my friends."[7]

The best explanation Vanzetti offered for lying repeatedly
was, "When I say the first thing false I have to say everything
false."[8] The jury could accept or reject this, but it certainly
revealed Vanzetti's logic. Yet Katzmann demanded it be stricken
from the record, and Thayer obliged. Exchanges harmful to
Vanzetti, however, were permitted to remain, no matter how
irrelevant. Earlier in the trial, when the arresting officer, Michael J.
Connolly, said that Vanzetti had put his hand in his hip pocket
where his gun was, Vanzetti cried out in the courtroom, "You are
a liar!"*[9]

Katzmann: You have a good strong voice, haven't you,
Mr. Vanzetti?

*At the Plymouth trial Connolly said nothing about Vanzetti reaching for his gun.

The C

Vanzetti:	Not very much now. It is more than one year I am in jail.
Katzmann:	Was your voice weak the day Michael J. Connolly was on the stand and you called him a liar when he said how you made a move to your hip pocket?
Jeremiah McAnarney:	Wait a minute.
Vanzetti:	I don't speak very high when I called that man a liar.
Katzmann:	You did not speak very high?
McAnarney:	I submit that is hardly,—I object to the question. His voice was whatever his voice was. My brother is putting this argumentative question to embarrass the witness, not to elicit any information.
Thayer:	I can't say it is for that purpose.
Vanzetti:	I don't speak more high than I speak now when I call that man a liar.
Katzmann:	Is that your recollection of the tone of voice you used that day?
Vanzetti:	Maybe the tone was different, because the sentiment was different.[10]

As though being an Italian radical was not sufficiently suspect, Katzmann continuously reminded the jury that Vanzetti was also a draft evader, though what this had to do with the crime at South Braintree was never explained.

Katzmann:	Had you any reason to believe that night [May 6] that I knew that you had run away to avoid the draft?

Vanzetti's reply, distilled from several answers, was, "I don't know if you know or not . . . but I know that in that time anybody you call . . . slacker was arrested."[11]

Katzmann mentioned the announcement of the anarchist meeting on May 9 that Vanzetti had written on the way to Bridgewater. Translated from the Italian, it read:

Fellow Workers, you have fought all the wars. You

have worked for all the capitalists. You have wandered over all the countries. Have you harvested the fruits of your labors, the price of your victories? Does the past comfort you? Does the present smile on you? Does the future promise you anything? Have you found a piece of land where you can live like a human being and die like a human being? On these questions, on this argument, and on this theme, the struggle for existence, Bartolomeo Vanzetti will speak. Hour_____ day_____ hall_____. Admission free. Freedom of discussion to all. Take the ladies with you.

Katzmann first tried to use the flyer to prove Vanzetti had lied when he said that he was afraid to tell the truth because he thought he had been arrested as a radical.

Katzmann: You had no fear, did you, about telling me about this meeting at which you were going to speak when I talked with you at Brockton? You did not have any fear about telling me that, did you?

Vanzetti: That isn't a question of fear. . . . You found the pamphlets in Nick's pocket speaking of this meeting.[12]

Then Katzmann used the flyer to prejudice the jurors another way.

Katzmann: Are you the man, Mr. Vanzetti, that on May 9th was going to address a meeting down at Brockton to your fellow citizens, saying: "You have fought in the wars, and you have worked for capitalists, and tried their ways"? Are you the man, sir, that was going to address the returned soldiers?

Vanzetti: Yes, sir.

Katzmann: You were going to advise in a public meeting men who had gone to war? Are you that man?

The

Vanzetti:	Yes, sir, I am that man, not the man you want me, but I am that man.[13]

When questioned by Katzmann at the Brockton police station, Vanzetti did not recall what he had done April 15. Actually, Katzmann's question had been maliciously leading and misleading. Katzmann had said, "You don't know where you were the Thursday before that Monday [Patriots Day, April 19], do you?" Vanzetti, not realizing the date was significant, had simply replied, "No." The district attorney read the question and answer to the jury at Dedham, then closed in.

Katzmann:	But after waiting months and months and months you then remembered, did you?
Vanzetti:	Not months and months and months, but three or four weeks after I see that I have to be careful and to remember well if I want to save my life.

*   *   *

Katzmann:	Weren't you careful, sir, when you were making your reply to that question?
Vanzetti:	Yes, but I never know in that time on the day 15th and the day 24th it was the day of the assault at South Braintree and Bridgewater. I don't know in that time.
Katzmann:	Didn't you intend to tell me the truth where you were on any day that I asked you?
Vanzetti:	I intend to tell you the truth, but I never can dream that you will say that on the 15th and the 24th I went to steal and kill a man.
Katzmann:	Then if you could not dream that you were to be charged with murder on the 15th of April, how was it you were so certain that you could not remember where you were on the 15th of April?
Vanzetti:	Because . . . the 15th of April is a day common to every other day to me. I peddled fish.[14]

Earlier in the cross-examination Vanzetti offered an even better response when he was asked why he could now remember what had happened on April 15.

Vanzetti: You can be sure that I can remember that I never kill a man on the 15th, because I never kill a man in my life.[15]

At Katzmann's request, Thayer struck this declaration of innocence from the record.

On redirect examination, Jeremiah McAnarney finally introduced the subject of Salsedo's death. McAnarney asked Vanzetti what he meant when he said earlier that he was afraid.

Vanzetti: I mean that I was afraid, for I know that my friends there in New York have jumped down from the jail in the street and killed himself. The papers say that he jump down, but we don't know.[16]

Further questions and answers established that the friend was Salsedo, that Vanzetti had learned about his death on May 4, and that previously he had gone to New York to find out what was happening to him. Katzmann objected several times but Thayer permitted Vanzetti to explain that he was told in New York that all literature should be picked up and concealed because there probably would be another roundup of radicals. Vanzetti added that a car was needed because there were some five hundred pounds of anarchist literature in the Boston area.

McAnarney made no attempt to demonstrate that similar raids had already taken place, particularly on the night of January 2, but his concluding questions to Vanzetti did go to the core of the defense.

McAnarney: Did either Chief Stewart at the Brockton police station or Mr. Katzmann tell you that you were suspected of robberies and murder?

Vanzetti: No.

McAnarney: Was there any question asked of you or any

The

	statement made to you to indicate to you that you were charged with that crime on April 15th?
Vanzetti:	No.
McAnarney:	In view of the questions asked of you, what did you understand you were being detained for at the Brockton police station?
Vanzetti:	I understand they arrested me for a political matter.

*   *   *

McAnarney:	Why did you feel you were being detained for political opinions?
Vanzetti:	Because I was asked if I was a socialist. I said, "Well,"——
McAnarney:	You mean by reason of the questions asked of you?
Vanzetti:	Because I was asked if I am a socialist, if I am I.W.W., if I am a communist, if I am a radical, if I am Blackhand.[17]

Except for a few questions, Sacco also testified without an interpreter, which was a serious error because his English was much worse than Vanzetti's, and the language problem crippled him badly, particularly during cross-examination. Fred Moore conducted most of the direct examination, leading Sacco through the story of his early life in Italy, his years in America, the decision to return to Italy, his efforts to get a *foglio di via*, and his alibi for April 15.

Moore attempted to present Sacco's activities on the night of May 5 by beginning with Salsedo's arrest and death, but Thayer would not permit this; the judge insisted Sacco be questioned about May 5 first. Moore replied, "Now, if your Honor demands, I will plunge immediately into May 5th and work backward. I would rather start at the bottom and work up."[18]

Under Moore's questioning, Sacco told about the night of his arrest. Asked if at any time he or Vanzetti reached for their guns, Sacco replied, "No, sir."[19] Yet a few minutes later, Judge Thayer, responding to one of Katzmann's objections, commented, "You claim that the attempt to draw a revolver is evidence of consciousness of guilt."[20] Thus Thayer implicitly rejected Sacco's denial; the issue was not whether he and Vanzetti reached for their guns, but why.

Moore asked Sacco if Stewart had asked him what he was doing April 15. Sacco said no. Moore asked Sacco why he thought he had been arrested. Sacco said, "I never think anything else than radical."

Moore:	What?
Sacco:	To the radical arrest, you know, the way they do in New York, the way they arrest so many people there.
Moore:	What made you think that?
Sacco:	Because I was not registered, and I was working for the movement for the working class, for the laboring class.
Moore:	Was there anything Chief Stewart said to you that made you think that?
Sacco:	Yes. He did ask me if I was a socialist.[21]

Sacco admitted lying to Stewart to protect his comrades. Moore asked if Katzmann had told him he was charged with the crime at South Braintree. Sacco said no. An attempt by Moore to discuss Salsedo and Elia was objected to by Katzmann and sustained by Thayer; however Moore was permitted to ask, over Katzmann's objections, "Did you know of various men who had been held and deported by reason of their ideas or opinions?" Sacco said yes.

Like Jeremiah McAnarney, Moore had a disconcerting tendency to skitter from one subject to another. He went from the deportations to Boda's Overland to the *foglio di via* to the two caps to the events of May 5 and May 6 within minutes, and he permitted Sacco to impair his credibility by giving some absurd answers. Moore should have known what a jury might believe, even if Sacco didn't. When Moore asked Sacco why he was carrying a pistol, Sacco said that his wife, while cleaning the house, had found the gun and bullets in a locked bureau drawer and had asked what he wanted to do with them. Sacco said he took them so he and Vanzetti could "go to shoot in the woods,"[22] but they started to talk instead, then Boda and Orciani came, and by then he had forgotten about the gun and bullets. It was not a convincing explanation, particularly since Katzmann was later able to point out that Sacco carried the gun in his waistband, not in his pocket.

Katzmann:	Are you telling this jury that you were not aware of the fact when you left your house on May 5th that you had this gun tucked in here? Are you telling them that?
Sacco:	Yes.
Katzmann:	Did not perceive the weight of it?
Sacco:	No, sir.
Katzmann:	Did not notice it?
Sacco:	No.
Katzmann:	Did not notice the 22 extra cartridges in your pocket?
Sacco:	No.[23]

Moore had Sacco describe how, at the Brockton police station, he was made to reenact the various details of the crime in order to help witnesses identify him. Sacco said that most of the witnesses had shaken their heads or said, "No, sir," but Katzmann insisted Sacco's observations be stricken from the record, and they were. After Sacco denied he had participated in the crime on April 15, Moore turned him over to Jeremiah McAnarney who had him repeat that he had lied to Stewart and Katzmann because he feared he had been arrested because of his radical activities.

Both attorneys, including the radical Moore, failed Sacco, just as McAnarney had failed Vanzetti. They had Sacco admit he was afraid, but did not demonstrate he had anything to fear. Yankee jurors not threatened by the Palmer raids, having no sense of alienation and no knowledge of discrimination, brutality, murder, suicide, or exile would never believe, unless shown, that it might be necessary to lie to protect oneself from a government which they found so worthy and which radicals found so ominous.

Katzmann opened his cross-examination of Sacco just as he had with Vanzetti by bearing in on the irrelevant but emotionally potent issue of draft evasion. When Moore asked Sacco why he came to America, Sacco had replied, "I was crazy to come to this country because I was liked a free country, call a free country."[24]

Katzmann:	Did you say yesterday you love a free country?
Sacco:	Yes, sir.
Katzmann:	Did you love this country in the month of May, 1917?
Sacco:	I did not say,—I don't want to say I did not love this country.

Katzmann kept insisting that Sacco say whether he loved America in May, 1917, and Sacco kept asking for a chance to explain. Moore objected, but Thayer ruled that Sacco had to answer.

Katzmann:	Did you love this country in the last week of May, 1917?
Sacco:	That is pretty hard for me to say in one word, Mr. Katzmann.
Katzmann:	There are two words you can use, Mr. Sacco, yes or no. Which one is it?
Sacco:	Yes.
Katzmann:	And in order to show your love for this United States of America when she was about to call upon you to become a soldier you ran away to Mexico?*
McAnarney:	Wait.
Thayer:	Did you?
Katzmann:	Did you run away to Mexico?
Thayer:	He has not said he ran away to Mexico. Did you go?

---

*This was unconscionable demagoguery on Katzmann's part, unconscionably abetted by Thayer, since Sacco, as an alien, could not have been drafted and, as a husband and father, probably would not have been even if he were a citizen. It is incredible that neither Moore nor McAnarney made these points.

The Ca

| Katzmann: | Did you go to Mexico to avoid being a soldier for this country that you loved? |
| Sacco: | Yes. |

* * *

Katzmann:	Is that your idea of showing your love for America?
Sacco:	Yes.
Katzmann:	And would it be your idea of showing your love for your wife that when she needed you you ran away from her?
Sacco:	I did not run away from her.[25]

Moore objected to this analogy and was overruled. After more of Katzmann's battering, Sacco finally managed to get in the words, "I don't believe in war,"[26] but they were lost as the district attorney drove ahead with his cross-examination which became famous and controversial because of the question of collusion with the Justice Department, because it was so savage and irrelevant, and because the contest was so pitifully unequal.

Katzmann:	Why didn't you stay down in Mexico?
Sacco:	Well, first thing, I could not get my trade over there. I had to do any other job.
Katzmann:	Don't they work with a pick and shovel in Mexico?
Sacco:	Yes.
Katzmann:	Haven't you worked with a pick and shovel in this country?
Sacco:	I did.
Katzmann:	Why didn't you stay there, down there in that free country, and work with a pick and shovel?
Sacco:	I don't think I did sacrifice to learn a job to go to pick and shovel in Mexico.
Katzmann:	Is it because,—is your love for the United States of America commensurate with the amount of money you can get in this country per week?
Sacco:	Better conditions, yes.

Katzmann:	Better country to make money, isn't it?
Sacco:	Yes.
Katzmann:	Mr. Sacco, that is the extent of your love for this country, isn't it, measured in dollars and cents?
McAnarney:	If your Honor please, I object to this particular question.
Thayer:	You opened up this whole subject.[27]

Thus Thayer, on the grounds that the defense had asked about Mexico first and that Sacco had said he liked a free country, permitted Katzmann to continue.

Katzmann:	Is your love for this country measured by the amount of money you can earn here?
McAnarney:	To that question I object.
Thayer:	Now, you may answer.
Sacco:	I never loved money.

*   *   *

Katzmann:	What is the reason you came back from Mexico if you did not love money, then?
Sacco:	The first reason is all against my nature, is all different food over there, different nature, anyway.
Katzmann:	That is the first reason. It is against your nature. The food isn't right.
Sacco:	Food, and many other things.

*   *   *

Katzmann:	You had Italian food there, didn't you?
Sacco:	Yes, made by ourselves.

*   *   *

Katzmann:	Couldn't you send to Boston to get Italian food sent to Monterrey, Mexico?
Sacco:	If I was a D. Rockefeller I will.
Katzmann:	Then, I take it, you came back to the United States first to get something to eat. Is that right? Something that you liked?
Sacco:	No, not just for eat.

The C

Katzmann:	Didn't you say that was the first reason?
Sacco:	The first reason——
Katzmann:	Didn't you say that was the first reason?
Sacco:	Yes.
Katzmann:	All right. That wasn't a reason of the heart, was it?
Sacco:	The heart?
Katzmann:	Yes.
Sacco:	No.
Katzmann:	That was a reason of the stomach, wasn't it?
Sacco:	Not just for the stomach, but any other reason.
Katzmann:	I am talking first about the first reason. So, the first reason your love of America is founded upon is pleasing your stomach. Is that right?
Sacco:	I will not say yes.
Katzmann:	Haven't you said so?
Sacco:	Not for the stomach. I don't think it is a satisfaction just for the stomach.
Katzmann:	What is your second reason?
Sacco:	The second reason is strange for me, the language.
Katzmann:	Strange language?
Sacco:	Yes.
Katzmann:	Were you in an Italian colony there?
Sacco:	If I got them? I can't get that, Mr. Katzmann.
Katzmann:	Pardon me. Were you in a group of Italians there?
Sacco:	Yes.
Katzmann:	When you came to America in 1908, did you understand English?
Sacco:	No.
Katzmann:	A strange language here, wasn't it?
Sacco:	Yes.
Katzmann:	What is the third reason, if there is one?
Sacco:	A third reason, I was far away from my wife and boy.

255

Katzmann:	Now, is there any other besides those three reasons why you loved the United States of America?
Sacco:	Well, I couldn't say. Over here there is more accommodation for the working class, I suppose, than any other people [place?], a chance to be more industrious, and more industry. Can have a chance to get anything he wants.
Katzmann:	You mean to earn more money, don't you?
Sacco:	No, no, money, never loved money.
Katzmann:	Never loved money?
Sacco:	No, money never satisfaction to me.
Katzmann:	Money never a satisfaction to you?
Sacco:	No.
Katzmann:	What was the industrial condition that pleased you so much here if it wasn't a chance to earn bigger money?
Sacco:	A man, Mr. Katzmann, has no satisfaction all through the money, for the belly.
Katzmann:	For the what?
Sacco:	For the stomach, I mean.
Katzmann:	We got away from the stomach. Now, I am talking about money.
Sacco:	There is lots of things.
Katzmann:	Well, let us have them all. I want to know why you loved America so that after you got to the haven of Mexico when the United States was at war you came back here?
Sacco:	Yes.
Katzmann:	I want all the reasons why you came back?
Sacco:	I think I did tell you already.
Katzmann:	Are those all?
Sacco:	Yes. Industry makes lots of things different.
Katzmann:	Then there is food, that is one?
Sacco:	Yes.

Katzmann:	Foreign language is two?
Sacco:	Yes.
Katzmann:	Your wife and child is three?
Sacco:	Yes.
Katzmann:	And better industrial conditions?
Sacco:	Yes.
Katzmann:	Is that all?
Sacco:	That is all.
Katzmann:	Among those four reasons, then, do you find any one that is called love of country? Have you named that reason?

Moore objected. Thayer ruled that Katzmann could ask the question if he omitted the last remark.

Katzmann:	Did you find love of country among those four reasons?
Sacco:	Yes, sir.
Katzmann:	Which one is love of country?
Sacco:	All together.
Katzmann:	All together?
Sacco:	Yes, sir.
Katzmann:	Food, wife, language, industry?
Sacco:	Yes.
Katzmann:	That is love of country, is it?
Sacco:	Yes.
Katzmann:	Is standing by a country when she needs a soldier evidence of love of country?
McAnarney:	That I object to, if your Honor please. And I might state now I want my objection to go to this whole line of interrogation.
Thayer:	I think you opened it up.
McAnarney:	No, if your Honor please, I have not.
Thayer:	It seems to me you have. Are you going to claim much of all the collection of the literature and the books was really in the interest of the United States as well as these people and therefore it has opened up the credibility of the defendant when he claims that all that

work was done really for the interest of the United States in getting this literature out of the way?[28]

Thayer's incoherent statement does not open up the credibility of the defendant, it opens up the credibility of the judge. The cross-examination shows that Sacco should never have been permitted to testify without an interpreter; that his lawyers had not prepared him, particularly on the draft evasion issue; that Katzmann was so cruel his methods might have been counterproductive if his victim were not an Italian radical; that most of Sacco's replies were senseless; and that either fear, confusion, the language problem, or the trap of anarchist dogma kept Sacco from explaining clearly why he did not want to go to war and why he doubted the American dream even though he had personally prospered.

Sacco's escape to Mexico was a fact of his life, but it had nothing to do with the murders at South Braintree. Anarchist literature had nothing to do with South Braintree either, but the trial seemed to revolve around it. The defense never claimed and never intended to claim that picking up the literature was in the interests of the United States; it was in the interests of keeping more anarchists from being deported. For Thayer to justify Katzmann's malevolent baiting of Sacco because it proved that Sacco did not have the interests of the United States at heart, on the grounds that this would be Sacco's justification for picking up the literature, was an assumption bordering on lunacy.

There followed a long argument, in the presence of the jury, concerning not what the defense claimed but what Thayer thought it was going to claim. Thayer, who became increasingly muddled and angry, kept asking McAnarney whether he was going to claim that Sacco's role in collecting the literature was in the interests of the United States "to prevent violation of the law by the distribution of this literature?"[29] McAnarney replied, "Absolutely we have taken no such position as that, and the evidence at this time does not warrant the assumption of that question."[30]

Thayer, now thoroughly belligerent, demanded to know just

The C

what the defense was going to claim. McAnarney said, "I am going to claim this man and Vanzetti were of that class called socialists. I am going to claim that riot was running a year ago last April, that men were being deported, that twelve to fifteen hundred were seized in Massachusetts."[31] It was a bold and striking statement, but McAnarney never followed it up and no supporting evidence was introduced. Instead, the dispute with Thayer continued with the judge parroting the same damning question over and over.

Thayer:	Are you going to claim that what the defendant did was in the interest of the United States?
McAnarney:	Your Honor please, I now object to your Honor's statement as prejudicial to the rights of the defendants and ask that this statement be withdrawn from the jury.
Thayer:	There is no prejudicial remark made that I know of, and none were intended. . . .
McAnarney:	If your Honor please, the remarks made with reference to the country and whether the acts that he was doing were for the benefit of the country. I can see no other inference to be drawn from those except prejudicial to the defendants.[32]

The debate between Thayer and McAnarney, joined by Katzmann and Moore, became even more confused over who meant to claim what, and just why Sacco was being pilloried in the first place. Thayer finally tried to make amends by telling the jury that he meant to make no remark prejudicing the rights of either defendant, though clearly he had done so by inanely and repeatedly asking whether the defense was going to claim that what Sacco did was in the interests of the United States.

When this matter finally had been laid to rest, Katzmann offered Sacco the opportunity to explain what he meant when he said that he liked a free country. Already wounded by incompetent counsel, a merciless prosecutor, and a biased judge, Sacco now proceeded to deliver the mortal blow himself.

Using poor English and worse logic, Sacco delivered an interminable lecture which had to infuriate the Yankee jurors since it came from an alien who earned a good salary, had saved $1,500, and stood before them an acknowledged radical and draft evader and an accused robber and murderer. Sacco said he could live as well in Italy as he could in America, work less, and eat better food. He said America put its best men, like Eugene Debs, in prison. He said the capitalists did not want the workers' children to be educated because they wanted to keep them subjugated. He said the poor could not afford to go to Harvard. He said wars were for the benefit of capitalists; "What right we have to kill each other?" he asked. He said he had nothing against the Germans; why should he kill them? "I don't believe in no war," he said, "I want to destroy those guns." He said he wanted to build, not demolish, and that was why he was a socialist.[33]

Looking at it generously, it was the speech of a good man blending truths, half-truths, and untruths, seasoned with a sprinkling of radical clichés, and served in a language he had not mastered. For the Yankee jurors, however, Sacco's English was so fractured it was incomprehensible at times; this foreigner was lecturing them on their own history and calling Jefferson "Abe"; and he dared to be critical even though he himself was proof that progress and upward mobility were possible in America. The ultimate error was for Sacco to say he could live better in Italy. Why then was he so afraid of being deported that he would lie to the authorities? Since no one ever explained to the jury the difference between going home and going into exile, they didn't know there was one. The blunt, outspoken Sacco had not only offended the jury in every way, but he had destroyed the alibi that he and Vanzetti had lied because they were radicals. If Italy was better than America, they could not have feared deportation as radicals as much as they feared execution as murderers.

In the event the jury overlooked anything in Sacco's torrent of words, Katzmann picked up some of the points and nailed them in.

Did he say life was better in Italy?

Sacco: No. Buy fruit more fresh for the working class, but no
           education and other things. It is just the same.

Did he know that Harvard gave scholarships to the poor?

Sacco: I can't answer that question, no.

Did he intend to condemn Harvard?

Sacco: No, sir.

Did his son go to public school?

Sacco: Yes.[34]

Repeatedly McAnarney objected but Thayer would not intervene; repeatedly Katzmann drew from a reluctant Sacco answers
that showed he was either ill-informed or ungrateful.

Katzmann then closed in on Sacco's radical beliefs. His aim
was twofold: to further destroy Sacco before the jury, if there was
anything left to destroy, and to keep his part of a bargain with the
Justice Department, in which the department had agreed to help
the district attorney secure a conviction and he had agreed to try
to get Sacco and Vanzetti to incriminate themselves as anarchists
so they could be deported if they weren't convicted.* Katzmann
asked Sacco if the newspapers and periodicals he read were
banned during the war. McAnarney objected on the grounds that
the "question is immaterial; the answer is immaterial." Thayer
overruled on the grounds that it was material to the defendant's
credibility; Sacco could not fear deportation if he wasn't a radical,
therefore the type of material he read and was going to collect was
relevant. Sacco had to admit he read publications that were
banned during the war.

With McAnarney's objections overruled by Thayer, Katzmann tried to force Sacco to say his views were the same as those
of an anarchist friend who had been deported. Sacco avoided a
direct reply but it was apparent that they were. Though this
justified Sacco's fear of deportation, it also marked him as a man

*See pages 324 ff.

for whom deportation would be justified. Also, Sacco's attorneys had referred to him, and he had referred to himself, as a socialist; Katzmann's questions made it clear he was an anarchist, which sounded much more threatening; anarchists, not socialists, used bombs.

Katzmann: And the books which you intended to collect were books relating to anarchy, weren't they?
Sacco: Not all of them.
Katzmann: How many of them?
Sacco: Well, all together. We are socialists, democratic, any other socialistic information, socialists, syndicalists, anarchists, any paper.[35]

Katzmann got Sacco to admit he and his friends were going to hide the literature, not destroy it.

Katzmann: After the time had gone by, were you going to bring them out, going to distribute the knowledge contained in them?
Sacco: Certainly, because they are educational for book, educational.
Katzmann: An education in anarchy, wasn't it?
Sacco: Why, certainly. Anarchistic is not criminals.[36]

Katzmann also asked Sacco about a conflict between his testimony and Vanzetti's. Vanzetti had said they were not going to pick up the literature the night they picked up the car; they had to find a hiding place first. Sacco said they were going to pick up the material that same night. When asked to explain this discrepancy Sacco said he was probably mistaken and Vanzetti was right. Actually, either man might have been lying in an attempt to protect others. It is also possible their plans were so uncertain that each had a different idea of what was going to happen once they got the car; too much organization conflicts with the spirit of anarchy. Sacco had not even removed incriminating literature from his own house.

By now the jury could be forgiven if they forgot this was a trial for murder and robbery since countless hours of testimony had been devoted to patriotism, draft evasion, Mexican food, and

The C

anarchist literature. When Katzmann finally got around to the robbery, it was not for long. He asked Sacco if he had removed Berardelli's gun as he lay dying on the sidewalk.

Sacco: No, sir.
Katzmann: Do you mean that, Mr. Sacco?
Sacco: Yes, sir, I mean it.[37]

Now Katzmann began to read what he claimed was the stenographic record of his interrogation of Sacco on May 6. He had asked Sacco, "Do you know Alessandro Berardelli?" Sacco had replied, "No. Who is this Berardelli?" Trying to prove that Sacco did know why he was arrested, Katzmann asked him at Dedham, "Didn't [you] have any idea when I asked you if you knew Berardelli? . . . "

Sacco: Well, fellows read one day the paper. He could not remember.
Katzmann: That did not bring anything back to your mind?
Sacco: No.
Katzmann: Three weeks afterwards?
Sacco: No. What a fellow can remember that?
Katzmann: Can't you remember back three weeks?
Sacco: Well, there isn't anything that interested me to remember.[38]

Katzmann had also asked Sacco on May 6, "Did you hear anything about what happened in Braintree?" Sacco had replied, "I read there was bandits robbing money." Katzmann had asked, "Where did they rob the money?" Sacco had replied, "Over near Rice & Hutchins."[39]

At Dedham, Katzmann insisted this oblique conversation should have made Sacco aware he was under suspicion for the robbery. Sacco replied, "Well, I don't think you mean . . . me."[40]

In the police station, Katzmann had asked Sacco if he was working the day before he read about the robbery in a newspaper on April 16; he did not ask Sacco what he was doing April 15. Sacco had replied, "I think I did." At Dedham, without noting he had never mentioned the date to the confused and frightened foreigner, Katzmann asked Sacco why he had lied about working on April 15. Sacco replied, "Well, of course, I never remember. . . . I could not remember exactly."

Katzmann: If you were in Boston on the 15th day of April, getting your passports, why didn't you tell me that the night I talked with you at Brockton?

Sacco: If I could remember I would tell you it right off.[41]

In October, 1917, Sacco had worked for the Rice & Hutchins shoe factory in South Braintree for seven or eight days, then left for a better job. When Katzmann asked Sacco on May 6 if he ever worked in Braintree, he had said no. Since Rice & Hutchins overlooked the holdup site, Katzmann asked Sacco why he had lied about working there.

Sacco: Because I am not registered. I am a slacker. Then, another thing, I don't want you to find that literature and then I won't be in trouble, that is all.

Katzmann: Are you telling this jury you falsified about ever working in Braintree because you were a slacker?

Sacco: Yes, sir.

* * *

Katzmann: The war was over, wasn't it, when you and I were talking?

Sacco: I know, but they could arrest me just the same, I suppose.

* * *

Katzmann: Did I ask you whether you had seen any service?

Sacco: No, but you could find out whether after.[42]

Katzmann continued to press Sacco about what working at Rice & Hutchins had to do with draft evasion, but Sacco did not give a credible reply until Moore questioned him later. He told Moore that, having just returned from Mexico, he was using a different name at the shoe factory. If Katzmann had checked he would have discovered that no one named Nicola Sacco had ever worked there, which would have forced Sacco to admit he had used another name because he was a draft evader subject to a year in prison for not registering.

The

As he did with Vanzetti, Katzmann demanded that Sacco explain why his memory was better in Dedham than it had been at Brockton.

Katzmann: Is your memory very good, Mr. Sacco? Good memory?

Sacco: Yes.

Katzmann: Working well?

Sacco: Not all the time.

Katzmann: How is it today?

Sacco: Pretty good.

Katzmann: How was it the night I talked to you?

Sacco: I was real disturbed.

Katzmann: Were you half as much disturbed when you were talking with me when you did not know what you were there for, as you say, as you are now when you are charged with murder?

Sacco: I would not say it is better than that time.

Katzmann: I am asking you to say which time were you better, now or that night?

Sacco: It looks to me now the charge is more bad.

Katzmann: Does that mean you were in better shape then as to memory than you are now?

Sacco: I did not know at that time they put in this murder. . . . I got to remember very particular things [now], because the charge is awful on my shoulders.

Katzmann commented sarcastically, "The worse the charge the better your memory?" Sacco replied, "I suppose so. [Man] have to remember where he was."[43] For Katzmann it meant just another joke; for Sacco it meant his life.

The first day of Sacco's testimony had been a disaster, partially because of his difficulty understanding and expressing himself in English. There must have been a conference with his attorneys afterward because the following morning Sacco asked for an interpreter. "I been thinking over last night I did answer something wrong," he said. "Probably I did not understand something."[44] But even with an interpreter the questioning was confused, repetitious, and pointless, punctuated by frequent protests from another interpreter, sitting in at the request of the defense, that the court interpreter was inaccurate.

When Moore took over for redirect examination, Sacco testified that on May 6 he couldn't remember what day he had gone to Boston for his *foglio di via*; since then he had checked all the dates carefully because he knew he faced a murder charge and it had to be April 15 because that was the only time he was away from work all day. He also said, in response to a question from Moore, that he did not believe in force or violence. Then came the reprise.

Moore: Mr. Sacco, in the discussion with Mr. Katzmann in the Brockton police station, was there at any time that Mr. Katzmann told you fully and definitely that you were being held on suspicion or on charge of being involved in the South Braintree murder?

Sacco: Never.

*   *   *

Moore: Mr. Sacco, at the time that you were talking with Mr. Katzmann, did you think at that time that you were charged with some matter involving your opinions and ideas?

Sacco: That is the only thing that I suspected.

*   *   *

Moore: What occurred with Mr. Stewart that made you think you were being held for radical activities?

Sacco: Well, because the first thing they asked me if I was an anarchist, a communist or socialist.[45]

Professor Edmund Morgan cogently summed up the Sacco-Vanzetti trial in one sentence: "Against a masterful and none too scrupulous prosecution was opposed a hopelessly mismanaged defense before a stupid trial judge."[46] Neither Sacco nor Vanzetti had expressed from the stand the very real fears of alien radicals of that period, nor had their attorneys offered evidence to prove their fears were justified. Timid attempts to do so were objected to by Katzmann who was sustained by Thayer, though the judge put

The C

no restraints on the prosecutor. Inanely chanting, "You opened it up," whenever the defense objected, Thayer permitted Katzmann to subject Sacco and Vanzetti—particularly Sacco because he was the easier victim—to blistering cross-examinations on issues that had nothing to do with what happened on April 15, but were certain to reinforce the fear, contempt, and hatred the jurors already felt for alien radicals.

Morgan called the summation for the defense "pitiable" and Katzmann's summation "cleverly devised and beautifully executed."[47] The prosecutor managed to twist, turn, and bend every bit of evidence to his favor, even when it clearly contradicted his case. Vanzetti could not have been the driver of the bandit car so Katzmann deftly moved him to the rear seat. Adroitly and dramatically Katzmann linked Austin Reed's testimony that Vanzetti had shouted at him to Vanzetti's outburst in the courtroom when he had cried, "You are a liar!" at police officer Connolly. Omitting Reed's claim that Vanzetti spoke unmistakable and clear English, Katzmann intoned:

> It fell to the man Vanzetti, the man who showed the gruff voice because he could not control himself because again he was facing his natural enemy, a police officer, Connolly, when he was on the stand, and he showed that same quality of gruff voice that he shows under emotion and excitement that Austin Reed told you about, the crossing tender at Matfield. . . . Will you ever forget the uncontrollable outburst of the defendant Vanzetti, keen enough to realize that [Connolly's testimony] condemned any consciousness of guilt theory of a minor offense, of which the authorities had no proof whatever. "You are a liar" burst from his lips when Connolly told about that move [to reach for his gun].[48]

The hard evidence against Sacco and Vanzetti for robbery and murder at South Braintree disintegrated under scrutiny. No one even claimed to have seen Vanzetti at the scene of the crime; the five witnesses who claimed to have seen him at all were contradicted by other witnesses, by logic, or by their own previous statements. Vanzetti was supposed to have been carrying Berardelli's gun when arrested, but there was no proof it had been removed from the repair shop and considerable proof it had not been; there was also the fact that Vanzetti's gun was a .38 while the repairman testified Berardelli's gun was a .32.

The seven witnesses who claimed to have seen Sacco were contradicted by other witnesses, by logic, or by their own previous statements. The found cap was discovered almost thirty hours after the crime; while the jurors did not know this, they could see in the courtroom that it did not fit Sacco. The jurors also did not know that the prosecution's testimony that the fatal bullet was fired from Sacco's gun was deceitful and probably tainted, but they had heard conflicting testimony from two experts for the defense. To believe Sacco was in South Braintree to kill Berardelli, the jurors had to discount all of his alibi witnesses, including the man he had seen on the train going home.

Reasonable doubt was supposed to rest with Sacco and Vanzetti but it never did. To accept the prosecution's case, the jurors first had to believe Sacco and Vanzetti were guilty and then substantiate their feelings with whatever seemed like proof. The defendants were Italian, radical, draft evaders. They lied. They were presumptuous. They behaved suspiciously. Some witnesses had identified them. Perhaps Vanzetti did have Berardelli's gun. Perhaps the cap did belong to Sacco. Perhaps Sacco had fired the fatal bullet. If Sacco and Vanzetti didn't commit this crime, they had probably committed another. Ripley, the jury foreman, had said it even before the trial began, "Damn them, they ought to hang them anyway!"

Katzmann understood that emotion rather than logic would determine the outcome, which is why nothing in his summation was as brilliant as his closing command: "Gentlemen of the jury, do your duty. Do it like men. Stand together you men of Norfolk!"[49] Stand together, you men of Norfolk County, against these foreigners who mongrelize our pure Anglo-Teutonic blood; stand together against these dissidents who eat our bread then question our values and call Jefferson "Abe." That atavistic call echoed three centuries of bigotry and intolerance in Massachusetts; it summed up the case against Sacco and Vanzetti.

The C

On the morning of July 14, 1921, Judge Webster Thayer delivered his charge to the jury. "The Commonwealth of Massachusetts called upon you to render a most important service," he said. "Although you knew that such service would be arduous, painful and tiresome, yet you, like the true soldier, responded to that call in the spirit of supreme American loyalty. There is no better word in the English language than 'loyalty.' For he who is loyal to God, to country, to his state and to his fellowmen, represents the highest and noblest type of true American citizenship, than which there is none grander in the entire world."[50]

Who could fail to recognize that Sacco and Vanzetti were not loyal to God, to country, to state, and were not American citizens? Who could forget that they ran away when America called them and that Sacco even had the audacity to criticize this country than which there is none grander in the entire world? It was a splendid opening, almost as effective as "Stand together you men of Norfolk!" except that at a trial there is at least one word in the English language better than loyalty; the word is "justice."

After his salute to patriotism, Thayer summarized the commonwealth's case at length paying loving attention to details that seemed incriminating. He discussed the behavior of Sacco and Vanzetti at the Johnson house on May 5 as evidence of consciousness of guilt without mentioning their alibi about needing the car to pick up radical literature and without mentioning that the prosecution never offered any other explanation for what Sacco and Vanzetti were doing at the Johnson garage.

Thayer made a mountainous thing out of policeman Connolly's accusation—never mentioned at Plymouth where Thayer was also presiding judge—that first Vanzetti then Sacco reached for their guns, and asked what was in their minds if they did. The possibility that they did not was covered by the brisk phrase "The defendants deny it."[51]

Thayer also said that the lies Sacco and Vanzetti told when arrested were evidence of consciousness of guilt if they knew they were suspected of robbery and murder. He noted their claim that they lied because they feared "some kind of punishment" because they were alien radicals, but did not dwell upon it.[52] Clearly he didn't believe it and didn't expect the jury to believe it either.

The judge never summarized the case for the defense or troubled the jury's deliberations by recalling testimony that could be considered favorable to Sacco and Vanzetti. Witnesses who testified to not seeing Sacco and Vanzetti at the scene of the crime were ignored, as were the clerk at the Italian consulate, the man on the train, the cloth peddler, and the Brinis. Evidence that showed Sacco and Vanzetti were elsewhere on the day of the crime was not mentioned by Judge Thayer. Neither was the fact that the prosecution had never offered the jury a motive for the crime, proof that either of the men had the stolen money, or the names of the other three robbers. There was no word from Thayer about the staggering illogic of the case: that two men who had taken part in a spectacular robbery and murder would resume their normal lives at once rather than leave the area or change their names or do whatever they had done simply to avoid the draft. Nor was there a word about the likelihood that two radicals who feared arrest and deportation would walk about with weapons in their pockets which linked them to a capital crime.

All Thayer said was, "An alibi is always a question of fact. Therefore, all testimony which tends to show that the defendants were in another place at the time the murders were committed tends also to rebut the evidence that they were present at the time and place the murders were committed."[53] So much for the alibi evidence presented by the defense.

After over thirty days in a hot courtroom listening to confusing and often contradictory testimony from 167 witnesses, no juror could be expected to remember all the details of the case. The jurors remembered only what they wanted to: the inept summary by the defense, the shrewd summary by the prosecution, Thayer's charge underscoring the prosecution's case, and Katzmann's appeal to stand together against the invader.

The jury went out to deliberate shortly after 2:30 P.M. They never asked for any excerpts from the testimony, they never asked any questions. At one point they sent for a magnifying glass to look at the ballistics evidence; every man was his own expert. At about 7:30 P.M. they were back with their verdict.

Thayer: Poll the jury, Mr. Clerk.

The C

The jury was polled.

Thayer: If the jury is agreed, you may please take the verdict.
Clerk: Gentlemen of the jury, have you agreed upon your verdict?
Ripley: We have.
Clerk: Nicola Sacco.
Sacco: Present.

Sacco stood.

Clerk: Hold up your right hand. Mr. Foreman, look upon the prisoner. Prisoner, look upon the Foreman. What say you, Mr. Foreman, is the prisoner at the bar guilty or not guilty?
Ripley: Guilty.
Clerk: Guilty of murder?
Ripley: Murder.
Clerk: In the first degree?
Ripley: In the first degree.
Clerk: Upon each indictment?
Ripley: Yes, sir.
Clerk: Bartolomeo Vanzetti.

Vanzetti stood.

Clerk: Hold up your right hand. Look upon the Foreman. Mr. Foreman, look upon the prisoner. What say you, Mr. Foreman, is Bartolomeo guilty or not guilty of murder?
Ripley: Guilty.
Clerk: In the first degree, upon each indictment?
Ripley: In the first degree.
Clerk: Hearken to your verdicts as the Court has recorded them. You, gentlemen, upon your oath, say that Nicola Sacco and Bartolomeo Vanzetti is each guilty of murder in the first degree upon each indictment. So say you, Mr. Foreman. So, gentlemen, you all say.
Jury: We do, we do, we do.
Thayer: (To the jury.) I can add nothing to what I said this

morning, gentlemen, except again to express to you the gratitude of the Commonwealth for the service that you have rendered. You may now go to your homes, from which you have been absent for nearly seven weeks. The Court will now adjourn.

Sacco: *They kill an innocent man! They kill two innocent men!*[54]

Vanzetti (far left) as a youth in Italy. In America, first he wore a Vandyke, then a moustache. *Courtesy Vincenzina Vanzetti © Herbert A. Feuerlicht*

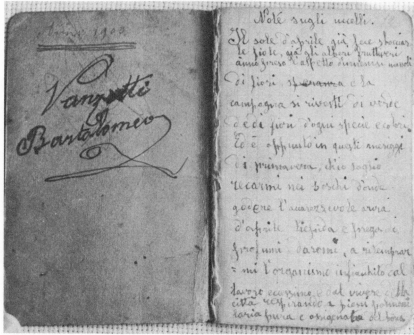

The book on birds Vanzetti wrote when he was twelve years old. *Courtesy Vincenzina Vanzetti © Herbert A. Feuerlicht*

Luigia and Bartolomeo Vanzetti with their parents. *Courtesy Vincenzina Vanzetti © Herbert A. Feuerlicht*

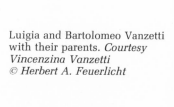

The photograph of Sacco with Rosina and Dante that was too large for the passport. *Courtesy S.H.M. Clinton*

Sacco being taken to the Dedham Courthouse.

Judge Webster Thayer.
Courtesy S.H.M. Clinton

The funeral procession. As the hearses approach, some of the bystanders remove their hats.

The armband.
Courtesy S.H.M. Clinton

The crowd on Hanover Street as the funeral procession left Langone's.

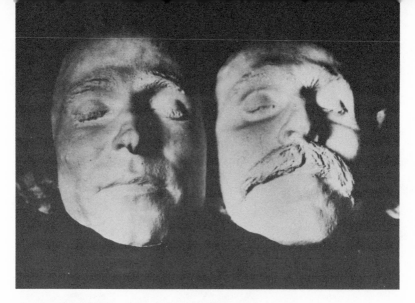

The death masks. *Courtesy S.H.M. Clinton*

The Vanzetti family plot at Villafalletto where one of the urns of mixed ashes is buried. © *Herbert A. Feuerlicht*

Luigia Vanzetti and Alfonsina Brini, both in mourning, pose together before Luigia returned to Italy. *Courtesy Vincenzina Vanzetti © Herbert A. Feuerlicht*

Dante Sacco (far right) visits Ettore, Vincenzina, and Luigia Vanzetti at Villafalletto in 1931. *Courtesy Vincenzina Vanzetti © Herbert A. Feuerlicht*

Sara R. Ehrmann.
© *Herbert A. Feuerlicht*

Vincenzina Vanzetti.
© *Herbert A. Feuerlicht*

below: Alfonsina Brini, aged
ninety-one. © *Herbert A. Feuerlicht*

bottom right: Beltrando Brini.
© *Herbert A. Feuerlicht*

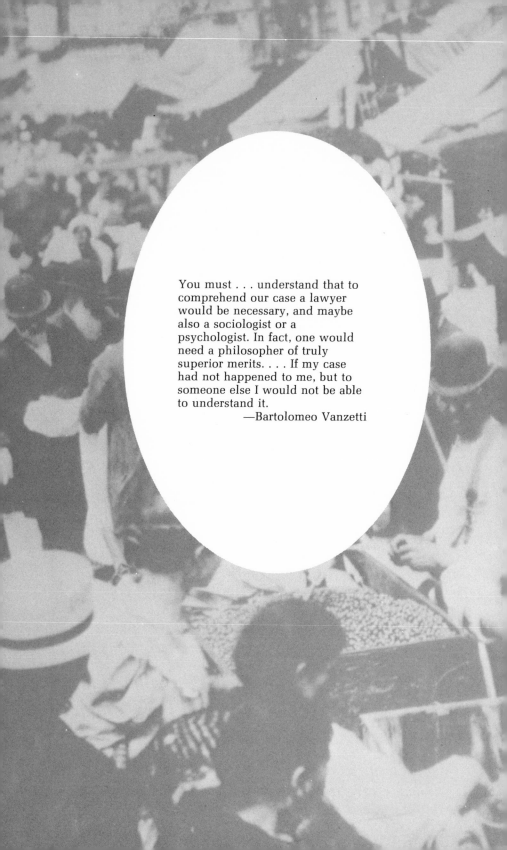

You must . . . understand that to comprehend our case a lawyer would be necessary, and maybe also a sociologist or a psychologist. In fact, one would need a philosopher of truly superior merits. . . . If my case had not happened to me, but to someone else I would not be able to understand it.

—Bartolomeo Vanzetti

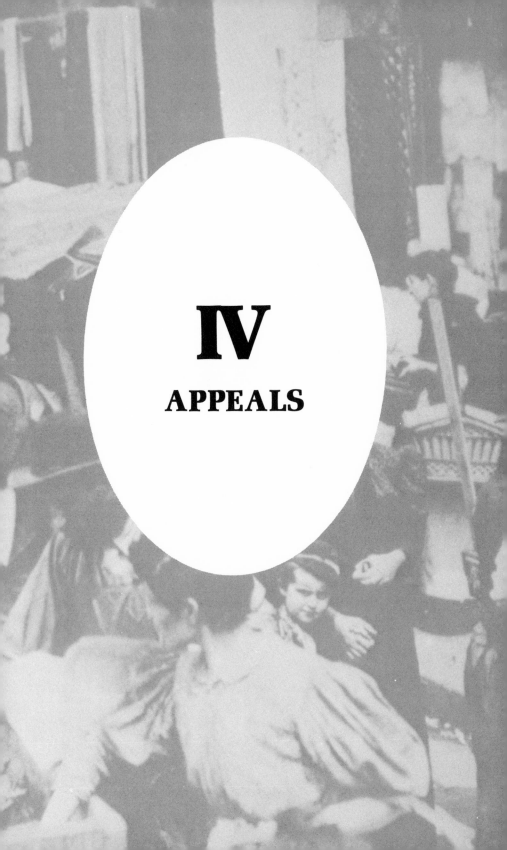

IV

APPEALS

19

Breakdown

Vanzetti to his sister Luigia, September 4, 1921:

It is impossible to explain in one letter a trial that lasted six weeks, especially a trial in which so many social forces, antagonisms, hates and prejudices came together.

Unfortunately you know what the outcome was. I was condemned for the second time for a crime which I did not commit; I have never even been in the place where it was committed. But the last word has not as yet been spoken. The case has been appealed. We will have the judge's answer in a few months. If it is negative we will go to the Supreme [Judicial] Court [of Massachusetts].

In that case we would have to wait a year for an answer. As you can see things move very slowly and patience is necessary. However, the lawyers are optimistic, they hope that the judge himself will grant a reversal. As for the newspapers and the information you wanted, I will do my best to see that you get them as soon as possible.

In Italy, approximately 200 newspapers are concerning themselves with my case. . . . Here, the Italians, and some Americans, are even more ready to help us than before the trial.

Therefore I ask you to be calm and strong. If you vacillate, what will happen to me? Nonetheless, I am in good health, and calm. I would be even better off if I knew that you were capable of strength of spirit. I have been in a great deal of danger; on my journeys, while working, and in New York, which is more dangerous than any jungle. Nonetheless I always came out with a whole skin. Why should I fall victim to a judicial error or a judicial vendetta? . . .

I do not think that you need to come here. What would you, a stranger who does not know the language, be able to do?

Vanzetti to Luigia, undated, same period:

You know everything; you know the general indignation that the unexpected verdict has raised on all sides, you know the generosity and the sympathy that the Italian population of America feels for us; you know how many influential persons are on our side and you know that the Italian proletariat is demonstrating for our release. These things should induce calm and courage.

But I have even better things to tell you: know that, although we have been condemned to death, this will never occur. A fervid campaign against the death penalty is underway, with the object of saving us from execution. Since the best elements in society are taking part in this campaign, there is hope that the outcome will be successful.

In addition, our innocence was clearly demonstrated at the trial. There is no one here who does not understand that we were condemned for reasons of racial and political hatred. We will never be abandoned.

The revolutionary press in Italy will start a campaign on our behalf. The Italian workers have our lives and our liberties in their hands. They have the power to make tyrants tremble; even if these tyrants hold sway across the seas, terror will bring about a sense of justice.

The Italian government will also be forced to intervene by the weight of popular pressure. The Spanish workers will also rise in our favor.

And here? Here, love, affection and solidarity will write an ineradicable page, if the capitalist inquisition does not spread its claws once again.

Why do I no longer place any faith in the process of law? Anyone who is willing to search the dregs of society for them will find a host of perjured witnesses; there are those who will do this in order to advance their career. The jury consists, in general, of the irresponsible, cretinous and fanatic poor, without even counting racial hatred, etc.

In any case I am waiting patiently to see what the law will do.

I study, read and exercise. I strive to remain strong and healthy.

Vanzetti to Luigia, April 4, 1922:

What you say is childish. Human life is uncertain, it is lived in the midst of so many dangers and so many plots, that not even the wisest of men can predict an hour ahead of time whether something will come out badly or well.

If I had remained in Italy, I could have died of melancholy, or of a thousand other sicknesses. I could have died in any sort of accident or, after having become an assassin myself, I might have died in that beautiful and holy war you so approved of. When were you ever thoughtless? When mother died you were only a child. Therefore you were not able to carry on mother's tasks, and no one could have expected that from you. You might have been a bit more adept—but what does this have to do with anything? Aunt Francesca told me that you became both good and skillful in a short period of time. Do not therefore delude yourself that you had anything to do with my present condition. Instead of losing yourself in this fantasy, try to know the truth, to face it and master it. . . .

My only hope, since I have seen that law and injustice are the same, is in the revolutionary proletariat.

It is the proletariat that has shouted its protests in a hundred languages. It is the proletariat that has exposed its chest to the steel of the police. The thieving and murdering bourgeoisie tremble under the feet of the proletariat. It is the proletariat that is forcing the executioners to understand, whether they be in togas, crosses, or gloves, that there has been enough misery, that there have been too many crimes, and that repayment will be demanded. A tooth for a tooth.

When we were arrested, when the trap was set for us, neither the police, nor the prosecutor, nor the judge thought the whole civilized world would take up our defense. . . .

Mrs. [Elizabeth Glendower] Evans . . . is really a marvelous woman. How much she has done for us!

She came to our defense on her own account, guided only by her conviction that we were innocent. . . . She is a millionaire and has one of the most respected names in America. She has done a great deal of work for political prisoners, and is still working for those who have not as yet been freed. She has given me several books and taught me some English.

After his second conviction, Vanzetti seems to have ceased

Appe

writing to his father; except for two brief notes, his letters home were to Luigia. This was probably a reaction to something his father had written to him; when Luigia came to America to see Vanzetti just before his execution, she told the press that the other members of the family were not anarchists and that "My father did not like some of the letters my brother wrote from America, and he scolded him for being so unwise."[1] Giovanni Vanzetti also considered his son a fool for working as a fish peddler in America when he could have been living comfortably in the role expected of him, relieving his aging father of the duties of running the family farm.

Vincenzina *My father kept saying, if he had stayed in Italy it*
Vanzetti: *would not have happened.*

Luigia obviously had said as much to Vanzetti,* which brought forth his indignant outburst "What you say is childish" and the list of calamities that might have befallen him had he stayed home. He could write such things to his younger sister, but he apparently did not know what to say to his father.

Vanzetti's letters home offer unedited insight into his thoughts and feelings. His love for humanity does not prevent him from adding to his sister's needless concern that she was somehow at fault for his leaving home by hinting that, at the age of 16, she might have been more adept at taking their mother's place. His love for justice does not inhibit him from calling down upon his persecutors an Old Testament vengeance the Puritans would have relished. His belief in the equality of man does not hinder him from pejoratively describing the jurors as poor, as well as cretinous and fanatic, or boasting that the best elements in society were trying to abolish the death penalty just to save his life. He had no reason to have faith in the courts but his prattling about the proletariat shows he was as much a victim of his anarchist illusions as he was of Massachusetts justice.

Because appeals were pending, Sacco and Vanzetti were not sentenced upon conviction. As one appeal followed another, one

---

*Vanzetti's family saved his letters but apparently he did not save theirs. Vincenzina Vanzetti doubts that any of the family letters exist, unless they are included among the papers of Aldino Felicani.

year followed another, and the two men were not actually sentenced until April, 1927. Though Vanzetti tried to reassure himself and his family that the masses were rushing to the barricades the world over, only a small but active group kept the case alive. At the center stood Aldino Felicani and the Sacco-Vanzetti Defense Committee.

Most people wakened to the injustice slowly, if at all. Gardner Jackson, who would later become a central figure on the Defense Committee, said that his wife first brought the case to his attention.[2] In 1921, Jackson, a wealthy Quaker born in Colorado and educated at Amherst and Columbia, was living in Boston and working as a cub reporter on the *Boston Globe.* At breakfast one morning his wife said, "I've been reading in the papers the accounts of this trial of these two Italians going on out at Dedham. I don't think that they're getting a fair break. . . . Will you try to find out?"[3]

Jackson talked to Frank Sibley, whom he and everyone else called "the dean of the Boston newspapermen." Sibley, who was covering the trial for the *Globe,* told Jackson, "She is perceptive. It's an outrage that's being perpetrated here."[4]

Gardner   *Sibley's accounts to me of what was going on in the*
Jackson: *courtroom, the expressions of prejudice, and so on, by the judge, Webster Thayer, the sneering, the whole gesture, led me to believe that the trial wasn't fair. Sibley was absolutely convinced early in the trial at Dedham that these two fellows were getting a dirty deal. The district attorney then, Fred Katzmann, employed techniques and methods that convinced Sib that this was really a frameup.*[5]

After talking to Sibley, Jackson went to the offices of the Defense Committee, which were now at 256 Hanover Street, where he met Aldino Felicani, whom he describes as "great, tall, gentle-mannered."[6] When Jackson offered to help the committee, Felicani said he would call upon him "to write stuff,"[7] but other propagandists were available, and while Jackson did occasional leaflets and throwaways, he did not plunge into full time committee work until the end of 1926.

App

Though Vanzetti's trial at Plymouth had been ignored by all but a few local newspapers and *La Notizia*, the trial at Dedham was covered by the Boston press and some out-of-town papers as well, in part because of the DeFalco scandal that preceded it. The Defense Committee also issued what Felicani calls "systematic publicity"; he handled the material for the Italian community while writers like Morris Gebelow, later known as Eugene Lyons, took charge of publicity for the "Americans."[8]

After the verdict, says Felicani, there were "explosions of protest from countries all over the world"[9] which was literally true in Paris where a bomb was thrown at police during a Sacco-Vanzetti rally and another bomb was mailed to the American ambassador. But though parts of Europe and Latin America reacted to the convictions, the response in Massachusetts, where it mattered, was resentment not of the verdicts but of the foreign demonstrations with their emphasis on violence, both real and threatened. Fred Moore and the Defense Committee were forced to disown "the lurid plots and threats" overseas as "thoroughly harmful to the effort being made to save the two men."

During 1922 and 1923, the Defense Committee concentrated on fund raising, publicity, and building public support for a new trial. "Moore did all this work," says Felicani. "I have to give him credit for all this."[10] Felicani also praises Roger Baldwin and the ACLU, as well as "the good ladies of Boston,"[11] the small group of influential women who assisted and solaced Sacco and Vanzetti. Contributions came not only from them but from labor unions, workers individually and in small groups, and from Italian communities and organizations. Every cent was needed because, according to Felicani, Moore was spending money at a terrible rate and had investigators working in every city where he had leads. The only city Moore didn't seem to investigate was Boston. If he had, he might have noticed the story in the *Boston Herald* on April 17, 1920, about the finding of the fraudulent Sacco cap almost thirty hours after the South Braintree murders.

Between 1921 and 1927 there were eight motions for a new trial for Sacco and Vanzetti.

The first, which asserted that the jury's decision was contrary to the evidence and warped by prejudice, was filed July 18,

1921, four days after the verdict, argued on November 5, and denied by Judge Thayer on December 24. Thayer wrote that the jury, having heard the witnesses and examined the exhibits, knew more than its critics and that, "I cannot—as I must if I disturb these verdicts—announce to the world that these twelve jurors violated the sanctity of their oaths, threw to the four winds of bias and prejudice their honor, judgment, reason and conscience. . . ."[12]

Moore expected this and had already filed what is referred to as the first supplementary motion (the Ripley-Daly motion) on November 8, 1921. This concerned the behavior of the jury foreman, Walter Ripley, who died October 10, a few months after the trial. Several jurors affirmed that during the trial Ripley carried several .38 caliber cartridges similar to those in Vanzetti's revolver and discussed them, even though the jurors were forbidden to consider anything not admitted as evidence. On October 1, 1923, a supplement to this motion was filed in which Ripley's friend, William H. Daly, swore that when he said he thought Sacco and Vanzetti were innocent, Ripley had replied, "Damn them, they ought to hang them anyway!"

The second supplementary motion (the Gould-Pelser motion) was filed May 4, 1922. Roy E. Gould, a peddler, was an eyewitness to the robbery; he was so close to the getaway car that one of the bandits fired at him, putting a hole through his coat. Gould had given his name and address to a police officer who verified this and said he had passed the information on to the state police. Gould's description of the man who fired at him did not fit either Sacco or Vanzetti, which is undoubtedly why the prosecution never summoned him. When the defense located Gould in October, 1921, Moore took him to see Sacco in prison. Gould said Sacco was not the bandit; after looking at photographs of Vanzetti, Gould cleared him as well.[13]

Louis Pelser was the witness who testified that Sacco was the "dead image" of the man he saw shoot Berardelli. On February 4, 1922, Pelser signed a statement for Moore in which he said that he had only had a glance at the man with the gun and did not see him clearly enough to identify him. He implied that Assistant District Attorney Harold Williams had persuaded him to identify the bandit as Sacco.[14] Two days after signing the affidavit, Pelser wrote to Katzmann to say that he had been drinking heavily the day he spoke to Moore, and that Moore had locked him in a room, given him a cigar, and persuaded him to repudiate his testimony.[15] Questioned by Williams on February 12, Pelser said he did not see any shooting but did see a man with a gun in his hand who looked like Sacco.[16]

The third supplementary motion (the Goodridge motion) was filed July 22, 1922. Carlos Goodridge was the man who rushed out of the poolroom when the shooting began and later testified that Sacco had pointed a gun at him from the getaway car, even though four friends testified that Goodridge had told them he could identify no one or had noticed only the pale, sickly driver. At the trial an attempt was made to show that Goodridge had pleaded guilty to a criminal charge before the same court and was on probation, but Thayer excluded this evidence.

Moore's investigators discovered that Goodridge's true name was Erastus Corning Whitney, that he had twice been convicted in New York for larceny, that he had fled a third larceny charge, and that he had been involved in other shady activities. Goodridge's former wife said, "he hated all persons that were of Italian nativity, and . . . on many and divers occasions, said that all Italians coming over on the ships to America ought to be sunk in the harbors."[17]

If some of the prosecution's activities were odious, Moore's handling of Pelser, Goodridge, and a third witness, Lola Andrews, raised a stench of its own. Pelser was bullied, threatened, and cajoled by Moore. The attorney trailed Goodridge to Maine and asked him what the district attorney had offered him to identify Sacco. When Goodridge denied receiving any concessions, Moore had him jailed on the larceny charge from which he had fled New York in 1911. After authorities in Maine checked with authorities in New York, who neither requested nor wanted Goodridge's arrest, he was released.

The fourth supplementary motion (the Andrews motion) was filed September 11, 1922. Lola Andrews was the woman who was job hunting the morning of April 15 and had tapped Sacco on the shoulder, while he was under a car, to ask for directions.

Mrs. Andrews, who was divorced, had a nineteen-year-old son who was located in Maine and persuaded by the defense to come to Boston and ask his mother to meet him in a hotel room. There Mrs. Andrews confronted not only her son but two of Moore's associates. They told her that her past had been investigated but, if she told the truth about the robbery, they would not divulge her secrets. Later, Mrs. Andrews, her son, and the two men went to Moore's house where two stenographers waited. One of Moore's men said to her, "You have never yet been known to be idle in the city of Quincy. . . . You have done all kinds of work and we have found that out. We have searched it." [18] Warned that the revelations would hurt both her and her son, Mrs. Andrews broke down and wept. Moore handed her a paper to sign repudiating her testimony. When she refused, her son said, "Mother, I want you to sign that paper, for it means a whole lot to me." [19] Mrs. Andrews signed the affidavit which stated she had lied at the trial under pressure from the prosecution. Two days later she signed another affidavit for Moore saying that the man she saw on April 15 was not Sacco. Mrs. Andrews eventually repudiated both affidavits as having been signed under coercion from Moore.

The fifth supplementary motion (the Hamilton-Proctor motion) was filed April 30, 1923. A supplement to this motion, relating to Captain Proctor, was filed November 5, 1923. In April, two experts, Albert H. Hamilton and Augustus H. Gill, examined the ballistics evidence under a high-powered compound microscope and concluded that neither the alleged fatal bullet nor the matching shell had been fired from Sacco's gun.* Hamilton also declared that the hammer on Vanzetti's revolver was not new, further contradicting the prosecution's claim that it was Berardelli's gun, based upon the repairman's testimony that he had replaced the hammer rather than the spring. The prosecution's experts, Charles J. Van Amburgh and Merton A. Robinson, disputed Hamilton and Gill about the bullet and shell but said nothing about Vanzetti's revolver, implicitly confirming that the hammer was not new.

While making a point in the courtroom, Hamilton took apart

*Whether they examined bullet III or a substitute will never be known.

and reassembled not only Sacco's gun but two new Colt automatics. In February, 1924, Harold Williams, now district attorney,* informed Judge Thayer the gun barrels had been switched; Sacco's gun had a new barrel and one of the new Colts had what was presumably Sacco's barrel. The discovery was made after William Thompson, who was not yet attorney for the defense but took part in the ballistics appeal, asked for additional test firings, a request Thayer ultimately denied.

This is how Vanzetti described the incident in a letter to Luigia dated March 10, 1924:

> As you may know, another mess has come up, someone has changed the barrel on Sacco's gun.
>
> I will tell you what I know of the matter. . . . Our lawyer, Thompson, went to the judge, who appears to alternate between being a tiger and being an ass, and said, "You cannot make an equitable decision in this matter until you have ordered one hundred shots fired from the gun, and had these bullets compared to the bullet that killed the [guard]. . . ."†
>
> The judge answered that he wanted to know the opinion of the prosecution first. The prosecutor announced that he wanted to see the weapon in question, and have it examined by an expert. . . .
>
> This expert arrived and, oh marvel of marvels, he noticed that the barrel had been changed. An expert hired by the defense came and confirmed this. The barrel has been changed and the hundred shots cannot be fired. But who did this? The judge immediately started an investigation into the matter (what a joke). The one who changed the barrel certainly did not do so in the presence of witnesses. . . .
>
> The head clerk of the court was called, since it was his job to look after the evidence. He said that

---

*Williams was elected district attorney in 1922, and Katzmann became his assistant.
†The defense did not yet suspect that bullet III might not be authentic.

the defense had never asked him for the weapon,* but that the prosecutor asked for the gun more than once and took it away with him, so that the clerk does not know what he did with it.

So the . . . prosecution took it away several times and did what it wanted with the weapon. Who then can have changed the barrels?

During the hearing before Judge Thayer, the defense claimed the barrels had been switched by the prosecution and that the old barrel on the new gun was not Sacco's, making it impossible to hold the test firings requested by Thompson. The prosecution claimed the old barrel was Sacco's and that Hamilton had switched barrels to give the defense a reason to demand a new trial.

Judge Thayer ruled that the old barrel found on the new gun was Sacco's. He did not say who had changed the barrels but clearly believed it was Hamilton. Since both Moore and the prosecution lacked scruples, either side could have been responsible. But if the district attorney had no reason to suspect the gun had been tampered with or did not want it tampered with, why didn't he simply agree or not agree to the new findings? His decision to have the gun checked first suggests consciousness of guilt. As in the matter of bullet III, the behavior of the prosecution raises questions about the integrity of the evidence, and the consequence is that with a doubtful bullet and a doubtful barrel, ballistics tests are meaningless.

The Proctor portion of the Hamilton-Proctor motion concerned Captain William Proctor's trial testimony that the fatal bullet was "consistent with" having been fired from Sacco's gun. In his affidavit of October, 1923, Proctor, who died five months later, asserted that what he meant was that the bullet had been fired by a Colt automatic, not that it had been fired by Sacco's Colt automatic, and that the questions asked him at Dedham were carefully framed to make it appear he thought Sacco was guilty when he didn't.

---

*Hamilton did examine the gun again on December 4, 1923, in the presence of the clerk, and later asserted the barrel had been changed by that date.

Appea

The five supplementary motions for a new trial were filed over a two-year period by Fred Moore and his associates. Two other attorneys, William G. Thompson and Arthur D. Hill, assisted in preparing and arguing the Hamilton-Proctor motion. Thompson was the distinguished lawyer who had been willing to take over the case when the first difficulties arose between Moore and Thayer, but Moore had refused to bow out and the Defense Committee had refused to fire him. Years later Felicani would say that if Thompson had handled the case from the beginning, the outcome would have been different.[20]

By 1924, tension between Moore and Felicani had reached such a peak that Moore decided to destroy the Defense Committee. He formed his own group, the Sacco-Vanzetti New Trial League, not only to perpetuate his role as chief counsel but to control the funds that were still being raised for Sacco and Vanzetti; Felicani says Moore demanded that all contributions sent to the Defense Committee be given to the New Trial League.[21] Moore's tactic very nearly succeeded because he took with him Mrs. Evans and other wealthy and influential backers of the Defense Committee, but the New Trial League had few Italian members and lacked the support of either Sacco or Vanzetti.

Sacco, who hated Moore from the start, whose wife wept when the committee wouldn't fire him, wrote the lawyer an apoplectic letter. His anger outracing his English, Sacco accused Moore of clinging to the case to further his own interests and to pocket the "sweet pay" he received. Sacco damanded that his name and photograph be removed from the letters and pamphlets of the New Trial League and ordered Moore to "please get out of my case." He also denounced Moore's "philanthropist friends"[22] and for a time refused to see them.But Sacco was always more realistic about the good women of Boston than Vanzetti, who lapped up their attention. Though Sacco liked Mrs. Evans and said she was like his own mother to him, he wrote another one of the women, "it is nice and noble to be rich and be kind and generous towards the poor exploit people, but it is much more noble the sacrifice of those who have none and divide his bread with his own oppressed brothers."[23]

The New Trial League collapsed, and Mrs. Evans and the

others returned to the Defense Committee which became more open to members who were not Italian. However, Gardner Jackson says that Mary Donovan, who came from a radical Irish group, was the only non-Italian actively involved in the day-to-day work of the committee until he joined it full time.

After the fiasco of the New Trial League, Fred Moore was finally fired. He officially withdrew from the Sacco-Vanzetti case in November, 1924, harboring a terrible bitterness. It was he who had turned the case from a routine murder charge against two Italian radicals into a major political trial, though it would not become the cause of the decade, and possibly the century, until Moore was gone. Of course if Moore had been a more accomplished lawyer Sacco and Vanzetti might never have had to become a cause; they might have been acquitted. But to be ignominiously dismissed before he could complete his masterpiece was a terrible humiliation for Moore, and he would exact a terrible revenge. He would later say "Sacco was probably, Vanzetti possibly guilty."[24] That would not only settle the score with Sacco and Vanzetti, but explain why Moore lost the case.

The Defense Committee, four years too late, now decided what was needed was a respectable, responsible, conservative Boston lawyer. They approached William Thompson, who was so reluctant to clean out Moore's stable that he asked for twenty-five thousand dollars in advance.

The Defense Committee managed to raise five thousand dollars and to obtain the balance as a grant from the Garland Fund, with the help of Roger Baldwin, who was secretary of the board of directors. The McAnarney brothers also withdrew from the case and William G. Thompson became attorney for Sacco and Vanzetti. At great cost to his practice he gave them the last full measure of devotion as a lawyer and as a man. He came to believe absolutely in their innocence and to regard Vanzetti with something close to religious awe. But that was later.

Aldino   *At the beginning he was very severe. Little by little*
Felicani: *things started to ease up [but] the relationship*
              between us remained that he was the aristocrat and
              we were the proletarian.[25]

During all of this manipulating and maneuvering, Sacco and Vanzetti suffered in their separate prisons, Vanzetti at Charlestown, where he was serving his sentence for his first conviction, Sacco at Dedham, where technically he was still waiting to be sentenced.

Prison was more unendurable for Sacco than for Vanzetti. Vanzetti was a thinker, a dreamer, a talker, who could easily pass an afternoon chatting with a friend, as he had the day of the South Braintree robbery. As a sentenced prisoner he was assigned work, and he filled the empty hours reading, studying, translating, writing. Sacco was different; he was physical rather than cerebral. His compact body compressed unlimited energy, yet as an unsentenced prisoner he was not put to work. Also, Sacco had a wife. Vanzetti, who loved everyone well but no one intimately, only partially understood Sacco's frustration. "Has Nick a wife?" Vanzetti wrote Mrs. Evans. "Yes, and a good one; but not being free, he must either think that she is consoling herself with somebody else, or that she is suffering the unspeakable agony of a loving woman compelled to mourn a living lover."[26] Besides the slur at Rosina Sacco, who did not deserve it, Vanzetti did not seem to understand the unspeakable agony of a loving man compelled to live apart from his wife.

Before the end of 1921, Sacco began to show signs of paranoia; he complained that something was being put into his food. In an attempt at therapy, Sacco was assigned to the prison shoe factory, but he was no longer the experienced edger who could earn eighty dollars a week with his skilled hands. He had so many accidents he was quickly removed.

Late in 1922, the paranoiac symptoms returned. On February 17, 1923, Sacco began a hunger strike.

Aldino Felicani:	*He was hoping . . . to precipitate more popular protest against the legal murder. . . . The publicity was terrific, as you can imagine.*[27]

Vanzetti to Luigia, March 15, 1923:

You must already know that Sacco has had recourse to a hunger strike. He is determined to be free or die. He has been without food for 29 days. . . .

He is very weak, if he continues he will not live long. He has, at the most, a week or two. His reason has undoubtedly been unseated by his misfortune. While he is fully conscious of what he is doing, there remains the fact that he hopes, in fact he is convinced, that this act will result in his freedom. This is an error that proves that his mind is a trifle disturbed. All supplications on the part of his friends and loved ones are useless.

The lawyer asked the committee, Nicola's wife, and me for authorization to have doctors examine Nicola, and take the measures necessary for his salvation; that is to say, force-feeding.

Then the lawyer himself assumed this responsibility, and asked the court to put Nicola into a hospital, in order to restore his mental health and save his life. I was furious but impotent, I bit my tongue and said nothing. . . .

The laws of the United States do not permit someone who is not in his right mind to be tried. Therefore all judicial action concerning Nicola will be suspended until he is declared cured. As you can see things have been, in his case, postponed for an indeterminate amount of time. But not for me. . . .

It is universally recognized that a separate trial is an advantage. In most cases the defense asks the court to permit this. The court forbade this the first time, now events have imposed this course. My lawyers are hopeful, but I am not, the first two trials were enough for me, my confidence is in the workers, not the law.

Nicola's tragic determination has shaken the civil conscience. There is electricity in the air and tension in men's souls. . . .

The fact remains that I am innocent, and that I am fully convinced of the innocence of Sacco, for this reason I would like to share his fate, as would probably be the case in a common trial. I will do my

best to bring this about. However the defense lawyers act according to other impulses. They often
overleap the barriers set up by my personal desires
and the desires of the comrades; we are not able to do
anything about this.

I hope that Nicola will come to his senses fast.
In the meantime, that which concerns me will take
its course, whether I wish it or not.

Today I was the object of a great demonstration
of affection on the part of the workers of Boston. . . .

America, dear sister, is called the land of liberty, but in no other country on earth does a man
tremble before his fellow men like here. Here, we
speak of liberty in order to have something to laugh
about.

Vanzetti was compared to Christ by several persons who
knew him, but this must have been one of the least Christ-like
letters he ever wrote. Since Vanzetti wanted more publicity, and
Sacco's fast was achieving it, why did Vanzetti object? Was it
because he lacked the will to fast himself? He wrote Mrs. Evans
that he was sorry for Sacco but after "serious consideration" he
himself had decided not to go on a hunger strike, though he was
ready to do so when it seemed "reasonable." [28] When would it
have been reasonable if not then, when a double protest would
have been doubly effective? If Sacco's fast had "shaken the civil
conscience" and caused "electricity in the air," how could
Vanzetti boast that the demonstration in Boston was for him
rather than for Sacco or for both of them?

Sacco was weak, but not near death; the commonwealth did
not dare let him die. When Vanzetti said Sacco would not live
long was he expressing a fact or a wish? If Vanzetti really wanted
Sacco to recover, why was he so furious at the possibility of his
being force-fed? Despite Vanzetti's exaggerated protests that he
did not want a separate trial, did he secretly hope Sacco's death or
insanity would improve his own chance for survival? Did the
defense lawyers really overleap his desires or was it less troubling
to put the onus on them?

It is neither just nor possible to judge a man in prison, particularly an innocent one, but one of the components of the split-guilt theory is that an innocent Vanzetti was willing to lay down his life rather than expose a guilty Sacco. At the time Vanzetti wrote this letter, it would seem he was willing to have Sacco die if it would help save his own life.

On March 16, after four weeks of fasting, Sacco was examined by three psychiatrists appointed by Judge Thayer. They described Sacco as "perfectly calm" as he told them that the state was trying to kill him slowly by putting poison in his food, blowing noxious vapors into his cell, and circulating electric currents under his bed.[29]

Sacco told the psychiatrists he had gone on a hunger strike because he refused to suffer any longer. Asked why he drank water, he replied that he didn't want to die too quickly because his lawyers were appealing for a new trial. Somewhere in his death wish the dim hope lingered that he might be saved after all.

The psychiatrists reported to Thayer that Sacco was "mentally disturbed" and Thayer ordered him sent to Boston Psychopathic Hospital for ten days of further examination. At the hospital, Sacco was told that if he didn't eat he would be fed through a tube. Sacco later explained, "I was too weak and could not fight them, so I said, 'I go ahead and eat.'" During his first few days at the hospital, Sacco felt better and behaved normally. He told the doctors how much he loved his family, nature, and his work. "I am soft-hearted," he said. "I cannot kill a chicken. I am kind, tender, I never kill anybody. I love my fellow man."

On the night of March 22, Sacco said he had a headache and asked for a wet towel for his head. When the attendant went to get one, Sacco rose from his bed and began to smash his head against the arms of a heavy chair, crying, "I am innocent! There is no justice!" It took four men to restrain him.

The next morning he was calm again. He told a doctor, "I am ashamed of what I done," but he also said he was tired of life and wanted to commit suicide. He did not repeat the episode, however, and the director of the hospital concluded there was "no evidence of insanity of any type." But the court ordered that he be held in the hospital for further observation, and his condition again deteriorated. He told Mrs. Evans, who visited him, that when he was sent back to jail he would give the judge twenty-four hours to decide the case one way or the other, and if he was not freed he would kill himself. After a visit from his wife, Sacco tried to bang his head against the edge of an open door. When he was restrained he became more violent and screamed that Rosina was a patient in the ward above him.

After that, periods of calm alternated with frenzied seizures during which he would shout that he wanted his freedom, that he wanted to go home to his wife and children. Psychiatrist Ralph Colp, Jr., in an article on Sacco's mental illness in *The Nation* (August 16, 1958), describes Sacco as suffering from "sensory deprivation." He had been deprived of "the three most important things in his life," writes Colp, "wife and children, job, and his exercise and contact with nature."

On April 10, the director of the hospital reported that Sacco was "of unsound mind, and definitely requires hospital care and treatment." On April 22, his thirty-second birthday, Sacco was committed to the Bridgewater Hospital for the Criminally Insane. There his condition improved dramatically. He was permitted to exercise, he shared a ward with others instead of being isolated in a room, and he spent his mornings working on the Bridgewater prison farm. He told a doctor that he wished he had succeeded in killing himself earlier, and though he would not attempt it at that point, he might in the future if he did not receive justice. On September 29, 1923, Sacco was discharged and returned to Dedham jail.

20

Those Anarchistic Bastards

During Sacco's breakdown and hospitalization, Vanzetti remained in Charlestown prison, keeping up his prodigious correspondence. A letter to Luigia on June 11, 1922, contains an important bit of news: "Two prisoners have confessed that they took part in one crime . . . which I have been accused of committing."

Late in 1921, Fred Moore had heard that two criminals, Frank Silva and James Mede, were involved in the unsuccessful Bridgewater robbery for which Vanzetti was convicted at Plymouth. Moore visited Mede, who happened to be in Charlestown prison where he taught English to his fellow prisoners, including Vanzetti. In return for an undisclosed sum of money, Mede told Moore he had planned the Bridgewater robbery with Frank Silva but did not take part in it because he was arrested on another charge first.

Moore went to Atlanta, where Silva was in prison, but Silva said he knew nothing about it. Not until 1928 did Silva sell his story—or a story—to *Outlook and Independent* magazine (October 31, 1928). Silva, who had worked for the L. Q. White Shoe Company and knew how the payroll was delivered, said that he had originally conceived the Bridgewater crime and invited Mede to participate. Since Mede was in prison, Silva decided to attempt the robbery without him on December 24, 1919, the day Vanzetti was delivering eels. Silva said the three other men who took part in the holdup were Joseph San Marco, Michael (Doggy) Bruno, and "Guinea" Oates; Doggy Bruno was the shotgun bandit. Bruno did not resemble Vanzetti, but he had the dark hair and closely cropped moustache the witnesses had originally described. *Outlook* magazine had a writer and a reformed burglar, who had helped persuade Silva to talk, drive to Bridgewater with Silva and Mede. They found that Silva recognized many places important to the crime and seemed to have an insider's knowledge of the details.

Since Silva was paid, there can be no assurance he told the whole truth or even a partial truth, or that he correctly identified his cohorts. His account eliminates C. A. Barr, who also resembled the shotgun bandit, but it makes better sense than Katzmann's case against Vanzetti; anything would. Four robbers are named, the shotgun bandit has the right kind of moustache, and the men are criminals of a low order of competence, the kind who would attempt a robbery but fail to pull it off.

The authorities of the Commonwealth of Massachusetts were not interested in Silva or Mede, however, since the party line held Vanzetti to be the villain, and Moore was unable to do anything with Mede's purchased confession which was not confirmed by Silva until Sacco and Vanzetti were dead. Vanzetti made the best of his disappointment by writing home on September 3, 1922, "There are . . . the confessions of the two prisoners, but the comrades and I feel it repugnant to take such a course. An old and heroic Italian comrade has said, 'As long as it is necessary to finance the defense of Sacco and Vanzetti, so that they may be defended by those means which the law itself permits, as long as it is necessary to protest their condemnation and to shout their innocence, as long as this is the case we are ready for anything. But we will not chase criminals in order to find the guilty parties . . . we cannot play the parts of policemen.' Our ancient and heroic comrade is right. It is disgusting to bow before the laws of knaves."

This attitude may explain the allegation by Eugene Lyons

that the Defense Committee told Moore to "lay off" one of his investigations,[1] though what Lyons said must be weighed against Felicani's assertion that he and Lyons often disagreed and had "many, many arguments about things."[2] The concept of an ancient and heroic anarchist urging his comrades to use only those means which the law permits is ludicrous, but it would take an anarchist to understand the anarchist view that it is immoral to help the state capture criminals. The nonanarchists on the Defense Committee were out of touch with the anarchists, and the anarchists were out of touch with reality.

In addition to informing his family about the latest developments in the case, Vanzetti's letters home were reassuring, angry, witty, boastful, naive, dogmatic, revealing, and rich in insights and aphorisms.

> The state does evil well and good badly. An honest man is soon thrown in jail and found guilty of any crime, but when the time comes to remedy an error, there are all sorts of complications and the state moves like a snail.[3]
>
> *   *   *
>
> I have received many tokens of esteem and friendship. . . . People come to see me whom I never would have met as a mere worker and agitator. This not only pleases me but has taught me a great deal.[4]
>
> *   *   *
>
> It is said that people speak well of you only if you are dead, but they also speak well of you if you are in jail.[5]
>
> *   *   *
>
> The lawyer is working as hard as he can to find the kind of evidence that will force a retrial. I say force, because the judge, our mortal enemy, who wants, if only he can, to ruin us, will not allow a retrial unless he is forced to it. Rendered ferocious by the obsessive necessity of defending his own class, he forgets the sort of fate that destiny reserves for tyrants. Above him is the Supreme Court of the

state, and above both there is the will of the proletariat of the world, and the conscience of all of civilized
humanity. In any case the lawyer feels optimistic.
Three witnesses for the prosecution have been anni-
hilated. Other important evidence is also going to be
produced against the twelve redskins [the jurors]
that condemned us.[6]

* * *

It is now election time over here and the
politicians are exchanging all sorts of insults. America is (if democracy is the same cynical joke that I
have always known) more democratic than Italy.
Here, those who pimp for the republic are elected by
popular vote.[7]

* * *

I have translated a monograph, dealing with the
Russian question, from English into Italian. This
work is of a theoretical-polemical nature, and will be
published in serial form by one of our newspapers
here, before coming out as a book. I am convinced
that I have accomplished a work of great utility to the
future development of humanity.[8]

* * *

I was expecting the judge's pronouncement last
month; this month is already almost gone, and he
has yet to say anything. Perhaps that Christian spirit
wishes once more to enliven my Christmas season
with his refusal?*[9]

* * *

Both my body and my soul remain strong. . . .
My writings, poor as they may be, are met with
sympathy and approval. In the thirteen years I spent
in this country, I never realized I had any talent at all
until this present misfortune took place. . . . If a
peaceful conscience and a firm heart mean Christmas, every day is Christmas for me.[10]

* * *

*The first motion for a new trial, on the grounds that the verdict was against the
weight of the evidence, was denied by Thayer on December 24, 1921.

You must be strong, melancholy does not do a bit of good. I know that this has been a violent and cruel blow, I suffer more for you and for the good people that I love than I do for myself. My shoulders are hard, I can carry my cross. You see, I am a rebel and would like to cut the tail off this vile and abject world. Nonetheless my spirits remain high. I love liberty, but I can continue to resist even behind bars. . . . It will take time but we will win. . . . In the meantime I am in excellent health. I read, work and write all the time. . . . I am active, I do not cry, and am very well loved.[11]

*   *   *

I just got back from school where I have been studying arithmetic. . . . Last year I got the first prize in English.[12]

*   *   *

The Americans are very democratic, if treated with sincerity and honesty they are happy. They like fruit (especially strawberries), salad, milk, and omelets. As you see, it will be easy to satisfy them.*[13]

*   *   *

You must . . . understand that to comprehend our case a lawyer would be necessary, and maybe also a sociologist or a psychologist. In fact, one would need a philosopher of truly superior merits. . . . If my case had not happened to me, but to someone else I would not be able to understand it.[14]

Luigia Vanzetti bore this bombardment with her customary sweetness and humility. Once she dared comment negatively on Vanzetti's repeated expressions of faith in the proletariat and was sharply reprimanded. "You have reason to be happy at the 'solidarity of so many good people,'" he wrote, "but do not refer to

---

*This was in reply to a question from Luigia on how to cope with one of Vanzetti's good ladies of Boston who was coming to visit Villafalletto. A pilgrimage to Vanzetti's village became obligatory for those of his supporters who could get to Italy.

it as 'ineffective as of this date.' . . . Be persuaded once and for all of this irrefutable truth: protest and revolt are full of good; cowardice, ignorance, and submission are fatal."[15]

Despite these fighting words, Vanzetti's letters reveal mounting confusion over his identity as well as conflict between the anarchist clichés he had lived by and the upper-class world that dazzled him. To a friend in Italy he ranted for paragraphs about how the proletariat had saved him from "the large companies," though with or without the proletariat he still would have had two trials and the right of appeal. Without pausing for breath he added, "The Americans have also been very helpful. I have met many doctors, lawyers and millionaires that I never would have gotten close to had I not been arrested. How they love me. They marvel at what I write, they visit me and bring me gifts, and they always write to me. If I were set free they would open the doors of their houses to me and let me in, they would help me in any way they could."[16]

In another letter, Vanzetti told Luigia, with pride that is painful to read, that Mrs. Evans "bless her soul . . . would like me to help her cultivate her garden" while another benefactor wanted him as a "handyman-son."[17] Elizabeth Glendower Evans, the bold dowager who gave Sacco and Vanzetti generous sums of money, visited them, and sent them gifts, had praised Vanzetti's poetry and wanted to translate his essays, but she did not offer to found a literary magazine for him if he were freed; she asked him to be her gardener. After all, he was Italian. And Vanzetti, who thought he was doing work of great utility to the future development of humanity, was flattered. "I would like to do it," he wrote Mrs. Evans. "I am not an expert gardener—but I think that you are so; and would it be possible, you would know what a worker I am, and what a garden I will plant and work out under your advice."[18]

The five supplementary motions for a new trial were argued before Judge Webster Thayer at the beginning of October and the beginning of November, 1923. On October 1, 1924, after virtually a full year had passed, Thayer handed down his opinion denying all five motions.

The Ripley-Daly motion concerned the jury foreman who

had carried and talked to other jurors about cartridges similar to Vanzetti's. Thayer wrote:

> It is true that said Ripley did show, to two or three of the jurors, at some time before the jury retired to consider their verdict, said three cartridges, and that there was some talk or discussion about them (but not the Vanzetti cartridges) and what that talk or discussion was, whether favorable or unfavorable to the defendant, does not appear, or when it was, before the jury finally retired; none of the jurors could recall. If the jurors would not recall what that conversation was, bearing in mind the tremendous gravity of the issues involved, it would not seem as though it could be very material or important, and if not, I fail to see how it could, or might, have created any disturbing influence in the minds of the jurors against these defendants.
>
> I therefore find that the mere production of the Ripley cartridges and the talk or discussion about them did not create such disturbing or prejudicial influence that might in any way affect the verdict.

"At any rate," Thayer added, "I am not willing to blacken the memory of Mr. Ripley. . . ."[19] He did not explain why the memory of the departed jury foreman was more important than justice for Sacco and Vanzetti, but he was so loathe to blacken Ripley's memory that he did not even mention the affidavit of William Daly, who swore that Ripley had said, "Damn them, they ought to hang them anyway!" The Daly portion of the appeal was simply ignored.

The Gould-Pelser motion had produced a new eyewitness, Roy Gould, who exonerated both Sacco and Vanzetti, and affidavits from Louis Pelser, who repudiated his testimony identifying Sacco as the "dead image" of the man who shot Berardelli, then partially repudiated his repudiation by saying that while the gunman looked like Sacco he did not see him fire. Concerning Gould, Thayer wrote, "This evidence only means the addition of one more eyewitness to the passing of the bandit automobile.

App

This, therefore, would simply mean one more piece of evidence of the same kind and directed to the same end, and in my judgment, would have no effect whatever upon the verdicts."[20] Thayer then stated his opinion that the verdicts did not rest on eyewitness testimony since the defense had produced more eyewitnesses to clear Sacco and Vanzetti than the prosecution had produced to incriminate them.

"The evidence that convicted these defendants," wrote Thayer, "was circumstantial and was evidence that is known in law as 'consciousness of guilt.' This evidence, corroborated as it was by the eyewitnesses, was responsible for these verdicts of guilty."[21] Thus eyewitness testimony did not convict the two men except when it corroborated circumstantial evidence; when it did not, as with Gould, Thayer dismissed it.

Thayer then digressed at length to discuss the guilty verdicts. He cited the lies told by Sacco and Vanzetti when they were arrested and, in a throwaway line, briefly noted the claim that they feared "some harm or punishment in some manner"[22] because they were radicals; Salsedo's death sent no chills down Thayer's spine. Thayer also said the defendants themselves introduced the subject of radicalism to explain their lies to Stewart and Katzmann, and that if they had not lied, they would not have had to bring up their beliefs to justify their behavior. He did not mention that if Stewart and Katzmann had told them the truth about why they were arrested, Sacco and Vanzetti might not have lied. The judge also made it clear that he believed Sacco and Vanzetti had tried to draw their guns and said that the jury "had a right to determine that radicalism had nothing to do with their carrying these guns and that radicalism had nothing to do with their attempt to use these guns upon the officers."[23] Thayer did not explain how being armed on the night of May 5 made Sacco and Vanzetti guilty of two murders that had occurred three weeks earlier.

Thayer continued:

> The defendants . . . claimed they were only consciously guilty of being radicals, which might subject them to deportation or other punishment, *but*

*not consciously guilty of the murder of Parmenter
and Berardelli.* No clearer cut question of fact was
ever tried out before any jury, and it became their
duty to pass upon the truthfulness of the claims
between the Commonwealth and the defendants. To
do this they would determine whether there was a
more logical, reasonable and probable connection
between the falsehoods and other conduct of the
defendants and radicalism, or the murder of Parmenter and Berardelli. If the jury under their oaths
believed that the murder of Parmenter and Berardelli
was the only true and logical determination of this
question, should I say, by setting aside their verdicts,
that they ought not to have so found?[24]

When Thayer was through justifying the jury's verdict, he
characterized Pelser's recantation to Moore as "not at all satisfac-
tory or trustworthy" since Pelser was drunk at the time and
withdrew his statement two days later. Thayer said Katzmann and
Williams had denied influencing Pelser's trial testimony "and I
find that their affidavits are true."[25]

The Goodridge motion concerned the witness with the
criminal record whom Moore trapped in Maine. Thayer correctly
pointed out that Goodridge's testimony had been "successfully
impeached" at the trial by other witnesses. The judge also
correctly excoriated Moore for having Goodridge arrested by the
Maine police in a futile attempt to coerce him into admitting he
had received concessions from the district attorney.[26]

The Andrews motion concerned Mrs. Lola Andrews who
repudiated her testimony when Moore confronted her with her
teenaged son and threatened to expose her past. Thayer commented that in obtaining Mrs. Andrews's affidavits, which she later
disowned, Moore was "guilty of unprofessional conduct." He
added, "Mr. Moore . . . seems to be laboring under the view that
an enthusiastic belief in the innocence of his clients justifies any
means in order to accomplish the ends desired."[27]

The Hamilton-Proctor motion concerned the ballistics opinions offered by Hamilton and Gill for the defense and Captain

App

Proctors's sworn statement that the questions asked of him at Dedham were designed to mislead the jury. Thayer decided the prosecution's ballistics experts were correct because they would not commit perjury; by implication the defense's experts would and did. As for Proctor, Thayer ruled that no deception or wrongdoing was involved. Unwilling to blacken the memory of the departed foreman Ripley, Thayer did not hesitate to blacken the memory of the departed Proctor by reproving him for charging Katzmann and Williams with "misconduct in their respective offices, which misconduct assailed their honor [and] their integrity."[28]

Vanzetti to Luigia, October 5, 1924:

> You will already know, by this time, that the judge denied our request for a retrial. Nothing else could have happened; and if, in my last letter I showed a certain degree of optimism, it did not come from conviction but was rather the result of certain rumors that had been repeated to me. That Jesuit had convinced everyone that came to see him that he would grant us a retrial.
>
> However, dear Luigina, I beg you to assure father and all our relatives and friends that there is no reason to become discouraged.
>
> Now our case will be presented to the supreme court of the state, which will announce a decision any time between six months and a year from now. If they do not concede our appeal there is always the federal Supreme Court.

The appeal to the Supreme Judicial Court of Massachusetts was prepared by William Thompson, who dropped the tainted Pelser, Goodridge, and Andrews motions. Thompson's appeal was based on the grounds that the conviction was unjust for certain specified reasons and on Thayer's denial of the Ripley-Daly, Gould, and Hamilton-Proctor motions. There was so much work to be done that Thompson, a thorough and meticulous attorney, did not argue the case before the supreme judicial court until January, 1926, fifteen months after Thayer's decision.

While Thompson prepared his case and Sacco and Vanzetti suffered doubt and dread in their cells, Thayer was perfectly content. In November, 1924, a month or so after he had denied the appeals, he went to a football game at his alma mater, Dartmouth. After the game he saw James P. Richardson, a professor of law and political science at the college. "Did you see what I did with those anarchistic bastards the other day?" Thayer crowed to Richardson. "I guess that will hold them for a while. Let them go to the Supreme Court now and see what they can get out of them!"[29]

This is the story Richardson told the Lowell Committee, but another version is found in the oral memoirs of Robert Lincoln O'Brien, editor of the *Boston Herald* during that period. O'Brien says Thayer saw Professor Richardson in a hotel washroom and said, "I've got those sons of bitches where I'm going to have them now. Those dagoes, I'm going to show them!"[30]

Vanzetti's response to Thayer's refusal to grant a new trial was presumably to suffer a nervous breakdown. Early in January, 1925, he was sent to the Bridgewater Hospital for the Criminally Insane where he remained until May, when he was returned to Charlestown prison. Psychiatrists diagnosed Vanzetti's condition as "hallucinatory and delusional."[31] Undoubtedly he was disturbed, but the possibility that his breakdown was staged is raised for the first time by his correspondence to Villafalletto.

Vanzetti's mail was read both at the prison and by authorities in Italy. Though he had his friends and attorneys smuggle out some of his letters, there were limits to what he could tell Luigia openly. On October 5, 1924, he wrote her he was upset that she had not met one of his American friends traveling in Europe because the woman "had a message which I do not wish to put down on paper." Vanzetti's friend had left for Europe in May; if the message concerned his breakdown, as the letter later suggests, he was considering this ploy at least five months before Thayer's decision.

The revealing portion of the letter begins in the cheerleader style Vanzetti often used to encourage Luigia: "I am well, I am strong, I want to win! Be of good spirits! Imitate my example, grant me the comfort of knowing that you are brave, strong and in

Appe

good health. Courage and faith!" Then he wrote, "In the meantime I will try to stay in the sun and in the fresh air as much as possible. I will try to make the most of my time, because I wish to reenter the great battle of life stronger and more fit than ever, so that I will be able to fulfill my dream. *Do not, in the future, believe everything that the news you get about me seems to portend.*" (Emphasis added.)

Vanzetti was apparently able to convince doctors he was mentally ill by improvising on some of Sacco's symptoms. He too felt electricity in the air and he barricaded his cell saying that men were coming to kill him. One night he smashed a chair to splinters, but he never attempted to kill or injure himself. Ironically, Vanzetti may have been more unbalanced by his ordeal than he realized or he would not have resorted to so futile a weapon. Pretending insanity might postpone his fate, but it would not alter it unless he could continue the farce indefinitely. His letters suggest his return to sanity was as deliberate as his decision to leave it. On May 6 he wrote Luigia he was back at Charlestown prison and that, "During my stay at the State Farm [the Bridgewater asylum] I gained strength and vigor, I have come back to Charlestown in much better health than I left it. The lawyer is happy that I came back, he was afraid that the judge would seize on the pretext of my illness to refuse to sign certain papers for the Supreme [Judicial] Court. That judge would like to see us suffer and die. . . ."

References to Vanzetti's mysterious behavior, which obviously worried the already distraught Luigia, continued after his return to prison. On May 8 he wrote, "I repeat, do not be alarmed or surprised at what you have heard or may hear. Understand." On June 17: "I cannot explain my way except through hints, which you constantly interpret incorrectly. I did not wish to allude to my idea nor to my battle, it was to the particular nature of our case, which forces me to do many things of which I would like to forewarn you. This however I cannot do. . . . I tell you that I have decided to take justice into my own hands. This does not necessarily mean that I am going to kill someone or commit suicide, or even that I have given way to desperation—it means that I wish to win, by whatever means are necessary. For this reason I must do many strange, clever things, play on almost everyone and everything. Do not, therefore, believe everything that is said." On August 16: "My health and my iron desire to win remain unimpaired. Do not be perturbed if I have chosen to be that which I am not, and to—do you understand? I wish to win." On September 16: "I can assure you that I am completely well, if you hear that I am ill do not believe it: understand?"

Vanzetti's letters from the mental hospital do not seem different from any of the others he wrote, though he may have had some aberrant moments, or moments he considered aberrant. On April 15 he wrote Luigia, "The doctors told me that, in my last letter, I wrote you that I wanted to get out of prison quickly, get rich fast, and return to Italy. . . . I know that I never wrote this, or said it, or even thought it. Moreover it is not in the least criminal, it is what 95% of the honest Christian swine of immigrants hope to do, and would do if they could."

On Christmas Day, 1925, Vanzetti informed Luigia that if there were no further delays the appeal would be argued before the Supreme Judicial Court of Massachusetts on January 11, 1926. "It is strange," he wrote, "I have an excellent lawyer, whose salary is costing a fortune; I have asked him a dozen times, and still I am not sure if I will be present at the hearing in the supreme court. I would like to be there if this is a right, but not if it were a special privilege. It is justice I am asking for, not privileges.

"In any case the question is not very important; my presence or absence in court would not affect the decision that is reached at all. In fact, I am completely convinced that those gentlemen already know what their decision is going to be."

Vanzetti's initial reaction to his new lawyer, Thompson, was negative. He wrote Luigia, "He laughs a lot and displays a great deal of optimism. I do not, however, put any confidence in this."[32] Another time he said, "The lawyer laughs his fat laugh, seems optimistic, talks about deportation and cuts off his sentences in the middle. I do not trust lawyers—and am completely sure that a legal defense, by itself, is completely inane and useless."[33] Feeling this way, Vanzetti was upset when Thompson opposed what Vanzetti believed would be his salvation, popular agitation. "He has asked my friends to discontinue that sort of activity completely," Vanzetti wrote.[34]

Thompson's order that there be no agitation displeased not only Vanzetti but the Defense Committee. Personally conservative, Thompson felt demonstrations exacerbated the very powers that would pass judgment on his clients. "He tied up our hands," says Felicani, yet the committee cooperated because they recognized that Thompson's reputation brought the case a kind of serious attention it would not have received otherwise. Every time Thompson went to court the press covered the hearings, which helped bring the Sacco-Vanzetti case back ino the limelight.[35]

Vanzetti to Luigia, January 11, 1926:

> Our case was discussed today. Neither Nicola nor I were present since the lawyer told us that we did not have the right to be. . . . However, I think that he lied. He probably wanted to avoid the great turnout of police in and around the courthouse that would have occurred had we been there. . . .
>
> It is said: "In two months we will have the decision, and it will be favorable." Perhaps this is true. . . .
>
> In the meantime, I am very busy translating the excerpts from *War and Peace* chosen by Proudhon, from Italian into English.

Vanzetti to Luigia, April 16, 1926:

> I have waited too long to write, as usual. The reason is that I thought that the supreme court would give its decision any day now.
>
> Nothing yet. . . .
>
> In any case—we will get a new trial.

Vanzetti to Luigia, May 16, 1926:

> I know that you are acquainted with the decision of the supreme court of the state. We must be brave, resist adversity, and refuse to allow it to make us despair.
>
> I see that I was wrong to write words of hope and encouragement because they must have made this blow even harsher and more unexpected.

> Mr. Thompson . . . is saddened and angered by this vile refusal; he has a great deal of sympathy for me. I am sure that he will do his utmost to defend us. Nonetheless I no longer have any hope. The conduct of the authorities of this state clearly demonstrates that they deliberately refuse to consider any evidence, reason or proof; they are determined to hold on to us at any cost. . . .
>
> I am unhappy that Sacco, who is completely disgusted by this whole mess, wants to discontinue all legal efforts. I think that we should see this through to the end. I hope that he will see the justice of my view.

On May 12, 1926, the Supreme Judicial Court of Massachusetts affirmed the convictions of Sacco and Vanzetti and upheld Thayer on all points, including his rejection of the motions for a new trial. At the time of this decision, the supreme judicial court did not have the power to review the facts of a case, it could only review questions of law; this has since been changed. The court found that Thayer had abused neither the law nor his discretion as trial judge. On some issues raised in the appeal, the court ruled that if Thayer had committed an error at one point, he had corrected it at another; virtually everything was swept under the enveloping cloak of Thayer's "discretion."

The cross-examination of Sacco, to which Thompson had objected, was upheld on the grounds that a defendant who testifies can be attacked on anything he has said, done, or believed in order to test his credibility; the claim of the defense that the true purpose was to fire prejudice against Sacco was rejected.

As for the motions for a new trial, the court ruled that Thayer's consideration of the Gould motion was sufficient; his decision to reject it was not subject to review. Thayer's ruling on Ripley and the cartridges was upheld, and his decision to ignore the Daly affidavit quoting the jury foreman's "Damn them!" was blinked on the grounds that Thayer did not have to believe Daly and was not obliged to explain why. The court also said Thayer

App

could believe whichever ballistics experts he chose, and his opinion that there had been no misconduct in framing Proctor's misleading testimony was final; neither issue being a matter of law, they were not subject to review.

It is often argued that if the supreme judicial court had the authority to review evidence as well as law, the decision would have been different. This is refuted by Robert Lincoln O'Brien who in his oral memoirs describes how two members of the supreme judicial court publicly agreed with his assertion that if the judges believed Sacco and Vanzetti were innocent, they would have found a way to force a retrial despite the limitations of their power of review.[36] The Supreme Judicial Court of Massachusetts had not reviewed the law, it had reaffirmed the guilt of Sacco and Vanzetti. Just as Thayer had gone out of his way to uphold the integrity of the jury and the prosecution, the supreme judicial court had gone out of its way to uphold the integrity of Webster Thayer. The Commonwealth of Massachusetts was standing together against the onslaught of the edge trimmer and the fish peddler.

Even before the supreme judicial court had delivered its decision, there had been a stunning new development in the case. On the afternoon of November 18, 1925, a convict in the Dedham jail named Celestino F. Madeiros called a trusty to his cell, handed him a note, and asked him to give it to Sacco. On his way to Sacco's cell, which was on the floor above, the trusty was given a magazine for Sacco by another convict. The trusty, who had read the note, put it between the pages of the magazine and handed the magazine to Sacco telling him there was a note inside.[37]

A few minutes later the trusty went back to Sacco's cell. Sacco was leaning against the wall, trembling. The note was in his hands and tears were in his eyes. "What is this?" Sacco asked the trusty. "Can't you read English?" the trusty replied.[38] The note was a confession signed by Madeiros in which he said he had taken part in the South Braintree robbery and that Sacco and Vanzetti were innocent.

21

Confession and Collusion

elestino Madeiros was one of life's losers. A Portuguese*
born in the Azores in 1902, he was brought to America
when he was two or three years old. Madeiros's family had
a history of epilepsy and insanity, and as he grew up he suffered
episodes of epilepsy and near-blindness. He was both a juvenile
and adult delinquent, with a criminal record that began when he
was fourteen. In November, 1924, during a bank robbery in
Wrentham, Massachusetts, Madeiros killed a cashier. He was sent
to Dedham jail to await trial and, after his conviction, to await the
outcome of his appeal to the supreme judicial court.

During his trial, Madeiros was placed in a cell next to
Sacco's. Several times Madeiros suggested that Sacco check with a
boy named Thomas who might have seen the South Braintree
bandit car; Madeiros even gave Sacco a map showing the location
of the Thomas house in Randolph. Since the Justice Department

*Since ethnic origin and political beliefs were obsessions during the Sacco-
Vanzetti case it seems necessary to point out that Madeiros was neither Italian nor
an anarchist.

had already tried planting a spy in the cell next to Sacco's, Sacco ignored Madeiros thinking he was either another spy or a madman.

Despite Sacco's rebuffs, Madeiros continued to try to communicate with him. After Madeiros was moved to another cell, he went to Sacco several times, in the bathroom or during exercises, and said, "Nick, I know who did the South Braintree job." One night Sacco told a prison guard that Madeiros had said to him, "I was the one that done the job,"[1] but this startling admission was ignored by the authorities, as all of Madeiros's confessions would be.

On November 16, 1925, Madeiros wrote a note:

> Dear Editor
> I hear by confess to being in the shoe company crime at south Braintree on April 15 1920 and that Sacco and Vanzetti was not there
> Celestino F. Madeiros

He signed this confession, put it in an envelope addressed to the *Boston American*, and gave the envelope to a trusty to mail, but it was turned over to a deputy sheriff and never left the prison.[2] When Madeiros learned this, he wrote the note the trusty delivered to Sacco, who immediately notified Thompson.

On November 19, Thompson met with Madeiros and Sacco in the Dedham jail. Madeiros told Thompson his story of the robbery at South Braintree, including details only a participant would have known. He was a freelance thug of eighteen, living in Providence, Rhode Island, when he was asked to help a local gang pull off the South Braintree job. The gang was well experienced, particularly in robbing the contents of freight cars. During the robbery, Madeiros sat on the back seat of the Buick, half-drunk and scared to death, clutching a Colt .38 with orders to hold back anyone who might rush the car. But Madeiros never fired; he said two members of the gang did all the shooting.[3]

Madeiros added two items that were not revealed at the trial. Two cars were used in the getaway, a Buick and a Hudson, not one as the prosecution had claimed. Also, there had been a delay while the criminals changed from one car to the other in the woods near Randolph. Both details later proved to be correct. In July, 1927, the defense discovered that Shelley Neal, the American Express agent who brought the payroll money from the railroad station to the factory in a small truck with two armed guards, testified at the inquest in 1920 that he had noticed two automobiles parked outside Slater & Morrill on the morning of April 15, their occupants obviously watching to see if the payroll arrived. At the trial, Neal mentioned only one car. Herbert Ehrmann speculated that the prosecution might have dropped the two-car evidence because it would eliminate the need for Boda's Overland and suggest too professional a criminal approach.[4]

The loss of time while changing cars near Randolph was confirmed by James E. King, an editor of the *Boston Evening Transcript* who, assigned by the newspaper to prove Sacco and Vanzetti were guilty, became convinced of their innocence. By checking railroad records which showed that trains had passed the two crossings at virtually the same time as the bandits, King found there was a delay getting from South Braintree to Matfield; this was because of the stop to change from the Buick to the Hudson.[5] Madeiros thought the Thomas boy had seen the bandits speed by his house in Randolph, which was why he mentioned him to Sacco in an attempt to help Sacco and Vanzetti without involving himself.

In telling his story, Madeiros, true to his own code of honor or perhaps fearing reprisals, gave false names and addresses for the other criminals; he later admitted this to Thompson. He did say, however, that three of the bandits were Italian and one was either a Pole or a Finn.

At the time Madeiros spoke to Thompson, his conviction for the murder of the bank cashier at Wrentham was under appeal. Thompson discussed Madeiros's confession with Dudley P. Ranney, an assistant district attorney who was now handling the Sacco-Vanzetti case for the commonwealth. Both men agreed nothing should be done about Madeiros until the supreme judicial court ruled on his appeal. On March 31, 1926, the supreme judicial court, which could find no flaws in Thayer's discretion, reversed Madeiros's conviction on the grounds that the trial judge had neglected to tell the jury that a defendant is presumed to be innocent until proven guilty. This meticulous concern for Madeir-

Appe

os's rights is admirable, though it contrasts sharply with the court's attitude in the Sacco-Vanzetti case; on the other hand, Madeiros was only a murderer, not an anarchist.

Once the supreme judicial court delivered its verdict, Madeiros was again innocent until he could be retried, but he made no attempt to retract his South Braintree confession. In May, 1926, Madeiros was tried a second time for the Wrentham murder and found guilty.

Thompson now asked the prosecution to join the defense in investigating the Madeiros confession, but Winfield M. Wilbar, then district attorney for Norfolk County, refused; he would neither participate in a joint investigation nor conduct one of his own. However, Dudley Ranney questioned Madeiros on June 28, while he was still waiting for the results of his second appeal to the supreme judicial court, and Madeiros freely implicated himself in the South Braintree crime. Madeiros's confession was volunteered and repeated at various times before he was finally condemned for the Wrentham murder; it cannot be dismissed as the attempt of a desperate man to delay his execution.

The only reason Madeiros ever gave for speaking out was that he "felt sorry for Mrs. Sacco and the kids,"[6] but no matter how sorry Madeiros felt for them, he still refused to name his confederates. "If I cannot save Sacco and Vanzetti by my own confession," he said, "why should I bring four or five others into it?"[7]

Since Madeiros was a murderer with a long criminal record and a history of illness and epilepsy, Thompson knew his word was worthless without corroborating evidence. Too overwhelmed with other details of the case to act as investigator as well, Thompson sought another attorney to look into the Madeiros confession. Roscoe Pound, the dean of Harvard Law School, recommended Herbert Ehrmann.

Born in Kentucky, a graduate of Harvard College and Harvard Law School, Ehrmann was a young Boston attorney who, according to his widow,* had no more than a "smattering" of

---

*Ehrmann died in 1970. His wife Sara not only assisted him in his work on the Sacco-Vanzetti case but was so affected by its outcome she became a leader of the movement to abolish capital punishment in America.

criminal law experience, but he had proved himself to Pound by doing an effective job of investigating Cleveland's criminal courts as part of a survey of criminal justice in that city which local citizens groups had asked Harvard Law School to arrange.

Sara   *We began assuming Sacco and Vanzetti were guilty.*
Ehrmann: *You always assume people are guilty if they're being*
            prosecuted. And we were away in Cleveland when
            the case was raging in Boston. When the Madeiros
            confession came, that was what brought Herbert into
            the case to assist Mr. Thompson in running down
            the evidence. And Herbert didn't expect it to hold
            up. He was advised, most strongly, by many who
            were close to him, not to touch it, not to take it, that
            this would certainly do him no good.

The first indication Ehrmann had that the confession might hold up after all was when he learned that after the South Braintree robbery, Madeiros, who had previously been penniless, had toured the United States and Mexico with a lady friend and $2,800, or what could have been his share of the stolen payroll.

Further clues began to accumulate.* Ehrmann visited the chief of police in Providence and asked if there was a local gang that specialized in freight cars; the chief said there was. It was the Morelli gang, a family operation run by the five Morelli brothers, all American-born Italians. Though they had formidable criminal records, three of them had been out on bail on April 15, 1920, waiting to go on trial in May. Ehrmann knew it was not uncommon for professional criminals to pay for their defense for one crime by committing another.

In New Bedford, Massachusetts, where one of the brothers, Mike Morelli, lived, Ehrmann discovered that the local police had suspected the Morellis as far back as April, 1920, when Mike Morelli was seen driving a new Buick which disappeared after the crime. "Madeiros, in his cell at Dedham," wrote Ehrmann, "could

*A full account of Herbert Ehrmann's odyssey in search of evidence to corroborate the Madeiros confession can be found in his book, *The Untried Case: The Sacco-Vanzetti Case and the Morelli Gang.* A shorter version appears in *The Case That Will Not Die.* See Bibliography.

App

never have falsely invented a story implicating as his guilty confederates this group of professionals *who had actually been under police surveillance in April 1920 as prime suspects.*"[8]

Actually the Morellis had been prime suspects not once but twice. In November, 1923, Emil Moller, a Danish-born criminal who was awaiting deportation, claimed he had information about the Sacco-Vanzetti case. When Fred Moore checked, Moller said he had shared a cell in Atlanta with Joe Morelli, who told him how his Providence gang had committed the South Braintree crime, including such details as changing cars in the woods. Moller also revealed that when Moore visited the prison in 1921 to investigate the Mede-Silva story, Joe Morelli panicked and asked Moller and two other prisoners, including Frank Silva, to agree to swear they were playing poker with him on April 15. Morelli's setting up an alibi for April 15 was clear evidence of consciousness of guilt, but Moore failed to follow up Moller's story. The Morellis were twice suspected and twice forgotten before Ehrmann began his search.[9]

Sara Ehrmann: *Herbert became convinced that Sacco and Vanzetti were innocent. He did the complete investigation of the Madeiros confession and he did not expect it to hold together and was amazed at every instance that either it was exactly as Madeiros had stated it or was so poorly concealed to protect other people that it was obvious. And then, when he talked with the law enforcement people who had been quite convinced that the Morelli gang were the ones who committed that crime and exchanged information with the police, he could not find any evidence at all of the guilt of Sacco and Vanzetti.*

When Ehrmann returned from New Bedford, he was so elated he called Assistant District Attorney Dudley Ranney, a classmate of his at Harvard, to tell him what he had learned and suggest that the case against Sacco and Vanzetti be dropped. Ranney replied, "Over my dead body."[10]

Disillusioned but undaunted, Ehrmann returned to Providence with his wife and asked her to check the indictments against the Morellis on file at the federal courthouse while he conferred with a lawyer who had defended them. When he met her later, she was "blazing with excitement." [11] She handed him her notes which showed that out of nine indictments for stolen shoe shipments, one was for a shipment from Slater & Morrill and four were for shipments from the adjoining factory, Rice & Hutchins. Five of the nine stolen shipments had originated at the holdup site in South Braintree. To know which freight cars to break into in Providence, the Morellis had to have spotters at the plants to note the numbers on the appropriate cars. A spotter would also notice when the payroll arrived, when and how it was carried from the upper factory to the lower factory, who carried it, how they were armed, and other details essential to plotting and carrying out the crime.

Sara Ehrmann: *After I had looked up the indictments against the Morelli brothers in Providence, which placed them right at the scene of the crime . . . Herbert was convinced that we had absolutely watertight evidence that would hold up against the Morellis . . . and that the prosecution would be very, very glad to have it. So he telephoned Dudley Ranney, and Dudley Ranney was thrilled and very excited. And we spent a whole night rejoicing and then word came—I don't know how soon—that the prosecution was sorry but it had no interest in getting any more criminals; they had them. That was it. Massachusetts had made up its mind.* *

Though the prosecution could not be moved, there were still the courts to appeal to, but Ehrmann wanted his case as convincing as possible. He visited Joe Morelli, then in residence at Leavenworth penitentiary, and asked him about the robbery. Morelli denied everything and wailed, "You are trying to spoil my record with my warden, my good record!" But when Ehrmann asked him directly about Sacco and Vanzetti, Morelli's guard

*Mrs. Ehrmann believes the decision was not made by Ranney, whom she said "suffered awfully, all through the case." Ranney later told Ehrmann that if he had been on the Sacco-Vanzetti jury, he would have considered the commonwealth's case "not proven." [12]

Appe

slipped slightly. "Sacco? Sacco?" he said. "See Mancini about that."[13]

Anthony Mancini, another member of the Morelli gang, was at leisure in the state prison in Auburn, New York, for killing a fellow criminal. Unlike Sacco and Vanzetti or Madeiros, Mancini had received a prison term rather than the death sentence for committing murder; the victim was another Italian. Up to a point Mancini talked freely with Ehrmann, saying of Sacco and Vanzetti, "They're not stick-up men . . . they're radicals. They believe in sharing what they have." But when he realized he was suspected of being one of the bandits, Mancini closed up. "I'm sorry I can't do something in this case—I would if I could," he said, "but there isn't anything I know."[14]

The following day Ehrmann went to New York City to check on Mancini's murder weapon. Joe Morelli owned several Colt .32 automatics, the same type of gun Sacco carried. A Colt .32 fired the bullet fatal to Berardelli, but what weapon was used to fire the other five bullets, including the one fatal to Parmenter, was never established. At the trial one of the ballistics experts for the defense had offered the opinion that these five bullets came from a 7.65 millimeter foreign automatic. Hamilton, the ballistics expert who testified for the defense during the appeals, agreed that a foreign gun had been used. In New York, Ehrmann learned that Mancini's weapon was a 7.65 foreign automatic.

By the time Ehrmann completed his investigation, he believed he could name the criminals who had robbed and murdered at South Braintree, and he did so in *The Untried Case.* Though the gang had been described as Italian, it lacked ethnic purity. According to Ehrmann, the five men in the Buick were Joe Morelli, Frank (Butsy) Morelli, Tony Mancini, and Celestino Madeiros; the fair-haired driver was a young criminal named Steve Benkosky or "Steve the Pole." A third Morelli brother, Mike, took care of the second car.[15]

Ehrmann not only identified the probable criminals but the appropriate weapons, the motive (cash was needed for an upcoming trial), and a method of operation (spotters at the shoe factories) that logically linked them to the crime. Physical descriptions matched those given by most of the witnesses; the pale, blond driver was accounted for and so was the man who spoke unmistakable and clear English since the Morellis were born in America. None of the alleged criminals bore the slightest resemblance to Vanzetti, but there was no credible eyewitness testimony putting Vanzetti at the scene of the crime. Both Joe Morelli and Tony Mancini were about the same height, weight, and coloring as Sacco, and he could easily have been mistaken for either one in a quick glance. Unfortunately for Sacco, his facial resemblance to Joe Morelli was startling. Shown photographs of Joe Morelli by Ehrmann and an investigator, witnesses for both the prosecution and the defense identified him as the man they had seen at South Braintree; several thought they were pictures of Sacco.

Ehrmann's investigation did not prove the men were guilty—only a jury could decide that—but he had amassed far more evidence against the Morelli gang than the prosecution had ever presented against Sacco and Vanzetti. The Morelli theory also included one critical item the Sacco-Vanzetti theory lacked, the confession of one of the participants.

One way to determine the truth beyond a reasonable doubt was for the prosecution to conduct its own investigation, bring the Morelli gang to trial, and let a jury decide whether or not the evidence was convincing. The prosecution refused. Speaking for the district attorney, Dudley Ranney said, "We believe we have found the truth, and . . . having found the truth, nothing else can matter."[16] Not even the truth.

Ranney's explanation strains credulity. The prosecution knew better than anyone how much tampering there had been with witnesses and evidence; how many questions remained unanswered; how determined the effort had been to prejudice the jury since evidence alone could not convict Sacco and Vanzetti. The refusal to do anything with the Morelli evidence except to try to discredit it shows consciousness of guilt on the part of the prosecution. Just as Thayer had shielded the jury and the prosecution, and the supreme judicial court had shielded Thayer, the prosecution was now shielding itself. No one in a position of responsibility in Massachusetts was willing to concede that a widening circle of officials were taking part in what had become a conspiracy to condemn two innocent men.

App

The Madeiros confession became the basis of a motion for a new trial, but the story of the Morellis continued long after Sacco and Vanzetti were ashes. Attorney Morris Ernst tried to get Joe Morelli to confess; Morelli denied he was involved but said his gang had done the job. However, Morelli demanded so much money for even this admission Ernst knew it was fatally compromised.[17]

Journalist Ben Bagdikian got Joe Morelli to promise to talk to him about the crime; in 1950, when Morelli was dying of cancer, Bagdikian was summoned. In a review of *The Case That Will Not Die*, Bagdikian wrote that when he entered the sickroom, Morelli lay in a terminal coma "with his lawyer shouting into his ears, 'Sacco, Vanzetti! Sacco, Vanzetti!'"[18]

Before he died, Joe Morelli presumably wrote his own account of the robbery in which he said it was his idea but carried out by Sacco, Vanzetti, Orciani, Boda, and Coacci who doublecrossed him by pulling it off a week ahead of schedule. Morelli did not explain why a pro, with his own gang at his command, should have recruited five anarchists for a major robbery, nor did he say why not even the prosecution accused Orciani, Boda, or Coacci, though it would have made the case more convincing to have had five criminals. He also slipped up in naming Coacci, who was dark and stocky, as the pale, sickly, fair-haired driver. Morelli did add one interesting detail; he said the guard Berardelli was his contact man inside the shoe factory and it was necessary to kill him so he wouldn't talk. This would explain why the bandits deliberately shot Berardelli even though he dropped his money box immediately.[19]

Unexpected confirmation of the Morelli theory appeared in 1973 in a book called *My Life in the Mafia* by Vincent Teresa. Teresa, who knew Frank (Butsy) Morelli, says that because Butsy did not want his adopted son to know about his criminal life, he sued a newspaper that printed an article implicating him in the South Braintree crime. According to Teresa, Butsy told him, "What they said was true, but it's going to hurt my kid."

As told by Teresa, Butsy Morelli said, "We whacked them out, we killed those guys in the robbery. These two greaseballs [Sacco and Vanzetti] took it on the chin. They got in our way so we just ran over them." Teresa asked, "Did you really do this?" Morelli replied, "Absolutely, Vinnie. These two suckers took it on the chin for us. That shows you how much justice there really is."

Teresa comments, "Butsey's [sic] dead now. I don't think he ever told the story to anyone else, except maybe a few close friends he had in the mob. The only thing I know for sure is that Butsey wasn't the kind of guy to tell tales. He didn't brag about anything—ever."[20] Though this is hearsay, and Morelli is dead, the story as told by Teresa is spontaneous, unsolicited, and has nothing to do with the balance of his book. Teresa may not have remembered Morelli's words verbatim, but there is no conceivable reason for reporting this confession unless he heard it.

The sixth supplementary motion (the Madeiros motion) for a new trial was filed May 26, 1926, and argued by Thompson in September. It was based not only on the Madeiros confession, but on the claim that the prosecution had suppressed evidence favorable to the defense and had cooperated with the Justice Department to secure a conviction. This motion, like all its predecessors, had to be argued before the trial judge, that same Webster Thayer who boasted about what he had done to those anarchistic bastards.

Vanzetti to Luigia, September 19, 1926:

> The discussion of the Madeiros motion started last Monday and ended last Friday. The *New York World* published a two-week series on the case, which is almost completely in our favor. . . . This series of articles has brought almost the entire capitalist press of Boston and of the United States over to our side.
>
> Thompson's discussion of the motion was magnificent. . . .
>
> The trial has taken on all the trappings of a national scandal, one in which the federal authorities are also involved.

App

Vanzetti to Luigia, October 1, 1926:

When the hearing was over, Thayer said . . . he would need several weeks to come to a decision. . . .

This excuse, that more time is necessary, is merely a blind, it is useful for pulling the wool over the eyes of fools. The truth is that Thayer does not wish to grant a retrial because he knows that we will win.

He knows that to grant a retrial and then not let it take place (as is sometimes done) would be to admit that all the criticism leveled against the authorities is founded in fact. To grant a retrial and let it take place would be even worse; all the errors, abuses, and falsehoods that occurred during the first trial would, one by one, be discovered; there would be a scandal of monumental proportions. There is only one way in which Thayer can win, to deny us a retrial. . . .

A reporter from the *New York World* who was present at the hearing in his professional capacity, and who studied the case minutely, wrote me a very optimistic and encouraging letter. . . .

I, however, who do not have the good fortune of being a great journalist, but have had the misfortune of having a certain degree of personal experience in this matter, am neutral if not pessimistic.

It is undeniable that Thompson is slowly winning the most influential elements of American society over to our side.

Vanzetti to Luigia, October 10, 1926:

If the judge does not announce a decision soon, and if I do not learn something positive, I will start a hunger strike; that will make him sing.

You must not be alarmed. They would not let me die of hunger, they would force-feed me; in fact, if it ever got to that point I myself would stop fasting.

Vanzetti to Luigia, October 24, 1926:

> Perhaps the news that the judge has rejected our appeal will reach you before you get my preceding letter.
>
> I was always sure that he would refuse. He is the worst assassin on earth.

Judge Webster Thayer denied the Madeiros motion on October 23, 1926. Dudley Ranney had not contested the Morelli evidence because he couldn't; instead he argued for the prosecution that Madeiros was a liar and a psychopath. Thayer seized upon this and wrote, "Madeiros is, without doubt, a crook, a thief, a robber, a liar, a rum-runner, a 'bouncer' in a house of ill-fame, a smuggler, and a man who has been convicted and sentenced to death for . . . murder. . . ."[21] It apparently did not occur to Thayer that such a man would be very likely to take part in a robbery and murder and very unlikely to confess to a crime he had not been accused of, at a time when he was not legally condemned. Thayer disregarded Madeiros's knowledge of some of the hidden aspects of the crime and dwelled upon details Madeiros had mistaken or forgotten. The judge also ignored the mountain of corroborating evidence amassed by Ehrmann, except to misstate and dismiss it. Felix Frankfurter, in a long article on the Sacco-Vanzetti case which appeared in the *Atlantic Monthly* in March, 1927, and was published as a book that same month, commented on Thayer's rejection of the Madeiros-Morelli evidence: "It was not for him to weigh the new evidence as though he were a jury, determining what is true and what is false. Judge Thayer's duty was the very narrow one of ascertaining whether here was new material fit for a new jury's judgment." That Thayer decided negatively Frankfurter found "amazing."[22]

The evidence suppressed by the prosecution because it might aid the defense concerned the Pinkerton reports which revealed that several of the eyewitnesses against Sacco had originally identified someone else and that Katzmann did not summon witnesses whose stories conflicted with his; Thayer's decision did not even take up the question of the suppressed evidence.

Ap

Most of Thayer's opinion dealt with the defense claim that the Justice Department had been in collusion with Katzmann to secure a conviction. Thompson had obtained affidavits from two former agents saying that the Justice Department was involved in the case and that proof and details could be found in the department's files. One of the agents, Fred J. Weyand, who had taken part in the Palmer raids, said that before their arrest, Sacco and Vanzetti were on a list of "radicals to be watched." He also said that he was one of several agents assigned to attend the Dedham trial to gather evidence of the radical activities of the two men or their associates.[23] Weyand's affidavit said, in part:

> Instructions were received from the Chief of the Bureau of the Department of Justice in Washington from time to time in reference to the Sacco-Vanzetti case. They are on file or should be on file in the Boston office.
>
> The understanding in this case between the agents of the Department of Justice in Boston and the district attorney followed the usual custom, that the Department of Justice would help the district attorney to secure a conviction, and that he in turn would help the agents of the Department of Justice to secure information that they might desire. This would include the turning over of any pertinent information by the Department of Justice to the district attorney. Sacco and Vanzetti were, at least in the opinion of the Boston agents of the Department of Justice, not liable to deportation as draft dodgers, but only as anarchists, and could not be deported as anarchists unless it could be shown that they were believers in anarchy, which is always a difficult thing to show. It usually can only be shown by self-incrimination.* The Boston agents believed that these men were anarchists, and hoped to be able to secure the necessary evidence against them from

*Weyand noted that the caustic criticism of the Justice Department by Judge George W. Anderson during the *Colyer* v. *Skeffington* case had made the agents more cautious about making arbitrary arrests.[24]

their testimony at their trial for murder, to be used in case they were not convicted of murder. There is correspondence between Mr. Katzmann and Mr. West [Boston head of the Bureau of Investigation's General Intelligence Division] on file in the Boston office of the department. Mr. West furnished Mr. Katzmann information about the radical activities of Sacco and Vanzetti to be used in their cross-examination. . . .

I am . . . thoroughly convinced, and always have been, and I believe that [it] is and always has been the opinion of such Boston agents of the Department of Justice as had any knowledge on the subject, that these men had nothing whatever to do with the South Braintree murders, and that their conviction was the result of cooperation between the Boston agents of the Department of Justice and the district attorney.[25]

The second affidavit, from former agent Lawrence Letherman, said, in part:

The Department of Justice in Boston was anxious to get sufficient evidence against Sacco and Vanzetti to deport them, but never succeeded in getting the kind and amount of evidence required for that purpose. It was the opinion of the department agents here that a conviction of Sacco and Vanzetti for murder would be one way of disposing of these two men. It was also the general opinion of such of the agents in Boston as had any actual knowledge of the Sacco-Vanzetti case, that Sacco and Vanzetti, although anarchists and agitators, were not highway robbers, and had nothing to do with the South Braintree crime. . . .

The Boston agents of the Department of Justice assigned certain men to attend the trial of Sacco and Vanzetti, including Mr. Weyand. Mr. West also attended the trial. There is or was a great deal of correspondence on file in the Boston office between Mr. West and Mr. Katzmann, the district attorney, and there are also copies of reports sent to Washington about the case. Letters and reports were made in triplicate; two copies were sent to Washington and one retained in Boston. The letters and documents on file in the Boston office would throw a great deal of light upon the preparation of the Sacco-Vanzetti case for trial, and upon the real opinion of the Boston office of the Department of Justice as to the guilt of Sacco and Vanzetti of the particular crime with which they were charged.[26]

When Thompson first learned about the Justice Department files on Sacco and Vanzetti, he wrote to Attorney General John G. Sargent requesting permission to examine them. Permission was denied, forcing Thompson to appeal to the courts. Thus the so-called Madeiros motion not only offered the identities of the probable criminals, but unmistakable proof that Sacco and Vanzetti had been tried for their beliefs after all; that the Justice Department, lacking evidence to deport them, was content to have them electrocuted; that Katzmann's cross-examination of both Sacco and Vanzetti attempted to elicit incriminating information about their beliefs and associates; and that the district attorney was aware he was prosecuting the two men for a crime the Justice Department was certain they did not commit.

In arguing the motion before Judge Thayer, Thompson had excoriated the attitude of the federal agents who were willing to have Sacco and Vanzetti die if they couldn't be deported. He declared:

> You never in the world can convince the common sense of mankind that it is justifiable to send two men to the electric chair when it stands unanswered and uncontradicted in the case that there is documentary evidence in the possession of your national government having the greatest possible bearing upon the innocence or guilt of these men and on the methods by which they were entrapped and

they [the Justice Department] refuse to produce it. . . . Think what is going to be said about it! The man who does not believe in private property in America may be killed whether he is guilty or not. That is going to be said from one end of the world to the other if this thing is allowed to go through. . . .

Is there anything so exalted in the office of the Attorney General of the United States that the inference that you draw against any other men who hold back documentary evidence should not be drawn in this case? . . . There is some reason of strong policy why those papers are not produced here. What can that reason be? What can it be? Are you going to say because Sacco and Vanzetti are Italians, because these are poor folks, because they are aliens . . . we will let [the attorney general] hold back what might set them free? . . .

This state cannot afford to execute men after a trial conducted in that way. There is something more important than punishing Sacco and Vanzetti for this murder, if they committed it, which we say they did not, and that is that the conviction of guilty men shall always be done under the rules of right and justice and fair dealing, openly and fairly, and without concealment or ulterior purpose. . . .

This case started with a background of persecutions, intolerance, and unwillingness to give men a chance to believe in their minds what they wanted to. . . . The quickest way to make this thing a running sore forever . . . is to give these people an opportunity to say that they have been oppressed and tyrannized over, that they have been made the victims of machination between the United States Government and the state, that there is evidence that would not be produced that would have acquitted them if it had been produced.

Give them a chance. Let us see whether there is any such evidence. That chance is worth more to this

App

state than the lives of Sacco and Vanzetti are worth to them.*[27]

Thayer's discussion of this portion of the appeal accused Thompson of "hysteria" for charging the Justice Department and Katzmann "with being in a conspiracy to send these two defendants to the electric chair, not because they are murderers but because they are radicals." Despite the uncontradicted affidavits of two former Justice Department agents, Thayer said he could find no "collusion between these two great governments,—that of the United States and the Commonwealth of Massachusetts."[28]

Thayer wrote, "It is fairly clear that counsel does not know what the evidence [in the possession of the attorney general] is. And if this is true, how can the Court find that there is such evidence in existence of any conspiracy that can be produced? Nothing can be produced that has no present existence."[29] But Thompson had conceded he didn't know what the evidence was; that was why he had appealed to the court to force the attorney general to reveal it. Two former agents had sworn that proof of collusion was in the files and the attorney general had implicitly confirmed this by refusing to release them, yet Thayer insisted the evidence had "no present existence."

Felix Frankfurter summed up his analysis of Thayer's decision on the Madeiros and Justice Department appeals by writing:

> I assert with deep regret, but without the slightest fear of disproof, that certainly in modern times Judge Thayer's opinion stands unmatched, happily, for discrepancies between what the record discloses and what the opinion conveys. His 25,000-word document cannot accurately be described otherwise than

---

*An unofficial summary of the files printed in the *Boston Traveler* the day Sacco and Vanzetti were executed said that they were known anarchists but not under surveillance; that a spy had been placed next to Sacco's cell; and that Katzmann had asked the Justice Department if the anarchist movement received a large sum of money after the South Braintree holdup and received a negative reply. Robert D'Attilio has sued the Justice Department under the Freedom of Information Act and has received a large part of the Sacco-Vanzetti material in their files. When he has the complete, or virtually complete files, he will publish his findings.

as a farrago of misquotations, misrepresentations, suppressions, and mutilations. The disinterested inquirer could not possibly derive from it a true knowledge of the new evidence that was submitted to him as the basis for a new trial. The opinion is literally honeycombed with demonstrable errors, and infused by a spirit alien to judicial utterance."[30]

It was Thayer who was hysterical, not Thompson. He was so determined to get those anarchistic bastards that as evidence of their innocence mounted he developed a siege mentality which was highly contagious. In January, 1927, Thompson and Ehrmann argued an appeal from Thayer's decision before the Supreme Judicial Court of Massachusetts. On April 5, the supreme judicial court ruled that Thayer was within his discretion in choosing not to believe Madeiros, that a prosecutor was not obliged to call witnesses "whose testimony contradicts what he is trying to prove,"[31] and that "no substantial evidence appeared that the Department of Justice of the United States had in its control any proof of the innocence of these defendants, or had conspired to secure their conviction by wrongful means."[32] In upholding Thayer's decision not to grant a new trial based on the Madeiros evidence, the court cited a decision in a civil case which read, "It is not imperative that a new trial be granted even though the evidence is newly discovered, and, if presented to a jury, would justify a different verdict."[33]

On April 9, 1927, four days after the supreme judicial court upheld Thayer's decision, almost seven years after their arrest, and almost six years after their conviction, Sacco and Vanzetti were brought back to the court at Dedham.

Clerk: Nicola Sacco, have you anything to say why sentence of death should not be passed upon you?

Statement by Nicola Sacco:
        Yes, sir. I am not an orator. It is not very familiar with me the English language, and as I know, as my friend has told me, my comrade Vanzetti will

Appe

speak more long, so I thought to give him the chance.

I never know, never heard, even read in history anything so cruel as this Court. After seven years prosecuting they still consider us guilty. And these gentle people here are arrayed with us in this court today.

I know the sentence will be between two class, the oppressed class and the rich class, and there will be always collision between one and the other. We fraternize the people with the books, with the literature. You persecute the people, tyrannize over them and kill them. We try the education of people always. You try to put a path between us and some other nationality that hates each other. That is why I am here today on this bench, for having been the oppressed class. Well, you are the oppressor.

You know it, Judge Thayer,—you know all my life, you know why I have been here, and after seven years that you have been persecuting me and my poor wife, and you still today sentence us to death. I would like to tell all my life, but what is the use? You know all about what I say before, and my friend—that is, my comrade—will be talking, because he is more familiar with the language, and I will give him a chance. My comrade, the man kind, the kind man to all the children, you sentence him two times, in the Bridgewater case and the Dedham case, connected with me, and you know he is innocent. You forget all the population that has been with us for seven years, to sympathize and give us all their energy and all their kindness. You do not care for them. Among that peoples and the comrades and the working class there is a big legion of intellectual people which have been with us for seven years, but to not commit the iniquitous sentence, but still the Court goes ahead. And I think I thank you all, you peoples, my comrades who have been with me for seven years, with the Sacco-Vanzetti case, and I will give my friend a chance.

I forget one thing which my comrade remember me. As I said before, Judge Thayer know all my life, and he know that I am never been guilty, never,—not yesterday nor today nor forever.[34]

Clerk: Bartolomeo Vanzetti, have you anything to say why sentence of death should not be passed upon you?

*Statement by Bartolomeo Vanzetti:**

Yes. What I say is that I am innocent, not only of the Braintree crime, but also of the Bridgewater crime. That I am not only innocent of these two crimes, but in all my life I have never stole and I have never killed and I have never spilled blood. That is what I want to say. And it is not all. Not only am I innocent of these two crimes, not only in all my life I have never stole, never killed, never spilled blood, but I have struggled all my life, since I began to reason, to eliminate crime from the earth.

Everybody that knows these two arms knows very well that I did not need to go in between the street and kill a man to take the money. I can live with my two arms and live well. . . .

Now, I should say that I am not only innocent of all these things, not only have I never committed a real crime in my life—though some sins but not crimes—not only have I struggled all my life to eliminate crimes, the crimes that the official law and the official moral condemns, but also the crime that the official moral and the official law sanctions and sanctifies,—the exploitation and the oppression of the man by the man, and if there is a reason why I am here as a guilty man, if there is a reason why you in a few minutes can doom me, it is this reason and none else. . . .

They all stick with us, the flower of mankind of

*The full text of Vanzetti's forty-five-minute statement can be found in the trial transcript and in several books about the case, including Ehrmann's *The Case That Will Not Die.* These are only brief excerpts.

App

Europe, the better writers, the greatest thinkers of Europe, have pleaded in our favor. The scientists, the greatest scientists, the greatest statesmen of Europe, have pleaded in our favor. The people of foreign nations have pleaded in our favor.

Is it possible that only a few on the jury, only two or three men, who would condemn their mother for worldly honor and for earthly fortune; is it possible that they are right against what the world, the whole world has say it is wrong and that I know that it is wrong? If there is one that I should know it, if it is right or if it is wrong, it is I and this man. You see it is seven years that we are in jail. What we have suffered during these seven years no human tongue can say, and yet you see me before you, not trembling, you see me looking you in your eyes straight, not blushing, not changing color, not ashamed or in fear.

Eugene Debs say that not even a dog—something like that—not even a dog that kill the chickens would have been found guilty by American jury with the evidence that the Commonwealth have produced against us. I say that not even a leprous dog would have his appeal refused two times by the Supreme Court of Massachusetts—not even a leprous dog.

They have given a new trial to Madeiros for the reason that the Judge had either forgot or omitted to tell the jury that they should consider the man innocent until found guilty in the court, or something of that sort. That man has confessed. The man was tried and has confessed, and the court give him another trial. We have proved that there could not have been another Judge on the face of the earth more prejudiced and more cruel than you have been against us. We have proven that. Still they refuse the new trial. We know, and you know in your heart, that you have been against us from the very beginning, before you see us. Before you see us you already know that we were radicals, that we were underdogs, that we were the enemy of the institution that you can believe in good faith in their goodness—I don't want to condemn that—and that it was easy on the time of the first trial to get a verdict of guiltiness. . . .

We were tried during a time that has now passed into history. I mean by that, a time when there was a hysteria of resentment and hate against the people of our principles, against the foreigner, against slackers, and it seems to me—rather, I am positive of it, that both you and Mr. Katzmann has done all what it were in your power in order to work out, in order to agitate still more the passion of the juror, the prejudice of the juror, against us. . . .

This is what I say: I would not wish to a dog or to a snake, to the most low and misfortunate creature of the earth—I would not wish to any of them what I have had to suffer for things that I am not guilty of. But my conviction is that I have suffered for things that I am guilty of. I am suffering because I am a radical and indeed I am a radical; I have suffered because I was an Italian, and indeed I am an Italian; I have suffered more for my family and for my beloved than for myself; but I am so convinced to be right that if you could execute me two times, and if I could be reborn two other times, I would live again to do what I have done already.

I have finished. Thank you.[35]

Thayer: . . . There is only one duty that now devolves upon this Court, and that is to pronounce the sentences.

First the Court pronounces sentence upon Nicola Sacco. It is considered and ordered by the Court that you, Nicola Sacco, suffer the punishment of death by the passage of a current of electricity through your body within the week beginning on

App▸

Sunday, the tenth day of July, in the year of our Lord, one thousand, nine hundred and twenty-seven. This is the sentence of the law.

It is considered and ordered by the Court that you, Bartolomeo Vanzetti——

Vanzetti: Wait a minute, please, your Honor. May I speak for a minute with my lawyer, Mr. Thompson?[36]

Vanzetti had remembered that he had more to say, including a tribute to Sacco. He was not permitted to speak again, but he gave his notes to a friend. "Sacco's name," Vanzetti was going to tell Thayer, "will live in the hearts of the people and in their gratitude when Katzmann's and your bones will be dispersed by time, when your name, his [Katzmann's] name, your laws, institutions, and your false god are but a dim rememoring of a cursed past in which man was wolf to the man."

Thompson: I do not know what he wants to say.

Thayer: I think I should pronounce the sentence.—— Bartolomeo Vanzetti, suffer the punishment of death——

Sacco: You know I am innocent. That is the same words I pronounced seven [six] years ago. You condemn two innocent men.

Thayer: ——by the passage of a current of electricity through your body within the week beginning on Sunday, the tenth day of July, in the year of our Lord, one thousand nine hundred and twenty-seven. This is the sentence of the law.[37]

That is so because Mr. Lowell has
found it to be so.
                    —William G. Thompson

V

THE CAUSE

22

Freedom or Death

Vanzetti to Luigia, April 11, 1927:
That which I had foreseen has come true. On
the 5th of this month the Court rejected our appeal.
Many people who thought that refusal would be
impossible, as in truth it should have been, are
grieved and indignant.

On the 9th we were taken to court and sentenced. When we entered the courtroom some of the
spectators got to their feet, and the rest would have
done the same, if the ushers had not told them to sit
down. When we were asked if we had anything to
say, Nicola said a few words, I on the other hand
spoke for a long time. When I had finished I looked
around and saw that women were crying, and that
men's mouths were all twisted and compressed, and
their faces contorted. . . .

[The newspapers] say that men who have been
condemned to death have never, in the history of
this state, or this nation . . . acted and spoken as we
did. I am proclaimed a true orator.

The *New York World* quotes Professor Frankfurter as saying that he never heard a speech that
moved him as mine did. . . .
I was more than astounded, as my chattering
did not come out well, I said things that were not
very important. . . . In any case, my words . . . may
have a great deal of influence on history, but none on
this case.

Vanzetti's modest comment that his chattering did not come
out well is closer to the mark than the emotional response of his
supporters. He was a speaker, writer, and thinker of limited ability
and unlimited prolixity; his best phrases were gold but they had
to be panned through streams of running words. Implicit in the
exaggerated praise accorded Vanzetti as a poet-philosopher was
the condescension of those who marveled that this self-tutored
Italian, who had not gone to Harvard, could express himself at all.
With the death sentence pronounced, the defense, on May 4,
formally applied to Alvan T. Fuller, governor of Massachusetts,
for clemency. Fuller's ancestors had emigrated to Ipswich in
1635,[1] but he definitely lacked the Brahmin touch; he had gone to
public school and a business college, rather than to Harvard, and
was a self-made millionaire who had started in the bicycle
business, taken over the Packard agency in New England, and
become one of the richest men in Massachusetts. Having con-
quered capitalism he turned to politics. As a member of the House
of Representatives he had, in November, 1919, called for "the
execution of the whole red scum brood of anarchists, Bolsheviks,
I.W.W.s and revolutionaries."[2] An independent Republican, he
was elected governor in 1924 and reelected in 1926. While one
eye was on the statehouse, the other was on the White House,
waiting for a vacancy.
The appeal to Fuller was signed by Vanzetti but not Sacco.
Writing to Luigia on December 5, 1926, Vanzetti said that if the
Supreme Judicial Court of Massachusetts upheld Thayer a second
time, he and Sacco would either have to appeal to the United
States Supreme Court or to the mercy of the governor. "Since the
other two courts denied us that which it seemed humanly

impossible to deny," he wrote, "there seems little reason to hope that the highest judicial authority, which is nothing but a servant of the plutocracy, will concede . . . what the others denied despite overwhelming evidence in our favor.

"On the other hand," he added, "we do not wish to ask the governor for mercy. The governor is a veritable louse, the governor is an ass that has been overloaded with gold and vanity, his mind is poor and one-sided, he is ferociously bigoted, and an unconscionable and obtuse reactionary. He hates us with a surpassing hatred, mostly because of our beliefs, which he is incapable of understanding. He would certainly refuse to commute our sentence, and we do not want him to."

In other letters to Luigia, Vanzetti not only spewed his contempt for Fuller in a similar vein—"he is . . . a fanatic, obtuse and ignorant, too fortunate, loaded down by ambition and gold, born an executioner"—but once wrote, "Some madman in Chicago had me in stitches with his letter to the governor. He wrote that, if we were not freed, he would burn the governor's house and family to ashes, and do the same to those of the barbaric Supreme [Judicial] Court and Thayer. . . . This letter was nice in that it made us laugh."[3] Yet on May 1, 1927, Vanzetti informed Luigia he was busy composing a clemency petition to Fuller.

It was during the last stages of the case that the differences between Sacco and Vanzetti emerged most clearly. Vanzetti had an overwhelming desire to live. "We are still alive," he wrote Luigia on November 14, 1926, "life is a victory, thus we are victorious." This thought was repeated in several letters home. Vanzetti wanted to live because prison was not as punishing for him as it was for Sacco. Sacco, the private man, had been deprived of what he most cherished: family, work, and nature. Vanzetti, the public man, had been deprived of nothing important; in a curious way, prison had liberated him. It had given him time to study and to write and, more important, an audience far beyond the closed circle of Italian anarchists. When he boasted of the important people "that I never would have gotten close to had I not been arrested" and how much they loved him and his work, the first part was true and he believed the second was as well.

When the question of a pardon first arose, Vanzetti scorned

the idea of life imprisonment. He said he would see how Sacco felt about it, but "were I fatherless, and alone in trouble, I would never sign the [petition for a] pardon." [4] Even as Vanzetti wrote this he was being disingenuous; he knew he was neither fatherless nor alone in trouble. Yet he could not seriously cite concern for his father, whom he had rejected years before and whose health was no problem; Giovanni Vanzetti died in 1931 at the age of eighty-two. Nor could Vanzetti cite Sacco who, without wavering, insisted upon freedom or death.

Without his father or Sacco to lean on, Vanzetti justified his petition to the governor by telling Luigia, "I wrote to satisfy my own conscience and out of respect for those people who have turned and are turning to the governor—they number in the millions and represent all the best elements of the human race, and lastly because Mr. Thompson asks me to." [5] Since he wrote a large part of the petition himself, though Thompson and Ehrmann enlarged, edited, and anglicized it, Vanzetti called it "legally splendid and passable as to principles," though he later complained Thompson had "emasculated" it. Vanzetti was angry with Sacco for refusing to sign the petition, which left him to bear the onus of pleading with the governor alone; Vanzetti called Sacco wrong, narrow, and intolerant and said it was "useless to reason with him." [6]

Thompson informed Governor Fuller that Sacco's refusal to sign the clemency petition was the same sort of aberration that had led him to a mental institution in 1923. Quite the contrary; in his article on Sacco's mental illness, Dr. Colp writes, "Not until April 9, 1927, when the sentence of death was finally and irrevocably passed upon him, did [Sacco] emerge at last from a series of emotional storms. . . . Once he knew he would die, Nick Sacco became more cheerful than at any time since his arrest. The integrity of his personality attained an apogee when, refusing the pleadings of Vanzetti and all his friends, he shunned any dealing with the authorities." [7]

When Sacco would not sign the petition, his attorneys had him examined by a noted psychiatrist, Dr. Abraham Myerson, who was one of the three doctors chosen by the court to check Sacco during his breakdown in 1923 and who had seen him

The Cau

occasionally since. Dr. Myerson spoke to Sacco on April 7, two days before the death sentence was pronounced. He wrote Herbert Ehrmann, "In my opinion, he is without signs of mental disease at the present time."

The psychiatrist reported that his conversation with Sacco covered everything from political philosophy to the impending executions. "He stated that he had been asked to sign a paper for further appeal to the governor and for a further continuance of the legal battle," wrote Dr. Myerson. "He said, 'I have always been against this battle. I have yielded because of the pleadings of the committee, my friends, my wife, and because Vanzetti wanted to fight. . . . Vanzetti signed this paper, but I would not. I told them I would have freedom or death.' This he repeated many times during the subsequent conversation, that he would have freedom or death. He had been guilty of no crime, and to spend the rest of his life in a jail was something he did not wish to do. He had seven years of it, and he did not know how he survived the seven years. He said, 'I am proud to die for my faith.' . . . If he had to die, he was not afraid to die [though] he would rather live and be free."[8]

Dr. Myerson suggested to Sacco that signing the petition would not violate his principles but honor the first law of nature, that of self-preservation. Sacco replied that nature did not reach into his cell. "The sunlight only comes in in small amounts, the air is different, it does not smell as sweetly," he said. "I am not in nature. I am not living in the world of nature, I am living in the world that man has made, so I will not fight in the way you state." When Dr. Myerson said Vanzetti was going to sign the petition, Sacco said, "Vanzetti loves the faith too; Vanzetti is a good, true friend and comrade, but he has a different philosophy than I have."[9]

In refusing to sign the petition, Sacco was thinking not only of himself but Rosina. Thompson explained to Governor Fuller that Sacco "believed that if he were dead and out of the way, that might relieve the suffering of his wife, in whom prolonged anxiety and worry might, he feared, result in a nervous collapse or something worse."[10] Sacco was aware that he and Vanzetti were not the only victims; Rosina, at the age of thirty-two, was a widow whose husband still lived. Only his death would free them both.

In a number of letters Sacco noted how ill and depressed Rosina was and once he wrote, "If they do not finish this iniquitous case sooner, I am afraid that they will kill her before long. It is . . . too much suffering all together inside and outside the prison."[11]

In an attempt to play on Sacco's emotions, Ehrmann asked his wife Sara to come with him to Dedham jail to urge Sacco to sign the petition not for himself but for his family.

Sara   *I pleaded with him that it would be so much better*
Ehrmann: *for his wife and his children if he were to live, and*
            he said it would be worse for them because unless he
            could be true to himself, he could never be true to
            them.

[*Rebecca Nurse: Would you have me belie myself?*]

Another person to whom Sacco explained how his death would help rather than hurt his family was Philip D. Stong, a feature writer for the North American Newspaper Alliance. "If I die," Sacco said, "my wife has no more worry—all over after a while. Not tied to me any more."[12] After the death sentence was pronounced, Vanzetti was permitted to remain in the Dedham jail with Sacco, and it was there Stong interviewed both men. During this interview, Vanzetti is supposed to have uttered the magnificent statement so often quoted:

> If it had not been for these thing, I might have live out my life talking at street corners to scorning men. I might have die, unmarked, unknown, a failure. Now we are not a failure. This is our career and our triumph. Never in our full life could we hope to do such work for tolerance, for joostice, for man's onderstanding of man, as now we do by accident. Our words—our lives—our pains—nothing! The taking of our lives—lives of a good shoemaker and a poor fish peddler—all! That last moment belongs to us—that agony is our triumph.

For some inscrutable reason, writers persistently have Vanzetti say this before being sentenced. He did not; unhappily, he may not have said it at all. Stong claimed he had taken notes on the margin of a newspaper during the interview, but in a letter to Upton Sinclair, read by Robert D'Attilio at the conference on Italian-American radicalism, Stong admitted "it was out of the question to take notes." He said he got "a bit more oratorical" than Vanzetti in reconstructing the conversation and had made up the phrase about the "lives of a good shoemaker and a poor fish peddler." Stong wrote Sinclair, "I confess to you that Bart said it somehow more simply, more powerfully and touchingly." It would be nice to know what Bart did say, because the quote that has been memorialized apparently owes more to Stong than it does to Vanzetti.

Though Sacco spoke to Stong about his wife's misery, very few persons close to the case seemed to understand how drained Rosina was, both emotionally and financially, and surprisingly few seemed to care.

Sara Ehrmann:	*Rosina Sacco was a small, dainty little person. I admired her tremendously; she was a beautiful little lady. I went out to her house—I forget exactly what stage it was—and they had no money at all. I don't know what they had done, whether they had sold everything that they had ever owned or what. I went out to this little house—and I can still see it—it was the cleanest little place I've ever seen, but there were bare floors, bare wooden chairs standing there, and nothing in the way of worldly things—comforts. And that was her house.*
Spencer Sacco:	*Moore had taken her complete life savings. The good women of Boston gave her food and clothing, but I know my grandmother did not expect sustenance from them.*

The petition to Governor Fuller that Vanzetti and his attorneys prepared concentrated on the argument that Judge Webster Thayer was so prejudiced against him and Sacco it affected his behavior at Dedham and his discretion in considering the motions for a new trial. This was substantiated by affidavits submitted with the petition and later by testimony before the Lowell Committee.

Vanzetti wrote:

> From the very beginning of the trial the Judge stirred up the political, social, religious, and economic hatred of the jurors, and their fears and antagonism against us, but covered himself by admonitions to the jury from time to time to treat us fairly and impartially; so that we were really tried not for murder, but for being radicals, draft evaders, and pacifists. Of course the Judge has many times denied this, but that that was his real attitude is conclusively shown by the affidavits which we are sending you with this request. . . . Can anyone bring himself honestly to believe that such persistent prejudice, hostility, and despisement as are disclosed in these affidavits did not affect the discretionary rulings of the Judge?[13]

Among the testaments to Thayer's bias was one from Lois B. Rantoul, who attended the trial on behalf of the Greater Boston Federation of Churches to see if it was fairly conducted. Mrs. Rantoul said:

> It was impossible to sit there day after day and not feel that [Judge Thayer] was convinced the defendants were guilty. I went twice to the Judge's room at the request of Judge Thayer to talk to him. At my first interview which was at the end of the case for the prosecution, and before the defense had presented their case, I told him that I had not yet heard sufficient evidence to convince me that the defendants were guilty. [Thayer] was much disturbed at this, showing it in both voice and gesture, and said that after hearing both arguments *and his charge* [emphasis added], I would come to him feeling differently. . . .
>
> At the second interview, I spoke to him in regard to testimony given by George Kelley the employer of Sacco in which Kelley praised Sacco's character while in his employ. The Judge was most

scornful, telling me in substance that Kelley didn't mean what he said, because he had heard that on the outside Kelley had said that Sacco was an anarchist and he couldn't do anything with him. It was most shocking to my sense of justice to have the presiding Judge attempt to make me believe hearsay, in place of testimony given under oath on the witness stand. . . . It gave me the feeling that if such a hearsay atmosphere was surrounding the Judge it was being felt by the jury also.[14]

Frank Sibley, who covered the case for the *Boston Globe*,* said:

My first impression of Judge Thayer was that he was conducting himself in an undignified way, in a way I had never seen in 36 years . . . of reporting. . . . He would come to the reporters' table—most of us eat at one table, six or eight of us—after eating his own lunch and spend a few minutes talking about the case. On one particular occasion Judge Thayer approached the table and said, "I think I am entitled to have printed in the newspapers a statement that this trial is being fairly and impartially conducted." None of us knew what to say. . . . He said, "Sibley, you are the oldest, don't you think this trial is being fairly and impartially conducted?" I said, "Well . . . we have talked it over, and I think I can say we have never seen anything like it," and he didn't say anything. . . .

It wasn't what he actually said on the bench, it was more his manner than anything that got into the record. . . . His whole manner, attitude seemed to be that the jurors were there to convict these men.

Sibley also said Thayer had called the defense lawyers "those

---

*Governor Fuller later told Robert Lincoln O'Brien that he "didn't take any stock" in Sibley's statements because of the way the reporter "wore his curious necktie."[15]

damn fools" and had ruled against them "with the air of prejudice and scorn."*[16]

Another journalist, John Nicholas Beffel, a radical who had worked for the Defense Committee, deposed that even before the jury was chosen, Thayer had said to the press, "Did you ever see a case in which so many leaflets and circulars have been spread broadcast saying that people couldn't get a fair trial in the state of Massachusetts?" Beffel said, "There was no mistaking that Judge Thayer was thoroughly angry. His remarks were uttered in a high voice and his face was flushed. . . . As he turned to leave the room he shook his fist and said to the other newspapermen: 'You wait till I give my charge to the jury. I'll show 'em!'"[17]

Elizabeth Rintels Bernkopf was a pretty young reporter whom Thayer liked to sit next to on the train to Dedham each morning when the motions for a new trial were being argued in 1923. "He conducted himself as no judge should," she said. "He talked continually about the case and the impression he gave was that he was decidedly antagonistic towards the defense. He referred to Moore as 'that long-haired anarchist from the West,' and [said] that he [Moore] couldn't come into his court and run things as he pleased, and that he might be able to get away with that sort of thing in the courts of California, but he was going to find out that he [Thayer] couldn't be intimidated by Moore, or anybody."[18]

Humorist Robert Benchley, a classmate of both Herbert Ehrmann and Dudley Ranney at Harvard, submitted an affidavit for the defense which said that during the Dedham trial, he and his wife were to meet a friend, Loring Coes, at the Worcester Golf Club. When Coes came out of the club, he said Thayer was there and, according to the affidavit:

> had just been telling what he, Judge Thayer, intend-
> ed to do to Sacco and Vanzetti, whom Judge Thayer
> referred to as "those bastards down there." Mr. Coes
> said that Judge Thayer had referred to Sacco and

---

*Louis Stark, who was sent to Boston by the *New York Times* to write about the case, found that all but one of the reporters he spoke to thought the trial had been unfair.

The Cau

Vanzetti as bolsheviki who were "trying to intimidate him" and had said that "he would get them
good and proper." Mr. Coes said that Judge Thayer
had told him and the other men that a "bunch of
parlor radicals were trying to get these guys off and
trying to bring pressure to bear on the Bench," and
that he "would show them and would get those guys
hanged," and that he, Judge Thayer, "would also like
to hang a few dozen of the radicals." Mr. Coes said
that Judge Thayer added that "no bolsheviki could
intimidate Web Thayer," and that he added in substance that Worcester would be proud of having such
a defender as Judge Thayer.[19]

Coes denied the story and told a reporter, "I do not recall any
such incident." When Benchley later testified before the Lowell
Committee he said he thought Coes "was pretty cross at me. . . . I
think he thought I violated the country club code of etiquette in
reporting a conversation of that nature and in dragging him into
it."[20]

James P. Richardson, Dartmouth's conservative professor of
law and political science, wrote Fuller, while the governor was
considering the clemency appeal, that "it would be a most
unfortunate thing if these men were allowed to go to the electric
chair without further careful examination of the case. . . . I know of
my own personal knowledge that Judge Thayer's mental attitude
during the progress of this case was such as to make him liable to
prejudge it. . . . I had a personal conversation with him . . . in
which it was very evident that Judge Thayer regarded these men
with a feeling which can only fairly be described as abhorrence."[21] Richardson told the Lowell Committee about Thayer's
comment "Did you see what I did with those anarchistic bastards
the other day?" and said that Thayer had also called Sacco and
Vanzetti "sons of bitches" and boasted, "They wouldn't get very
far in my court."[22] Dartmouth alumni were so enraged by Professor Richardson's sense of honor they offered the college a ten
thousand dollar contribution if he were fired.

George U. Crocker, a prestigious Boston lawyer and former

city treasurer, told the Lowell Committee that during the Dedham trial, Thayer spoke to him several times saying that Sacco and Vanzetti were "draft dodgers and anarchists and entitled to no consideration." Crocker said he couldn't remember the exact words but Thayer also said something to the effect that "we must protect ourselves against them, there were so many reds in the country, and he had a couple of them up in the trial at which he was presiding." The morning Thayer delivered his charge to the jury he read part of it to Crocker to show how he planned to counter one of Moore's arguments. "That will hold him," Thayer remarked.[23]

Crocker said of Thayer, "I have heard him discuss the evidence in a way that no judge should while the case is going on." Crocker also revealed that at least one of Thayer's diatribes was delivered to Judge John C. Crosby, a member of the supreme judicial court. "I know that he . . . talked to Judge Crosby much the same as he did to me," said Crocker.[24]

Vanzetti to Luigia, May 7, 1927:

> The Massachusetts constitution gives the governor, who holds the chief executive power in the state, the power to revoke or commute either for reasons of clemency or out of justice, any sentence that is passed in this state. The office of the governor is flooded by letters of protest, entreaty, threats and advice on what should be done. . . .
>
> The Catholics, Episcopalians, the Presbyterians, the Quakers, the free thinkers, the atheists, scientists, professors, writers, almost all the newspapers, and what is most important, almost the whole American people and almost all the college students are with us. . . .
>
> Our petition was presented to the governor two days ago. . . . Yesterday the newspapers had whole columns full of the contents of this document. . . . Various sworn declarations concerning the hate and enmity that Thayer bears us were presented at the

same time. . . . American friends write me that the whole thing had a great effect on the American people and authorities. . . .

The President of Harvard was in conference with the governor yesterday, and it is said that the latter will create a committee to inquire into our case. . . . This is exactly what we wanted. . . .

I do not think that the investigation will be over by the middle of July [the date set for execution]. If this is the case we will have a postponement. . . . I think the executioner will be left with empty hands and his mouth open.

If in his earlier letters Vanzetti exaggerated national and international interest, it was no longer necessary to do so, for by the spring of 1927, the Sacco-Vanzetti case was a flame that the final current of electricity would make eternal.

For more than six years, interest in the case was more or less concentrated among anarchists and other radicals, Italians and other immigrants, civil libertarians, and organized labor. Even within these groups there was indifference and opposition; some Italians were too offended by the radicalism and atheism of Sacco and Vanzetti to care about saving them. Though fund raising and propagandizing had continued all the while Sacco and Vanzetti were in prison, most of the country slumbered through the extended legal maneuvers, began to stir when the supreme judicial court first upheld Thayer, and awoke when Thayer rejected the Madeiros confession and the evidence of Justice Department collusion.

The Sacco-Vanzetti Defense Committee leaped back to life and published John Dos Passos's small book, *Facing the Chair*, which presented the evidence for the defense and called the case a "frameup." In addition to an irregular flow of books, pamphlets, and flyers, the committee issued one journal, *L'Agitazione*, for the Italians and another, the *Official Bulletin*, for what Felicani called "the Americans."

Propagandizing the Americans was made easier for the Defense Committee when Gardner Jackson ceased skirting the edges and became a member of the inner circle. In the fall of 1926, Jackson left the *Boston Globe* to take courses at Harvard. He had been there only a few months when Felicani asked for his help in arousing public opinion; if the courts would not save Sacco and Vanzetti it was time to turn back to the people. Jackson asked one of his professors, Arthur Schlesinger, Sr., what he should do. According to Jackson, Schlesinger replied, "You're now going to be fully participating in an event that will be the making of history, while all I do is just try to teach history. So I think it's more important for you to be doing this, than sitting in my classroom listening to my lectures."[25]

Aldino *[Jackson] performed a miracle. . . . Newspapermen*
Felicani: *started to come from everywhere. . . . Jackson talked*
     their language, not only professionally, but socially
     he was on the same level with them.[26]

Gardner Jackson spent not just time but money; Felicani says Jackson contributed at least $50,000 to the attempt to save Sacco and Vanzetti.[27]

Though the newspapers covered the Sacco-Vanzetti story, they did a "poor job" according to Professor Louis Joughin, whose social and literary history of the case constitute the larger portion of *The Legacy of Sacco and Vanzetti.* Joughin criticizes the press for neither investigating nor analyzing, but only superficially reporting. "A great many newspapermen knew a lot more than they wrote," he says.[28] Editorial writers were generally silent, at least until Thayer rejected the Madeiros motion. At that point the *Boston Herald* called for a new trial, saying, "The criterion here is not what a judge might think about [the Madeiros confession] but what a jury might think about it." The *Herald* also demanded that the Justice Department files be opened. Other newspapers agreed with the *Herald*, but protests were still muted pending the outcome of the appeal to the supreme judicial court. Meanwhile, Governor Fuller, to whom Sacco and Vanzetti supporters looked as a last hope, gave an extended magazine interview in December, 1926, to explain "Why I Believe in Capital Punishment."

Early in January, 1927, Fuller refused to reprieve three young men who had robbed the cashier at the Waltham carbarn in October, 1925; one had killed the night watchman who had tried to stop them. The murderer said he meant to fire at the ground and that he alone should be punished, but the court found otherwise. The three men were electrocuted in spite of a massive clemency campaign conducted in their behalf. All were Irish-Catholic veterans of World War I; the man who fired the fatal bullet was receiving a pension for mental problems resulting from his military service.

The execution of the carbarn bandits had a dolorous effect on the attempt to save Sacco and Vanzetti. Most Yankees already wanted Sacco and Vanzetti dead; now the Irish joined them. According to Robert Lincoln O'Brien, public sentiment was "Are you going to electrocute these carbarn boys and let these war slackers and anarchists and Italians go free?"[29] The proletariat Sacco and Vanzetti put their faith in, being largely Irish in Boston, and themselves victims for so long, would demand equal injustice.

In March, 1927, Professor Felix Frankfurter wrote the *Atlantic Monthly* article that atomized Judge Thayer and skillfully presented the arguments for a new trial; it was followed in April by the decision of the supreme judicial court not to grant one, and the pronouncement of the death sentence. Suddenly this was no longer an issue to be debated at leisure; Sacco and Vanzetti were going to die the week of July 10. The only hope lay with Governor Fuller, who had already demonstrated his belief in capital punishment. Now the campaign to save Sacco, who didn't want to be saved, and Vanzetti, who did, became desperate.

Aldino
Felicani:
We started to concentrate on a campaign that would lead to a revision of the case. . . . I think the suggestion of a committee to review the case came from our committee.[30]

The Defense Committee printed up tens of thousands of petitions to the governor and circulated them all over the country and the world, getting between 750,000 and one million signatures according to Gardner Jackson. The signed petitions were pasted together and wound around a stout stick.

Gardner
Jackson:
It was a huge roll, very heavy. Then Mary [Donovan] and I, with advance notice to the newspapermen

and the photographers, each carrying an end of that stick, walked up the steps of the statehouse into the governor's office with this roll.[31]

The Communist party, which had initially dismissed Sacco and Vanzetti as criminals, had long since seen them as a highly profitable investment and had undertaken an international campaign of agitation and fund raising. Jackson says the Communists raised over a half-million dollars for Sacco and Vanzetti, of which they gave the Defense Committee six thousand. "Of course they were using the case for their own purposes," he comments.[32]

In analyzing Sacco and Vanzetti's sources of support, Professor Joughin notes that, contrary to popular belief, most writers, clergymen, and educators were silent and remained silent about the case for seven years, though some finally spoke out at the very end when publicity was hottest and Sacco and Vanzetti were doomed.

Frankfurter's article forced many lawyers to take a stand; sixty-one law professors from colleges all over the country asked Governor Fuller to appoint a review commission. Others immediately condemned the idea as an "outrage" because it implied that the "courts of Massachusetts are incompetent to adjudicate fairly and honestly in criminal trials."[33]

In a *New Republic* article, "Boston's Civil War" (June 29, 1927), Bruce Bliven said he had been told that leaders of the Boston bar were about equally divided over the case but his own impression was that they were overwhelmingly against review. He wrote that, with some exceptions, the upper and middle classes were hostile to Sacco and Vanzetti, while the lower classes, also with some exceptions, were sympathetic to them. Bliven also noted that bookstores in Boston did not display Frankfurter's book but produced it from under the counter upon request, that it was forbidden to discuss the case in schools, and that there were economic and social reprisals against supporters of the two men.

When it was no longer possible to be neutral, the press began to commit itself on one side or the other. The *Springfield* (Massachusetts) *Republican* wrote that "a dog ought not to be shot

The C:

on the weight of the evidence brought out in the Dedham trial of Sacco and Vanzetti." William Allen White, editor of the *Emporia* (Kansas) *Gazette* and one of the most respected journalists in America, wrote Governor Fuller, "I have just returned [from New England] and I was surprised beyond words to find the bitterness and hate which had sprung up in New England, particularly in Massachusetts, among those who fear that Sacco and Vanzetti will not be executed."*

Arguments against review of the case ran along parallel paths. First, Massachusetts justice must be upheld. The dean of the Harvard Divinity School commented how shocked he was when he "first heard expressed the opinion that on the whole it was better that these men die than that faith in Massachusetts institutions should be shaken by a further review of the case."[34] Vanzetti himself wrote in one of his letters, "They must kill us to save the dignity and honor of their Commonwealth."[35]

Second, in the words of foreman Ripley, "Damn them, they ought to hang them anyway!" Even if they hadn't killed anyone, being Italian and anarchist was criminal enough. A letter to the editor of the *New Republic* (September 28, 1927) quoted a New Hampshire farmer who said, "Sacco and Vanzetti don't deserve to have civil rights. They are self-confessed draft dodgers and anarchists. I say Judge Thayer did right to find 'em guilty of that murder, evidence or not, so as to get rid of 'em. . . . America's for Americans, not for damned foreigners."

Third, since Sacco and Vanzetti were supported by radicals, both domestic and foreign, not to execute them would be to surrender to the Bolsheviks and other agitators; it would be un-American. Governor Fuller later explained, "The widespread support Sacco and Vanzetti enjoyed abroad proved that there was a conspiracy against the security of the U.S.A."[36]

The *New Republic*, in an editorial aptly entitled "Why

*This is the same William Allen White who on February 23, 1898, commented editorially, "A war with Spain over anything would be beneath the dignity of the United States. A gentleman cannot strike a sore-eyed, mangy, leprous beggar, no matter what provocation he may have. As between Cuba and Spain there is little choice. Both crowds are yellow-legged, garlic-eating, dagger-sticking, treacherous crowds. A mixture of Guinea, Indian, and Dago. One crowd is as bad as the other. It is folly to spill good Saxon blood for that kind of vermin."

Boston Wishes to Hang Sacco and Vanzetti" (May 25, 1927), put these rationalizations and other, unspoken ones into perspective when it explored the historical and psychological positions of the descendants of the Puritans:

> If Sacco and Vanzetti had been English or American communists [sic], it is most probable either that they would not have been convicted or that it would [not] have been necessary to arouse public opinion as to the need of a review of the justice of the conviction. It is the combination of their being foreigners and communists which is necessary to account for the resolution of good society in Boston that Sacco and Vanzetti shall die, no matter whether they have had or have not had a fair trial. The agitation for a review [of their trial] touches the Back Bay on its tenderest and most vulnerable spot. It is composed of an ethnic minority which still rules in some measure by virtue of wealth and social prestige. It resents the idea that the processes of this rule should be challenged by representatives of other and, in their opinion, inferior, peoples. . . .
>
> The first article in the creed of the Back Bay is that descendants of the early English settlers are entitled by a species of divine right to rule this country and particularly Massachusetts. Its apologists associate the welfare and security of the commonwealth with the unimpaired exercise of this sacred privilege. At present, however, the descendants of these early settlers, particularly those who live in large cities, are hopelessly outnumbered. They are afraid of being overwhelmed and submerged. They are peculiarly sensitive to any attack upon the part of the social machinery, such as legal administration, which they still partly control. They consider their own prestige and that of their class compromised by the challenge of the Sacco-Vanzetti verdict. Thus their stubborn and impassioned de-

The C

fense of a doubtful conviction is chiefly a matter of pathological class consciousness.

Governor Alvan Fuller understood this very well. As petitions, letters, and editorials for and against Sacco and Vanzetti overflowed the statehouse, he knew the next move was his. It would have been easy for him to ignore the pleas from abroad, from radicals, from unions—he would have been a hero if he had—but among those requesting a review of the case were influential, conservative lawyers, professors, millionaires, Brahmins, newspapers, and even the Episcopal bishop of Massachusetts. A shrewd politician, Fuller knew the best way to handle such heat was to deflect it by appointing a committee. Since the case concerned both the fallibility of justice in Massachusetts and the class consciousness of the descendants of the Puritans, the head of the committee had to be not only infallible but a visible saint.

23

We Three Kings

Vanzetti to Luigia, May 29, 1927:

I have some excellent news. . . .

Yesterday evening I saw Mr. Thompson in front of my cell.

I was eating one of the flavorful apples that Mrs. Jack never lets us lack. I was surprised to find him in a good mood. "Vanzetti, I have come to tell you that the governor has finally decided to nominate an investigative committee. . . . The President of Harvard is one of the members. . . ." Having said this he laughed one of his beautiful, sly laughs. . . .

I think that what I have told you about the hearing and the committee is the best news I could give you about the case.

The Massachusetts State Council of the Knights of Columbus, in a meek and ambiguous resolution on the case, prayed that Fuller would be guided by the light and strength of God. Since God would not head the committee, the governor's choice was the president of Harvard, Abbott Lawrence Lowell.

Fuller announced the appointment of his three-man advisory committee on June 1, 1927. Lowell was its chairman and engine; it immediately became known as the Lowell Committee. The other two members were Samuel W. Stratton, the president of MIT, and Robert A. Grant, a former judge of the probate court. Little was known about Stratton except that he had no legal education or training, had been recommended to Fuller by Lowell, and was expected to follow Lowell's lead in all things. Judge Grant, who had no experience in criminal law, was suspected of being anti-Italian and anti-Sacco and Vanzetti, which he denied, though when his luggage had been stolen during a trip to Italy he had characterized Italians as thieves. He also had hotly attacked the Felix Frankfurter article in the *Atlantic Monthly*.

The selection of Abbott Lawrence Lowell, however, brought enormous relief and satisfaction not only to Vanzetti, who could not have known better, but to those who should have. Ehrmann quotes a friend of his, who was also a friend of Lowell's, as saying, "Now we can sleep nights in the thought that the president of Harvard is on the committee."[1] Gardner Jackson persuaded the Sacco-Vanzetti Defense Committee to cancel all demonstrations while the three wise men were conducting their deliberations, to avoid any backlash.

Gardner   *I had such confidence in the ultimate intellectual*
Jackson: *probity of A. Lawrence Lowell—I scarcely knew*
           him, but my brothers had been at Harvard and I had
           always heard well of A. Lawrence Lowell—and was
           sure that we were going to get a completely objective
           appraisal.[2]

It is difficult to understand why the appointment of these particular men did not arouse greater criticism and alarm. The *New Republic* (August 3, 1927) noted that they were "drawn from the class in Boston most of whose members have sworn death to Sacco and Vanzetti." Lowell, Stratton, and Grant represented the outermost limits of Brahmin Boston; the life of an Italian anarchist was as foreign to them as life on Mars. Though they had not yet been chosen when Vanzetti wrote the phrase, they fitted to perfection his description of "Massachusetts' black gowned, puritanic, cold-blooded murderers."[3]

Abbott Lawrence Lowell, in whom so much hope rested, was

a direct descendant of the visible saints.[4] His paternal emigrating ancestor, Percival Lowle, as the name was then spelled, traced his line back to the time of William the Conqueror. Lowle was a sixty-eight-year-old merchant when, in 1639, he sailed with his family from England to Massachusetts. Lowell's maternal emigrating ancestor, John Lawrence, who sailed to New England in the early 1630s, traced his line back to the time of Richard I.

The Lowells and the Lawrences produced ministers, lawyers, public officials, scholars, Harvard men, a few poets, and millionaires. Abbott Lawrence Lowell's maternal grandfather, criticized for taking too much profit, retorted, "You cannot keep me from making money. I have always made money and I always shall make money."

The Lowells and the Lawrences were business associates. The textile centers of Lowell and Lawrence, both sewers of immigrant exploitation, were founded by members of the two families; the Lawrences invested in the mills at Lowell and the Lowells invested in the mills at Lawrence. Their wealth was exceeded only by their arrogance. When Abbott Lawrence Lowell's mother was a young woman she received a marriage proposal from the future emperor of France, Napoleon III. Her father rejected it, saying he would rather she marry an American. He was not disappointed; she married a Lowell.

Abbott Lawrence Lowell was born in Boston in December, 1856. A graduate of Harvard College and Harvard Law School, he became a member of the Massachusetts bar, but himself conceded, "I was a failure at the practice of the law." He had hoped to become a justice of the United States Supreme Court, but wrote, "as I never made any success in the law any dream of that kind long ago vanished."[5] Those who can't do, teach; after failing as a lawyer and dawdling in some public service tasks, Lowell was appointed a part-time lecturer in political science at Harvard in 1897. By 1900 he was a professor and in 1909 he was named president.

Lowell should have been disqualified from serving on the committee to judge Sacco and Vanzetti because for years he had been a vice president of the national committee of the Immigration Restriction League which was organized for the purpose of keeping men like Sacco and Vanzetti out of the country. Consistent with this position, Lowell tried in 1922 to introduce a quota system for Jews at Harvard; he also opposed the appointment of Louis Brandeis to the Supreme Court.

According to Gardner Jackson, Lowell cited as justification for limiting the number of Jews at Harvard the theft of some books from the Widener Library. Lowell said the books had been found in the room of a Jewish student, but a more careful investigation revealed only one of the missing books was in this student's room. Lowell, however, did not propose a quota system for Protestants, who had presumably stolen the remainder of the books. Even if the Jewish student had taken every book at Harvard, why were other Jews to be punished for his crime? Barbara Miller Solomon writes that Lowell's true purpose in proposing a quota for Jews was to apply "restrictionist thought to preserve the priority of the Anglo-Saxons in American colleges."[6]

Gardner Jackson:
In subsequent periods, and this has never been published and is not known, Felix Frankfurter and President Lowell engaged in a vitriolic correspondence over the quota-Jewish problem at Harvard. I am satisfied in my own mind that that had something to do with the whole case. Nobody but me has seen that exchange and it really was vitriolic. I am satisfied that the intensity of Lowell's animosity to Felix was a very large factor in what happened to his mind in the face of the evidence, since Felix had become the chief intellectual protagonist of the two Italians. . . . As a matter of human experience, I feel quite confident that President Lowell was not able to surmount the depth of his feeling of hostility to Felix Frankfurter. If that hadn't been the case, his decision in relation to the Sacco-Vanzetti case might have been altogether different.[7]

This was the man chosen to decide the fate of the two Italian anarchists. When Sacco and Vanzetti were summoned before the judgment seat of Abbott Lawrence Lowell, the history of Massachusetts had come full circle, and the circle was a hangman's noose. The Puritans were once again judging Anne Hutchinson and Mary Dyer; the Brahmins were judging the immigrants; old Massachusetts was judging new Massachusetts; death was judging life.

Since the Lowell Committee did not begin hearings until July 11, Governor Fuller postponed the date of execution from July 10 to August 10. Both Sacco and Vanzetti were still in Dedham jail, which Vanzetti preferred. "The location is healthier than at Charlestown," he wrote Luigia. "We are in the country, we have a great deal more light and air, and we are allowed to walk every morning in the courtyard-garden. Nicola and I walk together."[8]

Massachusetts law required that condemned prisoners be transferred to the death house ten days before execution. Even though the date had been postponed until August 10, at midnight on June 30, without warning or explanation, Sacco and Vanzetti were transferred from the prison at Dedham to the grim Cherry Hill section of Charlestown prison where the electric chair waited. Sacco wrote that they could now see nothing but "four sad wall and a lap of sky that disappear under the wing of a bird."[9]

Considering that seven years of legal proceedings, stacks of new documents and evidence, and two lives were involved, and that the three members of the Lowell Committee had absolutely no experience in criminal law, they worked with the incredible speed of the infallible. The hearings that began July 11 ended July 21. Arguments for the defense were delivered July 25. The committee's report was dated July 27. Herbert Ehrmann, who assisted William Thompson in arguing Sacco and Vanzetti's case before the Lowell Committee, wrote, "On such a time schedule the ablest Committee could not possibly have reached a considered conclusion. However, the Governor's Advisory Committee did not even require the few days at their disposal. Like the jury at Dedham, they knew the answers before their deliberations began: Sacco and Vanzetti were guilty."[10]

Ehrmann said that he and Thompson soon sensed that the members of the committee "regarded themselves as prosecutors, whose duty it was to expose or discredit anything pointing to the

The Ca

innocence of the men."[11] This was confirmed by an attendant in the statehouse who, at the beginning of the hearings, overheard Lowell and his associates in a discussion which revealed they believed Sacco and Vanzetti were guilty. At that point Thompson and Ehrmann decided to withdraw rather than lend credence to the pretense that the hearings were fair. Ironically, Felix Frankfurter was one of the men who dissuaded them. He still had faith in Lowell; he insisted that Lowell could be reached. Besides, in a public test of honor, Lowell would be victor; the public would assume the attorneys had surrendered because their clients were guilty.

During the hearings, frustration intensified futility. Thompson and Ehrmann were not permitted to be present when Lowell questioned Judge Thayer or the surviving jurors, nor were they informed what had been said. The attorneys were permitted to cross-examine Katzmann, but not to hear his direct testimony, putting them in the position of not knowing what points to challenge. They also were not informed that Lowell, the frustrated lawyer and would-be Supreme Court justice, had taken on the role of surrogate prosecutor and was privately conducting his own investigation to substantiate the case against Sacco and Vanzetti. When the hearings were over, the committee did not issue a complete transcript. They excised portions they wanted kept secret, including part of Katzmann's testimony, a statement from Thomas McAnarney that Judge Thayer had insisted Jeremiah McAnarney praise him in the courtroom for his fairness, and any evidence of Lowell's duplicity and errors.

On the fourth day of the hearings, the committee summoned two of Sacco's alibi witnesses, Professor Felice Guadagni and Albert Bosco, both of whom had testified they remembered meeting Sacco on April 15 because of the luncheon given that day for James T. Williams, Jr., the editor of the *Boston Evening Transcript.* Lowell asked Guadagni, "Why did it make such an impression on your mind then, by reason of the fact that you had to write it up for your paper?"

It was a clever question, designed to lead Guadagni into perjury, for Lowell had already checked the newspaper where Guadagni worked as an editor and knew there was no such article.

But Guadagni replied, "The impression, because I was invited. An Italian newspapermen's banquet. It was in a church."[12]

Then Lowell produced copies of Guadagni's newspaper and the *Boston Evening Transcript*, both of which said a banquet for Williams took place the evening of May 13. Guadagni became confused, and Thompson and Ehrmann were stunned; Lowell had shown that several of Sacco's witnesses were lying. Thompson suggested there might have been two banquets on two different dates, but the committee had already checked with Williams who said there had been only one, on May 13.

Even Thompson was so awed by Lowell he immediately conceded the point. He said to Guadagni, "You can believe what Mr. Lowell tells you because he has looked it up and he knows that the banquet did not take place until after Sacco was arrested and in the Dedham jail. What Mr. Lowell says is true, so Sacco could not have been in Boston the day before or the day after or that day [May 13]. We will take that for granted."[13]

After Guadagni left, Lowell paced back and forth saying, "A serious alibi has been destroyed."[14] But the next witness, Albert Bosco, insisted there had been a luncheon on April 15 and he had written up the story for *La Notizia*. Lowell snapped, "It is perfectly obvious that is not so."[15] Thompson, still overwhelmed by Lowell's infallibility, kept telling Bosco he was wrong, while Bosco kept insisting he was right. Thompson finally asked Bosco to bring in copies of *La Notizia* for April 14, 15, and 16, 1920. He then added, "Mr. Lowell knows that there was not any banquet which Mr. Williams attended on the 15th because there was not any such banquet. *That is so because Mr. Lowell has found it to be so.*"[16] (Emphasis added.)

Lowell ordered Bosco to bring in the copies of *La Notizia* the following morning, but Thompson and Ehrmann, too worried to wait, asked Bosco to bring the newspapers to Thompson's office that evening, which he did. The issue of April 16 had an article about a banquet held in Williams's honor the previous day and added that the Italian community would soon honor Williams with another banquet. There had been two banquets after all, one of them on April 15.

When Lowell read the article he acknowledged there had

been two banquets and apologized to Guadagni and Bosco, but when Bosco asked for permission to print an account of this incident in *La Notizia*, Lowell refused. When the transcript of the Lowell hearings was issued, the examinations of Guadagni and Bosco and the accusations that they were lying were fully recorded, but the events of the following morning were summarized as follows: "The witness Bosco who was on the stand yesterday afternoon again appeared, with the editions of the paper *La Notizia*, requested by the Committee, and the Committee, all counsel present, and the witness look in the books produced by the witness."[17]

That was all; there was not a word about Lowell's admission of error. The court reporter, asked about this omission, said he was following Lowell's orders. The president of Harvard had let the record show he had caught two of Sacco's witnesses lying and destroyed Sacco's alibi. Lowell finally did correct the record in December, 1928, sixteen months after Sacco and Vanzetti were executed.

In his role of surrogate prosecutor, Lowell also dredged up a witness even Katzmann dared not use, a woman from South Braintree named Carlotta Packard Tattilo, who insisted she had known Sacco since 1908 when they both worked at Rice & Hutchins. Unfortunately for Lowell, Sacco had just come to America in 1908 and was working in Milford, not South Braintree.

Lowell tried to make Mrs. Tattilo's story plausible by saying she "obviously" had the date wrong, but she insisted it was 1908. At the time of the trial, Mrs. Tattilo had told both Katzmann and Moore she had seen Mike [*sic*] Sacco along with Vanzetti in South Braintree on April 15, but before the Lowell Committee she became vague about this and said, "I don't say Mr. Sacco done it. I do not say it was him I saw that day."[18] Yet Lowell kept trying to transform her into a credible witness because she was the only person who claimed she knew Sacco before seeing him on April 15.

The reason the prosecution had not called her was not only apparent in her confused story, but in the testimony of other witnesses. Jeremiah Gallivan, Braintree's former chief of police, told the Lowell Committee, "That girl is a nut. . . . She ought to be out in the Brookline Psychopathic Hospital. . . . She is crazy, and she has been that way for years. She imagines things. She has pipe dreams, and that has been her makeup for years." A former co-worker said, "I will tell you, I think she is about twelve ounces to the pound."[19]

While the Lowell Committee was conducting its farcical review, Governor Fuller was working on his own investigation which was even more ludicrous than Lowell's. Fuller, a business-man, not a lawyer, knowing virtually nothing about the case, summoned witnesses at whim, peppered them with questions off the top of his head, and sometimes ended up quarreling with them. Instead of consulting an experienced criminal lawyer, the governor was occasionally assisted by his personal attorney, who handled his estate and other business matters, and knew no more about the case than he did. The defense lawyers were not permitted to speak to the witnesses Fuller called and were not even told who they were.

Perhaps because the entire case was too complex for Fuller to assimilate, he concentrated on certain details to the exclusion of everything else; he also seemed more interested in the simple holdup attempt at Bridgewater than the more complicated rob-bery and murders at South Braintree. Michael Angelo Musman-no, a young lawyer from Pittsburgh who originally came to Boston bearing a clemency petition from the Sons of Italy, stayed to help fight for Sacco and Vanzetti to the end. When Musmanno met with Fuller, the governor demanded to know why Vanzetti didn't take the stand at Plymouth. Musmanno explained that Vanzetti's lawyers had advised him not to because of his political views. Fuller would not accept this; several times he repeated that if Vanzetti was innocent he would have testified. In Musmanno's book, *After Twelve Years*, he commented that Fuller was un-doubtedly a good businessman but the Sacco-Vanzetti case was beyond his comprehension. Not even a lawyer, wrote Musmanno, could do what Fuller attempted—act as prosecutor, judge, and jury—and Fuller was not a lawyer.

Ehrmann wrote that Fuller also asked him why Vanzetti did not testify at Plymouth. Ehrmann tried to explain by pointing out that when Sacco and Vanzetti did testify at Dedham, "Mr. Katzmann murdered them!" To Ehrmann's surprise, Fuller replied, "I see. They were damned if they did and damned if they didn't."[20] But when Tom O'Connor, a Boston newspaperman who became deeply involved in the case, tried to discuss it with Fuller, the governor suddenly snapped, "Why didn't Sacco take the stand at Plymouth?" Sacco wasn't on trial at Plymouth; the question only revealed how thoroughly ignorant of the details Fuller was.

However, unlike Lowell, whom the defenders of Sacco and Vanzetti immediately recognized as an implacable foe, Fuller was unpredictable. Sometimes he seemed sympathetic, as in his remark to Ehrmann, and sometimes he even made them hopeful, though usually not for long. One of the men Fuller called to his office was Aldino Felicani who, refusing to go alone, took Gardner Jackson with him.

Gardner Jackson: *At the end of our conversation, with [Fuller] asking us considerable, detailed, searching questions, he said, "Well, gentlemen, if only all the witnesses had been as frank and as honest as you two have, I would have no problem at all in deciding this case. I haven't any doubt that you've been telling the absolute truth, insofar as you know it to be the truth." He shook hands and we got up and were walking out of his office walking on air, feeling that we had really gotten somewhere. Just as we were going out the door, he shouted at me from his desk, and said, "Mr. Jackson, there's one question that I haven't been able to get satisfied about in my mind. I'm a businessman. I want to see documentary evidence on everything. Vanzetti's alibi on the earlier crime for which he was tried and convicted . . . has never had any documentary evidence of any kind to support it." I went back into his office with Felicani and we both said, "Why, he was selling eels that day and there were twenty-one Italian families who bought eels from him at the very time that morning when he was supposed to have been participating in this holdup in Bridgewater." "Oh, Mr. Jackson," said Fuller, "those are Italians. You can't accept any of their words."*[21]

When Felicani and Jackson left the governor's office they were no longer walking on air. They went directly to Thompson's office and found he already knew the governor wanted documentary evidence to prove Vanzetti had sold eels seven and one-half years earlier. "It's impossible," said Jackson.[22]

Nothing was impossible for Felicani if it might save Vanzetti's life. He and Ehrmann went to the American Express office in Boston to see if they could find a receipt for the barrel of eels shipped in December, 1919, but receipts that old were not kept. Since Felicani remembered some of the fish dealers Vanzetti dealt with, he and Ehrmann set out for the piers.

They spent hours going from door to door, with one vendor after another telling them either that he had not sold fish to Vanzetti or that he did not keep old receipts. Finally, one dealer said he had a box full of American Express receipts in his attic. Ehrmann and Felicani searched through the box and found an American Express receipt book which showed that on December 20, 1919, a barrel of eels was picked up from Corso & Cannizzo to be shipped to B. Vanzetti, Plymouth, Mass. The eels would have been delivered in Plymouth on December 22 or 23, to be sold on the 24th. This was the documentary proof Fuller wanted.[23]

The receipt book was turned over to the governor. Later, Thompson and Ehrmann learned Fuller had said, "It is only twenty miles from Plymouth to Bridgewater. A pretty clever ruse—start with eels in Plymouth, then dash to Bridgewater for the holdup, then back to Plymouth to sell eels! Could there be a neater alibi?"[24] The receipt demanded by Fuller to prove Vanzetti's innocence had been twisted about to prove his guilt.

One of the witnesses questioned by Fuller was Beltrando Brini, who had helped Vanzetti deliver eels on the morning of December 24. Brini, who was twelve at the time of the Bridgewater robbery, was now a scholarship student at Boston University. The governor took Brini to lunch to discuss the Bridgewater crime. Brini told Fuller, "I saw Vanzetti at 7:30, just as we were

The Ca

about to start out, and [my father] sent me home to get my rubbers. I went home and came back at eight. Surely you don't believe that Vanzetti could travel to Bridgewater and back, change clothes twice, and commit the crime while I was getting my rubbers?"

Fuller replied, "Well, why couldn't he have done that?"[25]

When the Lowell hearings began, Vanzetti was naively optimistic. He wrote Luigia on July 14, "Last week we were interviewed by the governor's committee. It is composed of Professor Lowell, the president of Harvard University; Professor Stratton, the president of the Massachusetts Institute of Technology; and Justice Grant. The first two are great scholars, men of heart and spirit, they would only rule against us if they were sure that we were guilty. I am not afraid of this. They were very courteous; they approved openly of almost all of my arguments, and even of my beliefs and ideas. However, I got the impression that Grant does not wish to understand our evidence, that because his beliefs are different from ours he is our enemy."

Vanzetti's optimism quickly evaporated when he learned of the incident with Guadagni and Bosco; he and Sacco heard enough from their attorneys and friends to realize there was no hope. While Musmanno was visiting the two men, Vanzetti denounced both the Lowell and Fuller investigations and said, "We will do something about it. We will protest in the only manner left for us to protest. We will go on a hunger strike!"

"We cannot stop them from murdering us," said Sacco, "but we can let the world know they are murderers."[26]

Sacco and Vanzetti began their hunger strike on July 17. Vanzetti broke his fast after a few days; he later resumed and broke it several times. Sacco fasted for thirty days and surrendered only when threatened with force-feeding.

Vanzetti to Luigia, July 18, 1927:

> Yesterday Aldino [Felicani] of the committee and Mr. Thompson came to see me. I asked the former to send a telegram to Giacomo Caldera, for you. If this was done it is not necessary to tell you its contents.

I thought, at one point, that the evidence in the case, and the universal protest against the sentence would have induced the governor to come and see us, to understand us, and to make amends. I thought that the truth would be more than evident to anyone nominated to be a member of the investigative committee, if only they would wish to see and understand.

Instead it seems, from what little I hear, that both the governor and the committee are incapable or unwilling to see the truth. . . . They can't, and do not wish to, believe the defense witnesses.

It is for this reason that I started a hunger strike, and wanted you or Vincenzina to come over here.

Caldera received the radiogram on July 22:

VANZETTI IS WELL AND WOULD LIKE TO SEE A SISTER BEFORE AUGUST 10 DATE ON WHICH HE MUST DIE IF THE GOVERNOR DECIDES AGAINST HIM PREPARE FAMILY FOR TRAGIC CONSEQUENCES

SACCOVANZETTI COMMITTEE

Giacomo Caldera was the cousin from Villafalletto who had once worked in New York as a cook, had gotten Vanzetti his first job as a dishwasher, and had since returned home.

Vincenzina *They sent him the radiogram so as not to hurt us so*
Vanzetti: *much. He brought it to us. They sent it so that we would still see Bartolomeo and so that we would beg the governor for mercy. It said one of the sisters. Bartolomeo wanted to see one of the sisters.*

In 1921, after the Dedham trial, Luigia had offered to come to America but Vanzetti rebuffed her by writing, "I do not think that you need to come here. What would you, a stranger who does not know the language, be able to do?" Vanzetti had not known the language either when he first came, and many of his Italian friends in America still didn't, but perhaps he was being protective of his younger sister. But as execution drew closer and more likely, Felicani says Vanzetti began to speak of having Luigia come to visit him.

Felicani told him he had no right to ask his sister to come to see him die, but Vanzetti felt differently. According to Felicani, Vanzetti had another member of the committee send the radiogram.[27] Felicani does not explain why Vanzetti asked for "a sister" or "you or Vincenzina" if he was pining for Luigia. Luigia was the member of the family closest to him; he had not seen Vincenzina since she was five years old. During the years of Vanzetti's exile and imprisonment Luigia had been his confidante, bearing his sorrows, complaints, and homilies. If he wanted one last moment of communion with his family, he would naturally ask for Luigia. If he just wanted a female to shed tears for the governor, either sister would do. He did not ask to see his father nor did he write to him.

On July 22, Fuller went to Charlestown prison to speak to Sacco and Vanzetti. Sacco, true to himself regardless of the consequences, refused to discuss the case with the governor. When Fuller asked him why, Sacco replied, according to Musmanno, "Well, you see, governor, you are a millionaire, many times a millionaire, they tell me, and you just can't believe that a poor man has any rights. It would be just a waste of time for you to hear my story. I don't want to be discourteous . . . but why should I try to fool you by telling you I believe in you, and why should you try to fool me?"[28]

Vanzetti, who was certain he could persuade anyone willing to listen to him, did not hesitate to speak to the governor. Fuller was impressed by Vanzetti, as most people who knew him were. He came to see him twice and after the first visit said to the warden, "What an attractive man!" Nonetheless, one of the first questions Fuller asked Vanzetti was why he did not testify at Plymouth.

Because Vanzetti hadn't said all he wanted to Fuller—he was a compulsive talker and never said all he wanted—he received

Fuller's permission to put his remaining thoughts in a letter. It was dictated to Thompson's secretary on July 27 and sent to the governor the following day.

In his letter, Vanzetti spoke of his fears as a radical and wrote:

> I suppose you know that in Italy the common people has always been afraid of the police. It is hard to get over such ideas, especially when you know what they have done to our comrades in this country. . . . People don't seem to understand that Italians are unpopular anyway, especially if they are poor and laboring people. Their habits are not the habits of ordinary Americans, and they are suspected. They don't get the same chance before an American jury that an American would get. The jury cannot help being prejudiced against them, and then if on top of that the Italians turn out to be radicals, they have no show at all. . . . Before Americans will put an Italian on the same basis with themselves, and accept him as probably telling the truth, he has got to make money and own property.

Vanzetti discussed the witnesses and the evidence, then asked the critical question:

> Do you think, governor, that if I had been guilty of either one of these crimes, I would have been found on a streetcar carrying four buckshot cartridges in my pocket, and a revolver that was stolen from a murdered man? I think if I had committed a murder I should have been careful not to have any cartridges in my pocket, and certainly not to have a revolver that had belonged to a murdered man in my pocket. And when you think that the day I was arrested, May 5th, was five months after the Bridgewater crime and three weeks after the South Braintree crime, I don't think you would believe that anybody could possi-

bly have been such a fool as they tried to make me out, to keep carrying on my person the evidences of guilt. You cannot have it both ways. If we are clever bandits, then we don't do such things as that. If we do such things as that, we are not bandits. Bandits try to put away the evidence of crime, not to carry it around with them.

Near the close of the letter, Vanzetti wrote, "I see I have spent a great deal of time talking about the different points in these two cases; but what is the use talking about all these points when the case comes down to a very simple point. I am an Italian, a stranger in a foreign country, and my witnesses are the same kind of people. I am accused and convicted on the testimony of mostly American witnesses. Everything is against me—my race, my opinions, and my humble occupation."[29]

*Vanzetti to his family, July 28, 1927:**

I assure you that the fast is not hurting me—I am only weak. . . .

I spoke twice to the governor, an hour-and-a-half each time. He seemed much better than I had imagined him. He seemed, according to his lights, an honest and well-intentioned man. I believe that if he thinks we are guilty he will confirm the death sentence. I cannot understand how he could believe us guilty with all the evidence we have in our favor. I am afraid that he does not believe our witnesses, who are mostly Italian, and that he lets himself be convinced by the fact that the members of the juries that tried us are still convinced we are guilty.

I am afraid that he is not quite able to understand the great mass of legal documents connected with the case.

However, it seems that things are taking a turn

*Luigia had not yet left for America, but Vanzetti thought she had, so his salutation was, "Dearest ones." He still would not write to his father.

for the better. The lawyer and our friends are much more encouraged than they have been in the past. The governor said that I made a good impression on him and that he likes me very much.

On July 27, the Lowell Committee submitted its advisory report to Governor Fuller; its conclusions were not made public at that time. Fuller's decision on the fate of Sacco and Vanzetti was to be revealed at 5 P.M. on August 3. That very day, James Mede, accompanied by two attorneys, went to see the captain of the state police to confess to his part in planning the Bridgewater holdup, though it was attempted by four other men while he was in prison. Late in July, Mede had personally told his story to Governor Fuller, who insisted he tell it to the state police. But the police captain refused to take Mede's confession; "I can't take it and I won't take it," he said. One of the lawyers with Mede told the captain his refusal to record the confession could be interpreted as meaning that the state did not want to know the truth about the Sacco-Vanzetti case. "Well," the captain replied, "it is embarrassing. I think it will be damned embarrassing."[30]

Five o'clock came and went without any word from Governor Fuller; he was not even in his office. He finally arrived at 8:26, presumably to polish or dictate his decision. At 11 P.M. there was still no news. Shortly before 11:30, the governor's executive secretary appeared with a pile of sealed envelopes, each with the name of a newspaper. Louis Stark of the *New York Times* ripped open his envelope, flipped to the last page of the document, and shouted to a telegraph operator waiting for the story, "They die!"

The Ca

24

Motions and Mobs

Fuller's document was only five pages long, which permitted him to state his decision without seriously attempting to justify it.[1] The justification lay at the very beginning, where he said that his advisory committee, "men whose reputations for intelligence, open-mindedness, intellectual honesty and good judgment were above reproach," had "arrived unanimously at a conclusion which is wholly in accord with mine."

Having clutched at the security of the Lowell Committee, Fuller then explained that the purpose of his inquiry was to answer three questions. First: Was the jury trial fair? His reply was yes; Sacco and Vanzetti were not prosecuted and convicted because they were anarchists. Fuller did not mention the cross-examination of Sacco or the collusion with the Justice Department. He did note there were affidavits attesting to Thayer's bias, but "I see no evidence of prejudice in his conduct of the trial."

The second question was: Were the accused entitled to a new trial? No, said Fuller, none of the motions argued by the defense justified a new trial. "I give no weight to the Madeiros confession," he wrote. "It is popularly supposed he confessed to committing this crime,"* said the governor, who added "I am not impressed with [Madeiros's] knowledge of the South Braintree murders" and dropped the subject. Fuller did not say a word about the Morelli gang or the corroborating evidence accumulated by Ehrmann.

The third question was: Are they guilty or not guilty? Fuller said he had investigated the Plymouth trial and found "nothing unusual about this case except . . . that Vanzetti did not testify." He believed Vanzetti was guilty because witnesses had identified him. The governor said nothing about the cropped moustache, the Italian witnesses who identified Vanzetti as the man who had sold them eels that morning, or James Mede's confession.

As for South Braintree, the only alibi witness mentioned by Fuller was the clerk in the Italian consulate who had "no memorandum to assist his memory." The governor ignored all the other men who saw Sacco in Boston that day, as well as the surprise witness who rode home on the same train. Vanzetti's alibi was not even mentioned.

"As a result of my investigation," Fuller concluded, "I find no sufficient justification for executive intervention.

"I believe with the jury, that these men, Sacco and Vanzetti, were guilty, and that they had a fair trial. I furthermore believe that there was no justifiable reason for giving them a new trial."

The following morning, Thompson, Felicani, and Rosina Sacco went to Charlestown prison to tell Sacco and Vanzetti the grim news.

| Aldino Felicani: | *Vanzetti really took it very hard. He looked at me for minutes with eyes that were out of this world, just like a person who was losing his mind.*[2] |

Vanzetti kept repeating, "I don't believe it." Sacco, the

---

*This is one point where the mind bends in disbelief that such a statement could be made. Madeiros confessed, both orally and in writing, to taking part in the crime; this was not "popularly supposed" but fact. When Fuller interviewed Madeiros, the governor hinted that if he denied the South Braintree confession he might be spared execution for the Wrentham murder, but Madeiros, a crook, a thief, a robber, a liar, a rum-runner, a bouncer in a brothel, a smuggler, and a murderer, refused to save his life with a false retraction. In declining Fuller's bribe, Madeiros showed more integrity than the governor who offered it.

The C

realist, simply said, "I told you so. I told you so."[3] Felicani told both men that this was the time to send out a very strong message. Neither Sacco nor Vanzetti was in any mood to write exhortations, so Felicani admits he "almost dictated" the messages to them.[4] Both men dutifully attacked capitalism and said they were proud to die for anarchy.

While Sacco and Vanzetti were writing, Felicani spoke to Madeiros, whose execution for the Wrentham bank murder had been postponed should he be needed to testify about South Braintree. Since the commonwealth was determined not to know the truth about South Braintree, Madeiros would be executed with Sacco and Vanzetti; this time there would be two martyrs and one thief. Madeiros said to Felicani, "Too bad for them. I'm a criminal anyhow. I have a long record. But it's a shame for them."[5]

The report of the Lowell Committee was made public on August 7, four days after Fuller announced his decision.[6] Committee hearings had ended on July 21; at the close of that day, Lowell handed Grant and Stratton typewritten copies of a draft of his conclusions. The three men had not yet discussed the evidence, not all of the witnesses had been heard, and the defense lawyers had not made their arguments when Lowell dictated his decision. A true son of the visible saints, Lowell had his own theory of predestination; Sacco and Vanzetti were doomed before they could even present their case.

The Lowell report is the original edition from which Fuller prepared his pony. In more convoluted language it asks the same three questions and offers the same three responses. For the most part, no explanations are given; one must simply accept Lowell's divine judgment.

Was the jury trial fair? Indeed it was. The cross-examination of Sacco was justified to determine whether he was telling the truth when he said he was afraid of being deported as a radical. Evidence that the Justice Department had meddled in the case was not important because there was no proof that the government files, if opened, would show Sacco and Vanzetti were innocent. Judge Thayer tried to be "scrupulously fair"; true, he was "indiscreet in conversation with outsiders" but "we do not believe that he used some of the expressions attributed to him." The fatal bullet allegedly removed from Berardelli's body was genuine, and for the defense even to claim it was a substitute suggested "the case of the defendants must be rather desperate on its merits."

Were the accused entitled to a new trial? Indeed not. The favorable evidence of eyewitness Gould, who said Sacco and Vanzetti were not in the bandit car, was "merely cumulative" and "balanced by two other new witnesses on the other side," both exhumed by the committee. One was Mabel Hewins, whom the prosecution had not called because she insisted Sacco was the driver of the bandit car, and they were already surfeited with drivers. The other was Carlotta Packard Tattilo, who was not asked to testify because she was "twelve ounces to the pound." For Lowell, however, "the woman is eccentric, not unimpeachable in conduct; but the Committee believe that in this case her testimony is well worth consideration."

The foreman, Walter Ripley, did not influence the jurors by carrying cartridges in his pocket, and as for his having said, "Damn them, they ought to hang them anyway!" the committee decided "Daly must have misunderstood him, or that his recollection is at fault."

Proctor's testimony that the fatal bullet was "consistent with" being fired by Sacco's pistol was not meant to mislead the jury, nor did it. Concerning the additional ballistics opinions offered by Hamilton and Gill, the prosecution's experts "presented the more convincing evidence."

As for Madeiros, "The impression has gone abroad that Madeiros confessed committing the murder at South Braintree"; this deliberate lie—he confessed to taking part in the robbery, not to committing the murders—was undoubtedly the source for Fuller's absurd assertion that Madeiros had not confessed at all. After summarizing both the Madeiros confession and the confirming evidence as negatively as possible, carefully excising all credible points, the report stated, "it does not seem to the Committee that these affidavits to corroborate a worthless confession are of such weight as to deserve serious attention." There was no explanation as to why this decision should not have been left to a jury.

Are they guilty or not guilty? Here the Lowell report crammed in everything that might seen incriminating, without seriously considering its logic or validity. Both men were armed and both men lied because they were conscious of their guilt as criminals, not as radicals; why they were armed with incriminating weapons was not explained. Despite trial testimony that Berardelli's gun never left the repair shop, "there is no sufficient reason to suppose [it] was not in his possession at the time of the murder"; once again it is transformed from a .32 to a .38 and ends up in Vanzetti's pocket. When Lowell thought he had proved there was no banquet on April 15, he crowed, "A serious alibi has been destroyed." Once the alibi was restored, it was no longer serious; Sacco's alibi witnesses were not even mentioned. Lowell did not consider whether Sacco's alibi was convincing enough to make it doubtful he was in South Braintree; instead, the committee accepted the disputed bullet, the fraudulent cap, and the controverted eyewitnesses as proof that Sacco could not have been in Boston on April 15. Swallowing the prosecution's claims whole and disregarding Sacco's evidence entirely, "the Committee are of opinion that Sacco was guilty beyond reasonable doubt of the murder at South Braintree."

Vanzetti's alibi was discussed but found to be "decidedly weak." The cloth peddler was lying. Alfonsina Brini "had sworn to an alibi for him [Vanzetti] in the Bridgewater case," implying that she lied twice, though she never testified that she saw him the morning of the Bridgewater crime. The Lowell Committee did concede that the eyewitness evidence against Vanzetti was not exactly overwhelming, but decided that was because "he was evidently not in the foreground."

It was the discussion of Vanzetti's guilt that exposed the poverty of Lowell's logic. Vanzetti was guilty because a few witnesses claimed they saw him in South Braintree on April 15, and "there is no reason why, if he were there for an innocent purpose, he should have sworn that he was in Plymouth all day." The report denied the possibility that Vanzetti swore he was in Plymouth because that's where he was. It also ignored the fact that whether or not Vanzetti was in Plymouth, it was the prosecution's obligation to prove he was in South Braintree committing a crime, and even the Lowell Committee had trouble acknowledging this had been done. The paucity of the evidence against Vanzetti led the committee to conclude: "On the whole, we are of opinion that Vanzetti also was guilty beyond reasonable doubt."

Assuming the president of Harvard was functionally literate, he should have known that "on the whole" is a conditional phrase conveying uncertainty. One cannot "on the whole" be guilty beyond a reasonable doubt, yet that is what the Lowell Committee wrote and because of it Vanzetti was executed.

The Lowell report should have evoked derision, criticism, and a demand that Harvard hire a literate president. Instead it was as though Moses had appeared bearing the tablets of the Lord. If Abbott Lawrence Lowell said Sacco and Vanzetti were guilty, they were guilty. Ehrmann wrote that the Lowell report "did more to make the death of Sacco and Vanzetti acceptable to a doubting world than any decision of judge or jury."[7]

Robert Lincoln O'Brien:
> *I am greatly impressed by the testimony of A. Lawrence Lowell. I don't see how you could have a more judicial way of examining a case than this Lawrence Lowell committee.*[8]

William Lawrence, [Episcopal bishop of Massachusetts and Lowell's second cousin]:
> *I am satisfied with their report. I accept their judgment. I am willing the electrocution should go forward.*[9]

Boston Herald:
> *Most of the serious and earnest minded people who had misgivings as to the original verdict in Judge Thayer's court have had these dissipated by the calm and dispassionate recital of the evidences by President Lowell and his associates.*[10]

The New York Times:

> *It is a great public service which President Lowell, President Stratton and ex-Judge Grant have done in assuring the American people and the world that no intentional or notorious injustice has been done.*[11]

New York World:

> *Gov. Fuller made a very serious mistake in not publishing the report of the Lowell committee along with his own statement. For the report of the committee is an incomparably abler and more convincing document. It has the earmarks of fairness, consideration, shrewdness and coolness. This is the first time in seven years that the case against Sacco and Vanzetti has been plausibly and comprehensively stated.*[12]

Gardner Jackson reports that Felix Frankfurter was so incensed by the *World* editorial he went to New York to confront the editorial page editor, Walter Lippmann.[13] Four days later the *World* took a more critical view of the Lowell report, saying it "is not final and does not close the case" and that "open-minded men remain unconvinced."[14] Heywood Broun, a columnist for the *World* and a Harvard dropout, bitterly called the college "Hangman's House" and asked, "What more can these immigrants from Italy expect? It is not every prisoner who has a president of Harvard University throw on the switch for him."[15] The *New York Times* responded testily, "If we are to measure out condemnation for cowardly bomb throwers, we should not overlook men like Mr. Heywood Broun, who asks in The World whether 'the institution of learning in Cambridge which once we called Harvard will be known as Hangman's House.' Such an educated sneer at the President of Harvard for having undertaken a great civic duty shows better than an explosion the wild and irresponsible spirit which is abroad."[16]

Another writer who did not think killing Sacco and Vanzetti was a great civic duty was John Dos Passos. Dos Passos, a Harvard graduate, wrote an open letter to Lowell in which he called him an accomplice to "judicial murder" and asked, "Did the committee feel that the prosecution's case was so weak that they had to bolster it by fresh deductions and surmises of their own?" Dos Passos called the report "an apology for the conduct of the trial rather than an impartial investigation." He said, "Reading it, the suspicion grows paragraph by paragraph that its aim was not to review but to make respectable the proceedings of Judge Thayer and the district attorney's office. Not in a single phrase is there an inkling of a sense on your part or on that of your colleagues of the importance of the social and racial backgrounds of the trial."[17]

But Dos Passos, Broun, and other skeptics were the exception; as far as public opinion was concerned, particularly public opinion in Massachusetts, Sacco and Vanzetti were now guilty. This was not because the report argued the prosecution's case convincingly—its ineptness was embarrassing—but because it was signed by Abbott Lawrence Lowell.

To understand this acquiescence, it is necessary to return three hundred years to the era of the visible saints. Though the Puritan theocracy was long dead, American democracy had never vanquished the invidious idea that there was an elite in whom resided the conscience of the community. No matter that the Puritan conscience had always upheld bigotry, racism, reaction, and suppression; no matter that from Winthrop through Lowell the Puritans and their descendants had bent their principles to serve self-preservation; no matter that Sacco and Vanzetti had more moral authority than Abbott Lawrence Lowell. The Puritan myth still enshrouded Boston like a fog; it was impossible to penetrate. William Thompson, defender of Sacco and Vanzetti, unwittingly spoke for all those who believed the Lowell report when he told his own witness, "That is so because Mr. Lowell has found it to be so."

Of all those cowed by the immutable authority of Abbott Lawrence Lowell, only one mattered as far as Sacco and Vanzetti were concerned—Governor Alvan T. Fuller. During his investigation, Fuller had at times seemed genuinely uncertain of their guilt. Robert Lincoln O'Brien reports that while discussing the case with Fuller after commencement exercises at Boston University, he got the impression the governor was "on the leniency side."[18]

The Cas

The *New York Times* story on Fuller's decision to condemn Sacco and Vanzetti said it "stirred certain important men in Boston to private discussion of the case. These men, it may be stated on excellent authority, were taken into the Governor's confidence. They are declaring emphatically tonight that the Governor gave them every indication that he would pardon Sacco and Vanzetti or extend clemency to them. One of these men is a former high State officer. Nobody, however, wishes to talk for publication." The article added, "Not only did the Governor declare to confidants that the idea of sending the men to the electric chair on 'flimsy' evidence was 'abhorrent' to him, but he also said that he did not approve of having one Judge be the sole arbiter of the men's destinies, according to reliable sources tonight." [19]

Fuller was obviously considering some form of clemency; why did he change his mind? Three possibilities are usually cited. On August 2, President Calvin Coolidge announced he would not run in 1928. Coolidge, a former governor of Massachusetts, had been rocketed into national politics by his firm stand during the Boston police strike. Fuller may have decided an equally firm stand on Sacco and Vanzetti would send him to the White House the following year. Vanzetti, in one of his letters, wrote, "Fuller, to be President, will burn us all." [20] The second explanation is that Fuller was influenced by the Irish, a powerful political force in Boston, who wanted an eye for an eye; if the carbarn boys had to burn, so did Sacco and Vanzetti. The third theory is the one held by most observers of the case.

Roger
Baldwin:
I just don't think that Fuller was capable, being the kind of a man he was, of resisting the recommendations of men as highly placed as Lawrence Lowell and his two colleagues. The reflection on the courts of Massachusetts, the justice of the administration, was so great that I just don't think Fuller could have stood up to it. It would take a man of a great deal more courage than he had to say our courts were wrong and the president of Harvard University was wrong.

The three explanations are not incompatible. Fuller may have found Vanzetti a very attractive man, but he also found the

White House very attractive, and the Irish vote very attractive, and he was not about to do anything as unattractive as defy President Lowell of Harvard. If Lowell had decided differently, Fuller could have granted clemency, but Lowell would never have found for Sacco and Vanzetti. Justice is for gentlemen, not for beaten men from beaten races.

Edward S. Greenbaum, attorney:

> *I remember Al Smith once said something to me about this. He was saying that instead of President Lowell being appointed . . . he said, "Suppose they'd appointed me and Lillian Wald," and someone else he named, "as the committee of three. How would this have come out?" . . . With the same evidence, Lillian Wald, Jane Addams—that was the other—and Al Smith would, Smith said, unanimously have felt that these two fellows were not guilty. He said, "With Mr. Lowell's background, he would feel the other way."[21]*

When Governor Fuller announced his decision on August 3, Thompson and Ehrmann decided final appeals should be handled by another lawyer. They feared their passionate commitment to Sacco and Vanzetti had already offended Thayer, as well as others who would still be making decisions; the condemned men would benefit from having fresh, calm voices speak for them.

Arthur D. Hill, a prominent Boston attorney who assisted Thompson on one of the supplementary motions, took over the case, assisted by Musmanno and several other attorneys, while Thompson, Ehrmann, Frankfurter and other lawyers and law professors stayed in the shadows plotting strategy. Both Thompson and Ehrmann had entered the case skeptical of Sacco and Vanzetti's innocence; both died convinced not only of their innocence but of their greatness.

Sara Ehrmann:	*One day Herbert told me this very remarkable thing, that Mr. Thompson said that the character of Vanzetti was nearest the character of Christ than that of any man whom he had ever known.*

It is difficult to know how Hill felt about Sacco and Vanzetti, because he said different things to different people.

Robert L.
O'Brien

[Hill] said to me after it was all over, "Bob, mind you this. I never said to any human being that I thought these men were innocent. All I ever said was that I thought they had legal rights that should be protected."[22]

However, O'Brien also quotes Hill as saying "there is such a thing as an innocent man being hanged,"[23] while Ehrmann quotes Hill's comment that "Sacco and Vanzetti received as fair a trial as was possible—consistent with a determination to convict them."[24] Gardner Jackson heard Hill say that while he was not absolutely certain of their innocence, they would undoubtedly have been saved if not for the worldwide agitation in their behalf;[25] somehow, everyone was to blame but Massachusetts.

Both the legal and political strategies for the defense were compromised and possibly deliberately subverted at the end by the Communist party. Fully aware how well the case could be exploited, the Communists in the final weeks set up their own committee, appointed their own set of lawyers, and were openly antagonistic to the Sacco-Vanzetti Defense Committee. When the Defense Committee halted all demonstrations while Lowell and Fuller were deliberating, the Communists continued theirs, not only aggravating officials at a critical moment but falsely identifying Sacco and Vanzetti with the Communists and making justice even less likely. At another point, the Communists borrowed portions of the transcripts of both trials from the Defense Committee, and when the committee needed them again, the Communists insisted they were lost.[26]

Gardner
Jackson:

They quite clearly were trying to hamstring our operations. . . . Certainly in retrospect, and from hindsight, putting all the circumstances together, there's just no question in my mind that the Communists preferred Sacco and Vanzetti dead than alive. For their purposes the martyrdom of Sacco and Vanzetti was far more important than the actual rendering of justice.[27]

On August 5, a group of attorneys including Hill, Ehrmann, Frankfurter, Musmanno, and Francis D. Sayre, Woodrow Wilson's son-in-law, met to plan their last, desperate moves. On August 6, Hill appealed to the Superior Court of Massachusetts for a stay of execution which was denied. A petition for a stay of execution was also filed with Governor Fuller. That same day, Musmanno filed the seventh and final supplementary motion for a new trial based on the grounds that Thayer's bias denied Sacco and Vanzetti due process and equal protection of the laws in violation of the Fourteenth Amendment. The constitutional issue was raised in an attempt to open the way to an appeal to the federal courts. Hill requested the chief justice of the superior court to assign someone other than Thayer to hear the motion based on Thayer's prejudice. The chief justice replied that motions for a new trial were always argued before the judge who presided over the original trial: "In accordance with precedent and practice and sound reason, the motion should be and will be heard by Judge Thayer."

On August 8, Arthur Hill, compelled to ask Thayer to consider a motion in which he himself was now a defendant, urged the judge to withdraw from the case. "Every consideration of sound sense, good morals, and intelligent administration of law impels you to withdraw," Hill said.[28]

Thayer replied, "With reference to the question of prejudice, there is not any now and never was at any time."[29] As he spoke, the affidavits affirming his prejudice—"Did you see what I did with those anarchistic bastards?" and all the rest—lay before him. But Thayer was clever enough not to be trapped into ruling on his own prejudice; he took refuge in a technicality. No justice of the superior court had jurisdiction to hear a motion for a new trial once sentence had been passed. Since sentence had already been passed, he could not hear the new motion.

Arthur K. Reading, the attorney general of Massachusetts who was now arguing the case for the commonwealth, said Hill's arguments about Thayer's not ruling on his own prejudice were "the most preposterous" he had ever heard.[30] Reading also agreed with Thayer that it was too late to hear a motion for a new trial because sentence had been pronounced.

Hill then appealed to Thayer to revoke sentence and consid-

The Ca

er the new motion, but Thayer would do no such thing. He ruled immediately that he had no jurisdiction to consider the new motion because sentence had been passed and the following day denied the request that sentence be revoked.

On August 8, the same day Hill argued futilely before Thayer, he also argued motions for a writ of error, a writ of habeas corpus, and a stay of execution before Judge George A. Sanderson of the Supreme Judicial Court of Massachusetts. All were denied. Before Hill could appeal Sanderson's decision to the full supreme judicial court, he had to have Sanderson's approval. The appeal was filed on August 9. On August 10 defense and prosecution appeared before Sanderson to argue whether his decision should be brought before the full court. Sanderson listened, then asked the attorneys to return the following day, August 11, with their final arguments. There was just one problem; Sacco and Vanzetti were to be executed at midnight on August 10. Two days earlier Sanderson had said he had no authority to stay the executions. Unless Governor Fuller or someone else intervened, final appeals would be argued after Sacco and Vanzetti were dead.

Since Fuller gave no indication what he would do, it was decided to appeal immediately to the federal courts. Musmanno took a cab to Charlestown prison, where Sacco and Vanzetti were in the death house waiting for midnight. As he explained the petition for a writ of habeas corpus and asked them to sign it, Musmanno could hear noises in the next room where the executioner was testing the equipment. Vanzetti signed the petition; Sacco refused. "I have been crucified enough," Sacco said. "I won't let them crucify me again."[31]

Before Musmanno left, Vanzetti offered him a farewell gift, a two-volume history, *The Rise of American Civilization*, which Mrs. Evans had given him. Musmanno refused to accept the books, saying he would see Vanzetti again. "Mr. Musmanno," said Sacco dryly, "better take the books—I know."[32]

Arthur Hill and William Thompson, two paragons of Boston's legal profession, personally took the petition for a writ of habeas corpus to the summer home of Supreme Court Justice Oliver Wendell Holmes at Beverly Farms, Massachusetts. Holmes denied the writ at once. "I cannot think," he wrote, "that prejudice on the part of the presiding judge however strong would deprive the [state] Court of jurisdiction, that is of legal power to decide the case."[33] Privately Holmes told Thompson, "I am convinced that these men did not get a square deal, but we cannot take the United States government into state affairs and undermine the basic principles of the separate sovereignties of the state and federal governments."[34] The right to a fair trial is also a basic principle, and an agency of the federal government had conspired with the state to win a conviction. It should not have been difficult for the most brilliant and original mind on the Supreme Court to find a way to intercede, but Holmes had apparently forgotten he was descended from a political prisoner shipped to America as an indentured servant. The Holmes who ruled on Sacco and Vanzetti was the son of the original Brahmin; the judge who approved of sending that noted agitator Eugene Debs to jail for exercising his constitutional right of free speech; the aristocrat who did not wish to be run by either Jews or Catholics.

After Holmes denied the writ, it was presented to federal district court Judge George W. Anderson who had upheld the Constitution and the rights of immigrants after the Palmer raids. But Anderson also denied the writ, saying, "I have on this record no right to interfere with the legal processes of the Courts of Massachusetts."[35]

Unless Governor Fuller acted, Sacco and Vanzetti would die that night, with their appeal still pending before Judge Sanderson. Fuller either could not decide what to do or wanted to share the responsibility. He not only met with his advisory council but summoned all of the state's ex-attorneys general to request their opinions. At eight-thirty in the evening, with the execution scheduled for midnight, Arthur Hill spent two hours before the governor's council arguing that to execute two men while their case was still before the courts was not in the highest standards of justice.

All that day Rosina Sacco sat in the inner office of the headquarters of the Sacco-Vanzetti Defense Committee quietly waiting. Occasionally she crumpled pieces of paper in her hand. Once she spoke about her little daughter's kitten. Day passed into evening and there was still no news. Rosina Sacco quietly fainted and was taken to someone's home.[36]

In the death house, Sacco, Vanzetti, and Madeiros waited in

The Ca

their cells. The official witnesses also waited; the supper they would be served after the execution had been prepared. The largest number of newspapermen ever to cover an execution stood by; telegraph operators had their fingers poised over the keys.*

At 11:23 P.M. word finally came from the statehouse that Fuller had granted a stay of twelve days to permit the courts to complete their deliberations. Warden William Hendry of Charlestown prison rushed to the death house shouting, "Well, boys, it's all off." Madeiros and Sacco said nothing. Vanzetti said, "Well, I'm damned glad. I'd like to see my sister before I die." *[39]

The next morning Musmanno found Sacco and Vanzetti in a cheerful mood, though Sacco was weak from twenty-five days of fasting. Musmanno urged him to eat. "I want to register my protest against the infamy which keeps us here," Sacco replied. "Furthermore, why should I fatten myself for the execution?"[40]

The new execution date was August 22, 1927. The defenders of Sacco and Vanzetti had twelve more days to try to win their case in the courts of Massachusetts and the court of public opinion. They would fail in the former but triumph in the latter.

August, 1927, was Sacco-Vanzetti month not only in Boston but all over America and in much of the world. Without television for instant publicity and with radio a luxury rather than a household item, two obscure Italians had become the object of the greatest concern ever accorded two victims before that time and probably since. Musmanno wrote, "Never in recorded history was there such worldwide demonstration in behalf of two men condemned to death."[41] The *New York World* commented on the "extraordinary public interest in the outcome" and the "universal concern over 'what will happen to Sacco and Vanzetti.'"[42]

Liberals and intellectuals finally stirred themselves and over five hundred of them, including Jane Addams and John Dewey, signed a letter asking Fuller to stay the executions "until all

*So great was the interest in the fate of Sacco and Vanzetti that night, Boston police blotters were bare between 9:50 P.M. and 7:05 the following morning.[37]

*Luigia was delayed first in Italy, then in Paris, by passport complications, which raises the question of whether the United States tried to prevent her from coming and arousing more sympathy for Vanzetti.[38]

doubts are resolved." Governor Fuller told the delegation presenting the petition there were facts about the case that could not be made public. He couldn't say what they were, of course, because they could not be made public.

Anne
Hutchinson: I desire to know wherefore I am banished.

Governor   *Say no more, the court knows wherefore and is*
Winthrop: *satisfied.*

On August 7, the Sacco-Vanzetti Defense Committee issued a call to the "leaders of American letters, science, art, education and social reform" to demonstrate at the statehouse and at Charlestown prison. Several of the glamorous literary figures of the twenties answered the call, including Dorothy Parker, Edna St. Vincent Millay, and Katherine Anne Porter. Boston became the place to be that month. Picketing, being arrested and bailed, becoming involved for a few days would supply hours of chatter back at the safety of the Algonquin and perhaps an article or a poem besides. Gardner Jackson notes that one famous female of the day tried to bed him.[43]

Those who fought for Sacco and Vanzetti before the spotlights shone were bitter about the celebrities who appeared for curtain calls at the end. Jeannette Marks, in her account of the last two weeks of the case, *Thirteen Days*, described a vivid scene at Defense Committee headquarters on August 10. While Rosina Sacco was sitting there waiting to hear if her husband would die that night, a group of noisy, exhilarated demonstrators arrived. Mary Donovan evicted them, saying bitterly, "Think of their daring to come here on a day like this to enjoy themselves!"[44] People like Mary Donovan, Gardner Jackson and, more important, Aldino Felicani and Rosina Sacco, could only stare at the superstars and wonder where they had been for the last seven years.

What was a lark for a few literary lights was a terrifying experience for those who cared enough to risk everything to try to save Sacco and Vanzetti. Beltrando Brini, who had already spoken to Fuller, returned to the statehouse with six other witnesses who had testified at the Plymouth trial, including his mother and Mrs. Fortini, to confront the governor.[45]

Beltrando Brini:	*They were really frightened, trembling, shaking in their shoes; they seemed to be very much afraid. But I was quite desperate. I would have tried anything, short of violence, to do whatever I could. I didn't care if I had to go to prison or if it would jeopardize my career.*

The group was stopped by Herman MacDonald, the governor's executive secretary, who wanted to know what they had to say. Brini demanded that Fuller either arrest them for perjury for testifying for Vanzetti, or release Vanzetti and Sacco.

Beltrando Brini:	*MacDonald said, "You know the governor can't do that." I said, "It seems to me the governor can do anything if he can put to death two innocent men." And MacDonald said, "If you want to make a speech, go out into the Common." I said, "I was out there yesterday." I don't recall what else I said to Mr. MacDonald, but I was gently pushed out of the statehouse.*

August was a month of appeals, picketing, strikes, demonstrations, and bombings. There were explosions in a Philadelphia church, the home of the mayor of Baltimore, the New York City subway and elevated system, a theater in Sacramento, and the home of one of the Dedham jurors. The bombings may have been the work of psychopaths or radicals too outraged to be sensible; they may also have been the work of the Bureau of Investigation, the Communists, or any other group that wanted Sacco and Vanzetti to die, for they served only to reinforce public resentment of the two men. Because of the bombings, federal buildings were guarded, marines and troops stood ready to defend the Capitol, and the Washington Monument was closed to tourists. Guards were placed at public buildings, churches, subways, bridges, and other possible targets all over the country, as well as at American embassies abroad. Obviously, any two men who could create such havoc ought to be hanged anyway, damn them. Meanwhile, the Bureau of Investigation maintained its perfect record by failing to find any of the bombers.

Boston itself was armed for revolution. The arsenal at police headquarters included fifty-six shotguns, twelve submachine guns, and fifteen thousand rounds of ammunition. Charlestown prison was guarded by hundreds of police and troopers, plus fire companies with high-pressure hoses. It was rather heavy artillery considering the hundred-and-fifty or so persons who picketed the statehouse* or even the thousands who peacefully demonstrated on Boston Common until their meetings were broken up by police.

Across America there were more strike calls than strikes. The largest demonstrations were in New York. There, hundreds of thousands walked out, largely in the garment trades where most of the workers were immigrants. A march through Little Italy in lower Manhattan was broken up after what the *New York Times* described as a "running battle" between police and demonstrators.[46] Demonstrations in other cities were generally peaceful except for the usual skirmishes with police. In Chicago, however, the police used tear gas and gunfire and in Cheswick, Pennsylvania, troopers stormed a rally of striking miners, beating men, women, and children.

Overall, strike activity was sporadic and uncoordinated; there was nothing resembling a general strike or mass action on the part of labor. It was dangerous to demonstrate for Sacco and Vanzetti; the government had made that clear. On August 8, the chairman of the House Immigration and Naturalization Committee called Sacco and Vanzetti "bandits and murderers" and warned aliens who took part in Sacco-Vanzetti demonstrations that they "end their chances for citizenship" and were "liable for deportation." The Labor Department added that all demonstrations were being carefully monitored by government agencies.[47]

On August 11, the *New York World* printed a dispatch from Washington that said attempts would be made to prevent illegal aliens and radical aliens from being employed; all aliens would have to register with the government; and deportations of undesirable aliens would be resumed. The following day the *World*

*The pickets were arrested for loitering and other trivial charges, and some were beaten in the privacy of the police station. Most of the names on the police records are Jewish or Italian. It is a myth that the New York literary world turned out in force for Sacco and Vanzetti.

The C

reported that the government would renew its roundups of alien agitators and Congress would be asked to revoke the citizenship of foreign-born radicals so they could be expelled. Some of these threats were hollow, but they sounded ominous enough to serve their purpose which was to silence and intimidate the natural supporters of Sacco and Vanzetti. The proletariat in whom Sacco and Vanzetti put so much faith felt anguish, but not enough to forfeit their futures.

Overseas, where workers were safe from American bullying and fulminations, agitation was more organized and more intense. Hundreds of thousands struck and rallied in Paris and a number of other cities, including London, Belfast, Moscow, Berlin, Vienna, Budapest, Bucharest, Rome, and Madrid. There were demonstrations in Norway, Sweden, Denmark, Switzerland, Holland; in Japan and China; in North Africa and South Africa; in Mexico, Central and South America. Pleas for clemency came from the foreign press and almost every figure of stature abroad, including politicians, writers, scientists, and an earlier victim, Alfred Dreyfus.

Aside from public manifestations, how did the people really feel about Sacco and Vanzetti? The *Boston Evening Transcript* reported on August 8 that 80 percent of the telegrams and 99 percent of the letters received by Governor Fuller opposed clemency. Since the governor hoped to make political capital out of his decision to condemn the two men, it was in his interest to emphasize that public opinion supported him, so statistics emanating from his office through a newspaper that favored execution had to be suspect. The governor's executive secretary, Herman MacDonald, asked by Gardner Jackson what had become of a clemency petition sent by members of the British Parliament, cursed and said, "Do you think we pay any attention to this stuff? It comes in here by the barrelful and we shoot it right into the fire!"[48]

What Governor Fuller didn't burn were messages that read: "Congratulations to our future President, the 100 percent American, who has the courage of his convictions." "I am glad your trying ordeal is over. The country supports you." "Please accept congratulations upon your courageous decision in the Sacco-Vanzetti case and your maintenance of the principles of American law and justice." "I heartily congratulate you on your brave stand for law and order and decent government. All true and loyal Americans stand behind you."[49]

Letters and telegrams to Fuller and the press were not a reliable clue to public opinion because haters tend to be virulent and vocal. Only a psychotic could write, "If there is no one in Massachusetts who has the nerve to despatch Sacco and Vanzetti, let me know it, and I will come," but people such as this make themselves heard. Samuel Eliot Morison wrote Fuller, "My own support of the movement to obtain a retrial has been due as much to a desire to vindicate the honor of Massachusetts as to shield two men from further punishment for a crime which I believe they did not commit." Morison was an articulate historian who could make a commitment eloquently and without fear of reprisals, but what about the silent majority, the vast number of immigrants who suffered with Sacco and Vanzetti and shared their fears and their pain but had neither the courage nor the standing nor the words to express their feelings? Vanzetti wrote Luigia that fifty million signatures had been collected for him and Sacco world-wide,[50] but there were others who did not sign petitions (some couldn't write), or march, or strike. They could only weep and wonder why even in the land of their dreams, the awesome machinery of the state should be crushing out the lives of two innocent men. If this could happen in America, there was no refuge anywhere.

Whatever the figures were on a national or international scoreboard, there is no doubt that in Massachusetts, hatred of Sacco and Vanzetti was rabid. Professor Joughin estimates "probably 80% of the citizens of Massachusetts desired to have the men executed. . . . Fear for the safety of the established order led to hatred of that order's critics, and finally to a belief that the exercise of mercy would indicate a strategic defeat."[51] For too many people in Massachusetts, whatever their backgrounds, the Sacco-Vanzetti case, originally an outgrowth of earlier anxieties and crises, had by now produced anxieties and crises of its own which could be relieved only by human sacrifice.

25

You Kill Two Innocent Men

While agitation continued and pleas poured in, lawyers frantically sought some way to save Sacco and Vanzetti. On August 11, Judge Sanderson ruled the defense could appeal to the full Supreme Judicial Court of Massachusetts. Hill argued the appeal on August 16, declaring that "Judge Thayer is just as much a defendant in this case as if in the dock, and to allow him to hear any question on it is to make him in effect a judge in his own case."[1] Attorney General Reading argued that no motion for a new trial could be made after the death sentence had been imposed.

On August 18, the justices of the supreme judicial court wrote their decision, locked it in a safe, and went on vacation, leaving instructions that the decision not be released until the following morning, when they were safely out of town. That same day, August 18, Sacco, certain he was going to die, said farewell to his fourteen-year-old son Dante. He spoke to the boy, then embraced and kissed him. When Dante left, his father's eyes followed him until he was out of sight, then Sacco lay on his cot and sobbed.[2]

When the decision of the supreme judicial court was released on August 19, it took the judges five pages to affirm the narrow, technical point that "a motion for a new trial in capital cases comes too late if made after sentence has been pronounced"; therefore "the judicial conduct of the trial judge . . . need not be discussed." The request that sentence be revoked was the same as a motion for a new trial and could not be considered because motions for a new trial came too late if made after sentence had been pronounced.[3]

Attorneys for Sacco and Vanzetti immediately presented a plea for a stay of execution to the chief justice of the Superior Court of Massachusetts and a petition for a writ of habeas corpus to a federal district court judge. Both were denied.

Musmanno went to Charlestown prison to tell Sacco and Vanzetti the decision of the supreme judicial court. Before he said a word, Vanzetti looked at his face and said, "Mr. Musmanno, you don't need to tell me what happened." Sacco said he had expected it.[4] After Vanzetti's initial calm reaction, he suddenly went berserk. Eyes glaring, he began to shout, "Get the million men!" and he wrote an incoherent letter to Thompson ordering "all the nations of the world" to mobilize and attack the United States.[5]

That afternoon, Sacco and Vanzetti, who had been moved to the Cherry Hill section of Charlestown prison when Fuller granted them a stay of twelve days, were taken back to the death house. At about the same time, the ship that carried Luigia Vanzetti across the Atlantic docked in New York.

Luigia Vanzetti was a slender, devout, and melancholy woman, aged far beyond her thirty-six years. Snatched from a small farm-town and thrust into an international glare, she spoke simply and from her heart. She told reporters her father had said he hoped she and Bartolomeo would come back together, but he was very pessimistic because he had spent two years in America "and spoke of the hatred against the Italians here." She also said "my mission is one of peace and solace" and that she had come to persuade her brother to return to the church "whether he lives or dies."[6] The members of the Sacco-Vanzetti Defense Committee who had come to greet Luigia must have gagged on this statement and urged her to take a more positive approach because in a later radio broadcast she said, "I have a great hope in my heart that this

The Ca

great country in which millions of people have found liberty and happiness will not allow my brother and Sacco to die."

Luigia was met in New York by Rosina Sacco and Aldino Felicani, as well as a group of some three hundred sympathizers. Before she left Villafalletto, Luigia had received her father's imperious command that, if it were possible, "When you return, be sure to bring Barto back with you." During the drive from New York to Boston Felicani told her what she could realistically expect.[7]

Luigia and Bartolomeo Vanzetti, who had regained control of his sanity, were reunited in the death house the following day. Rosina Sacco had begged Warden Hendry to permit Luigia, whom she called "my sister in misfortune," to enter through a side door sparing her the regular route to the death cells which led through the execution chamber and past the electric chair, a route Rosina took every time she visited her husband. At Vanzetti's request, Rosina also asked the warden to permit him to leave his cell for Luigia's visit so he would not have to greet her through bars one inch thick, one inch apart, and covered with mesh. Though both requests violated prison rules, Hendry agreed. He unlocked Vanzetti's cell so he could stand in the corridor to embrace the sister he had not seen for nineteen years.

Luigia collapsed in Vanzetti's arms. Warden Hendry caught her as she fell, while Rosina Sacco ran to get water. When Luigia recovered, she and Bartolomeo sat together weeping and recalling their childhood in Italy. It was not a joyous childhood, but it must have seemed so at that point. They did not discuss either religion or politics.

Vanzetti later regretted having asked one of his sisters to come to America. In his last note to Luigia he wrote, "My dear sister, how happy I was to see you and hear your sweet words of encouragement and hope. Nonetheless I think it was a terrible mistake to make you cross the ocean to come and see me here. You cannot know how much I suffered in seeing your agony."

After the reunion, Luigia was put to the task for which she had been summoned, to beg for her brother's life. Felicani suggested taking her to see William Cardinal O'Connell, spiritual leader of Boston's Catholics. Luigia, Rosina Sacco, and Felicani were driven to the cardinal's summer home, where the women received tea and sympathy from Cardinal O'Connell, while Felicani waited outside in the car.[8]

It was now Saturday, August 20; execution was two days away. Musmanno was in Washington, D.C., that morning, where he filed an appeal with the United States Supreme Court, citing the Fourteenth Amendment. While he was in the capital, he also went to the Justice Department to request that the files on Sacco and Vanzetti be released. Attorney General Sargent was on vacation, but an assistant said there was nothing he could do. The assistant told several other petitioners for Sacco and Vanzetti the files would be made available if Fuller or the Lowell Committee requested them. No such request was made.

That same Saturday, Arthur Hill returned to Beverly Farms to ask Justice Oliver Wendell Holmes for a stay of execution so the Supreme Court could consider whether the constitutional rights of Sacco and Vanzetti had been violated. "I assume that under the Statute my power extends to this case although I am not free from doubt," wrote Holmes in his memorandum of rejection. "But it is a power rarely exercised and I should not be doing my duty if I exercised it unless I thought that there was a reasonable chance that the Court would entertain the application and ultimately reverse the judgment. This I cannot bring myself to believe."[9]

The great dissenter would not dissent on behalf of Sacco and Vanzetti; he would not even let them live long enough to have their case considered by the Supreme Court because he *believed* the Court would decide against them. Prognostication is also a power rarely exercised by a Supreme Court judge. Holmes had said privately he felt the two men had not gotten a square deal, yet he would not let the Court hear their appeal because he had made up his mind it would be rejected. Holmes also noted in his rebuff that he had "received many letters from people who seem to suppose that I have a general discretion to see that justice is done. They are written with the confidence that sometimes goes with ignorance of the law." This supercilious sneer implied that belief in justice revealed ignorance of the law, a position confirmed by Holmes's behavior.

Oliver Wendell Holmes was now the one person in the

The Ca

country who might have saved Sacco and Vanzetti, not just with a stay of execution but permanently. He was probably correct in anticipating that the conservative Supreme Court would rule against the two alien anarchists, though this was up to the Court to decide, not Holmes. But he was also the one man in Massachusetts with more moral authority than Abbott Lawrence Lowell. Holmes's bloodline was not quite as pure as Lowell's, but Holmes more than compensated for it by his magisterial position as the most honored member of the Supreme Court. A blistering dissent on the Sacco-Vanzetti case written by Oliver Wendell Holmes, the pride of the Brahmins, would have reverberated around the world, including Boston. It would have virtually forced Fuller to grant clemency or given the governor the justification he sought to act as he was privately inclined. But instead of being bold and compassionate, Holmes chose to follow the narrow, inhumane path of his Puritan ancestors.

On Sunday, August 21, Hill appealed to the only other liberal on the Supreme Court, Louis Brandeis. Brandeis felt he was in an awkward position. Privately sympathetic to Sacco and Vanzetti, he had let Rosina Sacco use his home in Dedham during the trial. His wife and daughter were openly partisan to the two prisoners, and Felix Frankfurter and Elizabeth Glendower Evans were family friends. Brandeis spent less than three minutes with Hill, meeting him on his porch and not even letting him into the house. Hill later explained, "Justice Brandeis, on being informed on what case we were acting, stated that because of his personal relations to some of the people who had been interested in the case he felt that he must decline to act on any matter connected with it." [10]

Gardner Jackson says he understood and sympathized with Brandeis's position, but Felicani and others on the Defense Committee were bitter. It does seem Brandeis was cutting too fine a point on a matter that involved life or death. He was not being asked to resolve the case but to let Sacco and Vanzetti live long enough to permit the Supreme Court to resolve it.

That same day, August 21, Musmanno sent three telegrams, several hours apart, to President Calvin Coolidge, who was vacationing in Rapid City, South Dakota, asking him to intercede, though the president had already received and rejected similar pleas. Silent Cal remained silent. At 5 P.M. Musmanno called Rapid City and spoke to a presidential secretary. He was told the president felt the matter was out of his jurisdiction. When Musmanno asked if he could speak to Coolidge, he was told the president was resting; he was still tired from fishing the previous day.

After being rejected by Brandeis, Arthur Hill set out to find Supreme Court Justice Harlan Fiske Stone, who was vacationing on an island off the coast of Maine, while Musmanno telephoned Chief Justice William Howard Taft, who was vacationing in Canada. Both justices were asked to stay the execution. Both refused.

While lawyers were making their futile appeals that Sunday, Boston was mobilized for a major assault. All two thousand police were on duty. Firemen were armed not only with water hoses but with pickaxes and guns. Police cars patrolled the streets. Small planes flew overhead, watching for signs of disorder.

Police banned any meeting on Boston Common, but there was a demonstration anyway, which was broken up. Pickets marching in front of the statehouse were arrested for "sauntering and loitering." One of them, George L. Teeple, Harvard '97, told the judge, "I am a native-born American citizen, of American breeding and American antecedents, as far back as my knowledge goes in both branches of my family; and I feel that such citizens have a peculiar responsibility in doing all that they can to see that full and exact justice is done to the foreign-born who come to our shores."

The judge replied, "There may be some excuse for foreigners who are ignorant to violate the law, but there is very little excuse for an American and a graduate of Harvard to do the same thing."[11]

On Monday morning, August 22, 1927, the Sacco-Vanzetti case was theoretically pending before the United States Supreme Court, but unless a judge or Governor Fuller granted a stay of execution so the case could be heard, Sacco and Vanzetti would die that night.

Musmanno went to Fuller's office early that morning, before

the governor, and asked MacDonald if Fuller had acted on five affidavits Hill had delivered on Saturday. "What difference does it make?" said MacDonald. "The men are guilty."[12]

Fuller arrived at the statehouse at 10:40 A.M. He said cheerfully to the waiting reporters, "Good morning, gentlemen. It's a beautiful morning, isn't it?"

Musmanno had left by then to petition a superior court judge for a stay of execution; the judge said he had no power to grant it. With Arthur Hill still in Maine, where he had gone to find Justice Stone, a group of volunteer attorneys of the highest caliber prepared still another petition for a writ of habeas corpus, to be presented to the federal district court. Musmanno took the petition to Charlestown prison, where Vanzetti signed it and Sacco refused.

Musmanno wrote that while he was there, Rosina Sacco and Luigia Vanzetti came to say goodby. According to the *New York World* (August 23, 1927), Musmanno was at the prison from 2:30 to 3 P.M. Luigia and Rosina went three times that day, at 11 A.M., at 4:30 P.M., and suffered a final, five-minute farewell at 7 P.M. Either the hours given in the *World* are incorrect, or Musmanno related the scene as told to him by someone else.

There was one small space between the bars through which food and other necessities were passed. Vanzetti grasped his sister's hands through this opening. "Oh, Luigia, why did you come?" he cried. "You have given yourself so much pain." He wept while Luigia prayed.

In the next cell Sacco clasped his wife's hands. "Rosina," he said, "I love you and always will."

"Nick," said Rosina Sacco, "I am dying with you."[13]

At 5 P.M., federal district court Judge James A. Lowell heard the arguments of the volunteer attorneys and refused to grant a stay because he could find no federal question involved. Immediately, two of the attorneys went to Oliver Wendell Holmes to appeal for the third time and to be rejected for the third time.

Musmanno returned to Fuller's office, where all day long men and women had come and gone making their last appeals. One of them was Congressman Fiorello La Guardia, who told reporters, "there's one chance in a thousand of a reprieve."[14]

Musmanno again pleaded the case with Fuller. The governor listened for a while, then said, "Answer me this: why didn't Vanzetti take the stand at the Plymouth trial?" Eventually, perhaps to be rid of him, Fuller told Musmanno to speak to Arthur Reading, the commonwealth's attorney general. The governor told Musmanno he would accept Reading's recommendations.[15]

Musmanno went to Reading's office. The attorney general said that while he agreed Sacco and Vanzetti had a right to be heard by the Supreme Court, "I do not yet see any obligation on our part to continue granting reprieves."[16] Reading would not concede that if the governor did not grant a reprieve no one would; all he would say was that he would think about it and report to Fuller.

Musmanno returned to Fuller's office and was there at 9 P.M. when Rosina Sacco and Luigia Vanzetti came to plead with the governor. Musmanno, who spoke Italian, volunteered to translate for Miss Vanzetti. The scene between the two women and Fuller, as recorded in *After Twelve Years*, belongs in a play; a tragedy.[17]

"Governor," said Rosina Sacco, "you are a man of family. You have a wife and children. My husband has a wife and children. Please look upon this case as a family man. Can you let my husband and family man die on the word of a woman like Lola Andrews? My husband was always good and faithful to me. He was devoted to his home. Is that the way bandits act? How can you kill my husband on that kind of story? Miss Andrews says that my husband was seen under the automobile. My husband knows nothing about automobiles. He never ran one, never fixed one. You are an automobile man, governor. Why don't you give my husband a test? Find out if he knows anything about automobiles and if he does not, then he cannot be the man Lola Andrews saw.

"Here is poor Miss Vanzetti. How can you kill her brother, a man who is so good that there is not a person in Plymouth where he lived who will say that he ever did an unkind act—and you know that the men who committed that murder were not kind men."

"Your Excellency," said Luigia Vanzetti, "my brother believes in you. When you shook his hand he accepted it as the

handshake of a brother, of an understanding brother. His innocence is assured. Of that there can be no doubt. God has recorded
that on the books; the only problem in this long case has been to
have those in authority read God's handwriting. . . .

"Please, please, please, governor, save my brother. He is too
young to die. He has too remarkable a brain, too big a heart, to die.
He is too innocent to die. Please, governor, also save that good
man Sacco."

Fuller told the two women he didn't expect them to understand the case the way lawyers and judges did and that he could
do nothing.

Luigia said, "But governor, I understand you can do something. They tell me you have the supreme power to help my
brother and Mr. Sacco. You are a governor. Let me take my Barto
back to Italy. The last words of my father before I sailed were,
'Bring Barto back with you.'

"In Italy, we look upon America as a land of opportunity, a
land of freedom, of happiness, of justice, and of mercy. And you
have the power of mercy. And will you not extend that mercy for
these two poor, tortured men, who have already suffered seven
long years? Imagine how my heart was cut to pieces when, after
nineteen years, I saw Barto so weak, thin, and consumed with
worry, worry about me and the millions who are sorrowing for
him. Has this great, good government of America not tortured him
enough already? On my knees, oh governor! I implore you, do not
let America become known as the land of cruelty instead of
mercy. I beg of you, I pray you for mercy, mercy, mercy!"

Luigia Vanzetti fell to her knees clutching her rosary. "I am
very sorry," said Fuller, "I regret it very much. There is nothing,
absolutely nothing I can do and remain true to the oath of my
office."

Luigia screamed. Rosina Sacco and Musmanno raised her to
her feet and led her to the antechamber where some of their
friends, including Felicani and Gardner Jackson, were waiting.

Gardner   *The most vivid aspect of that wait was the callous*
Jackson: *cynicism and wisecracking of the governor's secre-*
            tary, Herman MacDonald, who offered us cigars and

*told us to take it easy, not to take it so hard, that after
all they were just a couple of wops.*[18]

It was now 10:35 P.M. Musmanno returned to Fuller's office
and asked the governor if he would still be guided by the
recommendations of Attorney General Reading. Fuller said he
would but he had not yet heard from him. Musmanno went back
to the antechamber to wait.

When Musmanno saw Vanzetti earlier that day, Vanzetti told
him he wanted to speak to attorney William Thompson once
more. Thompson, weary and heartsick, had gone to New Hampshire to rest, but as soon as he received the message, he left for
Charlestown prison, arriving in the early evening. After he spoke
to Vanzetti, Thompson went to his office to make notes of the
conversation. A prison guard who overheard the discussion
verified Thompson's account which appeared as an article in the
Atlantic Monthly (February, 1928).[19]

There were three cells in the narrow room adjacent to the
execution chamber. Madeiros was in the cell nearest the electric
chair, Sacco was in the middle, and Vanzetti was in the third cell.
When Thompson entered the room, Vanzetti was sitting at a small
table, writing. Vanzetti stood, smiled, and shook hands. As they
spoke, Thompson sat on a chair in front of Vanzetti's cell.

Thompson told Vanzetti that though he was certain of his
innocence, he could be mistaken. "I thought," wrote Thompson,
"he ought for my sake, in this closing hour of his life when
nothing could save him, to give me his most solemn reassurance,
both with respect to himself and with respect to Sacco. Vanzetti
then told me quietly and calmly, and with a sincerity which I
could not doubt, that I need have no anxiety about this matter;
that both he and Sacco were absolutely innocent of the South
Braintree crime, and that he (Vanzetti) was equally innocent of the
Bridgewater crime."

Vanzetti told Thompson that, looking back, he could see
why some of the things he and Sacco did seemed suspicious, but
"no allowance had been made for his ignorance of American
points of view and habits of thought, or for his fear as a radical and

The Ca

almost as an outlaw, and that in reality he was convicted on evidence which would not have convicted him had he not been an anarchist, so that he was in a very real sense dying for his cause. He said it was a cause for which he was prepared to die."

Vanzetti thanked Thompson for all he had done, and asked him to do what he could to "clear my name." Then the two men discussed violence and vengeance. Thompson asked Vanzetti to issue a statement asking his friends not to retaliate. Vanzetti replied that "he desired no personal revenge for the cruelties inflicted upon him; but he said that, as he read history, every great cause for the benefit of humanity had had to fight for its existence against entrenched power and wrong, and that for this reason he could not give his friends such sweeping advice as I had urged. . . . He asked me to remember the cruelty of seven years of imprisonment, with alternating hopes and fears . . . and whether I thought that such refinement of cruelty as had been practiced upon him and upon Sacco ought to go unpunished."

Vanzetti went on to say that all great movements for progress, including Christianity, began idealistically and had then been corrupted. Thompson said he didn't think Christianity was entirely corrupt and pointedly reminded Vanzetti that Christ had forgiven his enemies. Vanzetti became angry and asked whether "he could forgive those who had persecuted and tortured him through seven years of inexpressible misery." Thompson, who had not suffered those seven years and was not scheduled to be executed within a few hours, said love was a stronger force for good than hate, and if Vanzetti forgave his enemies it would win more adherents to his cause and strengthen the belief in his innocence. Vanzetti said he would think about it. Thompson said that though he knew Vanzetti did not believe in immortality, "if there was a personal immortality he might hope to share it." Vanzetti said nothing.

Vanzetti's final remarks were about the evils of society which allowed the powerful "to oppress the simple-minded and idealistic among their fellow men." He said he feared that only violence would change the system by which the few exploited the many.

"At parting, " wrote Thompson, " he gave me a firm clasp of

the hand and a steady glance, which revealed unmistakably the depth of his feeling and the firmness of his self-control."

Thompson then turned to Sacco who was lying on his cot in the center cell. Sacco rose and said "he hoped that our differences of opinion had not affected our personal relations, thanked me for what I had done for him, showed no sign of fear, shook hands with me firmly, and bade me goodbye." Thompson noted that it was "magnanimous" of Sacco not to be more specific about their differences of opinion, since Sacco had always argued that nothing would save them "because no capitalistic society could afford to accord him justice. I had taken the contrary view," concluded Thompson, "but at this last meeting he did not suggest that the result seemed to justify his view and not mine."

When Thompson left Charlestown prison it looked like a fortress under siege. Eight hundred police guarded the building, machine guns and searchlights were mounted on the roofs and catwalks, and police boats patrolled the nearby river. The surrounding area was roped off so no one could approach without special permission.* The streets of Boston and all major public buildings, including Governor Fuller's Packard showroom, were blanketed by police, state constables, detectives, and private guards of every kind. Police arrested pickets and broke up attempts to hold street demonstrations. There would be no violence in Boston that night except as sanctioned by the commonwealth.

Did officials who so zealously guarded their right to kill Sacco and Vanzetti seriously believe a mob would rush the death house to rescue them? It was no longer possible, but before he resigned himself to death, Vanzetti considered ways of eluding it.

Roger
Baldwin:
Vanzetti was a romanticist. Once, when Mrs. Evans and I were talking with him in his cell in Charlestown state prison, he outlined a scheme to force a jail delivery by arms. He had friends among the Pennsylvania miners, he said, who were prepared to

---

*An unidentified man somehow penetrated the blockade and managed to reach the warden's office, where he gave a letter to one of the guards and disappeared. [20]

> *dynamite the prison to get him out. Mrs. Evans and I*
> *demurred, explaining its folly, and he dropped it.*[21]

Gardner   *I still have in my files a design of the interior of the*
Jackson: *prison drawn by Vanzetti's own hand that outlined*
           an escape method from the prison. . . . [Jack] Grey
           [an ex-convict] did try to connive with some of the
           guards in those last weeks to try to get Vanzetti
           escaped from the prison.[22]

Jackson says nothing further about this escape plan and Felicani says nothing about it in his oral history. Nor does Felicani mention an even more bizarre plot Jackson reveals.

Gardner   *There was an attempt by Felicani, through an ex-*
Jackson: *convict named Jack Grey, who was a safe-cracker*
           and had spent twenty years in prison, to bribe the
           electrician at Charlestown prison so that the electro-
           cution would not take place at the appointed time. It
           was successful to this extent. The bribe was passed
           and the electrician agreed. He was figuring it out two
           days before the electrocution night. In monkeying
           with the electricity set-up in the prison it went flooey
           on him, all the lights in the prison went out, and all
           hell broke loose. It was discovered so that it didn't
           materialize. It was just supposed to be a delaying
           action. . . . My reaction when Felicani told me he
           had done this was that it showed very little sympa-
           thy for the feelings of Sacco and Vanzetti. He did it
           without consulting any of us. It was the only thing
           that he did, through my long association with him,
           without consultation.[23]

Jackson later adds, "I cannot remember, in our discussion of this particular episode, but I believe I'm right in saying that Felicani did talk with Vanzetti about it before, and that Vanzetti was prepared to participate in the delay."[24]

If this is true, both Felicani and Vanzetti showed very little sympathy for the feelings of Sacco who, though opposed to the authority of the state, accepted the Socratic view that the state had the right to kill him; indeed, it had to in order to preserve itself. All he wanted was to die and be done with it. To have allowed Sacco to be strapped into the chair and not be electrocuted would have been a punishment so cruel and inhuman as to be inconceivable. "I think it is true to say," says Jackson, "that Felicani didn't worry about Sacco to the extent he did about Vanzetti."[25]

At 11 P.M., Musmanno still waited in the governor's office for final word on whether Sacco and Vanzetti would die in one hour. Unable to bear the suspense any longer, Musmanno wrote Fuller a note asking whether a decision had been reached. At 11:03, Fuller summoned him.

"Mr. Musmanno," Fuller said, "The attorney general has just sent me a letter in which he says that he does not recommend a stay of execution."

"And what do you say, Governor Fuller?"

"That is my decision."

"And on that decision will you stand for all time?"

"For all time."[26]

Warden William Hendry and a Catholic priest notified Sacco, Vanzetti, and Madeiros they would die that night. Sacco, who was writing a letter to his father, asked Hendry to be sure it was mailed. Vanzetti flung his arms wide and said, "We must bow to the inevitable." Madeiros, who was sleeping, said, "All right," rolled over, and went back to sleep.

The priest offered the men the sacraments of the church, but all three refused. He told them to send for him if they changed their minds; they never did.

Celestino Madeiros, who had to be wakened and was described as "semi-comatose," entered the execution chamber at 12:02:47, a guard on either side. He sat in the electric chair without a word and was pronounced dead at 12:09:35. He was twenty-five years old.

Nicola Sacco entered the execution chamber at 12:11:12. He was pale and weak from the thirty-day fast he had been forced to end just a few days earlier, but he walked without assistance. He

The C

sat in the chair and shouted in Italian, "Long live anarchy!" Speaking rapidly in English, as though he wasn't certain how much time he had left, he said, "Farewell, my wife and child and all my friends." Looking at the seven witnesses in the room taking their roles in the ritual murder, he said politely, "Good evening, gentlemen." His final words were English, then Italian: "Farewell, *mia madre*." During Sacco's long fast his body had lost salt and water, which conduct electricity, so he was given higher voltage than the other two men. He was pronounced dead at 12:19:02. He was thirty-six years old.

Bartolomeo Vanzetti entered the execution chamber at 12:-20:38. He shook hands with three of the guards and Warden Hendry, whom he thanked "for all you have done for me." He sat in the chair, looked at the witnesses, and slowly said, "I wish to tell you I am innocent. I never committed any crime, but sometimes some sin. I thank you for everything you have done for me. I am innocent of all crime, not only of this one, but of all. I am an innocent man." Then Vanzetti made his final, futile concession to Thompson's world. He said, "I wish to forgive some people for what they are now doing to me." He was pronounced dead at 12:26:55. He was thirty-nine years old.

Rosina Sacco and Luigia Vanzetti waited together in an apartment with some sympathizers. When the call came telling them the men were dead, the screams and sobs of the two women could be heard throughout the neighborhood.* In America and around the world, others wept, raged, and cursed. No one of age would ever forget the night of August 22, 1927; it was one of those events by which people mark their lives.

One of the most vivid examples of the intensity and universality of feeling took place in New York City. At Union Square, a crowd of fifteen thousand had gathered. A reporter for the *New York World* noted that when word came that Sacco and Vanzetti were dead, men and women wept, screamed, fainted, and some "aimlessly" tore at their clothes.[27] The tearing of the clothing was

---

*Years later, when a member of the family was ill, Dante's wife assured Rosina Sacco, "I've done everything I can. I've even prayed." Rosina Sacco replied, "Oh, don't pray. I tried it once and it didn't work."

not aimless; it is the most extreme expression of grief known to Orthodox Jews who could vent their anguish only by the traditional act of *keriah*, rending their garments. An Orthodox Jew is obliged to do this upon the death of his closest relatives: parents, siblings, children, or spouse. It is not done for distant relatives or friends or non-Jews. But all immigrants were brothers that night; a little of each of them died with Sacco and Vanzetti.

Abroad, a wave of fury and hatred broke over all things American; there were riots, strikes, and violent demonstrations in France, Switzerland, England, Germany, Scandinavia, Portugal, Mexico, Argentina, Australia, and South Africa. Mobs attacked American embassies, shops and buildings, overturned American cars, defaced American monuments, burned American films and flags. Probably no single act committed by American authorities ever triggered such worldwide revulsion as the execution of Sacco and Vanzetti.

For Rosina Sacco and Luigia Vanzetti there was nothing left except to bury their dead in peace, but they were not even granted that; now their friends came forward to exploit the two men in death as both friends and enemies had exploited them in life.

Felicani claimed the two bodies, which were released on Tuesday, after autopsies. The funeral was planned for Sunday, prolonging the pain for Rosina Sacco and Luigia Vanzetti, but assuring a great turnout. A decision was made, presumably by the Defense Committee, to cremate the men, though there is no indication that either Sacco or Vanzetti wanted to be cremated. In several references to his death in his American correspondence, Vanzetti said he expected nothing from the state but a cheap coffin and a hole in the ground. A few hours before he died, Sacco told Warden Hendry he wanted his body sent home to Italy for burial;[28] presumably he gave his wife the same instructions. Cremating the men was not only contrary to their wishes but an additional blow for the devout Luigia, since it is forbidden by the church.

Vincenzina *I don't know whether the committee made the deci-*
Vanzetti: *sion to postpone the funeral and whether Rosa and*

The Ca

Luigina were consulted. I do not know who decided to cremate the bodies. I know that Luigina was against it.

Felicani had originally planned to have the bodies on view at the headquarters of the Defense Committee, but when the owner of the building had the janitor nail a two-by-four upright in the doorway so the coffins could not be carried in, the committee decided to display the bodies at Langone's funeral parlor on Hanover Street, the last stop of most Italians before they departed Boston permanently.

Sacco and Vanzetti were embalmed and placed on view at Langone's from Thursday evening through Sunday morning, surrounded by wreaths which carried such messages as "Revenge" and "Massachusetts the Murderer." When Langone's doors opened to the public, the press came first to photograph the bodies. Posing at the head of the coffins was Mary Donovan, holding a large placard with the words "'Did you see what I did to those anarchistic bastards?' Judge Webster Thayer." When Langone asked her to leave, she went outside and handed her placard to a reporter to copy. A police sergeant seized it, and Mary Donovan was arrested for inciting to riot and distributing anarchistic literature.

Eight thousand persons passed by the coffins that first night; an estimated one hundred thousand came in all. Some were anarchists, some were mourners, some were merely curious; Madeiros's body, on view in Providence, drew ten thousand spectators in one day. Lines began to form outside Langone's at 6 A.M.; it took as long as four hours to get from the end of the line to the small, flower-filled room with the two open coffins. Felicani said the viewers came from "nowhere and everywhere."[29]

Both the Defense Committee and Boston prepared for Sunday's funeral. Felicani ordered thousands of red armbands with the words "REMEMBER! JUSTICE CRUCIFIED AUGUST 22, 1927" lettered in black. Meanwhile, the city had men digging up streets so the funeral procession could not pass the statehouse.

In many respects, the funeral as planned was typically Italian, with a band, huge floral displays, and the coffins to be borne aloft by pallbearers. But the police would not allow the band and insisted the coffins stay in the hearses. All that remained were the flowers, which Sacco and Vanzetti loved, and the mourners, who loved them.

The two hearses bearing the coffins of Sacco and Vanzetti left Langone's about 2:30 P.M. on Sunday, August 28. They were preceded, followed, and surrounded by floral displays, some carried, some banked in flower-cars. After the flower-cars came two limousines. In one, behind drawn curtains, rode Rosina Sacco, her son Dante, Luigia Vanzetti, and Aldino Felicani. The other limousine was for members of the Defense Committee who began the procession on foot but intended to ride later on.

Behind the limousines were thousands of mourners, eight or ten abreast, arms linked. Though it was raining, they were determined to take part in what was called the March of Sorrow, the eight-mile walk to the crematory at Forest Hills cemetery. Mounted police led the procession and surrounded the hearses and the limousines. Sympathizers and the curious lined the streets; estimates of the number of persons who watched the funeral procession ranged from two hundred thousand to millions.

From the start the funeral continued the seven-year contest of wills between the supporters of Sacco and Vanzetti and the representatives of the commonwealth. At Scollay Square, tension rose when the marchers passed a newsstand displaying copies of the *Nation*, which had a cover sympathetic to Sacco and Vanzetti. Immediately men bought and distributed the magazine.[30] The marchers had been ordered to begin the procession with their armbands in their pockets; now they put them on and the streets blazed with the message in black and red: JUSTICE CRUCIFIED.

Now that this was becoming less of a funeral and more of a demonstration, the police became openly hostile. At one point trucks were parked curb-to-curb to block the marchers. As the crowd inched around the obstacles, one man was accidentally pushed through a plate-glass window. When the lines formed again, mounted police rode directly at the marchers, clubs flailing. Jeannette Marks wrote that the police tried to break up the funeral procession "by every strategy in their power. . . . They

The Ca

ordered opposite tides of traffic into the marchers, they even diverted traffic into the cortege, they threw trucks across the way, they rode straight into bystanding groups of sympathizers, and they clubbed."[31]

Marchers who survived the rain, which was falling heavily, and the police, finally reached the Forest Hills area, close to the cemetery. Forest Hills was an Irish ghetto, and the Irish, remembering the carbarn boys as well as their own abuse at the hand of the Yankees, jeered the marchers with racial epithets, while the police again attacked. Marks wrote, "Arm linked in arm [the marchers] were swinging on bravely and silently when suddenly at Forest Hills Elevated Station came the sharp command, 'Get over there!'

"And police charged them, together with an automobile from the station house in which a patrolman ran down the crowd. Not a half minute was given the procession to obey before clubs began to swing and marchers to sprawl. There were curses, blows and kicks, and the guardians of law and order drew their guns."[32]

By the time the marchers escaped, the coffins were already in the crematory chapel and the marchers were left standing outside the locked gates of the cemetery. The small chapel held only about one hundred persons; thousands of mourners who had come by other routes surrounded the crematory. Rosina Sacco, Dante, and Luigia Vanzetti remained in their car, an eloquent expression of how they felt about the cremation and the circus their friends and foes had made of this last homage to the men they loved.

Gardner Jackson had written a eulogy for Aldino Felicani to read, but Felicani had never sought the spotlight and he refused it now. The eulogy was read by Mary Donovan. By any standards it was dreadful; a fair example was the line, "Horrible enough would it be if the killing of you had been ordered by the political and material powers alone." Anything written or said by Sacco or Vanzetti would have been better, but the only words of the two men that were quoted were those Vanzetti probably did not say: "If it had not been for these thing . . . "

From the time Sacco and Vanzetti were arrested, every moment of what remained of their lives was marked by controversy; not even their ashes would know peace. Instead of giving

Rosina Sacco an urn containing only her husband's ashes, and Luigia Vanzetti an urn containing only her brother's ashes, the committee mixed the remains of the two men together so they would be inseparable in death, though they had not been inseparable in life. One urn of mixed ashes was given to Mrs. Sacco, a second to Miss Vanzetti, and a third was kept by the committee for a memorial.

Before she returned to Italy, Luigia Vanzetti gave a portion of her ashes to Alfonsina Brini, to express her gratitude to the Brinis for taking the place of Vanzetti's own family. Alfonsina Brini kept the urn for a number of years, then decided to bring it to Italy to give to Vincenzina Vanzetti, by then Vanzetti's only surviving sister. Before she could do so, the Brini house was robbed. Though the urn of ashes was not touched, Mrs. Brini was more concerned about it than any of her own possessions. She wrote Aldino Felicani who came and took the ashes from her.[33] The urn now appears to be missing, and no one seems to know what happened to the urn the committee kept for a memorial. Actually, considering the proprietary attitude of some members of the committee, the ashes may have been divided into more than three parts, and there may be more urns about than is generally known.

Only three urns of ashes are definitely accounted for. One is in the possession of Rosina Sacco; the other two are in Italy. Luigia Vanzetti, the dutiful daughter and loving sister, obeyed her father's orders to bring Barto home with her.

Vincenzina Vanzetti: *My sister brought the ashes of Sacco and Vanzetti in one urn. The ashes came to the Villafalletto railway station in a lead-lined railway car, a funerary car. At Villafalletto the ashes were divided by an employee of the town. While the bells were ringing, one urn was carried past our house, through the village, where every shop was closed in mourning. Bartolomeo's ashes were buried in the village cemetery. All the people were there; it was like a funeral. The other urn remained at the railway station with the police guarding it and then went on to Sacco's town, Torremaggiore.*

The Ca

In October, 1927, the United States Supreme Court dropped the case of Sacco and Vanzetti from its docket. The courts of Massachusetts and the courts of the United States were through with Sacco and Vanzetti; they were physically and legally dead. The court of public opinion would judge them differently and grant them eternal life.

Don't cry, Dante, because many
tears have been wasted, as your
mother's have been wasted for
seven years, and never did any
good. So, Son, instead of crying,
be strong, so as to be able to
comfort your mother.
> —Sacco's last letter to his son

None of my enemies will be
mourned as I am.
> —Vanzetti's last letter to his
> family

Afterword

That's why they wept, my parents and all the others. They wept not only for Sacco and Vanzetti but for themselves and for the American dream. To the extent that it existed, the American dream had always been somewhat selective, but the execution of Sacco and Vanzetti confirmed that liberty and justice could be as fraudulent in America as they were everywhere else. America had come of age.

In one sense, the execution was superfluous except to gratify an emotional need, for the nativist racists had won their tenacious battle to keep America white, Anglo-Saxon, and Protestant, not with a literacy test but with an outright quota system. In 1921, Congress passed a law limiting the number of immigrants admitted annually from each nation to 3 percent of the number of persons of that nationality living in the United States in 1910. A more blatantly racist law followed in 1924. It required divining how many persons of which nationalities populated the country in 1790, how many descendants they had by 1920, how many immigrants of which nationalities came during the nineteenth century and, without benefit of calculators or computers, setting up new quotas. When the arithmetic was done and the entrails were read, Great Britain, Ireland, and Germany received more than two-thirds of the 150,000 yearly allotment, while the annual quota for Greece was 307 persons. The national origins quota system was not abolished until 1965.

Even after quotas were established, the Immigration Restriction League did not disband; eternal vigilance is the price of bigotry. I did not choose to follow its fortunes, but did, by chance, come upon a confidential memorandum prepared by the league while Hitler was stoking his ovens. The memo warned members of the league to prepare for battle, lest misplaced sympathy for the Jews cause Congress to offer them refuge.

Since Massachusetts made certain that Sacco and Vanzetti died amid so many doubts, several questions still cling to the case even after the story has been told.

First, the three asked by Lowell and Fuller. *Was the jury trial fair?* Of course not; neither Vanzetti's trial at Plymouth nor the joint trial at Dedham was fair. Tampered evidence, abused witnesses, perjured testimony, and a biased judge and jury do not constitute justice. Two things that can be said incontrovertibly are that Sacco and Vanzetti did not receive a fair trial and were not proved guilty beyond a reasonable doubt.

Were the accused entitled to a new trial? Indisputably. Juries do make errors even in nonpolitical cases. With Sacco and Vanzetti, given the time and place, the slow poisons of the Puritans and the rapid doses administered by Palmer, it is dimly possible to conceive how a Yankee jury, influenced by a biased judge, repelled and unpersuaded by an offensive and inadequate defense, and bombasted by a brilliant prosecutor, could find enough justification in what appeared to be evidence to find two Italian anarchists guilty. What defies reason is that in the course of six years and eight appeals, Sacco and Vanzetti were unable to win a retrial on any grounds: Proctor's misleading testimony, Ripley's "Damn them!," the affidavits from the agents of the Justice Department, Thayer's prejudice, Madeiros's confession. Clearly, the commonwealth was determined not to give the two men a second chance. Attorney William Thompson said, "I do not believe they would indict 'Joe' [Joseph Morelli] in this case if two angels from heaven came down with an affidavit in each hand saying they saw him commit the murder."[1] If such angels had appeared, Thayer undoubtedly would have found their testimony merely cumulative, the Supreme Judicial Court of Massachusetts would have ruled it was within Thayer's discretion to do so, and Lowell would have wanted to know why the angels were in South Braintree that day if they had not been there for a guilty purpose.

Are they guilty or not guilty? This is the question that is hardest to put to rest. It is too well known that just as innocent persons are sometimes convicted, guilty persons are sometimes acquitted. Sacco and Vanzetti did not have a fair trial, were not proved guilty beyond a reasonable doubt, and should have been granted another trial; but is it possible that they were guilty anyway? The incontestable proof of their innocence is the refusal of the commonwealth to try them again in the face of national and international outrage. If Sacco and Vanzetti were not innocent, there would have been no such reluctance; a second guilty verdict would have silenced the world, but that was a gamble Massachusetts dared not take.

In 1961, new ballistics tests were sponsored by a writer named Francis Russell. Russell believes that Sacco was guilty and Vanzetti innocent except as an accessory after the fact because he carried Berardelli's revolver,[2] that wondrous weapon that changed back and forth from a .32 to a .38 and alternately needed a new spring or a new hammer. The experts were Jac Weller and Frank Jury who, with Julian Hatcher, had written a book in 1957 called *Firearms Investigation Identification and Evidence.* In it they stated, "there can be no doubt that Sacco's pistol fired one cartridge case and one of the fatal bullets."[3] In a dwarfed summary of the case they omitted most of the evidence but managed to find room to describe Sacco and Vanzetti as "admittedly not very patriotic" and to assert that "strong efforts were made by various organizations, many of which were Communistic, to arouse sentiment for these two individuals."[4] The authors also wrote that both Proctor and Van Amburgh "indicated in their original testimony that the [Sacco] pistol, the bullet, and the

After

cartridge case all matched;"[5] there was not a word about Proctor's affidavit repudiating his testimony.

After the 1961 tests, which involved examination of the evidence with comparison microscopes, as well as test firings,[6] Weller and Jury confirmed the conclusions they had reached four years earlier. Because the gun barrel was rusty, they cleaned it by firing two preliminary shots.[7] Rust is iron oxide; the iron for the iron oxide came from within the gun barrel. In cleaning out the rust, particularly with something as forceful as a bullet rather than with oil, did the experts alter any of the minute markings and measurements that are so critical in ballistics testing?

Also, if the gun had deteriorated, what about the bullet? In October, 1975, seven ballistics experts who examined evidence concerning Robert F. Kennedy's assassination reported they could not determine whether three of the bullets tested had been fired from Sirhan Sirhan's gun because the deterioration of the bullets made identification impossible.[8] This was after only seven years; what might happen to a bullet after forty years? *

The key question still is whether Weller and Jury were testing Sacco's gun barrel and bullet III. Since there is no proof and much doubt that the bullet is authentic, there is no point to testing it. If the bullet was substituted by the prosecution and the barrel is Sacco's, they will match. What is needed are not more ballistics tests but unimpeachable evidence that what is being tested is the fatal bullet. Anyone who is certain that it is should feel obliged to locate the Colt .32s owned by Joe Morelli and see if the bullet matches any of them. Perhaps he can also find the fingerprints taken from the abandoned Buick and check whether they belong to Sacco and Vanzetti or the Morelli mob.

To fire the fatal bullet, Sacco would have had to be in South Braintree on April 15, so Russell eliminates all of Sacco's alibi witnesses with one blow. He writes of Sacco's alibi, "Thirty years after the trial, that evidence was to turn paper thin with the

---

*In an informal, off-the-record talk with a ballistics expert at the New York City Police Department, I was told that bullets do deteriorate and that even today ballistics experts disagree and make mistakes. This was not said in reference to the Sacco-Vanzetti case, which he would not discuss since he did not have the evidence, but as a general background briefing.

admission of a former Boston anarchist, Anthony Ramuglia, that he had been coached to present a false alibi for Sacco." Russell says Ramuglia had agreed to testify that he had seen Sacco in Boni's restaurant, then remembered he had been in jail on April 15. "On learning this," Russell writes, "the anarchists picked another comrade whose perjury would be less liable to discovery."[9] Russell does not name the witness who perjured himself.

Even if Ramuglia's story were true, it does not mean that all the witnesses lied or that Sacco was not in Boston or at Boni's; it could mean that Sacco's friends were too zealous in strengthening his story because they knew the prosecution was playing a deadly game and they had to play it too. But is Ramuglia's story true? Russell does not make it clear that the Ramuglia story is hearsay. After the first edition of Russell's book was published, he received a letter from a writer in San Francisco named Paul Jacobs who reported that Ramuglia had told him this story ten years earlier.[10] Unfortunately, Ramuglia was dead, so there was, is, and never will be any way of verifying it. Robert D'Attilio, who has spent a considerable amount of time tracing the witnesses and other figures related to the case, has found that a man named Anthony Ramuglia did live in Boston during the appropriate period, but he has not been able to uncover any evidence that Ramuglia was involved with the anarchist movement.*[11]

A letter reporting an unverifiable story told by a dead man, whose existence as an anarchist has not been confirmed and who believed Sacco was innocent anyway, cannot be considered weighty enough to discredit the sworn testimony of all of Sacco's witnesses. Yet in words reminiscent of Thayer's charge to the jury at Plymouth ("Because the [defendant's] witnesses are Italian no inference should be drawn against them"), Russel concludes, "I could only feel that if the other Italians had been telling the truth

---

*Ramuglia told Jacobs he was an anarchist during the 1920s, but Jacobs has no corroborating evidence. According to Jacobs, though Ramuglia told him he was asked to lie for Sacco, Ramuglia did *not* believe Sacco was guilty. Ramuglia repeated the standard observation that Sacco was more capable of committing a crime than Vanzetti—a credo no one has yet justified—but he believed he was asked to provide an alibi not because Sacco was at South Braintree but because he had spent part of his day in Boston on a personal or political mission he did not want revealed in court. *Telephone interview with Paul Jacobs, April 18, 1977.*

After

there would have been no need to coach Ramuglia in perjury."[12] As for John D. Williams, the advertising agent, Russell says he discovered Williams was a radical,[13] though this was never a secret; it was known at the time of the trial.* In impeaching Sacco's witnesses, Russell does not mention Hayes, the Yankee Sacco saw on the train.

Russell also believes Sacco was guilty because the Italian radical, Carlo Tresca, is supposed to have said so to Max Eastman and others.[14] Roger Baldwin, who knew Tresca well, says Tresca never said a word to him about Sacco being guilty.[15] At the conference on Italian-American radicalism held in Boston in November, 1972, Russell was one of the speakers in a panel discussion, "The Sacco-Vanzetti Case Reconsidered." Carlo Tresca's daughter, Beatrice, who was in the audience, told Russell that during the period of the case she was a college student and that when she saw her father, which was at least once a week, she always asked him, "Quick, what's the latest?" Miss Tresca added emphatically, "I never heard him say that he had a doubt of either one."

Another panelist, Dr. Nunzio Pernicone, who is writing a biography of Tresca, said that in trying to track down just what Tresca had said to whom about the case, he had spoken to Luigi Quintiliano who, said Pernicone, knew as much or more about Sacco and Vanzetti than Tresca; it was Quintiliano who told Vanzetti, during his trip to New York, to get rid of the literature. Quintiliano told Pernicone that he knew how Tresca felt about Max Eastman "and his dubious political opinions" and that if Tresca thought Sacco was guilty "he would have died ten times before revealing it to Max Eastman." Pernicone also said Tresca had told Baldwin, Norman Thomas, and others that Sacco was as innocent as Vanzetti.

Exactly what Tresca said or believed will never be known

---

*Russell writes that in 1917 Williams "had been associated with Trotsky and Bukharin in New York." According to Theodore Draper, *The Roots of American Communism* (New York: Viking, 1957), p. 80, on January 14, 1917, about 20 left-wing socialists met at the home of Ludwig Lore in Brooklyn. Trotsky and Bukharin were present—as was Williams, who represented the Socialist Propaganda League of Boston. The most important decision made at the meeting was to publish a bimonthly periodical.

because when Russell cited him as proof of Sacco's guilt, Tresca, like Ramuglia, was dead. In order to have Tresca's hearsay opinion—if it was Tresca's opinion—convict Sacco, Russell asserts that "of all the people in the United States, outside of the actual participants in the South Braintree murders, Tresca was the one who should have known the truth. For the anarchists he was their admired and much loved leader. . . . He knew their innermost secrets."[16] Robert D'Attilio, who was moderator for the panel discussion, pointed out that, on the contrary, Tresca was not even considered an anarchist by the group to which Sacco and Vanzetti belonged; that there was a feud at least ten years old between their leader, Galleani, and Tresca; and that one of the mysteries of the case was "how Tresca managed to send Fred Moore to Boston." D'Attilio said that far from being an insider, Tresca was very much on the outside in this situation, and he wondered "just what Tresca did know" about the Sacco-Vanzetti case. Tresca knew Vanzetti little; Sacco less. His friend at court was Fred Moore.

No matter which way one turns, which lead one follows, the prime source of the split-guilt theory seems to be Fred Moore. In evaluating Moore's verdict, the correlation between his failures and his views of Sacco and Vanzetti should be charted. When the case began, Moore believed so firmly in the innocence of both men he was able to persuade the McAnarney brothers, and he had to believe Sacco was innocent or he would not have requested ballistics tests. As the bitterness between Moore and Sacco mounted, Moore began to hint of Sacco's guilt, while Vanzetti remained unblemished. After Moore was fired, he cast a shadow over Vanzetti as well by telling Upton Sinclair, "Sacco was probably, Vanzetti possibly guilty."

Moore admitted to Sinclair that neither Sacco nor Vanzetti nor any of their friends had said anything privately to justify this opinion.[17] Sinclair checked Moore's statement with the lawyer's former wife who said she was "astounded." She explained, "I worked on the case with him all through the years, and I knew about it as intimately as he did. He never gave me a hint of such an idea, and neither did anyone else. I feel Fred is embittered because he was dropped from the case, and it has poisoned his mind."[18]

Afterw

Roger Baldwin was one of the persons to whom Moore expressed doubts about Sacco, while they were riding in a car with Elizabeth Glendower Evans after a visit to Vanzetti in Charlestown prison.

Roger Baldwin: *I didn't credit Moore's remarks to me with much weight because of Moore's disagreement with the Defense Committee and because of his reported strange conduct. . . . I heard from other people that there were some doubts about Sacco, but then whenever I asked about it, it always came back to Moore.*

No other attorney close to the case agreed with Moore. The McAnarney brothers joined the defense only after they were convinced by Moore, as well as Sacco and Vanzetti, that the two men were innocent; when the McAnarneys testified before the Lowell Committee in 1927, that conviction still held. William Thompson and Herbert Ehrmann entered the case as doubters and became converts. Arthur Hill seemed ambivalent but, except for assisting on one motion, he joined the battle only in the last few weeks. Ehrmann has said Hill preferred to assert he was fighting for the integrity of justice in Massachusetts rather than take the socially unacceptable position of fighting for Sacco and Vanzetti.

Upton Sinclair gave the split-guilt theory a boost by reporting that he did not get the cooperation he expected from Rosina Sacco when he went to her seeking information for his novel about the case, *Boston*. "I felt certain that there was some dark secret there," Sinclair wrote. "Nobody would be frank with me, and everybody was suspicious even though I had been introduced and vouched for by Mrs. Evans, a great lady of Boston who had led and financed the fight for freedom of these two Italians."[19] Mrs. Evans was extremely sympathetic and helpful, but to say she led and financed the fight was an exaggeration, though she did offer Vanzetti a job as her gardener. The very condescension of the sentence—Mrs. Evans is a "great lady" while Sacco and Vanzetti are "these two Italians"—explains why Sinclair received such a cold reception. Rosina Sacco, who was the great lady in the case, was through crawling.

Spencer Sacco: *Sinclair was writing a book called* Boston *and he did approach my grandmother's household. Now here's*

> *a five-foot-one-or-two Italian immigrant who speaks
> very, very little and very, very poor English at the
> time, and here arrives on the scene an American
> white Anglo-Saxon Protestant and he wants infor-
> mation. Naturally she's going to turn him away. He
> hadn't encountered any big, dark secret; he encoun-
> tered a small, frustrated Italian. I believe she was
> sick of being used.*

Russell believes the dark secret sensed by Sinclair was that Sacco was guilty and this explained the silence of the Sacco family, particularly of Sacco's son, Dante. Russell asserts that "never once have they [the Saccos] even appeared on a public platform"[20] at any event to honor or vindicate Sacco and Vanzetti. Though they may not have been on the platform, Dante Sacco did appear at such meetings and his wife was present when a futile attempt was made in the Massachusetts legislature in 1959 to grant the two men a posthumous pardon.

Roger Baldwin remembers seeing Dante Sacco at memorial meetings for his father and Vanzetti.

Roger   *He spoke to me, very shyly. . . . We never sat down*
Baldwin: *to discuss the case. What would he say, anyhow? He*
           had to assume that his father was innocent. . . . He
           wanted to be himself [but] I don't think he did
           anything disloyal. He could have changed his name
           but he didn't. Dante certainly could have saved
           himself a lot of trouble if he had changed his name.

Dante Sacco was fourteen years old when his father died; all he could have known about the case was what his mother told him, which was that his father was innocent. The Sacco family has been silent not because of some hideous, dark secret but because once Sacco was dead, there was nothing more to say. For some time after the execution, Rosina and Dante continued to be the widow and son of Nicola Sacco, doing what others demanded of them. Then it finally became apparent they were being used; the Vanzetti family did not feel this way because, except for Luigia's brief visit, they were in Italy the entire time, too distant to be exploited. Rosina Sacco had been used by a host of people who promised her everything then gave her an urn of ashes, mixed. With Sacco's death, more users appeared. At some point Rosina and Dante decided they had had enough. They did not change their name or move to another part of the country, but they decided to be something other than a martyr's relics.

Rosina Sacco ceased writing to Luigia Vanzetti in Italy and severed her connections with the good ladies of Boston. She sought privacy; "the publicity of the case just killed her, always," said Mrs. Ehrmann. In 1943, sixteen years after Sacco's execution, Rosina Sacco married another Italian anarchist.

The children, Dante and Ines, grew up, married, had families of their own. They tried always to shield their mother from press and publicity because, said Spencer Sacco, "the woman had been hurt, deeply, and you don't go around opening new wounds." But Spencer Sacco said the case was not a dark secret in his own home, though Dante Sacco and his family were not obsessed by it because they had other, healthier things to live for.

On August 22, 1971, the Sunday magazine section of the *Boston Herald* published a condensed version of the new foreword Russell had prepared for the McGraw-Hill edition of his book in which he argues his view that Sacco was guilty and writes that "the Saccos after half a century are still bound to their dark secret." At the time, Dante Sacco was literally on his deathbed; he died two days later.

After Dante Sacco was dead, Russell wrote an article for a magazine called *Metro Boston* (February, 1972), in which he said Dante had made "no attempt to vindicate his father's name" because "Dante Sacco knew that his father was guilty." What proof was there of Sacco's guilt? For one, Dante's silence, "the silence of the Sacco family, unbroken for half a century." The technical term for this kind of logic is *petitio principii*. Russell is assuming to be true what has to be proved; his assumption is his conclusion and his conclusion is his assumption. Informally, logicians call this "begging the question" or "going around in circles."

Nine months later, during the panel discussion of the case at the conference on Italian-American radicalism, Russell repeated his belief that Sacco was guilty. Several speakers on the panel and in the audience challenged him. Then a young man seated near the rear of the room stood. His first words were not quite audible because the audience was chattering, and only after he said "You have confused and have abused my family, and upset my family" did Russell realize who was speaking. Russell said, "You're Dante's son, are you?" and those were the last words Russell spoke that afternoon.

The young man was Spencer Sacco, one of Dante's three sons. His voice breaking with tension and emotion, bells pealing at a nearby church underscoring his words, Spencer Sacco spoke out for his father and his grandfather. He tried to explain how his family felt about many things, including Russell's attacks. He listed specific errors of fact in the *Metro* article and asked Russell, "Where do you get your information?" He said his father did not run up to people and say, Hey, I'm Dante Sacco, son of the famous anarchist, but that when asked, neither his father nor any other member of the family denied the relationship. He made it clear his father had not only wanted to protect Rosina Sacco, but to find an identity other than as the son of a celebrated victim, and that he had succeeded. "At my father's funeral," said Spencer Sacco, "there was a full church of 460 *friends*, not 460 people that wanted to write books, not 460 people that wanted to know him because he was the son of Nicola Sacco."

When Spencer Sacco was through, there were tears and applause, but no reply from Russell. None of the two hundred or more people in the room could forget Spencer's appearance except, apparently, Francis Russell. Nine months later, the *National Review* (August 17, 1973) published an article by Russell in which he again said Dante Sacco had been silent because his father was guilty and listed as one of the reasons he believed Sacco was guilty "the silence of the Sacco family, unbroken for a half-century." But as Russell knew, the silence had been broken. Using Russell's logic, since the Sacco family was no longer silent, Sacco was no longer guilty.

The entire concept of family accountability is insupportable; viewing it from the opposite end, Richard Nixon was innocent because his daughter, Julie Nixon Eisenhower, defended him so vigorously. Russell makes a point of saying he was warmly received by the Brini family because "the friends of Vanzetti have nothing to hide."[21] I too was warmly received by the Brinis—that is their manner—but that is not why I believe Vanzetti was innocent. I would believe it even if the Brinis had slammed the door in my face, for the more relevant reason that there is no proof of his guilt. On a matter as serious as murder, no man should be convicted by the behavior of his family or friends, or by spectral hearsay attributed to Carlo Tresca, or by the unconfirmed claims of an unconfirmed anarchist.

The wisdom of the decision made by the Sacco family to rebuild their lives is confirmed by the fate of Luigia Vanzetti, which no one has troubled to check before. By submerging the tragedy, the Saccos were able to function normally. Luigia Vanzetti brought the tragedy home with her, went mad, and died.

Vincenzina Vanzetti: *My sister became prematurely old. She suffered and cried so much that something went out in her brain. She kept getting more and more depressed. She could not move her legs, her back. She had a total nervous breakdown, but she was conscious to the end.*

If Sacco were guilty, Vanzetti presumably would have known, particularly if he carried Berardelli's gun. The belief that Vanzetti nobly gave his life for Sacco weakly hinges on an unconfirmed tale told, of course, by Fred Moore. Moore said he advised Vanzetti at Dedham that because there was so little evidence against him, he could push harder for his acquittal, but since the jury was bound to want one victim, they would "soak" Sacco. Moore asked what he should do and Vanzetti replied, "Save Nick. He has the woman and child."[22] Vanzetti may have said it, but did he mean Moore should save Sacco at his expense or that Sacco should also be saved because he was also innocent?

Perhaps Vanzetti the ikon, Thompson's concept of Christ, would have died rather than betray a guilty comrade, but not the real Vanzetti who wrote those letters to Villafalletto; who endangered his family when he knew they were under Fascist surveillance by writing them anti-Fascist harangues; who sent for a sister to plead for him, costing Luigia her sanity and her life; who wrote, "I wish to win, by whatever means are necessary. For this reason I must do many strange, clever things, play on almost everyone and everything." No one as desperate to escape death as Vanzetti would have died for a guilty man. He did not have to compromise his honor by betraying Sacco publicly; the right word to the right person would have done it.

Vanzetti was not the man to die for Sacco, nor was Sacco the man to let him. Sacco died for himself and his wife; he had no need to kill Vanzetti too. In a letter to Vanzetti in December, 1924, when they were in separate prisons, Sacco wrote, "You are quite right when you say—that after all we are still on our feet—of course, because we are always keep in our soul the hope and faithful in our innocent . . . "[23] If Sacco were guilty he would not speak of his innocence to Vanzetti and risk provoking him. Besides, Sacco wanted to die, not Vanzetti. All Sacco had to do was confess; if he didn't it was because he had nothing to confess. Sacco had a better perception of reality than Vanzetti; the Myerson report confirms Sacco was neither a fanatic nor a fool.

In addition to the three questions asked by Lowell and Fuller, at least one other should be considered: *Who killed Sacco and Vanzetti?* There are such obvious villains as Thayer, Katzmann, Chief Stewart, and the justices of the supreme judicial court, but the list of those who contributed to the crime by what they did or did not do is painfully long. It includes various parties to the prosecution, those who tampered with the evidence, witnesses who lied, and witnesses who belatedly discovered their integrity. Fred Moore should not be overlooked, nor should the Communists. A special place should be found for Governor Fuller, who had doubts about the guilt of Sacco and Vanzetti but let them die presumably because he wanted to be president.

Assistant District Attorney Dudley Ranney felt the case against Sacco and Vanzetti was "not proven," but fought for their execution because that was his job; he did not resign. Judge George W. Anderson told a Bureau of Investigation agent he should have resigned rather than obey orders during the Palmer raids, but when the Sacco-Vanzetti case came before him during

Afterw

the final appeals, Judge Anderson could find "no right to interfere" and did not resign. Justice Louis Brandeis, who believed in
their innocence, would not grant Sacco and Vanzetti a stay of
execution so the Supreme Court could hear their case.

In the end, the fate of Sacco and Vanzetti was left to two
Brahmins. Either Lowell or Holmes might have saved them, but
Lowell chose to prove them guilty beyond the prosecution's
doubt, and Holmes chose to dismiss those who begged for justice
as ignorant of the law. Not only did the Puritan legacy kill Sacco
and Vanzetti, but their ultimate executioners were its two most
prominent legatees.

In writing this book, the most dismaying realization has been
how little things have changed. The government's preoccupation
with silencing critics and dissenters is a matter of record, a record
which includes the period of the Vietnam War and Watergate. A
fraction of the abuses of the FBI have finally been exposed, but
that can of worms will never be fully opened. Good men still
wallow in muck and blood to promote or protect their careers.
Prosecutors, for unfathomable reasons, continue to send people to
prison or death knowing they are innocent.

Anti-Catholicism, America's oldest prejudice, is now the
most acceptable one. The October 18, 1976, issue of the *Village
Voice*, a New York weekly that can be described as liberal or
left-liberal, published a cartoon strip in which a maniacal cardinal
tells a young priest that once the church gets an anti-abortion
amendment passed, it can get a constitutional amendment out-
lawing birth control devices, prohibit the teaching of Darwin's
theory, and then "we'll once again be able to decree that the Earth
is the center of the Universe." A Jewish intellectual I know well,
Ph.D., chairman of a department at a major university, told me
that Catholics will eventually be a majority in America "and then
we can have an Inquisition."

The greatest scorn is still reserved for Italians. In an article
called "Respectable Bigotry" (*The American Scholar*, Autumn,
1969), Michael Lerner writes that a "brilliant" Yale professor,
irked that an Italian dared challenge John Lindsay for mayor of
New York, said, "If Italians aren't actually an inferior race, they do

the best imitation of one I've seen." Lerner added, "Everyone at the dinner table laughed."

My son was astonished to discover that in more than two hundred years, America has had only one president who was not white, Anglo-Saxon, and Protestant, and his friends refuse to believe it; obviously the significance of John F. Kennedy's victory and Al Smith's defeat are not part of the school curriculum. The WASP, or whoever can impersonate one, remains the American; the rest still float in ethnic limbo. The Democratic party, once considered the haven of immigrants and ethnics, seems unable to understand anything but the value of their votes. During the 1968 presidential primaries, Eugene McCarthy said, "The polls seem to prove that [Robert F. Kennedy] is running ahead of me among the less intelligent and less well-educated voters of the country. On that basis, I don't think we're going to have to apologize or explain away the results in the state of Oregon."[24] McCarthy was inviting the voters to prove they were superior to the blacks and ethnics who were voting for Robert Kennedy by voting for *him*. They rose to the challenge; Oregon was the only state where McCarthy defeated Kennedy.

In 1972, Democratic candidate George McGovern, at a meeting with ethnic leaders in Cleveland, was quoted as saying, "I don't see why all these people just can't become Americans like everybody else."[25]

In 1976, Jimmy Carter's comment about ethnic purity—a curious phrase redolent of racist rhetoric and not at all what ethnics want—caused a commotion, but his remarkable clarification went unremarked. Carter said, "If you have a lower-status neighborhood that is black primarily or Latin American primarily or Polish primarily or of Germanic descent primarily, I see nothing wrong with that."[26] The press never asked Carter why black, Hispanic, Polish, and German neighborhoods are lower status.

Since it is their book, the last words should be spoken by and about Sacco and Vanzetti. Vanzetti had an insatiable need to be loved and respected, so he defined himself by what others thought

Afterw

of him and became what they wanted him to be. This trait, combined with genuine charm, wit, and intelligence, enabled him to endear himself to everyone from the Brini children to Felicani to Fuller. Sacco, secure in the love of his family, his work, and his garden, did not bend to suit others; he was never anyone but himself. For this reason, Vanzetti has always had the better press; he is profound, philosophical, lovable, while Sacco has acquired the reputation of being hardheaded, volatile, truculent.

Sara Ehrmann: *I've always wondered why that was. I thought Sacco was delightful, the few times I saw him. He was young, his eyes were smiling and flashing when we chatted. I can remember when I visited him out in the Dedham jail I had my two children with me and he was joking away with the children and laughing about things and very gay with me. He was an attractive, active, stimulating man—bright. He wasn't bitter in his attitudes, except when he was pressed to do something that was definitely against his own moral beliefs.*

Yet for most of those who knew them, Vanzetti was the scholar, Sacco the peasant. Therein, perhaps, lies the acceptability of the split-guilt theory; if anyone did it, it was Sacco, surely not Vanzetti. Even some who believed both men were innocent said that, unlike Vanzetti, Sacco was *capable* of committing a crime, blinking the fact that both men were armed and that a man psychologically and philosophically opposed to violence will not carry a gun even in self-defense. Also involved is a kind of anarchist machismo, which was evident at the conference on Italian-American radicalism. Almost every radical who spoke— and all were male—said in essence, We know Sacco and Vanzetti were innocent of this particular crime, but that's not because they couldn't have committed crimes; after all, they were anarchists. Though this was said about both men, the burden of being the more likely culprit has always been borne by the dynamic Sacco rather than the dreamy Vanzetti. Perhaps Sacco and Vanzetti carried weapons not just to defend themselves against their enemies, either official or in the movement, but as an expression of this same anarchist machismo which says, Don't think that because I'm an idealist I'm weak.

Vanzetti believed in violence, as he told Thompson a few hours before he died. His letters and fantasies often expressed violence, but there is no evidence that he ever committed any. There is no evidence that Sacco ever did either.

Sara Ehrmann:	*Those two individuals could not have committed that crime. They could not have done it. Any person who was close to them at all would have known it.*
Roger Baldwin:	*I never did believe the talk about Sacco's guilt. . . . My relations with Sacco and Vanzetti, personal relations, were such during those years that I saw them in jail, in the many hours that I spent with them, I never came to distrust their stories. . . . In the situation that they were in, never been out of jail from the moment they were arrested, they showed extraordinary courage and self-restraint. . . . They bore their fate with great dignity and with philosophical detachment. . . . Generally speaking, they were quite lovable. . . . They weren't resentful and bitter; Sacco was indignant but not bitter. They were idealists. Both of them were idealists. They were about as far away from murderers and thieves as anyone you could think of.*

Nicola Sacco to his seven-year-old daughter, Ines, July 19, 1927:

I would like that you should understand what I am going to say to you, and I wish I could write you so plain, for I long so much to have you hear all the heart-beat eagerness of your father, for I love you so much as you are the dearest little beloved one.

It is quite hard indeed to make you understand in your young age, but I am going to try from the bottom of my heart to make you understand how dear you are to your father's soul. If I cannot succeed in doing that, I know that you will save this letter and read it over in future years to come and you will see and feel the same heart-beat affection as your father feels in writing it to you.

I will bring with me your little and so dearest letter and carry it right under my heart to the last day of my life. When I die, it will be buried with your father who loves you so much, as I do also your brother Dante and holy dear mother.

You don't know Ines, how dear and great your letter was to your father. It is the most golden present that you could have given to me or that I could have wished for in these sad days.

It was the greatest treasure and sweetness in my struggling life that I could have lived with you and your brother Dante and your mother in a neat little farm, and learn all your sincere words and tender affection. Then in the summer-time to be sitting with you in the home nest under the oak tree shade— beginning to teach you of life and how to read and write, to see you running, laughing, crying and singing through the verdant fields picking the wild flowers here and there from one tree to another, and from the clear, vivid stream to your mother's embrace.

The same I have wished to see for other poor girls, and their brothers, happy with their mother and father as I dreamed for us—but it was not so and the nightmare of the lower classes saddened very badly your father's soul.

For the things of beauty and of good in this life, mother nature gave to us all, for the conquest and the joy of liberty. The men of this dying old society, they brutally have pulled me away from the embrace of your brother and your poor mother. But, in spite of all, the free spirit of your father's faith still survives, and I have lived for it and for the dream that some day I would have come back to life, to the embrace of your dear mother, among our friends and comrades again, but woe is me!

I know that you are good and surely you love your mother, Dante and all the beloved ones—and I am sure that you love me also a little, for I love you much and then so much. You do not know Ines, how often I think of you every day. You are in my heart, in my vision, in every angle of this sad walled cell, in the sky and everywhere my gaze rests.[27]

Bartolomeo Vanzetti's last letter to his family, August 4, 1927:

I swear to you that I am completely innocent of this or any other crime. Do not be ashamed of me. There will come a day in which my life will be known for what it is, and whoever bears the name of Vanzetti will hold up his head in pride. Everyone who knows me already loves and respects me. I have written my epitaph with twenty years dedicated to justice and liberty for all. If I must die through the injustice of men and circumstances, you may be sure that none of my enemies will be mourned as I am.

I do not want you to cry for me. I want you to be serene and strong, and continue my work for me. I want you to sing of me, rather than cry for me, I want to live in your hearts, which must be whole and strong and happy.

I will fight to the end to win.

Vanzetti was right; none of their enemies were mourned as he and Sacco have been. The bones of their oppressors have been dispersed by time, while Sacco and Vanzetti live in legend, poetry, plays, novels, on film, in countless serious studies, and where they wished most to be, in the hearts of the people.

The Sacco-Vanzetti case marked the ultimate attempt of the WASPs to assert control over the immigrants. The two men were murdered because they were aliens who still believed in the perfect world their enemies had enunciated and abandoned; they had to be destroyed because they were unwanted reminders of what America might have been. But the reach of the WASPs exceeded their grasp; in winning the case they lost their souls, and

Afterwo

their moral authority passed to immigrants like Sacco and Vanzetti.

The Puritan concept of a visible saint was of someone who, having been supremely tested, evolved greater strength and faith. By the Puritans' own standards, Sacco and Vanzetti were visible saints.

Bibliographies and Notes

The following are works consulted on the Sacco-Vanzetti case. In addition, specialized bibliographies precede several sections and chapters. Certain magazine articles, books, and pamphlets are cited in the text or in footnotes. Newspapers consulted include *The New York Times*, the *New York World*, the *Boston Herald*, the *Boston Post*, the *Boston Evening Transcript*, and the *Boston Globe*.

*The starred titles are indispensable sources for information about the case.

Adlow, Elijah (Judge). Transcript of taped interview. Boston: Boston Public Library Oral History Collection, February 4, 1970.
AIHA Conference. *Italian American Radicalism: Old World Origins and New World Developments. Proceedings of the Fifth Annual Conference of the American Italian Historical Association*, November 11, 1972. Staten Island, New York: The American Italian Historical Association.
Baldwin, Roger N. The Reminiscences of Roger N. Baldwin (Part 1). New York: Columbia University Oral History Collection, 1954.
Carpenter, Albert. Taped interview (no transcript available). Boston: Boston Public Library Oral History Collection, November 13, 1968.

Dos Passos, John. *Facing the Chair.* Boston: Sacco-Vanzetti Defense Committee, 1927.

* Ehrmann, Herbert. *The Case That Will Not Die.* Boston: Little, Brown, 1969.

————. *The Untried Case: The Sacco-Vanzetti Case and the Morelli Gang.* New York: Vanguard, 1960.

Evans, Elizabeth Glendower. *Outstanding Features of the Sacco-Vanzetti Case.* Boston: New England Civil Liberties Committee, 1924.

Felicani, Aldino. The Reminiscences of Aldino Felicani. New York: Columbia University Oral History Collection, 1954.

Fraenkel, Osmond. *The Sacco-Vanzetti Case.* New York: Knopf, 1931.

Frankfurter, Felix. *The Case of Sacco and Vanzetti.* New York: Grosset & Dunlap, 1962.

Frankfurter, Marion, and Gardner Jackson (eds.). *The Letters of Sacco and Vanzetti.* New York: Dutton, 1960.

Greenbaum, Edward S. The Reminiscences of Edward S. Greenbaum. New York: Columbia University Oral History Collection, 1965.

Jackson, Gardner. The Reminiscences of Gardner Jackson. New York: Columbia University Oral History Collection, 1955.

*Joughin, Louis and Edmund Morgan. *The Legacy of Sacco and Vanzetti.* Chicago: Quadrangle, 1964.

Lyons, Eugene. *The Life and Death of Sacco and Vanzetti.* New York: International Publishers, 1927.

Marks, Jeannette. *Thirteen Days.* New York: Boni, 1929.

Musmanno, Michael A. *After Twelve Years.* New York: Knopf, 1939.

Myerson report: Letter and report from Dr. Abraham Myerson to Herbert Ehrmann, April 7, 1927. The Herbert B. Ehrmann Papers, Manuscript Division, Harvard Law School Library, Cambridge, Massachusetts.

O'Brien, Robert Lincoln. The Reminiscences of Robert Lincoln O'Brien. New York: Columbia University Oral History Collection, 1951.

Russell, Francis. *Tragedy in Dedham.* New York: McGraw-Hill, 1971.

Sinclair, Upton. *Boston.* New York: Boni, 1928.

*Trial transcript. *The Sacco-Vanzetti Case: Transcript of the Record of the Trial of Nicola Sacco and Bartolomeo Vanzetti in the Courts of Massachusetts and Subsequent Proceedings, 1920–1927* (5 vols.); New York: Henry Holt, 1928. *Supplemental Volume*: a sixth volume which deals primarily with the Plymouth trial. New York: Henry Holt, 1929. All six volumes were reprinted by Paul P. Appel, Mamaroneck, New York, in 1969.

Vanzetti, Bartolomeo. (Autobiography) *The Story of a Proletarian Life*, translated by Eugene Lyons. Boston: Sacco-Vanzetti Defense Committee, 1923.

I BEGINNINGS

1 The Crimes

1. Ehrmann, *The Case That Will Not Die*, p. 17.
2. Trial transcript, p. 752.

2 The Men

1. Letters shown to author by Spencer Sacco, June, 1973.
2. *Il Messaggero*, interview with Sabino Sacco, February 1, 1976. Sabino Sacco died in May, 1976, at the age of 92.
3. Trial transcript, p. 1818.
4. *Il Messaggero*, interview with Sabino Sacco, February 1, 1976.
5. Myerson report, p. 3.
6. *Il Messaggero*, interview with Sabino Sacco, February 1, 1976.
7. Evans, *Outstanding Features of the Sacco-Vanzetti Case*, p. 46.
8. Ibid., p. 27.
9. Ibid.
10. Ibid.
11. Trial transcript, p. 5230.
12. Ibid., p. 5231.
13. Ibid.
14. Ibid., p. 1606.
15. Evans, *Outstanding Features of the Sacco-Vanzetti Case*, p. 26.
16. Ibid., p. 27.
17. Ibid., p. 26.
18. Hymie Kaplan to author, October 11, 1971.
19. Myerson report, p. 1.
20. Vanzetti, autobiography, p. 5.
21. Ibid., p. 6.
22. Ibid., p. 7.
23. Ibid.
24. Ibid., p. 18.
25. Ibid., p. 19.
26. Vanzetti to his Aunt Edvige, December 15, 1914.
27. *Letters of Sacco and Vanzetti*, p. 166.
28. Ibid., p. 196.
29. Ibid., p. 178.

II BACKGROUNDS

Books consulted or recommended for chapters 3 and 4 include:

Erikson, Kai T. *Wayward Puritans*. New York: Wiley, 1966.
Feuerlicht, Roberta Strauss. *The Life and World of Henry VIII.* New York: Crowell-Collier, 1970.
Morgan, Edmund S. *Visible Saints*. Ithaca, New York: Cornell U. Press, 1965.
Simpson, Alan. *Puritanism in Old and New England*. Chicago: U. of Chicago Press, 1955.
Starkey, Marion. *The Devil in Massachusetts*. New York: Knopf, 1950.
Wertenbaker, Thomas Jefferson. *The Puritan Oligarchy*. New York: Grossett & Dunlap, 1947.
Ziff, Larzer. *Puritanism in America*. New York: Viking, 1973.

3 The Visible Saints

1. Barbara Miller Solomon, *Ancestors and Immigrants*, (Chicago: U. of Chicago Press, 1972), p. 31.
2. Quoted in Melvin Steinfield, ed., *Cracks in the Melting Pot*, (Beverly Hills, Calif.: Glencoe Press, 1970), p. 58.

4 The Accursed Group

1. Yves Simon, *Community of the Free*, (New York: Henry Holt, 1947), pp. 63–72. See also, Carey McWilliams, *Witch Hunt*, (Boston: Little, Brown, 1950), pp. 263–269.
2. Ray Allen Billington, *The Protestant Crusade, 1800–1860*, (Chicago: Quadrangle, 1964), p. 7. Professor Billington's definitive study includes such statements as, "Clearly the foreign-born, removed from the restraints of the old world and intoxicated by the freedom of the new, had not yet adjusted themselves to the standard of a society which they appreciated more than they understood." The foreign-born I knew adjusted easily to sweatshops and discrimination, which they understood more than they appreciated.
3. Marcus Lee Hansen, *The Atlantic Migration, 1607–1860*, (New York: Harper Torchbooks, 1961), p. 32.

5 The Oldest Prejudice

1. Louis Wright, *The Cultural Life of the American Colonies*, (New York: Harper Torchbooks, 1962), pp. 46–47.

2. Michael Novak, *The Rise of the Unmeltable Ethnics*, (New York: Macmillan, 1973), p. 74.
3. Milton Barron, ed., *Minorities in a Changing World*, (New York: Knopf, 1967), p. 307.
4. Ray Allen Billington, *The Protestant Crusade, 1800–1860*, (Chicago: Quadrangle, 1964), pp. 3–4.
5. Mary H. Cadwalader, "Charles Carroll of Carrollton," *Smithsonian*, December 1975, pp. 64–70.
6. Billington, *The Protestant Crusade*, p. 5.
7. Ibid., p. 16.
8. Ibid., p. 30.
9. Marcus Lee Hansen, *The Atlantic Migration, 1607–1860*, (New York: Harper Torchbooks, 1961), pp. 57–59, 65–66.
10. Maldwyn Allen Jones, *American Immigration*, (Chicago: U. of Chicago Press, 1960), p. 80.
11. Ibid., p. 82.
12. Ibid., p. 86.
13. John Higham, *Strangers in the Land*, (New York: Atheneum, 1968), p. 210. This is an essential and standard work on American nativism from 1860 to 1925, continuing the history begun by Billington.
14. Jones, *American Immigration*, p. 24.
15. Ibid., p. 45.
16. Antonia Fraser, *Cromwell, The Lord Protector*, (New York: Knopf, 1973), pp. 328, 338.
17. Billington, *The Protestant Crusade*, p. 43.
18. Ibid., p. 70.
19. Ibid., pp. 70–71.
20. Ibid., pp. 71–75.
21. Ibid., p. 89.
22. Ibid., p. 88.
23. William Shannon, *The American Irish*, (New York: Macmillan, 1966), p. 43n.
24n. *New York Times*, October 16, 1960.
25. Billington, *The Protestant Crusade*, p. 239.
26. Oscar Handlin, *Boston's Immigrants*, (New York: Atheneum, 1974), p. 49.
27. Billington, *The Protestant Crusade*, p. 240.
28. Ibid., p. 324.
29. Handlin, *Boston's Immigrants*, pp. 73-75.
30n. Ibid., pp. 69, 177, 205.
31. Billington, *The Protestant Crusade*, p. 386.
32n. Marcus Lee Hansen, *The Immigrant in American History*, (Cambridge: Harvard U. Press, 1940), pp. 111–112, 105.

6. The Master Racists

1. Clarence Winthrop Bowen, *The History of Woodstock, Connecticut; Genealogies of Woodstock Families,* (Worcester, Mass.: The American Antiquarian Society, 1943), p. 83.
2. Barbara Miller Solomon, *Ancestors and Immigrants,* (Chicago: U. of Chicago Press, 1972), pp. 1, 3, vii.
3. Ibid., p. vii.
4. Oscar Handlin, *Boston's Immigrants,* (New York: Atheneum, 1974), p. 142.
5. Solomon, *Ancestors and Immigrants,* p. 53.
6. Ibid., pp. 37, 41.
7. Maldwyn Allen Jones, *American Immigration,* (Chicago: U. of Chicago Press, 1960), pp. 179, 197, 205.
8. Yves Simon, *Community of the Free,* (New York: Henry Holt, 1947), p. 62.
9. Oscar Handlin, *Race and Nationality in American Life,* (Boston: Atlantic Monthly Press, 1957), p. 84.
10. John Higham, *Strangers in the Land,* (New York: Atheneum, 1968), pp. 9–10.
11. Ibid., p. 143.
12. Ibid. See also, Solomon, *Ancestors and Immigrants,* pp. 69–77.
13. Solomon, *Ancestors and Immigrants,* p. 74.
14. Larzer Ziff, *Puritanism in America,* p. 68.
15. Solomon, *Ancestors and Immigrants,* pp. 99–102. Dr. Solomon's book is an invaluable history of the Immigration Restriction League.
16. Ibid., p. 110.
17. Ibid.
18. Ibid., pp. 169–170.
19. Ibid., p. 126.
20. Ibid., p. 123.
21. Handlin, *Race and Nationality in American Life,* p. 90.
22. Higham, *Strangers in the Land,* pp. 154–155.
23. Ibid., p. 156.
24. Ibid.
25. Handlin, *Race and Nationality in American Life,* p. 96.

7 Pests and Pogroms

Books consulted on Italian-American history include:

DeConde, Alexander. *Half Bitter, Half Sweet: An Excursion into Italian-American History.* New York: Scribner's, 1971.
Gambino, Richard. *Blood of My Blood.* New York: Doubleday, 1974.

Iorizzo, Luciano, and Salvatore Mondello. *The Italian-Americans*. New York: Twayne, 1971.

Tomasi, Silvano, and Madeline Engel (eds.). *The Italian Experience in the United States*. New York: Center for Migration Studies, 1970.

1. DeConde, *Half Bitter, Half Sweet*, pp. 1, 15.
2. Ibid., p. 77.
3. Barbara Miller Solomon, *Ancestors and Immigrants,* (Chicago: U. of Chicago Press, 1972), p. 167.
4. For a full account of the New Orleans lynching, see Richard Gambino, *Vendetta*, (New York: Doubleday, 1977).
5. DeConde, *Half Bitter, Half Sweet*, p. 123.
6. *New York Times*, March 15 and 16, 1891.
7. Solomon, *Ancestors and Immigrants*, p. 109.
8. Iorizzo and Mondello, *The Italian-Americans*, p. 223.
9n. Melvin Steinfield, ed., *Cracks in the Melting Pot*, (Beverly Hills, Calif.: Glencoe Press, 1970), p. 33.
10. DeConde, *Half Bitter, Half Sweet*, p. 168. Also, the *New York Times*, August 8, 1920.
11n. John Higham, *Strangers in the Land*, (New York: Atheneum, 1968), p. 278.
12. Andrew M. Greeley, *Why Can't They Be Like Us?* (New York: Dutton, 1971), p. 30.
13. Solomon, *Ancestors and Immigrants*, p. 197.
14. For a thorough analysis of the Dillingham report, see Oscar Handlin, *Race and Nationality in American Life*, (Boston: Atlantic Monthly Press, 1957), chap. 5.

8 Economic Wars

1. Yves Simon, *Community of the Free*, (New York: Henry Holt, 1947), p. 41.
2. John Higham, *Strangers in the Land*, (New York: Atheneum, 1968), p. 138.
3. Ibid., p. 55.
4. Henry David, *The History of the Haymarket Affair* (New York: Collier Books, 1963), p. 47.
5. Ibid., p. 24.
6. Thomas Brooks, *Toil and Trouble: A History of American Labor*, (New York: Dell, 1964), p. 3.
7. Ibid., p. 29.
8. Ibid., p. 50.
9. David, *The History of the Haymarket Affair*, p. 25.

10. Ibid., p. 50.
11. For a definitive account of the Haymarket bombing, see David, *The History of the Haymarket Affair*.
12. For a biography of Czolgosz, see A. Wesley Johns, *The Man Who Shot McKinley*, (South Brunswick, N.J.: Barnes, 1970).
13. William Preston, Jr., *Aliens and Dissenters: Federal Suppression of Radicals, 1903–1933*, (New York: Harper Torchbooks, 1966), p. 31.
14. "The Liberator of Masetti," *La Folla*, Milan, Italy, January 11, 1914. This article is attached to the transcript of the Reminiscences of Aldino Felicani in the Oral History Collection of Columbia University.
15. Felicani, A., Reminiscences, p. 16.
16. Frederick Lewis Allen, *The Big Change*, (New York: Bantam, 1961), p. 24.
17. Preston, *Aliens and Dissenters*, p. 36.
18. See George Lowry, *Theodore Roosevelt and the Progressive Movement*, (New York: Hill & Wang, 1960). For a superb overall biography, see Henry F. Pringle, *Theodore Roosevelt* (New York: Harcourt, Brace, 1956).
19. For a biography of Debs, see Ray Ginger, *Eugene V. Debs*, (New York: Collier Books, 1962).
20. See Paul F. Brissenden, *The I.W.W.*, (New York: Columbia U. Press, 1920); Joyce Kornbluh, ed., *Rebel Voices: An I.W.W. Anthology* (Ann Arbor: U. of Michigan Press, 1964); and Patrick Renshaw, *The Wobblies* (New York: Anchor Books, 1968).
21. Renshaw, *The Wobblies*, p. 94.
22. Kornbluh, *Rebel Voices*, pp. 168, 158–159.
23. Ibid., p. 159.
24. Margaret Sanger, *An Autobiography*, (Elmsford, N.Y.: Maxwell Reprint Co., 1970), p. 81.
25. Kornbluh, *Rebel Voices*, p. 161.
26. Ibid., p. 181.

9 Silencing Dissent

For this chapter, see Roberta Strauss Feuerlicht, *America's Reign of Terror: World War I, the Red Scare, and the Palmer Raids*, (New York: Random House, 1971).
1. Arthur S. Link, *Woodrow Wilson and the Progressive Era*, (New York: Harper Torchbooks, 1963), p. 148.
2. Henry F. Pringle, *Theodore Roosevelt*, (New York: Harcourt, Brace, 1956), p. 406.
3. John Higham, *Strangers in the Land*, (New York: Atheneum, 1968), p.200.
4. Ibid., pp. 198–199.

5. A. J. P. Taylor, *A History of the First World War*, (New York: Berkley, 1966), pp. 90–92.
6. John C. Farrell, *Beloved Lady: A History of Jane Addams' Ideas on Reform and Peace*, (Baltimore, Md.: Johns Hopkins Press, 1967), p. 171.
7. Ray Ginger, *Eugene V. Debs*, (New York: Collier Books, 1962), p. 349.
8. William Preston, Jr., *Aliens and Dissenters: Federal Suppression of Radicals, 1903–1933*, (New York: Harper Torchbooks, 1966) p. 292.
9. Link, *Woodrow Wilson and the Progressive Era*, pp. 281–282.
10. Ibid., p. 282.
11. William E. Leuchtenburg, *The Perils of Prosperity, 1914–32*, (Chicago: U. of Chicago Press, 1958), pp. 17, 30.
12. Taylor, *A History of the First World War*, p. 110.
13. Pringle, *Theodore Roosevelt*, p. 408.
14. Leuchtenburg, *The Perils of Prosperity*, p. 34.
15. Ibid., p. 44.
16. George Creel, *How We Advertised America*, (New York: Harper, 1920), p. 3.
17. Phillip Knightley, *The First Casualty*, (New York: Harcourt Brace Jovanovich, 1975), p. 123.
18. Higham, *Strangers in the Land*, p. 210.
19. Ibid., p. 209.
20. Harold Hyman, *To Try Men's Souls: Loyalty Tests in American History*, (Berkeley and Los Angeles: U. of California Press, 1959), pp. 271–272.
21. Ibid., pp. 272–284.
22. James Mock and Cedric Larson, *Words That Won the War: The Story of the Committee on Public Information*, (Princeton: Princeton U. Press, 1939), pp. 37–38.
23. Preston, *Aliens and Dissenters*, p. 129.
24. Donald Johnson, *The Challenge to American Freedoms: World War I and the Rise of the American Civil Liberties Union*, (Lexington: U. of Kentucky Press, 1963), pp. 56–59.
25. Zechariah Chafee, Jr., *Free Speech in the United States*, (New York: Atheneum, 1969), p. 52n.
26. Ibid., p. 70.
27. Ibid.
28. Ibid., p. 52n.
29. Ibid., p. 51.
30. Patrick Renshaw, *The Wobblies*, (New York: Anchor Books, 1968), p.188.
31. Preston, *Aliens and Dissenters*, pp. 128, 130.
32. Renshaw, *The Wobblies*, p. 181.
33. Ibid., pp. 174–175.

34. Ginger, *Eugene V. Debs*, pp. 366, 374, 369.
35. Ibid., pp. 376–377.
36. Ibid., p. 377.
37. Ibid., pp. 387–390.
38. Ibid., pp. 393–394.
39. Chafee, *Free Speech in the United States*, p. 80.
40. Ibid., p. 81.
41. Ginger, *Eugene V. Debs*, p. 426.
42. Ibid.
43. Mark DeWolfe Howe, ed., *Holmes-Pollock Letters*, vol. II, (Cambridge: Harvard U. Press, 1961), p. 7.
44. Ibid., p. 8.

10   The Red Scare

The standard work on most of the material in this chapter and the following one is Robert K. Murray, *Red Scare: A Study in National Hysteria, 1919–1920*, (New York: McGraw- Hill, 1964). See also, Roberta Strauss Feuerlicht, *America's Reign of Terror*, (New York: Random House, 1971).

1. A.J.P. Taylor, *A History of the First World War*, (New York: Berkley, 1966), p. 169.
2n. Ibid., pp. 168–169.
3n. See Donald Johnson, *The Challenge to American Freedoms: World War I and the Rise of the American Civil Liberties Union* (Lexington: U. of Kentucky Press, 1963).
4. Ibid., pp. 114, 110.
5. Murray, *Red Scare*, p. 9.
6. Ibid., p. 93.
7. William Slosson, *The Great Crusade and After*, (New York: Macmillan, 1930), p. 81.
8. Arthur Waskow, *From Race Riot to Sit-In*, (New York: Anchor Books, 1967), p. 177.
9. Ibid., pp. 110–119.
10. For a complete account of the Chicago riot, see William Tuttle, Jr., *Race Riot: Chicago in the Red Summer of 1919*, (New York: Atheneum, 1970).
11. For a critical study of the first 40 years of the FBI, see Max Lowenthal, *The Federal Bureau of Investigation*, (New York: Sloane, 1950).
12. Ibid., p. 5.
13. Ibid., pp. 24–35.

14. Ibid., pp. 67–68.
15. Robert W. Dunn, ed., *The Palmer Raids*, (New York: International Publishers, 1948), p. 16.
16. Stanley Coben, *A. Mitchell Palmer: Politician*, (New York: Columbia U. Press, 1963), p. 205.
17. Murray, *Red Scare*, p. 79.
18. Ibid., p. 81. See also Lowenthal, *The Federal Bureau of Investigation*, p. 72.
19. Waskow, *From Race Riot to Sit-In*, pp. 189–191.
20. Lowenthal, *The Federal Bureau of Investigation*, p. 51.
21. Ibid., pp. 56–57.
22. Ibid., pp. 56–58.
23. Murray, *Red Scare*, pp. 84–86.
24. Ibid., p. 91.
25. Ibid., pp. 87–90.
26. See Patrick Renshaw, *The Wobblies*, (New York: Anchor Books, 1968), pp. 163–165; Joyce Kornbluh, ed., *Rebel Voices: An I. W. W. Anthology*, (Ann Arbor: U. of Michigan Press, 1964), pp. 255–256; Murray, *Red Scare*, pp. 182–184.
27. See Renshaw, *The Wobblies*, pp. 165–166; Murray, *Red Scare*, p. 188; and Walker C. Smith, *Was It Murder? The Truth About Centralia*, (Centralia, Wash.: Centralia Publicity Committee, 1925), p. 8.
28. Coben, *A. Mitchell Palmer*, p. 196.

11 America's Reign of Terror

1. For a full biography of Palmer, see Stanley Coben, *A. Mitchell Palmer: Politician*, (New York: Columbia U. Press, 1963).
2. Max Lowenthal, *The Federal Bureau of Investigation*, (New York: Sloane, 1950), p. 84.
3. Ibid.
4. Ibid., p. 91.
5. "Report upon the Illegal Practices of the United States Department of Justice by Twelve Lawyers," (Washington, D.C.: National Popular Government League, 1920), p. 65; hereafter, NPGL report.
6. Murray, *Red Scare*, p. 196.
7. NPGL report, p. 37.
8. Ibid., p. 18.
9. Ibid., p. 19.
10. Ibid., pp. 19–20.
11. Ibid., p. 20.

12. *New York Times*, November 8, 1919.
13. Ibid., November 9, 1919.
14. NPGL report, pp. 11–13.
15. Ibid., p. 27.
16. *New York Times*, November 9, 1919.
17. Murray, *Red Scare*, p. 197.
18. Ibid., p. 211.
19. Zechariah Chafee, Jr., *Free Speech in the United States,* (New York: Atheneum, 1969), p. 212.
20. NPGL report, pp. 37–40.
21. Ibid., p. 55.
22. Ibid. See also, Lowenthal, *The Federal Bureau of Investigation*, p. 169.
23. NPGL report, p. 55.
24. Ibid.
25. Ibid., p. 45.
26. Ibid.
27. Ibid.
28. Ibid., p. 46.
29. Ibid., p. 62.
30. Ibid., p. 63.

III The Case

12 Into the Trap

1. Trial transcript, p. 1924.
2. AIHA conference, pp. 30–37. I was present at the conference and have detailed notes on material and discussions not included in the AIHA report.
3. Dos Passos, John, *Facing the Chair*, p. 56.
4. AIHA conference, p. 34.
5. Dos Passos, *Facing the Chair*, p. 57.
6. Robert D'Attilio to author. This has been verified by another anarchist historian. Since Canada is much closer to New England, the fact that Sacco and Vanzetti went all the way to Mexico also tends to confirm the existence of an escape route.
7. Felicani, A., Reminiscences, p. 44.
8. Max Lowenthal, *The Federal Bureau of Investigation*, (New York: Sloane, 1950), p. 74.
9. Ibid.
10. Trial transcript, p. 859.
11. Ibid., pp. 1833–1834.

12. Ibid., pp. 1707, 1712, 1713, 1714.
13. Ibid., p. 1927.
14. Ibid., pp. 1715, 1716.
15. Ibid., p. 1850.
16. Ibid., pp. 1716–1717, 1761.
17. Ibid., pp. 1718–1720.

13 Bricks without Straw

1. Ehrmann, *The Case That Will Not Die*, pp. 53–54.
2. Felicani, A., Reminiscences, p. 65.
3. Trial transcript, p. 1715.
4. Ibid., p. 1725.
5. Ibid., p. 3387.
6. Ibid., pp. 3388–3389.
7. Ehrmann, *The Case That Will Not Die*, p. 50.
8. Trial transcript, pp. 1945-1946.
9. Ibid., p. 1802.
10. Ehrmann, *The Case That Will Not Die*, pp. 58-59.
11. Myerson report, p. 3.
12. Felicani, A., Reminiscences, p. 2.
13. Ibid., pp. 7–8.
14. Ibid., pp. 10, 19.
15. Ibid., pp. 12, 14.
16. Ibid., p. 41.
17. Ibid., pp. 45, 55, 48.
18. Ibid., pp. 49–50.
19. Ibid., p. 50.
20. Ibid., pp. 61–62.
21. Ibid., p. 63.
22. Ibid., p. 64.

14 Plymouth: I Could Tell He Was a Foreigner

1. Trial transcript, supp. vol., p. 365.
2. Ibid., p. 366.
3. Ibid., p. 367.
4. Ibid., pp. 7, 10, 9.
5. Ibid., pp. 17, 18.
6. Ibid., pp. 23, 26.
7. Ibid., pp. 75, 78.
8. Ibid., p. 49.
9. Ibid., p. 90.

10. Ibid., p. 128.
11. Ibid., pp. 132–133.
12. Ibid., p. 129.
13. See Ehrmann, *The Case That Will Not Die*, chap. 8, for a complete discussion of the shells.
14. Trial transcript, p. 1863.
15. Ibid., p. 2057.
16. Trial transcript, supp. vol., p. 149.
17. Ibid., p. 313.
18. Ibid., pp. 327–328.
19. Ibid., pp. 328–329.
20. Brini family to author.
21. Trial transcript, supp. vol., p. 226.
22. Ibid., p. 236.
23. Ibid., p. 252.
24. Ibid., p. 258.
25. Ibid., p. 260.
26. Ibid., p. 259.
27. Ibid.
28. Ibid., p. 260.
29. Ibid., p. 220.
30. Ibid., p. 260.
31. Ibid., p. 262.
32. Joughin and Morgan, *The Legacy of Sacco and Vanzetti*, p. 42.
33. Trial transcript, supp. vol., pp. 228–229.
34. Ibid., pp. 231-232.
35. Ibid., p. 235.
36. Ibid., p. 249.
37. Ibid., p. 252.
38. Ibid., p. 277.
39. Ibid., p. 274.
40. Ibid.
41. Ibid., pp. 274–275.
42. Bartolomeo Vanzetti, *Background of the Plymouth Trial* (Boston: Road to Freedom Group, 1926), p. 34.
43. Ibid., p. 35.
44. Trial transcript, supp. vol., p. 332.
45. Ibid., p. 334.
46. Ibid., p. 335.
47. Ibid., p. 336.
48. Ehrmann, *The Case That Will Not Die*, p. 109.
49. Ibid., pp. 109–110.
50. Ibid., p. 110.
51. Ibid.

52. Ibid., p. 111.
53. Ibid., pp. 112–113.
54. Ibid., p. 114.

15   The Cutting of the Throat

1. Felicani, A., Reminiscences, p. 58.
2. Ibid., p. 57.
3. Ibid.
4. Ibid., pp. 66–67.
5. Ibid., pp. 82–83.
6. Ibid., p. 68–70.
7. Ibid., p. 110. See also Patrick Renshaw, *The Wobblies* (New York: Anchor Books, 1968), p. 186.
8. Ehrmann, *The Case That Will Not Die*, p. 153.
9. Felicani, A., Reminiscences, p. 68.
10. Ibid., p. 71.
11. Ibid., p. 73.
12. Ibid., p. 89.
13. Ibid., p. 87.
14. Ibid., p. 92.
15. Ibid., p. 95.
16. Ibid.
17. Ehrmann, *The Case That Will Not Die*, p. 159.
18. Felicani, A., Reminiscences, p. 109.
19. Carpenter, A. Taped interview.
20. Trial transcript, p. 4991.
21. Ibid., pp. 4992, 4991.
22. Ibid., p. 4992.
23. Ibid.
24. Ehrmann, *The Case That Will Not Die*, p. 156.
25. Trial transcript, p. 5047.
26. Ibid., p. 5049.
27. Felicani, A., Reminiscences, pp. 73–74.
28. *Boston Herald*, January 29, 1921.
29. Felicani, A., Reminiscences, pp. 74–76.
30. *Boston Herald*, January 29, 1921.
31. Felicani, A., Reminiscences, p. 77. See also, *Boston Herald*, January 28 and 29, 1921.
32. *Boston Herald*, January 29, 1921.
33. Ibid., February 1, 1921.
34. Ibid., February 2, 1921.
35. Ibid., February 4, 1921.

36. Ehrmann, *The Case That Will Not Die*, p. 169.
37. Ibid., p. 166.
38. *Boston Herald*, April 24, 1920.
39n. E. Adlow, Taped interview, pp. 35–36.
40. Trial transcript, p. 5062.
41. Ibid., p. 5253.
42. Ibid., pp. 3579–3580.

16   Dedham: The Prosecution

1. Trial transcript, p. 216.
2. Ibid., pp. 205, 206.
3. Ibid., pp. 482–485.
4. Ibid., p. 501.
5. Ibid., p. 520.
6. Ibid., p. 295.
7. Ibid., pp. 1167–1168.
8. Ibid., p. 545.
9. Ibid., p. 337.
10. Joughin and Morgan, *The Legacy of Sacco and Vanzetti*, p. 77.
11. Trial transcript, p. 240.
12. Ibid., pp. 224, 252.
13. Ibid., p. 466.
14. Ibid., p. 464.
15. Joughin and Morgan, *The Legacy of Sacco and Vanzetti*, pp. 79–80.
16. Trial transcript, p. 5179.
17. Ehrmann, *The Case That Will Not Die*, p. 179.
18. Trial transcript, pp. 417–418.
19n. Ehrmann, *The Case That Will Not Die*, pp. 178–180.
20n. Trial transcript, pp. 1974, 1728.
21. Ibid., pp. 68, 69.
22. Ibid., p. 2215.
23. Ibid., pp. 595–597.
24. Ibid., pp. 615–616.
25. Ibid., pp. 732–733.
26. Ibid., pp. 426–427.
27. Ibid., pp. 490, 495.
28. Joughin and Morgan, *The Legacy of Sacco and Vanzetti*, pp. 80, 81.
29. Trial transcript, p. 3514.
30. Ibid., p. 1157.
31. Ibid., p. 809.
32. Ibid., p. 1687.
33. Ibid., p. 196.
34. Ibid., pp. 200, 198.
35. Ibid., p. 200.

36. Ibid., pp. 815–816.
37n. Ibid., p. 5235.
38. Ibid., p. 798.
39. Ehrmann, *The Case That Will Not Die*, p. 208.
40. Trial transcript, p. 854.
41. Ibid., p. 857.
42. Ibid., pp. 1928–1929.
43. Ibid., p. 5170.
44. Ibid., p. 3642.
45. Ibid., pp. 5185–5186.
46. Ehrmann, *The Case That Will Not Die*, p. 261.
47. Trial transcript, pp. 3642, 896.
48. Ibid., pp. 3642–3643.
49. Ibid., p. 2254.
50. Ibid., p. 920.
51. Ehrmann, *The Case That Will Not Die*, p. 283.
52. Ibid., p. 284.

17 Dedham: The Defense

1. Trial transcript, p. 4993.
2. Ibid., pp. 1700–1703.
3. Ibid., p. 1554.
4. Ibid., p. 1555.
5. Ibid., p. 2192.
6. Lefevre Brini to author.
7. Trial transcript, p. 1538.
8. Ibid., pp. 1539, 1540.
9. Ibid., pp. 1823–1824.
10. Ibid., p. 1825.
11n. Ibid., p. 1979.
12. Ibid., pp. 1825–1826.
13. Ibid., p. 1942.
14. Ibid., p. 853.
15. Ibid., p. 869.
16. Ibid., pp. 2266b–2266c.
17. Ibid., p. 2266c.
18. Ibid., p. 4929. See also Clay C. Burton, "Italian-American Relations and the Case of Sacco and Vanzetti," AIHA conference, pp. 65–74.
19. Trial transcript, pp. 2014–2016.
20. Ibid., p. 2021.
21. Ibid., p. 2022.
22. Ibid., p. 2023.
23. Ibid., p. 4995.

24. Ibid., p. 4993.
25. Ibid., p. 1707.
26. Ibid., p. 1710.
27. Ibid., pp. 1721–1722.
28. Ibid., p. 1726.
29. Ibid., pp. 1726–1727.
30. Ibid., p. 1728.
31. Ibid., p. 1729.
32. Ibid., pp. 1731–1732.
33. Ibid., p. 1733.
34. Ibid., p. 1734.
35. Ibid., p. 1737.

18 Dedham: The Heretics

1. Trial transcript, p. 1737.
2. Ibid., p. 1738.
3. Ibid., p. 1744.
4. Ibid., pp. 1742–1743.
5. Ibid., p. 1771.
6. Ibid., p. 1758.
7. Ibid., p. 1762.
8. Ibid., p. 1797.
9. Ibid., p. 752.
10. Ibid., p. 1767.
11. Ibid., p. 1777.
12. Ibid., p. 1761.
13. Ibid., p. 1778.
14. Ibid., pp. 1802–1803.
15. Ibid., p. 1769.
16. Ibid., p. 1808.
17. Ibid., p. 1812.
18. Ibid., p. 1831.
19. Ibid., p. 1841.
20. Ibid., p. 1844.
21. Ibid., p. 1845.
22. Ibid., p. 1858.
23. Ibid., pp. 1903–1904.
24. Ibid., p. 1818.
25. Ibid., pp. 1867–1868.
26. Ibid., p. 1869.
27. Ibid., pp. 1869–1870.
28. Ibid., pp. 1870–1873.
29. Ibid., p. 1873.

30. Ibid.
31. Ibid.
32. Ibid., p. 1874.
33. Ibid., pp. 1875–1877.
34. Ibid., pp. 1877–1880.
35. Ibid., pp. 1889–1890.
36. Ibid., pp. 1890–1891.
37. Ibid., p. 1893.
38. Ibid., p. 1911.
39. Ibid., p. 1946.
40. Ibid., p. 1947.
41. Ibid., p. 1948.
42. Ibid., p. 1912.
43. Ibid., pp. 1918–1919.
44. Ibid., p. 1950.
45. Ibid., pp. 1964, 1967, 1968.
46. Joughin and Morgan, *The Legacy of Sacco and Vanzetti*, p. 94.
47. Ibid., p. 107.
48. Trial transcript, pp. 2207–2208.
49. Ibid., p. 2237.
50. Ibid., p. 2239.
51. Ibid., p. 2260.
52. Ibid., p. 2262.
53. Ibid., p. 2263.
54. Ibid., pp. 2265–2266.

IV   APPEALS

19   Breakdown

1. *New York Times*, August 20, 1927.
2. Jackson, G., Reminiscences, p. 114.
3. Ibid.
4. Ibid., p. 115.
5. Ibid., pp. 115–116.
6. Ibid., p. 152.
7. Ibid., p. 160.
8. Felicani, A., Reminiscences, pp. 96, 100.
9. Ibid., p. 96.
10. Ibid., p. 104.
11. Ibid.
12. Trial transcript, p. 5563.
13. Ibid., p. 3505.
14. Ibid., pp. 5567–5569, 5576.
15. Ibid., p. 5584.

16. Ibid., pp. 5592, 5589.
17. Ibid., p. 3807.
18. Ibid., p. 3938.
19. Ibid., p. 3917.
20. Felicani, A., Reminiscences, p. 111.
21. Ibid., p. 125.
22. *Letters of Sacco and Vanzetti*, pp. 21–24.
23. Ibid., p. 45.
24. Russell, Francis, *Tragedy in Dedham*, p. 17.
25. Felicani, A., Reminiscences, p. 112.
26. *Letters of Sacco and Vanzetti*, p. 135.
27. Felicani, A., Reminiscences, p. 116.
28. *Letters of Sacco and Vanzetti*, p. 89.
29. See Ralph Colp, Jr., "Sacco's Struggle for Sanity," The *Nation*, August 16, 1958, pp. 65–70.

20   Those Anarchistic Bastards

1. Russell, *Tragedy in Dedham*, p. 462.
2. Felicani, A., Reminiscences, p. 101.
3. Letter to Luigia Vanzetti, June 11, 1922.
4. Ibid.
5. Ibid.
6. Ibid., September 3, 1922.
7. Ibid.
8. Ibid., October 20, 1922.
9. Ibid.
10. Ibid., undated.
11. Ibid., April 6, 1924.
12. Ibid., March 10, 1924.
13. Ibid., July 28, 1923.
14. Ibid., November 27, 1925.
15. Ibid., July 15, 1924.
16. Letter to Elvira Fantino, June 25, 1923.
17. Letter to Luigia Vanzetti, July 28, 1923.
18. *Letters of Sacco and Vanzetti*, p. 97.
19. Trial transcript, pp. 3602–3603.
20. Ibid., p. 3514.
21. Ibid.
22. Ibid., p. 3516.
23. Ibid., p. 3519.
24. Ibid., p. 3523.
25. Ibid., p. 5597.

26. Ibid., pp. 3888, 3891.
27. Ibid., p. 3950.
28. Ibid., p. 3703.
29. Ibid., p. 5065.
30. O'Brien, R. L., Reminiscences, p. 176.
31. See Ralph Colp, Jr., "Bitter Christmas: A Biographical Inquiry Into the Life of Bartolomeo Vanzetti," The *Nation*, December 27, 1958, pp. 493–495.
32. Letter to Luigia Vanzetti, April 15, 1925.
33. Ibid., May 8, 1925.
34. Ibid., December 25, 1925.
35. Felicani, A., Reminiscences, pp. 127–128.
36. O'Brien, R. L., Reminiscences, pp. 164–165.
37. Trial transcript, pp. 4496–4497.
38. Ibid., p. 4497.

21   Confession and Collusion

1. Trial transcript, pp. 4398, 4585.
2. Ibid., p. 4574.
3. Ibid., pp. 4416–4418.
4. Ehrmann, *The Case That Will Not Die*, p. 400.
5. Ibid., pp. 416–417.
6. Ehrmann, *The Untried Case*, p. 33.
7. Ibid.
8. Ehrmann, *The Case That Will Not Die*, p. 413.
9. Ehrmann, *The Untried Case*, pp. 105–106; Russell, *Tragedy in Dedham*, pp. 278–279; A. Carpenter, taped interview. Carpenter, who met with Moller, says Moore was "encouraged" by Moller's story, but does not explain why Moore did not pursue it.
10. Ehrmann, *The Case That Will Not Die*, p. 413.
11. Ibid., p. 414.
12n. Ibid., *The Case That Will Not Die*, p. 389.
13. Ibid., *The Untried Case*, pp. 107–111.
14. Ibid., *The Untried Case*, pp. 114–118.
15. Ibid., chap. 5.
16. Trial transcript, p. 4390.
17. Ehrmann, *The Case That Will Not Die*, p. 429.
18. Ben Bagdikian, review of *The Case That Will Not Die*, New York *Times Book Review*, March 30, 1969, p. 32.
19. Ehrmann, *The Case That Will Not Die*, pp. 429–432.
20. Vincent Teresa, *My Life in the Mafia*, (New York: Doubleday, 1973), pp. 44–46.

21. Trial transcript, p. 4726.
22. Frankfurter, *The Case of Sacco and Vanzetti*, p. 103.
23. Trial transcript, pp. 4500–4502.
24n. Ibid., p. 4501.
25. Ibid., pp. 4503–4504.
26. Ibid., p. 4506.
27. Ibid., pp. 4379, 4381–4383.
28. Ibid., pp. 4748, 4750.
29. Ibid., p. 4751.
30. Frankfurter, *The Case of Sacco and Vanzetti*, p. 104.
31. Trial transcript, p. 4893.
32. Ibid.
33. Ibid., p. 4889.
34. Ibid., pp. 4895–4896.
35. Ibid., pp. 4896–4904.
36. Ibid., p. 4904.
37. Ibid., pp. 4904–4905.

V THE CAUSE

22 Freedom or Death

1. William Hyslop Fuller (comp.), *American Fuller Genealogy*, vol. III, Palmer, Mass., 1914, p. 175.
2. New York *World*, August 9, 1927.
3. Letters to Luigia Vanzetti, January 21, 1927, May 7, 1927.
4. *Letters of Sacco and Vanzetti*, p. 161.
5. Letter to Luigia Vanzetti, May 1, 1927.
6. *Letters of Sacco and Vanzetti*, pp. 254, 256, 252, 254.
7. Ralph Colp, Jr., "Sacco's Struggle for Sanity," The *Nation*, August 16, 1958, pp. 65, 70.
8. Myerson report, p. 4.
9. Ibid., p. 5.
10. Trial transcript, p. 4908.
11. *Letters of Sacco and Vanzetti*, p. 27.
12. Philip D. Stong, "The Last Days of Sacco and Vanzetti," in Isabel Leighton, ed., *The Aspirin Age* (New York: Simon & Schuster, 1949), p. 186.
13. Trial transcript, p. 4916.
14. Ibid., pp. 4943–4944.
15n. O'Brien, R. L., Reminiscences, p. 167.
16. Trial transcript, pp. 4954–4957.
17. Ibid., pp. 4929–4930.
18. Ibid., pp. 4964–4965.

19. Ibid., p. 4928.
20. Ibid., p. 5019.
21. Ibid., p. 5068.
22. Ibid., pp. 5065–5066.
23. Ibid., pp. 4947, 4969.
24. Ibid., pp. 4972, 4970.
25. Jackson, G., Reminiscences, p. 184.
26. Felicani, A., Reminiscences, pp. 131, 129.
27. Ibid., p. 133.
28. Joughin and Morgan, *The Legacy of Sacco and Vanzetti*, pp. 241–242.
29. O'Brien, R. L., Reminiscences, p. 174.
30. Felicani, A., Reminiscences, p. 137.
31. Jackson, G., Reminiscences, p. 201.
32. Ibid., p. 255.
33. Joughin and Morgan, *The Legacy of Sacco and Vanzetti*, p. 259.
34. Ibid., p. 238.
35. *Letters of Sacco and Vanzetti*, p. 234.
36. Musmanno, *After Twelve Years*, p. 401.

23 We Three Kings

1. Ehrmann, *The Case That Will Not Die*, p. 484.
2. Jackson, G., Reminiscences, p. 223.
3. *Letters of Sacco and Vanzetti*, p. 231.
4. For a complete biography, see Henry A. Yeomans, *Abbott Lawrence Lowell, 1856–1943* (Cambridge: Harvard U. Press, 1948).
5. Ibid., p. 44.
6. Barbara Miller Solomon, *Ancestors and Immigrants*, (Chicago: U. of Chicago Press, 1972), p. 205.
7. Jackson, G., Reminiscences, p. 280.
8. Letter to Luigia Vanzetti, April 11, 1927.
9. *Letters of Sacco and Vanzetti*, p. 63.
10. Ehrmann, *The Case That Will Not Die*, p. 485.
11. Ibid.
12. Trial transcript, p. 5086.
13. Ibid., p. 5097.
14. Ehrmann, *The Case That Will Not Die*, p. 381.
15. Trial transcript, p. 5103.
16. Ibid., p. 5104.
17. Ibid., p. 5109.
18. Ibid., p. 5112.
19. Ibid., pp. 5173, 5195.
20. Ehrmann, *The Case That Will Not Die*, p. 535.

21. Jackson, G., Reminiscences, pp. 220–221.
22. Ibid., p. 221.
23. Felicani, A., Reminiscences, pp. 142–143. See also Ehrmann, *The Case That Will Not Die*, p. 536.
24. Ehrmann, *The Case That Will Not Die*, p. 537.
25. Musmanno, *After Twelve Years*, p. 246.
26. Ibid., p. 279.
27. Felicani, A., Reminiscences, p. 147.
28. Musmanno, *After Twelve Years*, p. 248.
29. For full text, see *Letters of Sacco and Vanzetti*, pp. 381–397.
30. *Outlook and Independent*, October 31, 1928, p. 1074.

24 Motions and Mobs

1. For full text, see Trial transcript, pp. 5378c–5378h.
2. Felicani, A., Reminiscences, p. 148.
3. *New York Times*, August 5, 1927.
4. Felicani, A., Reminiscences, p. 148.
5. Ibid.
6. For full text, see Trial transcript, pp. 5378i–5378z. For a devastating analysis of the report, see Ehrmann, *The Case That Will Not Die*, chap. 29.
7. Ehrmann, *The Untried Case*, p. 182.
8. O'Brien, R. L., Reminiscences, p. 171.
9. Ibid., p. 170.
10. *Boston Herald*, August 9, 1927.
11. *New York Times*, August 8, 1927.
12. *New York World*, August 8, 1927.
13. Jackson, G., Reminiscences, p. 226.
14. *New York World*, August 12, 1927.
15. *New York World*, August 6 and 5, 1927.
16. *New York Times*, August 7, 1927.
17. *New York Times*, August 8, 1927.
18. O'Brien, R. L., Reminiscences, p. 166.
19. *New York Times*, August 5, 1927.
20. *Letters of Sacco and Vanzetti*, p. 232.
21. Greenbaum, E., Reminiscences, pp. 128–129.
22. O'Brien, R. L., Reminiscences, p. 172.
23. Ibid., p. 175.
24. Ehrmann, *The Case That Will Not Die*, p. 161.
25. Jackson, G., Reminiscences, p. 282.
26. Ibid., pp. 253, 214, 255.
27. Ibid., pp. 255, 215.
28. Musmanno, *After Twelve Years*, p. 294.
29. Ibid.

30. Ibid., p. 296.
31. *New York World*, August 11, 1927.
32. Musmanno, *After Twelve Years*, p. 11.
33. Trial transcript, p. 5532.
34. Musmanno, *After Twelve Years*, p. 300.
35. Trial transcript, p. 5533.
36. Marks, *Thirteen Days*, pp. 5–6, 10, 13, 14.
37n. *New York World*, August 12, 1927.
38n. Ibid., August 4, 11, 13, 1927.
39. Ibid., August 11, 1927.
40. Musmanno, *After Twelve Years*, p. 304.
41. Ibid., p. 323.
42. *New York World*, August 4, 1927.
43. Jackson, G., Reminiscences, p. 230.
44. Marks, *Thirteen Days*, p. 10.
45. *New York World*, August 9, 1927.
46. *New York Times*, August 10, 1927.
47. Ibid., August 9, 1927.
48. Musmanno, *After Twelve Years*, p. 337.
49. *New York World*, August 5, 1927.
50. Letter to Luigia Vanzetti, July 18, 1927.
51. Joughin and Morgan, *The Legacy of Sacco and Vanzetti*, p. 297.

25   You Kill Two Innocent Men

1. Musmanno, *After Twelve Years*, p. 311.
2. *New York Times*, August 19, 1927.
3. Musmanno, *After Twelve Years*, p. 312.
4. Ibid., p. 313.
5. Ralph Colp, Jr., "Bitter Christmas: A Biographical Inquiry Into the Life of Bartolomeo Vanzetti," The *Nation*, December 27, 1958, p. 499.
6. *New York World*, August 20, 1927.
7. Felicani, A., Reminiscences, pp. 147–148.
8. Ibid., p. 152.
9. Trial transcript, p. 5516.
10. *New York World*, August 22, 1927.
11. Musmanno, *After Twelve Years*, p. 344.
12. Ibid., p. 359.
13. Ibid., pp. 362–363.
14. *New York World*, August 23, 1927.
15. Musmanno, *After Twelve Years*, p. 366.
16. Ibid., p. 374.
17. For the full account, see Musmanno, *After Twelve Years*, pp. 382–387.

18. Jackson, G., Reminiscences, p. 239.
19. Thompson's article is reprinted in full in Ehrmann, *The Untried Case*, pp. 246–252.
20n. *New York Times*, August 23, 1927.
21. Baldwin, R., Reminiscences, p. 232.
22. Jackson, G., Reminiscences, p. 251.
23. Ibid., p. 250.
24. Ibid., p. 251.
25. Ibid.
26. Musmanno, *After Twelve Years*, pp. 389–390.
27. *New York World*, August 23, 1927.
28. *Letters of Sacco and Vanzetti*, pp. 117, 133; *New York Times*, August 23, 1927.
29. Felicani, A., Reminiscences, p. 157.
30. Ibid., p. 159.
31. Marks, *Thirteen Days*, pp. 58–59.
32. Ibid., pp. 59–60.
33. Alfonsina Brini to author.

Afterword

1. Trial transcript, p. 4749.
2. Russell, *Tragedy in Dedham*, p. XXII.
3. Julian S. Hatcher, Frank J. Jury, and Jac Weller, *Firearms Investigation Identification and Evidence*, (Harrisburg, Pa.: The Stackpole Co., 1957), p. 466.
4. Ibid., p. 463.
5. Ibid., p. 466.
6. Francis Russell, "How I Changed My Mind About the Sacco-Vanzetti Case," *Antioch Review*, Winter, 1965–1966, p. 605.
7. Ibid.
8. *New York Times*, October 7, 1965.
9. Russell, *Tragedy in Dedham*, p. 466.
10. Francis Russell, "Sacco-Vanzetti: The End of the Chapter," The *National Review*, May 5, 1970, p. 465. The Jacobs letter is among the papers given by Francis Russell to the Boston Public Library for its Sacco-Vanzetti collection.
11. Robert D'Attilio to author.
12. Russell, *Antioch Review*, p. 599.
13. Ibid.
14. Russell, *Tragedy in Dedham*, pp. 463–464.
15. Roger Baldwin to author.
16. Russell, *Antioch Review*, p. 599.

17. Russell, *Tragedy in Dedham*, pp. 256–257.
18. Ibid., p. 257.
19. Ibid., p. 463.
20. Ibid., p. XXI.
21. Ibid., p. XXII.
22. Evans, *Outstanding Features of the Sacco-Vanzetti Case*, p. 29.
23. *Letters of Sacco and Vanzetti*, pp. 24–25.
24. Jules Witcover, *85 Days: The Last Campaign of Robert F. Kennedy*, (New York: Ace, 1969), p. 209.
25. Michael Novak, *The Rise of the Unmeltable Ethnics*, (New York: Macmillan, 1973), p. XVI.
26. *New York Times*, April 10, 1976.
27. *Letters of Sacco and Vanzetti*, pp. 67–68.

Index

471

I

American Legion assault on,
120–121
and Bisbee incident, 99–100
and Lawrence (Massachusetts)
mill strike, 84–88
suppression of, 100–101
and World War I, 91, 99

Jack, Cerise, 11–12
Jackson, Gardner, 290, 353–354,
381, 390, 399, 403–404, 407,
408, 413
on Communist party, 385
and Defense Committee, 282,
351–352
and Fuller, 367–368
on Lowell, 359, 361
Jacobs, Ellsworth C., 7
Jefferson, Thomas, 51, 52, 53
Jewish immigrants, 64, 68–69
Johnson, Simon, 8
Joughin, Louis, 352, 354
Jury, Frank, 421
Justice Department, 312
and Katzmann, 234, 253, 261,
325–327
and Palmer raids, 135, 136, 149
Sacco-Vanzetti files of, 327–329
and suppression of evidence,
159–160

Kaplan, Hymie, 86, 133
Karas, Peter, 126
Katzmann, Frederick G., 158, 159,
160, 162, 183, 202, 282
and ballistics evidence, 219,
222
and cross examination of
defendants, 216–217, 233,
241–248, 251, 252–259,
260–265
at Dedham trial, 215, 224–225,
233–234
and DeFalco incident, 196, 197,
198

and interrogation of defendants,
158
and justice Department, 253,
261, 325, 326–327
before Lowell Committee, 363
at Plymouth trial, 163, 165,
169–170, 172–174, 178,
179, 180
and summation at Dedham
trial, 209, 214, 267, 268
and suppression of evidence,
324
Katzmann, Percy, 196, 197, 198
Kelley, George, 12, 14
testimony of, 150, 215, 216,
217, 228, 346
Kelley, Michael F., 12–13
Kennedy, John F., and
anti-Catholicism, 56
King, James E., 314
Know-Nothing Party, 57–58
Kravchuck, Semeon, 126
Ku Klux Klan, 119

Labor unions (see Unions)
LaGuardia, Fiorello, 401
Langone's funeral parlor, 411
Lavrowsky, Mitchel, 125–126
Lawrence (Massachusetts), IWW
strike in, 84–88
Lawrence, William, 380
Lawrence family, 360
Lawyers, stand of, 354
League of Nations, 108
Letherman, Lawrence, 326–327
Leuchtenburg, William, 92
Levangie, Michael, 6, 207–209,
210
Lewis, John L., 110, 111
Lippmann, Walter, 381
Literacy test
Dillingham report on, 72
enactment of, 73
and immigration restriction, 64
Lodge, Henry Cabot, 63, 64, 88,
91, 108

473

Ir